BURMA

ART AND ARCHAEOLOGY

BURMA
ART AND ARCHAEOLOGY

Edited by

Alexandra Green and T. Richard Blurton

ART MEDIA RESOURCES

© 2002 The Trustees of The British Museum

First published in 2002 by The British Museum Press
A division of The British Museum Company Limited
46 Bloomsbury Street, London WC1B 3QQ

First published in the United States in 2002 by
Art Media Resources, Ltd.
1507 South Michigan Avenue, Chicago, IL 60605
info@artmediaresources.com
www.artmediaresources.com

A CIP catalogue record of this book is available
from the Library of Congress

ISBN 1–58886–024–8

Project management by Swales & Willis
Cover design by Bettina Newman
Typeset in Plantin Light by Exe Valley Dataset, Exeter
Printed and bound in the UK by Cambridge University Press

Contents

Foreword

In 1994 when my wife Ruth and I left Burma we decided to give our collection of Burmese lacquer to the British Museum. Unwittingly we set off a chain of events which culminated six years later in the exhibition 'Visions from the Golden Land: Burma and the Art of Lacquer'. This was accompanied by a sizeable catalogue and by a varied programme of educational activities, which included the conference organised jointly by the British Museum and the School of Oriental and African Studies. The present publication collects some of the papers given at SOAS in June 2000, and this Foreword gives me an opportunity of expressing my deep satisfaction that scholars and researchers in many fields and from many lands were able to come together and share their common interest in the history, art and culture of Burma.

The pleasure is tinged with bemusement, as I trace the origin of this important meeting back to the collection we started in 1989 and gifted in 1994.

Collecting is in varied proportions recreation and passion. The finely crafted Burmese lacquerware which so captivated me in the 1990s may seem to have nothing in common with the targets of my previous collections, both of natural history specimens – beetles inland and sea-shells on the coasts of Africa in the 1960s and 1970s. If there is any link, it is literally a superficial one: the rounded surface in all three groups is hard, glossy, brightly coloured and attractively patterned. Forest paths and offshore island reefs alike were out of bounds in Burma in 1989. Huge tracts of country were closed to all foreigners, especially diplomats. My collecting energies were perforce diverted from natural objects to man-made artefacts.

I made the switch to lacquer at the Christmas Charities Fair held at the British Ambassador's Residence in Rangoon in December 1989. At the curios stall a round water-pot with *yun* decoration of elephants on the base and a maker's inscription at the rim caught my eye. It became Catalogue Number 1. Over the next four years the collection grew steadily. Used lacquerware was cheap, and simple domestic pieces were being discarded. We even collected a few from rubbish heaps. Sylvia Fraser-Lu's 1985 book *Burmese Lacquerware* was invaluable as a collector's aid, with its many illustrations of techniques, forms of vessels and names of the many decorative patterns.

Gradually my Burmese improved until I could 'talk lacquer' with sellers and makers, and start to read the inscriptions on many vessels. My British Council colleagues' help was enlisted to decipher and interpret them. I was struck by the way such inscribed objects could reveal the cultural values and beliefs of their makers and users. The more I learned, the more I wanted to understand. These inscriptions became a special study.

Short leaves spent in Britain were a chance to see Burmese lacquer pieces in the Victoria and Albert Museum and in the British Museum. Richard Blurton of the BM visited Burma and I was asked to purchase a range of ordinary twentieth century artefacts for the BM. This led to close friendship and collaboration. I was asked to commission from Mandalay craftsmen a new throne in lacquered and gilt wood for a wonderful large hollow lacquer Buddha image which had been in the BM since at least 1826.

In Burma the Buddhist practice of making donations for merit is all-pervasive. Insidiously the idea grew of giving our entire collection to a museum in order to share with many others our pleasure in the beauty of the objects and in the skill of the makers. By our last year in Burma this resolution had hardened into a decision. The gift was unconditional, but scarcely disinterested. We knew the BM would carry out essential conservation, allow access to students and keep the collection together, postponing for a few lifetimes the dispersal inevitable in a world of impermanence. And we naturally expected that from time to time some of the objects we had donated would go on display to the public.

Quite unexpected was the scale of the Museum's response to our gift. They would mount an exhibition devoted to the culture of Burma, the first to be seen in London since 1826. Vessels from our gift would join forces with other artefacts made with lacquer – sculpture, manuscripts, musical instruments, furniture – to illumine many aspects of Burmese life, art, culture, beliefs and values.

A flurry of activity followed. Richard Blurton and I read widely. Lacquer objects were studied, compared, their inscriptions deciphered. Key objects not represented in the BM's collections were tracked down in museums all over England. The V&A were persuaded to lend their magnificent shrine. The British Library generously loaned manuscripts never before displayed to the public. Richard and I visited Cambridge, Liverpool, Brighton, Ipswich and the National Trust's Kedleston Hall in Derbyshire, which houses Lord Curzon's Indian Museum. We also saw several fine private collections, including the outstanding Missorten Foundation in Belgium. At Kew, the Institute for Economic Botany yielded magnificent pieces and tools from the mid nineteenth century.

Slowly the catalogue grew, with Richard and I sharing the labour. Computers shuddered in protest as they were asked to integrate into the English text all the Burmese inscriptions in Burmese script. Our editor showed patience in almost Burmese fashion with the many delays. We only just avoided following the example of the Director of the great Delhi Exhibition of Indian Art Manufactures, Sir George Watt, whose 1903 catalogue was issued some months after the exhibition closed.

The beauty of the BM exhibition was a complex combination of the objects, their wonderful lighting, design and variety. It was a great pleasure for us to hear the comments and questions of those who came to admire and to learn. I guided groups of adults and children and learned from them. But a very special pleasure was to attend the conference and see both seasoned scholars and complete newcomers passionately involved with the history and art and achievements of Burma. As their contributions are being edited for publication in this volume, the 'Visions' exhibition has gone on tour to Exeter, Bath and Sunderland. In 2003 it will cross the Atlantic to New York. Let us hope that in future Burmese scholars will be able to join in and share their findings in international gatherings.

Ralph Isaacs

Preface

This volume has grown out of the conference, *New Research in the Art and Archaeology of Burma*, which was held in London over the weekend of 17–18 June 2000. It was organised jointly by the British Museum and the School of Oriental and African Studies (University of London). The conference was planned to coincide with the exhibition at the British Museum, *Visions from the Golden Land: Burma and the Art of Lacquer*, which ran from 8 April to 13 August that same year. This in its turn came into being through the generous gift to the British Museum by Ralph and Ruth Isaacs of their collection of over 250 items of Burmese lacquer. We believe that the exhibition was the first major examination of the art of Burma, in London, since 1826, and as such we felt it was appropriate to convene a meeting where the present state of the study of the art and archaeology of Burma could also be assessed. This study has, after all, been marginalised now for many years, for a variety of political, social, and economic reasons. However, this subject is relevant to the University, where it is taught, and to the Museum, which holds important collections reflecting Burmese civilisation from the earliest times to the present day. Here was an opportunity which we felt we could not forgo.

A particular concern of the conference organisers, Elizabeth Moore, Alexandra Green (both of SOAS) and Richard Blurton (British Museum), and then the editors, was for all the chapters to report on *new* research in the area of Burmese art and archaeology. This was to be a forward-looking undertaking, encouraging scholars again to take more interest in the remarkable cultures of the largest country in mainland Southeast Asia. We wanted to advertise that an array of scholarly work was actually being carried out, contrary to accepted views. The chapters cover a very wide range of subjects, from prehistory to the twentieth century with the definition of art sometimes close to that of anthropology. However, the editors feel that the compartmentalisation suggested by these terms is, in Burma, sometimes merely a reflection of Western scholarly constraint, and thus not always useful. We have been pleased to reflect this very broad view of the cultures of Burma in this publication.

The first three chapters are concerned with the archaeology of Burma. Elizabeth Moore *et al.* examine the regional variety of grave goods, particularly bronzes and rings made of stone or glass, in the Chindwin and Samon River valleys. A diversity of pre-historic cultures in Burma is further confirmed by this evidence, with the Chindwin area possibly revealing the inception of bronze casting and the Samon region indicating the transition between the Bronze and Iron Ages, and the Pyu period.

Historical myths claim that the first kings of Pagan settled in the area as early as the second century AD. Bob Hudson *et al.* have attempted to determine the locations of the legendary nineteen founding villages, and in the process reveal early settlement patterns in the area which had an impact upon later monuments at Pagan.

Votive tablets are extensively found in the Burmese archaeological record. They substantiate acts of devotion performed by the Buddhists of Burma. The easy mobility of both the tablets, and the moulds for their manufacture, creates inherent difficulties in establishing the origin of tablet finds. John Guy discusses the variety of tablets, and indicates how the similarities between Pagan period votive tablets and eastern Indian motifs further blur distinctions between types.

From this archaeological perspective of Burma, the chapters shift to art historical concerns. Pamela Gutman examines the influences that Mon sculpture and images, particularly those from the Kaw-gun caves at Pa-an in Lower Burma, may have had upon the classic Sukhothai walking Buddha. The distinctive Kaw-gun type that emerged in the eleventh century was influenced by Pala, Mon-Khmer, and Srivijayan sculpture. Interactions between the Mon and Thai monks may have influenced the transfer of sculptural styles, as the physiognomy and the placement of robes of the Kaw-gun images are later found in the Sukhothai type.

Charlotte Galloway addresses the visual expressions of the Buddha's Enlightenment in the Ananda temple at Pagan, which in the past have been regarded as deriving solely from the Theravada Buddhist tradition. In comparing the imagery with both Mahayana and Theravada texts describing the Enlightenment, it becomes clear that categorising Pagan religions as separate entities dominated by the Theravada is no longer a viable scholarly position.

In writing on the Burmese sculptures in the British Museum in London, Richard Blurton makes clear how little is known about the chronology of Burmese bronze sculptures, especially those of the post-Pagan period. Only by comparing Burmese images with dated pieces, by using archival data, and through scientific analysis of the sculpture will it be possible to attribute pieces more fully than current vague identifications, such as 'Burma, seventeenth to eighteenth centuries'.

Two chapters address the painting traditions of Burma. In the first, Alexandra Green applies Vidya Dehejia's narrative mode categorisation to seventeenth and eighteenth century wall paintings of the twenty-eight previous Buddhas, scenes from the life of Gotama Buddha, and the last ten Jataka tales, but ultimately rejects this system for a simpler classification where enlightenment defines the pivotal point in the narrative construction of the paintings. The use of narratology also illustrates how Burmese artists prioritised space over time in the expression of religious and social issues in the murals.

Patricia Herbert's chapter on Burmese manuscripts focuses on representations of Buddhist cosmology, and also examines the variety of styles and conventions found in the manuscripts. This enables a comparison of significant scenes, ranging from the highest heaven to the deepest hell, and reveals differences in the organisational and spatial presentation of the imagery.

Bénédicte Brac de la Perrière addresses a less well-known aspect of Burmese religious beliefs by examining the statues in *nat* sanctuaries. The antiquity of the statues' function within *nat* cults seems to date primarily from the nineteenth century, though the cults themselves are considerably older. It may be that during the reformation of local rituals during this time, issues associated with kingship became incorporated into such rites and were expressed by the use of permanent *nat* images in *nat* palaces.

The rapid physical disintegration of Burmese monastic architecture is explored by Sylvia Fraser-Lu. The difficulties of preserving these buildings and the interest, or lack thereof, in supporting the survival of indigenous wooden buildings dating from the beginning of the colonial period to the present day are charted here. Greater concern has always been expressed for temples and stupas, but it is only within the past decade that the Burmese government has turned its attention to wooden buildings.

Turning to areas of Burma that have been considered peripheral to its cultural studies, the next three chapters consider how identity is created among Kachin and Karenni groups and how textiles are used to affirm political connections. Mandy Sadan writes on how the *manau* festival with its painted wooden posts, the *manau shadung*, has become the main symbol of the Kachin people within Burma. However, this symbol did not necessarily have the all-encompassing meaning that it has today, and this may be due to actions taken by the colonial government, as well as economic changes in the early twentieth century.

Susan Conway illustrates how female dress was used to express political affiliations and authority in the Shan States. Female dress was conservative in comparison to male dress, and thus when women married into different courts, they continued to wear their traditional dress. A king or prince could reveal the extent of his strategic political connections by showing off his wives. At certain periods of time, however, when traditional dress did not accord with ideas of cultural uniformity, it was suppressed.

'Traditional' Karenni clothing also expresses meanings and values, currently those of the exiled Karenni people. Sandra Dudley explores how women's clothing in particular has become a part of tradition essential in the definition of a modern Karenni person and exiled refugee. The tensions between new arrivals in refugee camps in Thailand and the pre-existing refugee community over issues such as history, morality and identity seem to be expressed in part through opinions over clothing. Women's dress has considerable significance in defining the 'traditions' of the Karenni and their 'nation'.

Finally, the chapters turn towards European collectors of Asian material, whether it be objects or images. Uta Weigelt discusses the *yun* lacquer collection of Lucian and Christine Scherman. The forms of these objects are varied, including boxes, bowls, and plates. Some photographs in the collection and Mrs Scherman's diary entries also reveal the steps in lacquer production. The identification of lacquer producers and workshops and the translation of inscriptions provide valuable data for future analyses of Burmese lacquer.

The discovery of an important historical archive at the Royal Geographical Society in London prompted the final chapter of this book. Joanna Wright brought hitherto unpublished negatives by Max and Bertha Ferrars to the attention of Richard Blurton. The editors felt that the reproduction of as many of these photographs as possible would complement the new research presented by the other contributors. Many of these images are similar, but not identical, to those in the well-known book by Max and Bertha Ferrars, *Burma* (1901), and thus are presented here with the appropriate caption or relevant quotes from the Ferrars' text.

In editing this diverse compendium of chapters, the editors initially felt that standardisation of terminology should be achieved throughout the publication. However, it soon became apparent that this was not going to be possible – or indeed desirable. We therefore present these chapters with, for the most part, the usages that the individual authors requested in their original texts. This is particularly so in the thorny matter of the use of Pali or Sanskrit for religious terms. Pali seemed more appropriate for a Theravada country, but Sanskrit terms are, for the most part, better known. Thus, generally, we have used 'Bodhisattva', not 'Bodhisatta'; 'stupa' and not 'thupa', but we have not been doctrinaire in all such matters. Only in one area have we kept to one standard – the use of established geographical spellings, as opposed to new spellings. We have for the sake of clarity and established practice, elected to use the word 'Burma' to describe the country, and not 'Myanmar', which is so little known. Similarly, we have used 'Pagan' and not 'Bagan'; 'Pegu' and not 'Bago'; 'Irrawaddy' and not 'Ayeyawaddy'. We feel certain that this usage will allow the information we are presenting in this volume to reach a wider public.

We have greatly benefited from the advice of the doyen of Burmese studies in Britain, John Okell, and we thank him for spending so much precious time on reading the contributions. Others we thank are Ralph Isaacs, our editors Teresa Francis (initially) and then Nina Shandloff (subsequently), and of course the authors who have responded to our enquiries and requests with commendable celerity. Elizabeth Dell at the Green Centre in Brighton generously assisted with the supply of photographs, and Graham Millington of the British Council in Rangoon very kindly acted as courier between Britain and Burma. Ann Searight prepared the map in record time. Both editors are grateful for the support of colleagues in the British Museum. Richard Willis and Colin Morgan of Swales and Willis have been scrupulous in their editing

and design of this volume. Finally, Martin Williams and Jens Johansen both gave considerable general support for which we are greatly appreciative.

In our endeavours we are most grateful to the funding bodies which enabled us to go ahead with the conference and the subsequent publication of the proceedings, using contributions which had been raised for the education programme accompanying the exhibition. These charitable bodies were the Burma Project (Open Society Institute, New York), the Paul Hamlyn Foundation, and the Charles Wallace (Burma) Trust. Without this support we would not have been able to make the necessary arrangements. We also acknowledge the considerable assistance of John Reeve and his staff in the Education Department of the British Museum, and, importantly, the support of the School of Oriental and African Studies for allowing us use of the fine new lecture facilities in the Brunei Building. The organisers of the conference had no idea how many people would attend, so the presence of at least sixty people over what was one of the hottest weekends of the summer was a happy result. The conference also included a private view of the exhibition devoted to Burmese lacquer at the British Museum. The rarity of the event coupled with the response of those who attended, encouraged us to publish these proceedings and we are grateful to the British Museum Press for supporting this project.

We present this volume in the sincere hope that it will encourage more scholars, in a variety of disciplines, as well as the general public, to think seriously again about the beauty and interest of the artistic and historical traditions of this remarkable country.

Alexandra Green and
T. Richard Blurton

INDIA

CHINA

KACHIN

HUKAWNG VALLEY

R.Mali

R.Nmai

R.Chindwin

Myitkyina

YUNNAN

R.Irrawaddy

Bhamo

Namkham

0   300 km

Tagaung

Lashio

Po Win
Daung ■

CHIN

Shwebo

Monywa
Kyaukka   Mingun

SHAN

Sagaing • Mandalay
Ava • Amarapura

B   U   R   M   A

Pakkoku

Nyaung-U

Laihka

Kengtung

Pagan   Thazi

R.Samon

LAOS

Salay
(Sale)   *Mt.Popa* ▲ Meiktila

Taunggyi

L.Inle

Ywama

YAWNGHWE

Loikaw

THAILAND

KAYAH
KAREN

THAILAND

ARAKAN

Prome

R.Sittang

LANNA

BAY

OF

BENGAL

Pegu

R.Salween

Rangoon

Thaton

Pa-an
Martaban
Moulmein

TENASSERIM

TENASSERIM

THAILAND

Tavoy

BURMA

1 Prehistoric grave goods from the Chindwin and Samon river regions

U Nyunt Han, U Win Maung (Tanpawady) and Elizabeth Moore

Continuing research by the Department of Archaeology in Burma is rapidly adding data to the understanding of prehistoric cultures in the Chindwin and Samon River regions. For example, the Mandalay Branch has excavated in the Chindwin area at cemetery sites near Nyaunggan and at Monhtu, 30 miles east of Nyaunggan, both in Budalin Township. In the Samon region, excavations have been carried out at U Pok Kyi's field near Myin U Hle village and at Hnawgan village in Mahlaing Township. Koko Kha Hla in Wundwin Township, Nyaungyan village in Thazi Township and Inn Te in Taungtha Township have also been the focus of archaeological investigation.[1] The bead-working site or 'bead mound' of Padi Kon on the Pyaw Bwe side of the Samon River has also been excavated.

In this chapter, grave goods from cemetery sites in the Chindwin and the Samon River valleys are used to define prehistoric regions within Upper Burma.[2] Chindwin and Samon artefacts were made from a range of materials, including stone, bronze, terracotta, iron, glass and lead. They are equally diverse in form. Out of the many artefacts recovered from these sites, the focus here is on ceremonial rings, beads, and bronzes. The characteristics, material and form, are used to divide the cemeteries into two provisional groups: a Bronze Age one and a somewhat later transitional Bronze to Iron Age one.[3] Secondly, this paper suggests that transitional sites may overlap with at least the early part of the first to ninth century AD Pyu period. Many artefacts from Samon locations are very similar to Pyu objects in material or form, and some transitional items have even previously been labelled Pyu. Some Pyu sites, like Halin in the Chindwin area, also reveal evidence of prior Bronze and transitional age occupation with such items as stone rings and bronze tools (Figure 1.1).[4]

THE CHINDWIN BURIAL SITES

The Chindwin sites (*c.* 20–24° N by 94–96.5° E) are north of Monywa on both sides of the river in Sagaing Division, and are within the arid zone of the country. Rainfall in the area is low, around 6.75 cm per annum, and virtually all of it falls between May and October. Between November and March there is seldom more than 1.3 cm of rain.[5] Transportation is provided by the Chindwin River.

The Chindwin region has rich copper deposits and abundant sources of stone such as basalt, rhyolite, serpentine-bearing rock and silicified tuffs. These materials were used to make tools and rings; the use of bronze is seen in a variety of implements, from axes to spears and halberds. Human remains of *Homo erectus* were recovered from Nwe Gwe, east of Monywa,[6] and other examples of prehistoric occupation were found at a number of Chindwin locations, including the Chin So Kon mound west of Mogyo Byin village in Salingyi Township. Here a range of stone tools and megaliths has been recorded.[7]

Casting and forging were well developed by the period of the Nyaunggan burials, with the smelting of copper deposits on the opposite bank of the Irrawaddy River likely.[8] Rich porphyry copper deposits around the Sabedaung, Kyinsindaung and Letpadaung mountains may have provided the raw material for the copper goods found at the Chindwin sites.[9] The main deposits being mined today are several hundred metres below surface level, but in the Bronze Age low-level sources of ore near the surface may have been exploited. Evidence from kilns at Kyaukmyet, along the banks of the Chindwin, probably date only to the historic period, although suggestions of prehistoric use have also been made.[10]

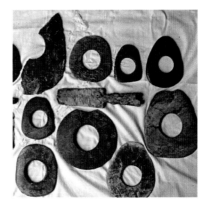

Figure 1.1 Stone rings and bronze tool from Halin (Nyaungkobin Monastery). Photo courtesy Office of Strategic Studies.

Most of the Chindwin material discussed in this chapter is from Department of Archaeology excavations at Nyaunggan in the Budalin Township of Sagaing Division (22.24° N by 95.63° E). Northwest of Monywa is a line of craters, and the Nyaunggan Bronze Age cemetery is located on the northwest rim of one of these craters.[11] As mentioned, Nyaunggan is a Bronze Age site with inhumation burials and one, if not more, secondary burial urns, which have not yet been dated.[12] In 1998, U Pauk Pauk directed several excavations at the Nyaunggan cemetery, which is located 65.1 metres above sea level on a sloping surface measuring some 180 by 75 metres and with a surface soil of sandy mud. The excavations yielded thirty-seven human skeletal remains and four animal skulls. Grave goods included pottery; bronze axes and spears; stone rings, tools and beads; and terracotta and shell beads.[13]

The excavated stone rings are of various shapes, ranging from round or oval to square and triangular. They are not made of precious materials, such as jade, but from locally available stones, both igneous and sedimentary.[14] Stone tools include pounders (round at one end and pointed at the other) and polished shouldered axes (Figure 1.2).

Twenty-three stone beads recovered from the burials were almost all elongated barrel-shaped, some 2.5 to 5 cm in length. Two beads were about 17 cm long with a diameter of about 1 cm in the middle (Figure 1.3).[15] Terracotta beads were surface finds, as were two lead rolls similar to finds from the Pyu site of Maingmaw and also Dvaravati sites in Thailand.[16] No carnelian, green stone or crystal beads were excavated at Nyaunggan.

THE SAMON BURIAL SITES

The Samon River valley (c. 19–22° N by 95–97° E) is located south of Mandalay, and, like the Chindwin River valley, lies within the country's arid region. It has less precipitation than the Chindwin area and little moisture-creating ground vegetation, but it does have stream access to main waterways. The river, which enters the Irrawaddy River just south of Mandalay, runs south and is bounded to the east by the Shan Plateau.[17] To the west the area rises slightly, with intermittent streams flowing both into the Samon River and west towards the Irrawaddy River. The river valley is adjacent to ore resources, such as the copper-bearing sites at the foot of the Shan Plateau, including Kye Taung or 'Copper Mountain' located east of Beinnaka in Pyawbwe Township. No sites have yet been surveyed on the Shan Plateau, although this eastern uplift may well have been an ore source for the Samon sites. The distribution of sites in the Samon River region includes locales south of Mandalay, east of Magwe, and north of Pyinmana in the Mandalay and Magwe Divisions.

The Samon sites included here are more numerous than those from the Chindwin valley, but although in part based on recent excavations by the Department of Archaeology, many objects come from less secure contexts where village reports have provided the only information. The Samon cemetery sites described below are found in or near villages within eight townships of Mandalay Division.[18]

Bronze grave goods include axes, spears, kye doke (bronze packets), miniature spears, curvilinear 'coffin' ornaments, bells, and thin sheet reliefs depicting female 'mother goddess' figures. Iron spears are often set in bronze handles. Objects made from iron, stone, and glass have also been recovered (Figure 1.4 and 1.5). The stones include red, orange, brown and white carnelians and green stones, most commonly chalcedony. Glass recovered is frequently of turquoise blue or pale green colour, but violet, sapphire blue, golden brown, dark green and emerald green pieces have also been found. Bead finds include spheres, discs and zoomorphic forms (Figure 1.6). The kye doke, bronze 'mother goddess' figures, certain types of glass, and the stone ceremonial

Figure 1.2 Stone rings, discs and pounder from Nyaunggan (National Museum). Courtesy of Office of Strategic Studies.

Figure 1.3 Long stone beads (*c.* 17.5 cm) and terracotta disks and beads from Nyaunggan, Budalin, Chindwin region (National Museum). Courtesy of Office of Strategic Studies.

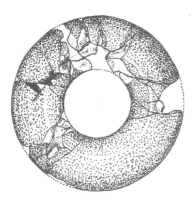

Figure 1.4 Blue glass ring from Tatkon, Samon region. Outer diameter, 12.5 cm; inner diameter, 6.25 cm. Courtesy of U Win Maung (Tanpawady) Collection.

Figure 1.6 Carnelian tiger bead from Myo Hla, Yamethin, Samon region; length, 8.75 cm. Courtesy of U Maung Maung Tin Collection.

Figure 1.5 White marble stone ring from Kha Bo, Samon region. Outer diameter, 11.75 cm; inner diameter, 6.25 cm. Courtesy of U Win Maung (Tanpawady) Collection.

rings (Figures 1.4, 1.5, 1.7 and 1.8) have to date only been located at transitional sites, such as Nyaungyan in Thazi Township of the Samon region, and are not found at Bronze Age sites.

Although most of the Samon grave goods described here are of the transitional Bronze to Iron Age period, there is evidence of occupation from other periods. For example, at sites east of Beinnaka such as Pin Thaung and Myauk Mi Kon, long polished chisels (*c.* 40 cm) and small glass beads have been found. Pyu coins depicting a rising sun have been found in the Tatkon mound at the transitional site of Tha Hpan Chaung in Pyinmana Township. The Pyu sites of Beinnaka and Maingmaw have yielded both Pyu and pre-Pyu artefacts.[19] At Beinnaka, the Pagan period Nan U Zedi was unearthed from a mound east of the site. These details illustrate the range of finds from the sites described here, but sites

from other areas of Burma, including the Chindwin region, are equally varied in the objects recovered and the structures found.

COMPARISON OF ARTEFACTS FROM THE SAMON AND CHINDWIN REGIONS

The Samon and Chindwin regions offer valuable comparative material. Both areas have sites with stone but no metal; some have only bronze and others reveal bronze, iron and glass. Ceremonial rings and bronze tools are found in both areas, although the forms differ. A few artefacts, such as *kye doke* (bronze packets), miniature spears, curvilinear 'coffin' ornaments, bells, and thin bronze repoussé female figures, here called 'mother goddesses', primarily derive from the Samon River region.

Kye doke (bronze packets) and other bronze items

Kye doke, miniature bronze spears, and 'coffin' ornaments have been found at transitional sites throughout the Samon area and further afield (Figure 1.7).[20] Many villagers associate the bronze packets with male burials; apparently, female burials contain beads, but no bronze. The packets are some 7.5 cm long.[21] Each is made up of a variable number of bronze wires; some of these are half a centimetre wide. The tips of the wires are sharp, suggesting they were cut or twisted from a longer wire. They break easily, possibly an indicator of a high tin content. Each bunch is wrapped around the middle with wire, and some of the wrapping wires bear traces of cloth.[22] The packets are assembled to form bundles, which may include ten or more packets. *Kye doke* are generally found with inhumation burials, and are placed on either side of the shoulder, on the chest, or gripped in the upturned hands of the skeleton. At Shwe Ku Kon near Nyaungyan village, inhabitants reported finding some burials with seven small packets held in the closed hand of

3

the skeleton, and in other cases three to five packets. Some *kye doke* were found on the chest, in either a vertical or horizontal row. Up to thirty, found on different parts of the body, have been reported from a single burial.

Miniature bronze spears, but not axes, have been found laid lengthwise below the lower arm. The spears range in size from about 2 to 10 cm, with some thinner than others. These spears are usually bound up in bundles of five or six pieces. At some sites, villagers have recovered bronze bells, with perforations on the sides and a clapper; these are placed above the head of the corpse. There are also curvilinear and round conical bronze pieces (respectively, about 10 to 12.5 cm high and around 7.5 cm in diameter). Villagers report finding the curvilinear pieces laid out both horizontally and vertically. Both conical and curvilinear ornaments have small holes, possibly to fasten on to wood with bamboo 'nails'. Because the conical pieces have been found in a layer above the curvilinear ornaments, they may have been sewn to a cloth coffin cover. These hypotheses are clearly subject to revision following further excavations.

'Mother goddess' figures

Thin bronze sheet reliefs of female 'mother goddess' figures have been recovered from transitional Samon burials only; they are not found in Bronze Age Chindwin burials (Figure 1.8). To date, nine examples have been recovered.[23] All measure between 60 to 90 cm high and vary in width from about 12 to 60 cm. The sheets are easily broken, suggesting a high tin content. However, as the alloy has not been assessed, this could be a result of their thinness and method of manufacture, which presumably involved beating the material, not casting it. The curvilinear and conical ornaments found are thicker than the figures, and remain slightly pliable even today.

Most of the 'mother goddesses' are shown singly, but two depict a pair of females within an outer figural form. One double figure has two curvilinear designs linking the 'neck' and torso. One 'mother goddess' is in triple form. The double and triple figures are placed within an enclosing form with only two legs, thereby conveying a sense of one female. On the single figures, the legs have

been bent under at the knee, which is shown only on these figures. Each figure varies, but they are uniformly headless with prominent breasts and womb. The breastbone, backbone and legbones are seen on both single and double 'mother goddesses'. The figure is elongated above the breasts, possibly representing a 'head', although the backbone reaching to the top of the figure suggests otherwise.

'Mother goddesses' have been recovered *in situ* from a burial at only one site. In this grave a single figure was placed horizontally on top of a skeleton, and a double figure was laid below the skeleton. The feet of the 'mother goddesses' pointed towards the head of the burial, and had the legs not been bent under they would have covered the face of the skeleton. However, several figures have small holes around the edges, including the bottom of the leg, suggesting they were once laid out flat and fixed to a flat surface, possibly wood, on top of the skeleton. These images, like the curvilinear ornaments described in the previous section, may possibly have been coffin decorations.

The skeleton also had carnelian beads on the neck and waist, and *kye doke* and bronze tools were recovered from the same burial. This may indicate a link between male burials and 'mother goddesses'. If so, these images may be explained in a number of different ways, including a hope for (various) female companions in a next life or an assurance of abundant offspring.

Ceremonial rings

Rings made of stone (*kyauk gwin*) and of glass have been found at many sites in the central zone divisions of Mandalay, Sagaing and Magwe.[24] The shape of the rings may be circular, triangular, ovoid, rectangular, or round with multiple points.

On the Nyaunggan rings (Chindwin area), the outer diameter varies from 10 to 18.75 cm, and the diameter of the inner hole from 3.75 to 5.75 cm.[25] The hole is always a perfect circle, although not always centred. Some rings have holes drilled in adjoining sections, allowing repair, possibly with bronze wire.[26] Rings were found on the wrist, the leg, by the shoulder, and on the pelvic area. One burial had three rings: one under the upper left shoulder, one on the pelvic area, and a third underneath the left arm. Ritual concepts, including fertility, may have dictated the various placements of the rings on the body.

In the Samon region a variety of shapes and stone-types characterise the *kyauk gwin*. A number of the stone rings are made of a white stone, and at some sites both white stone and round blue glass rings have been recovered.[27] However, at Bu Lu Kon in Wundwin Township, a *kyauk gwin* made of a marbled dark green stone has been recovered. A white triangular *kyauk gwin* has been reported from Beinnaka, and a white ring with eight

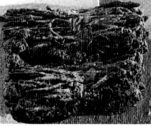

Figure 1.7 Two *Kye doke* or bronze packets from the Samon region. Courtesy of U Win Maung (Tanpawady) Collection.

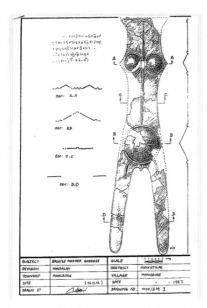
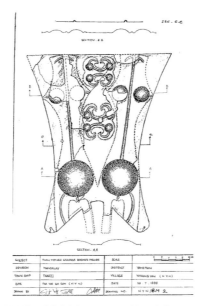
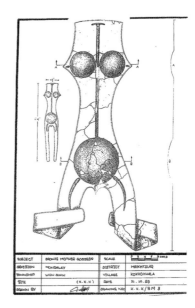

Figure 1.8 Single mother goddesses: Myin U Hle, Mahlaing Township (left) and Koko Kha Hla, Wundwin Township (right). Double mother goddess, from Nyaungyan, Thazi Township (centre). Courtesy of U Win Maung (Tanpawady) Collection.

points recovered from Kha Bo (Figure 1.5), demonstrating that not all Samon rings are circular. Many of the ring forms remain consistent between regions, but some are found at Bronze Age burials with only bronze implements, while others are from transitional bi-metallic bronze and iron burials. In addition, most rings are made from local stone, though the blue glass rings raise questions about the chronology and extent of cultural exchange between the Samon and Chindwin River regions.

Beads

A wide variety of beads have been found from both Bronze Age and transitional period areas. Bronze Age beads are most frequently barrel-shaped and are made of stone or shell. For instance, excavations at the Nyaunggan site yielded only stone and gastropod shell beads.[28] To date, with the exception of Halin, in the Chindwin area such beads are surface finds rather than from burials.

Beads from Samon burials are made from a range of materials. These include opalised wood (*ingyin kyauk*), agate, amethyst, crystal, carnelian and green stone (usually chalcedony).[29] People report that green stone beads are often found with bronze tools and red carnelian beads with iron in burials at the Samon village of Ywa Htin Kon in the Yanaung area of Thazi Township. Transitional beads are found on the neck, wrists or other body parts of inhumation burials. Glass beads, both discs and short tubular types, are usually found at the waist level of the skeleton. They are often called Pyu, although in the Samon area most of the glass beads have been recovered from inhumation burials at transitional sites in the Pyawbwe area.

Semi-precious stone beads carved in a variety of forms are seen at most transitional sites of the Samon area. Beads may be round, barrel-shaped, flat or one of a number of zoomorphic forms.[30] These include elephants, tigers, lions, bulls, ducks, long-tailed birds, tortoises, frogs, dogs, rodents, rhinoceroses, crocodiles, fish, and owls. A few non-zoomorphic forms also exist, for instance, a seated man and pots. These are identical to Pyu beads, but at Pyu sites *in situ* beads have generally been recovered from urns, not on skeletons.[31] Elephants with tusks are the most common zoomorphic bead shape at both Pyu and Samon sites. In the Samon region, like other animal beads, they are generally recovered from the neck of skeletons.[32] Although usually made from green stone, other materials are evident. For example, a blue glass elephant was found with a Pyu silver bowl in Myin Mu Township in Sagaing Division, and another in a Samon context at Kyut Kan village in Wundwin Township.

Bronze tools

The eleven bronze tools excavated from the Nyaunggan Bronze Age cemetery in the Chindwin region range in weight from 9 to 222.52 grams. There are two small socketed axes measuring 5 by 3.75 cm and two medium socketed axes with a round bottom measuring 7.5 by 5 cm. Arrowheads include one large example of 12.5 by 3.75 cm and four smaller ones, 7.5 by 2.5 cm. There is one spear measuring 4 by 20 cm and a halberd-type flared-edge axe measuring 15 cm square.[33] Other halberds have also been reported from the Chindwin region.

Examples of longer socketed bronze spears (some 30 cm) with an iron shaft have been found in both the

Samon and Chindwin areas. Iron swords set in finely made bronze shafts have also been recovered from some Samon sites. The greatest difference between the Samon and Chindwin bronzes is in axe shape and length. The Chindwin axes are rounded whereas the Samon type tends to be longer, almost rectangular with a rounded edge. The rounded bronze axes of the Chindwin area are rare in the Samon valley, where the axes often have a much longer socket (*c.* 10 cm) with small flanges. This latter type, however, is seen also in samples from the Shan Plateau published by T.O. Morris and held in the British Museum.[34]

CONCLUSION

A range of artefacts has been recovered from cemetery sites in the Chindwin and Samon regions. Excavations and surveys to date suggest that the majority of Chindwin sites are Bronze Age in date, while those of the Samon region are primarily transitional. Bronze is the main metal found in Bronze Age burials, and iron swords with bronze handles have been recovered from transitional sites in both the Samon and Chindwin regions. Occupation of the Samon valley may post-date that of the Chindwin area, given the mortuary use of complex bronzes, the mixture of bronze and iron, and the range of semi-precious stone beads. Because of these differences in material, form and burial assemblages, a distinction between Bronze Age and transitional Bronze to Iron Age burials has been proposed.

Still to be studied is the relationship between material and form. For instance, stone rings occur in a range of shapes and stone types, but glass rings tend to be round and blue. Only round rings are flanged, but they may be stone or glass. In addition, the wide distribution of the *kye doke* may support the suggestion that the transitional period products included regional variations. This is also upheld by the widespread distribution of the Samon axe type.

Continuities between the Samon and Chindwin cultures and the Pyu period exist in site location and the materials used to produce grave goods. Transitional sites in the Samon are often labelled Pyu as they have rich bead assemblages. Iron, which is also used at transitional sites, is the principal material of tools from the Pyu period, when the employment of bronze is restricted to simple ornaments.[35] It is believed that 'Pyu' culture is principally urban, whereas the Samon sites are villages without the brick walls and putative moats characteristic of Pyu cities. Future research may show that transitional sites are contemporary with at least the early part of the Pyu period.

Regional comparisons of the variety of grave goods may offer a means by which to begin mapping prehistoric routes of cultural and technological exchange. While the archaeology of the Chindwin region may best inform us about the inception of bronze casting in Upper Burma, the Samon area may offer insight into the transition from a Bronze and Iron Age to the Pyu period.

ACKNOWLEDGEMENTS

The authors are grateful for the research support of U Win Sein, the former Minster of Culture and the staff of the Departments of Archaeology and the Cultural Institute. The logistical support of Col. Than Tun, Maj. Bo Bo, Maj. Khin Maung Win and the staff of the Office of Strategic Studies has been greatly appreciated. The help of many Township Heads has been invaluable in visiting the sites described here. Finally, many thanks are extended to the management and staff of Zaykabar Company Ltd. All errors, however, remain our responsibility.

NOTES

1 Bronze objects recovered from Nyaungyan village in Thazi Township are displayed at the National Museum in Rangoon. The Inn Te site is located near the stream of Sin Te Wa Chaung, which flows into the Irrawaddy River.

2 The material presented here primarily draws on research carried out by the authors from 1998 to the present. Some of the Chindwin material is presented in E. Moore and Pauk Pauk, 'Nyaung-gan: A Preliminary Note on a Bronze Age Cemetery near Mandalay, Myanmar (Burma)', *Asian Perspectives*, vol. 40, no. 1, 2001, pp. 35–47. The Samon data has not been published elsewhere. For the Chindwin region, reference is also made to the proceedings of the Universities Historical Research Centre's *Workshop on Bronze Age Culture in Myanmar* (Rangoon, 7 January 1999).

3 None of the Chindwin or Samon sites has yet yielded material from which it has been possible to obtain absolute Carbon 14 dates, although attempts were made to date the bones from Nyaunggan (personal communications, Dr Zsuzsa Szanto, Institute of Nuclear Research of the Hungarian Atomic Research Institute [HAS], Debrecen, Hungary; Prof. Charles Higham, New Zealand) Thus only estimates have been possible, e.g. an initial founding of around 1000 BC and a span of some three hundred years, from *c.* 900–600 BC. (See respectively, Kyaw Han, 'Burial Practice at Nyaunggan Bronze Age Site', *Proceedings of the Workshop on Bronze Age Culture in Myanmar (Yangon, 7 January 1999)*, Yangon: Universities Historical Research Centre, 1999, p. 55, and I. Glover, 'Observations on a Visit to the Nyaunggan Archaeological Site, Myanmar, January 2–4, 1999 and Comments on the Future Possibilities of Research there', *Proceedings of the Workshop on Bronze Age Culture in Myanmar (Yangon, 7 January 1999)*, Yangon: Universities Historical Research Centre, 1999, p. 87.)

4 For example, a large number of bronze tools and stone rings have been found at Halin (22.27° N by 95.49° E), collected at Nyaungkobin Monastery, while a carnelian tiger bead, *kye doke*, and a blue glass ring have been recovered from an inhumation burial south of the city wall.

5 *Burma Gazetteer – Lower Chindwin District*, Rangoon: Office of the Superintendent of Government Printing, Burma, 1912, p. 1.

6 Than Tun, 'History of Myanmar Culture', *Myanmar Two Millennia Conference, December 15–17, Proceedings*, pt. 4, Yangon: Universities Historical Research Centre, 1999, p. 1. See also, Thaw Tint and Sein Tun, *The Quaternary*

Stratigraphy and Palaeolithic–Neolithic Evidences from Central Burma, Yangon, 1985.

7 Three of the megaliths from the Chin So Kon mound are now kept at Monywa University History Department. A typology of the tools was carried out by U Than Tun Aung, titled *The Stone Implements from Moegyobyin: A Typological Study,* under the supervision of Dr Toe Hla, Mandalay University, December 1997.

8 Nyunt Htay and Khin Maung Win, 'Report on the Investigation of Metallic Implements Found in Nyaunggan Village, Budalin Township', *Proceedings of the Workshop on Bronze Age Culture in Myanmar (Yangon, 7 January 1999),* Yangon: Universities Historical Research Centre, 1999, pp. 71–3.

9 Moore and Pauk Pauk, 2001. For example, around Letpadaung, there are shafts about one metre in diameter. The interiors of these shafts are highly vitrified, but their function and dating need further examination.

10 See Nyunt Htay and Khin Maung Win, 1999, p. 70, for suggestions of earlier use and Glover, 1999, p. 85, on reasons for dating their use to the historic age.

11 Pe Maung Than and Win Naing, 'Geological Observations on the Nyaunggan Burial Ground (A Preliminary Report)', *Proceedings of the Workshop on Bronze Age Culture in Myanmar (Yangon, 7 January 1999),* Yangon: Universities Historical Research Centre, 1999, p. 11. See also, Moore and Pauk Pauk, 2001.

12 Kyaw Han, 1999, p. 54. Nyunt Han, 'Archaeological Findings at Nyaunggan Bronze Age Site' *Proceedings of the Workshop on Bronze Age Culture in Myanmar (Yangon, 7 January 1999),* Yangon: Universities Historical Research Centre, 1999, p. 31. C.F.W. Higham, 'The Bronze Age of Southeast Asia: Notes on the Nyaunggan Site, Myanmar', *Proceedings of the Workshop on Bronze Age Culture in Myanmar (Yangon, 7 January 1999),* Yangon: Universities Historical Research Centre, 1999, p. 91. Moore and Pauk Pauk, 2001. Other Chindwin sites include Ok-aing village in Budalin Township; Ywatha, Min Gwe Daung, Moktaw and Aing Daung villages in Kani Township; Htauk Ma Kon, Sar Htoon and Mogyo Byin villages in Salingyi Township; burials near Chaung-U village in Monywa District; sites around the copper-bearing formations of Sabedaung, Kyezindaung and Letpadaung on the west bank of the Chindwin River; and Shwe Taung Kon, Letpanchebaw, Kyaw Hmaing village in Nyaung-U Township. Letpanchebaw (21.16° N by 95.03° E) was excavated in 1978 and 2001. The excavations yielded Neolithic remains; a more recent survey of the eroded bank on the Irrawaddy River revealed a potsherd sequence spanning the Neolithic, Bronze, Pyu, Pagan and Ava periods. Stone rings and bronze tools were also found. The site has remnants of a circular brick wall, and has been identified as one of the nineteen Pyu villages of Pagan. Win Maung (Tanpawady), 'Pukan – 19 Ywa' (Bagan – 19 Villages), paper read at Maha Loka Mayazein Kuthodawgyi Hpaya in Mandalay for the 83rd birthday celebration of Sayagyi U Maung Maung Tin (Mahaweiza), 1999, p. 11.

13 Pauk Pauk, 'Excavation at Nyaunggan Bronze Age Site', *Proceedings of the Workshop on Bronze Age Culture in Myanmar (Yangon, 7 January 1999),* Yangon: Universities Historical Research Centre, 1999, p. 26.

14 Pe Maung Than and Win Naing, 1999, p. 2.

15 San Nyein, 'Beads from Nyaunggan', *Proceedings of the Workshop on Bronze Age Culture in Myanmar (Yangon, 7 January 1999),* Yangon: Universities Historical Research Centre, 1999, p. 78. Nyunt Han, 1999, p. 35.

16 Aung Myint, personal communication, 1999. Glover, 1999, p. 86.

17 Country Township and Division Map (Pyeh Neh Hnit Taing Mye Pon), Forestry Department, Yangon, 1997 [1 cm=13 km]; One Inch (1:63,360) Map Series, Third Edition, 1946.

18 (1) Wundwin Township: Bu Lu Kon hill near Shwe Taung village, Koko Kha Hla and Shaw Bin villages; (2) Mahlaing: fields outside Myin U Hle village, Myo Gon and Hnaw Kan villages; (3) Thazi: Shwe Ku Kon hillock near Let Htut Gon village and Nyaungyan village; (4) Pyaw Bwe: Aye Tha Yar, Ywa Htin Kon, Yanaung, Si Bin Tha, Htoon Bo, Myauk Mi Kon, Pin Thaung and Beinnaka villages; (5) Yamethin: Myo Hla village (Figure 1.6); (6) Pyinmana: Tatkon village (Figure 1.4); (7) Kyaukse: Kha Bo village; and (8) Taungtha Township: Inn Te village.

19 No Brahmanical or Buddhist objects have been recovered from Maingmaw. Than Tun, 'Brahmanical and Buddhist Iconography of Pyu, Mon, Rakhine and Myanma', paper read at the 50th Anniversary of the Sanatana Dharma Swayamsevak Sangh, Ramakrishna Mission, Rangoon, 14 January 2000, p. 1.

20 Bronze packets have been found at sites just south of Mandalay, around Pyinmana, in the Minbu area opposite Magwe, at the foot of Mount Popa, and at Halin. This covers a much wider area than the present Samon valley.

21 *Kye doke* recovered from Halin in the Chindwin region are much smaller, some 1.5 cm in length. Like examples among the Samon *kye doke,* they were placed on the hands of the skeleton, and wrapped to make packets (*ahdoke*).

22 Traces of cloth have also been reported on bronze axes recovered from Samon sites.

23 Three are from Koko Kha Hla (Wundwin), one from Myin U Hle (Mahlaing) and five from Nyaungyan (Thazi). The double figures were recovered from Koko Kha Hla and Nyaungyan. The triple figure is also from Nyaungyan.

24 While the most common glass colour is sky-blue, other colours such as greenish blue and dark green have been recovered. Also, rings of other materials have recently been found. For example, a round bronze ring (*c.* 5.5 cm in diameter) has been recovered from Pyaw Bwe Township. During the 2001 excavations at Letpanchebaw in Ywa Hmaing village a terracotta ring (*c.* 5.5 cm square) was found.

25 Nyunt Han, 1999, p. 35.

26 *Ibid.*

27 A different type of glass ring has been found in Mahlaing Township at Myo Gon, west of Koko Kha Hla, Wundwin Township. Made up of six turquoise blue bangles cast as a unit, the bracelet is 1.8 cm in height and with an inner diameter of 6.5 cm.

28 Nyunt Han, 1999, p. 35.

29 The identification of the green stone was made to the Director of the National Museum by the Gems Museum (Yangon), on the occasion of the Myanmar Necklaces (Beads) Exhibition at the National Museum, 18 August–30 September 2000. Beads decorated with white lines made from fossil wood (*ingyin kyauk*) or carnelian, are sometimes seen at transitional sites in the Samon region, but are more common at Pyu sites. See E. Moore and Aung Myint, 'Beads of Myanmar (Burma): Line Decorated Beads amongst the Pyu and Chin', *Journal of the Siam Society,* vol. 81, no. 1, 1993 [published 1995], pp. 54–87.

30 Flat disc glass beads vary in size and colour. Examples include a sapphire blue disc measuring 8.5 mm in diameter from Beinnaka; violet discs, *c.* 2.3 cm in diameter, from

Htoon Bo; and from Aye Tha Yar village, a deep blue one tinged with violet, *c.* 3.8 cm in diameter.

31 Myint Aung reported inhumation burials at Halin at several excavation sites. He also noted that, '. . . [there are] Neolithic ground and polished implements in different kinds of stones. The common types among them are adze and ring stone. There is not enough evidence to decide their place in the Halin cultural assemblage.' Myint Aung, 'The Excavations at Halin', *Journal of the Burma Research Society*, vol. 53, pt. 2, 1970, p. 61.

32 Planetary significance in current ritual may be relevant to the shape of both rings and beads, two of the grave goods recovered from prehistoric burials. For example, '. . . the elephant with tusks is associated with the planet Mercury, whose influence lasts 17 years. Placed on the south, Mercury is linked to Wednesday morning. When counting the eight planets counter-clockwise according to their period of influence, the final planet is always Mercury. For example, the duration of the Moon is 15 years, associated with the east and the tiger. Counting counter-clockwise 15 times, the ending planet is Mercury' (personal communication, U Win Maung). While this is cited in reference to elephant beads, planetary association may also prove relevant to the variety of ring shapes. In recording ring shapes at many villages, particularly in the Chindwin region, it has been noted that in every case there are rings in a number of different shapes. In the Samon area, there are different ring shapes and a range of zoomorphic beads. Any consideration of the significance of bead form needs to be in the context of other artefacts. For instance, Samon bead and ring forms relate to the 'mother goddesses', the *kye doke* and the design of the curvilinear 'coffin' ornaments, a pattern seen on the 'mother goddess' figures as well. The above astrological explanation is a hypothesis given to illustrate the complexity of present-day practice, as the range of grave goods described in this chapter suggests a similarly complex prehistoric ritual practice.

33 Nyunt Han, 1999, p. 34.

34 See T.O. Morris, 'Copper and bronze antiquities from Burma', *Journal of the Burma Research Society*, vol. 28, no. 2, 1938, pp. 95–9.

35 See Aung Thaw, *Report on the Excavations at Beikthano*, Rangoon: Ministry of Culture, Union of the Government of Burma, 1968, p. 55.

2 Digging for myths: archaeological excavations and surveys of the legendary nineteen founding villages of Pagan

Bob Hudson, U Nyein Lwin and U Win Maung (Tanpawady)

INTRODUCTION

Pagan (also commonly transliterated as Bagan) is an urban centre in Upper Burma (Myanmar) which reached its peak between the eleventh and thirteenth centuries AD. During this period, more than 2,000 brick temples, stupas, and monasteries were erected for the glory of Buddhism and the spiritual advancement of those who sponsored the construction (Figure 2.1).[1] The dating is well attested by epigraphic material from foundation stones.[2] Scientific evidence for activity at Pagan before this period has been sparse, although it has been determined by radiocarbon dating that pottery production was taking place at Otein Taung, an extensive earthenware site in what is now the geographical centre of the city, perhaps as early as AD 670–980.[3]

The origin of the city, or at least the origin of settlement in the general area that later became Pagan, is traditionally attributed to a confederation of nineteen villages dated to AD 107.[4] Our recently collected data, ranging from oral history to archaeological survey and excavation, has pinpointed on the Pagan map most of the contenders for founding or 'root' village status. The historiographical approach of the authors to this issue is divided. All generally agree with the conventional view that the direct provenance of the documentary evidence only goes back to AD 1520 or so.[5] However, the indigenous authors of this chapter are convinced that the parts of the chronicles relating to the origins of Pagan are facts, albeit facts that may be cloaked in ancient metaphor, which have been passed on through tradition and possibly through now-

Figure 2.1 Monuments within the Pagan archaeological zone. Photograph by the author.

lost, earlier documents. The Western author leans more toward the notion that humans have a remarkable propensity to create stories about themselves, and to believe firmly that these stories are true.[6] What may thus be 'invented traditions' should be viewed with great care. However, rather than argue these issues, the authors will content themselves with presenting the data, and offer the pleasure of critique to others.

CHRONICLES

The written history of Pagan was summarised in 1829 by a panel of scholars who were charged with 'sifting all credible records in the books'.[7] The result was the *Hmannan Yazawin*, later translated as the *Glass Palace Chronicle* by Pe Maung Tin and G.H. Luce,[8] which attempted to integrate inscriptions, earlier chronicles, and histories of individual pagodas, monasteries or towns. The *Glass Palace Chronicle*, as mentioned above, dates the first moves toward urbanism in the Pagan area to AD 107. It says that at that time, the Pyu founded Yon Hlut Kyun, a name with folkloric origins, about fourteen kilometres from Pagan on the eastern side of Mount Tuyin.[9]

The local story is that Pyu soldiers fleeing from a war saw a hunter and his dogs chasing a rabbit. The rabbit turned on his pursuers and drove them away, and this was taken as an omen that such a place would be a site worth defending against enemies. Despite such obstacles as a malicious flying squirrel and other aggressive faunal and floral totems, King Thamoddarit then 'began to build a city with the dwellers in nineteen villages'.[10] His son-in-law Pyusawhti, a hero who according to the chronicles killed the squirrel and several other beasts, has become a key symbol of modern Pagan. His bronze image even graces the forecourt of Pagan's museum, at the expense of the kings of the historical era.

The chronicles agree that the earliest civilisation in Burma was that of the Pyu. Four chronicles compiled between AD 1672 and 1829 mention the founding of Sri Ksetra, also called Thayekittaya, and all have it precede Pagan.[11] The four largest Pyu settlements, Beikthano, Halin, Mongmao and Sri Ksetra, which all enclose areas of 600 hectares or more within brick walls, have been the subject of extensive archaeological investigation. Beikthano appears to be the earliest, according to the available radiocarbon dates, possibly operating between the second century BC and seventh century AD. Radiocarbon dates have indicated activity at Halin between the first and eighth centuries AD. Mongmao, at the south end of the Kyaukse valley, has been assigned on stylistic grounds to the second to sixth century. Sri Ksetra is considered the latest, occupied between the fourth and tenth centuries AD.[12] The Pyu are also identified as having been present at Waddi,[13] a smaller walled site west of Mongmao, and at a cluster of settlements around Binnaka. The latter, located at E 96.15° N 20.5666° in

the Samon River valley, appears to have been continuously occupied from the Pyu to the Konbaung periods.[14] Pyu landscape and irrigation systems have also been investigated.[15] The Old Burmese tribes were seen by Luce as migrating by way of the Shan state to Kyaukse in the eighth century AD, and later continuing westward to Pagan.[16] This would make them late arrivals in terms of the radiocarbon dates, let alone the traditional ones.

The *Glass Palace Chronicle* lists the founding villages of Pagan as Nyaung-u, Nagabo, Nagakyit, Magyigyi, Tuti, Kyaussaga, Kokkethein, Nyaungwun, Anurada, Tazaunggun, Ywamon, Kyinlo, Kokko, Taungba, Myegedwin, Tharekya, Onmya (with a quibble as to whether this should actually be Singu), Yonhlut and Ywasaik.[17] We will take these names and their English spellings as a guide, while providing variants from other chronicles or oral sources. A version of the list had earlier appeared during the Nyaung Yan period (AD 1597–1752) in the *Maha Yazawingyi* or *Great Chronicle*, by U Kala, and continued to be reproduced in subsequent chronicles (including the *Glass Palace Chronicle*), pagoda histories, biographies and guide books for pilgrims.[18]

SURVEY METHODS

Collection of data on the sites mentioned in the list of nineteen villages has ranged from a re-examination of English and Burmese documentary sources and inch-to-the-mile survey maps to interviews with local residents, including the abbots of monasteries, who are often *de facto* custodians of local history. Win Maung made several field trips to survey sites and collect oral history. Bob Hudson and Nyein Lwin conducted a major excavation of the putative palace of the founding King Thamoddarit at Yonhlut, and did test excavations, surveys and sampling of some of the other possible founding villages and their environs. The locations of places that may not easily be found again, such as abandoned habitation sites, were pinpointed with a Global Positioning System (GPS) receiver. All site locations are reported in this chapter in decimal degrees, which is the standard form of longitude and latitude used in computer mapping.[19] The sites are listed in the order of their distance from the walled medieval elite centre now known as 'Old Pagan' (Figure 2.2). Also provided at the beginning of each entry is a list of variant spellings of the site name.

THE NINETEEN VILLAGES

Nagabo (Nagobo, Nagasaing, Nagaso, Nagasit, Nagabol, Nagasate, Nagasi, Nagaaing, Pagan Myo). Map 84 K/16, E 94.8757° N 21.1767°

This site is now a palimpsest of Pagan era and later buildings, located to the east and southeast of modern Taungbi village.

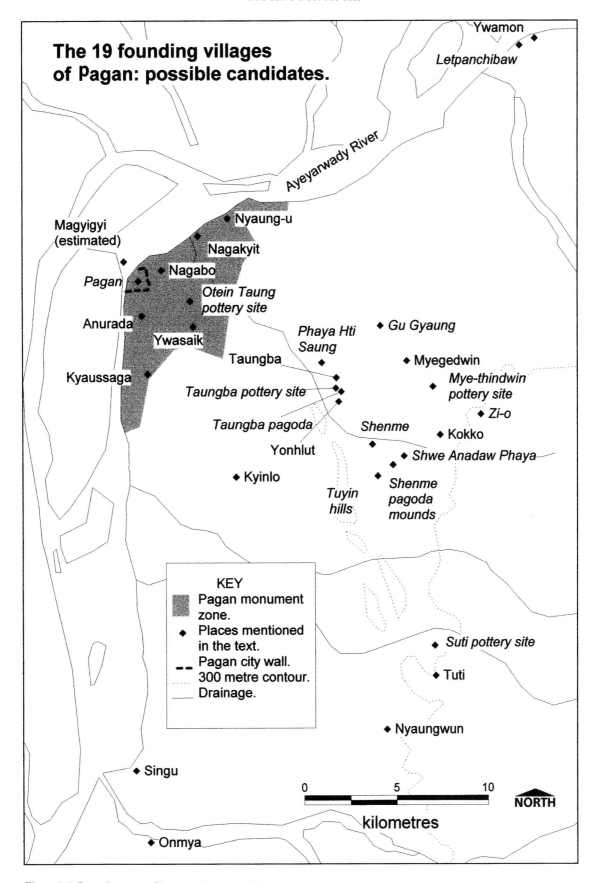

Figure 2.2 Location map: Pagan and surrounding area.

Nagakyit (Naga Kyee). Map 84 K/16, E 94.8946° N 21.1929°

An inscription in the Shwezigon pagoda mentioned that this village, 'Naga Kyitmaw', was nearby. The location is between the Wetkyi-in stream and the Shwezigon pagoda. Some of the buildings nearby have Pyu bricks marked with finger-strokes.

Anurada (Anuradha, Anutara, Anurudha, Myingaba). Map 84 K/16, E 94.8654° N 21.1552°

Now called Myinkaba, Anuradha is the only Pali name found among the nineteen villages. There are Pyu bricks with fingermarks or characters south and north of the present village and around the Nga Kywe Na Daung pagoda where the old village was supposed to be. A version of the *New Chronicle* says the present day 'Old Pagan' was on the site of the original Anurada village, and moved when King Pyinbya founded his new capital in AD 846.[20]

Ywasaik (Yworsiet, Ywasit, Ywaseik, Ywasait, Ywasite, Thitmahti, Phwasaw, Tampawaddy). Map 84 K/16. Estimated location E 94.8918° N 21.15°

Phwasaw, the name mentioned in the *New Chronicle*, was also the name of a later queen of Pagan. The 'third palace', said to have been founded by King Thaik-taing-min in AD 514, is believed to have been located here on the perimeter of the Pagan archaeological zone. The palace site, south of West Phwasaw village, is today marked by an inscribed brick and concrete pillar, as are Pagan's other supposed palaces. According to local informants, the old village of Ywasaik was located north of the Dhammarajika (Dhammayazika) pagoda. Pyu bricks with fingermarks are also found here, and village elders in West Phwasaw told Win Maung that a gold scroll inscribed in the Pyu language and script was once discovered in the bed of a stream running west of the Dhammarajika pagoda.

Nyaung-U (Nyaung-oo). Map 84 K/16, E 94.9101° N 21.2011°

A modern market town and administrative centre, Nyaung-U retains its archaic name. Housing developments in the area make new archaeological discoveries difficult, though open excavations from construction work remain potential sources of information.

Kyaussaga (Kyauk Saga). Map 84 K/16, E 94.8681° N 21.1277°

The village is situated east of the present day Thiripyitsaya village, south of New Pagan and on the southern bank of Ye-O-Zin stream. Two sandstone Buddha images in the Kyauk Saga temple are said to be of a pre-eleventh century date, executed in a Gupta-influenced style. Old Pyu bricks with fingermarks are also found here.

Thiripyitsaya is said to have been the second capital, located near the Lokananda pagoda, a riverside structure that prominently marks the southern extent of the city. The putative site of the 'second palace' is today marked just west of New Pagan's main crossroad by an inscribed brick and concrete pillar. The move of the locus of power to Thiripyitsaya is mentioned with a curious casualness in the *Glass Palace Chronicle*. In a saga otherwise full of dramatic deeds of men, gods and spirits we are merely told that in the reign of Thinlikyaung (AD 344–377) 'the group of nineteen villages was dissolved, and he founded and built the city of Thiripyissaya [sic] at the site of Lokananda where he lived'.[21]

Kyinlo (Krin-lo, Kra-lo, Krin-lon, Jin-lon). Map 84 K/16, E 94.9133° N 21.0792°

This site is in a cultivated field east of Kinka on the Pagan-Chauk road, and north of Kyaukkan. Potsherds, elephant-shaped pendants and spherical and barrel shaped green and orange beads have been discovered in this village.[22] Field survey has located fingermarked bricks and old furnaces for smelting iron, with iron slagheaps. In a monastery compound north of Kyaukkan village there stands a ruined brick building with elements that suggest an architectural style earlier than the eleventh century AD. Archaeological excavation at Kyinlo in 1906 recovered iron implements, a stone image of the Buddha, stone receptacles supposed to be reliquaries, and mutilated bronze figures of the Buddha and two disciples.[23]

Taungba (Taung-pa, Taung-ma, Taung-fa, Taung-pan, Taung-mae). Map 84 K/16, E 94.9656° N 21.1259°

The present village of Taungba was relocated in modern times due to highway construction. It is now east of the road between Nyaung-U and Kyaukpadaung, and within view of the Tooth Relic Pagoda on Tuyin Mountain. The name Taungba literally means a place near a mountain. There are several local sites of historic and archaeological significance here.

Hti Ta Hsaung Pagoda. Map 84 K/16, E 94.9581° N 21.1329°

The Phaya Hti Saung or Hti Ta Hsaung pagoda, located one kilometre northwest of Taungba village, is the major monument extant in this eastern hinterland area of Pagan, apart from several monuments on Mount Tuyin. A stupa-topped temple, it is reputed to enshrine bodily relics of the medieval monk, Shin Arahan, who is credited with being the spiritual mentor to King Anawrahta.[24] It was most recently restored in 1985, and is an active religious site, with an attached monastery.

Taungba Pagoda. Map 84 K/16, E 94.9681° N 21.1193°

On the southern side of Taungba village is a small pagoda that was restored in 1907, according to an ink inscription inside. There is evidence to support local opinion that it was originally a medieval structure. A circular stone slab, now used as a stepping stone at the entrance, resembles the capstones found in old relic chambers. Part of a stone capsule or container, possibly a reliquary, was found among brick debris nearby, in a depression formed by a disused water tank. This site appears on the 1945 British Army survey map 84 K/16 as a monastery.

Earthenware site

This area is located between the modern village and the site from which Taungba was moved when the highway was built. An ash lens (Map 84 K/16, E 94.9652° N 21.1209°), dense with potsherds, was excavated and sampled at Taungba for radiocarbon dating. The sample, OZE 765, had a radiocarbon age of 530±40 BP, giving a calendar date range of AD 1300–1450 at 95.4 percent probability.[25] The evidence suggests that this site was used for the production, by open-field or pit firing, of a diverse range of domestic earthenware products. Samples recovered included lamps and containers with rim diameters of up to 40 cm. No sprinkler pots, the standard ritual items of the Pagan period, were found in the ash lenses. The earthenware had a bright red, coarse fabric, with visible quartz inclusions. Some pieces were burnt through, suggesting overheating during manufacture. Pottery was noted over an area of at least 100 by 200 metres. Material collected on the surface often had a much finer fabric, suggesting different phases of use at the site. Surface finds included bowl and stem fragments of smoking pipes, which we would attribute to the post-Pagan period, as pipes must have followed the introduction of tobacco from the New World.

Ruined pagoda

About 300 metres west of the earthenware deposits there is a mound, apparently a pagoda ruin. It is 15 metres in diameter, 2.5 metres high, with a hollow on top suggestive of past efforts to recover relics. There are pieces of worked sandstone among the debris. It fits the description of, and is therefore probably the same as, a mound 'near Taungba village' excavated early last century.[26]

Yonhlut (Yon Lut, Yon Hlut, Yon Lwe, Yon Hlut Kyun). Map 84 K/16, E 94.9647° N 21.1133°

This name has been variously translated as Free Rabbit Island, Free Animal Forest, a Jungle where Rabbits Were Set Free, or the Place of the Hare's Release. The archaic word 'kyun' is still used for 'jungle' in this area, though it more generally means 'island'. To confuse matters, an island in the Irrawaddy (Ayeyarwady) River opposite Pagan is also called Yon Hlut Kyun,[27] although its claim to historical status barely goes back 50 years. The current residents appear to have forgotten the names of the villages that were mapped there in 1945 (Map 84 K/16)

Figure 2.3 Excavations at Yon Hlut Kyun. Photograph by the author.

and a field survey in 1999 indicated that the location of the villages on the island, as well as the island's shape, has changed due to regular inundation. The ancient Yonhlut, while ten kilometres or more from the Irrawaddy, is itself effectively an island, at least in the wet season. It sits on relatively high ground, with a seasonally active stream to its south, and what appears to be a vestigial branch of the stream, largely now filled by agriculture and affected by local canal building, to its north.

In 1905, the archaeologists at Pagan spent 200 rupees to erect masonry pillars marking all of the old palace sites mentioned in the chronicles. This included a pillar at Yon Hlut Kyun identifying it as the home of Pagan's first dynasty. The masonry pillars were referred to only peripherally in a list of 'expenses sanctioned and incurred', with no explanation as to why the particular sites were chosen.[28] However, a handwritten manuscript of the *New Pagan Chronicle*, by Saya Be contains a drawing of brick foundations at Yon Hlut Kyun,[29] so the site may have been well known locally at the time the monument was erected. Local people say there is a tradition of

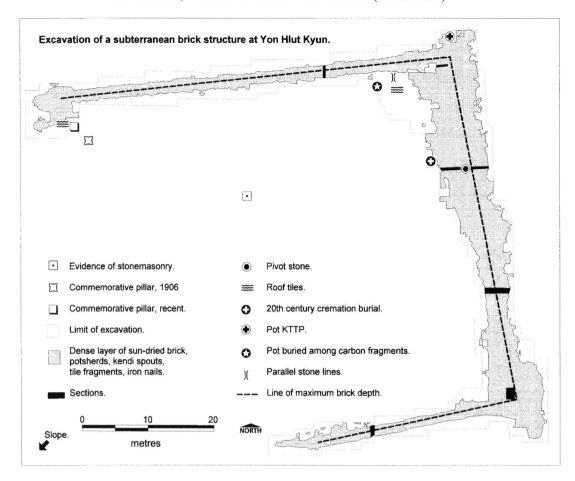

Figure 2.4 Plan of the Yon Hlut Kyun excavation.

sprinkling a handful of earth from this auspicious spot over new construction sites. The authors have observed visitors taking away bags of soil which they indicated were for ritual purposes.

In 1999, Bob Hudson and Nyein Lwin investigated Yon Hlut Kyun at the suggestion of the Director of Archaeology at Pagan, U Aung Kyaing. The brief was, in effect, to find scientific evidence to prove or disprove the legends. By this time there was no above-ground structure visible. The excavation programme resulted in the discovery of a 60-metre square structure made of sun-dried brick with roof tiles, iron nails, a pivot-stone from a doorway and earthenware pottery fragments that included *kendi*, or ritual sprinkler pots (Figures 2.3 and 2.4).[30] The structure is located on the eastern approach to Pagan from Mount Popa, a well-known pilgrimage site, beyond which is the medieval rice-growing area and putative homeland of the Burmans, Kyaukse. No charcoal samples were found in any context that would justify radiocarbon dating, and a chronology for the building is still an open question. Comparison of some of the artefacts excavated with material from Pagan has produced inconclusive results.

Pottery
Earthenware potsherds were found throughout the Yon Hlut site, including several spouts from libation or sprinkler pots. These pots appear in Pagan-period wall paintings illustrating the Buddhist ritual of pouring water.[31] Two round-bottomed pots with cordmarked decoration on the outside were found substantially complete. Pot KTTP (Figure 2.5) was found at a depth of one metre, under the deepest layer of rubble located during the excavations. Two other pots that were located appear to represent continuing use of the site for ritual purposes. One earthenware pot was found sitting in a discrete mass of soil and carbon fragments, with a distinguishable edge between this soil mass and the surrounding matrix of red earth. This suggests that a hole may have been dug, and the pot either burned or heated in the hole, or buried in the hole along with burnt material. The third major ceramic find consisted of a twentieth-century Chinese porcelain bowl in close context with burnt human bones.[32] This was found on the edge of the brick structure, with no overlying brick. It was again sitting in what appeared to be a deliberately dug hole, and stands as evidence of the continuing ritual use of the site.

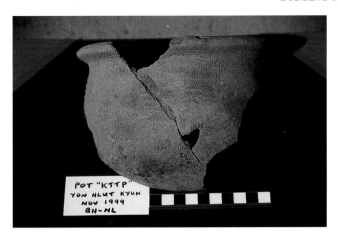

Figure 2.5 Pot KTTP, nicknamed 'King Thamoddarit's Toddy Pot'. Photograph by the author.

Bricks

Bricks at Yon Hlut Kyun appear to be sun-dried rather than fired. Most have deteriorated to rubble, but at least one survived virtually complete, if not intact, to allow accurate measurement.[33] There was no sign on any of the

brick segments that were excavated of the fingermarks typical of Pyu bricks. When measurements of bricks from a number of archaeological sites in Burma were subjected to statistical comparison by multivariate analysis, the bricks at Yon Hlut Kyun corresponded closely with samples from Gu Gyaung, a Pyu-style monument several kilometres to the north (see below), and also with Pagan bricks of the twelfth and thirteenth centuries.[34] The distance on the graph (Figure 2.6) between the brick samples indicates relative differences in size. The correlation between the samples from Yon Hlut Kyun and Gu Gyaung needs to be viewed in the light of both being limited events. There is just one structure at Yon Hlut Kyun, and a pair of apparently associated buildings at Gu Gyaung. The other samples are from Pyu sites and from Pagan. These sites saw construction over some centuries, during which time there was quite a variation in brick size. The graph also indicates that Hiram Cox, visiting Pagan two centuries ago, appears to have accurately determined a minimum and maximum size range of the bricks used there.[35] Popular wisdom among archaeologists and historians in Burma is that 'old bricks are bigger'. Many early Pyu bricks compare in size with

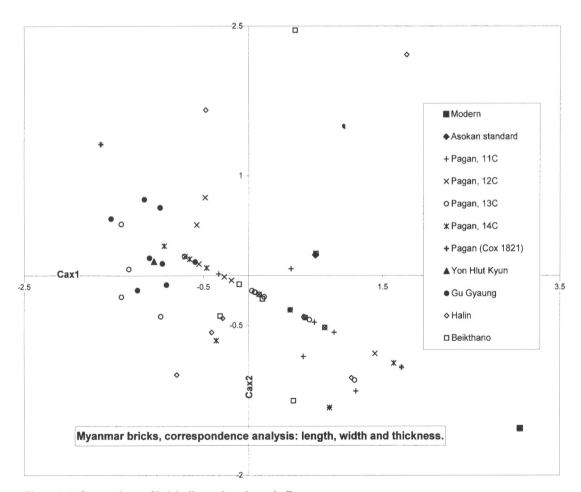

Figure 2.6 Comparison of brick dimensions in early Burma.

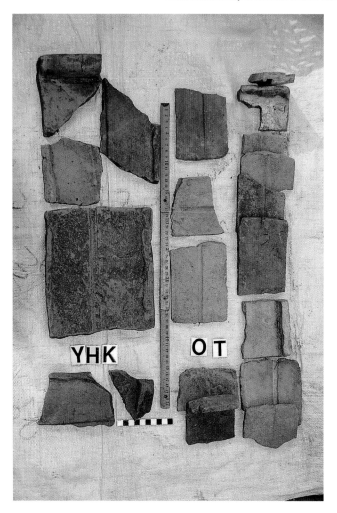

Figure 2.7 Two styles of roof tile, from Yon Hlut Kyun and Otein Taung. Photograph by the author.

Figure 2.8 One of several iron nails from the Yon Hlut Kyun excavation. Photograph by the author.

the large 'Asokan standard' of 50 by 26.25 by 8.75 cm that originated in India and field measurements indicate that bricks at Pagan generally tend to be smaller than this.[36] There are encased pagodas where the outer bricks are larger than the inner ones, so a direct chronology should not be implied. However, the clustering of bricks according to their mathematical characteristics certainly does appear to tell a story, and in this instance, suggests a relationship between Yon Hlut Kyun and buildings much later than the traditional second century AD origin of this 'first palace' site.

Tiles

Deposits of roofing tiles were found at Yon Hlut Kyun, and tile fragments were scattered generally across the site. The tiles appeared to have been fired, but not glazed. They were turned under at one end and had raised ridges along the top edges of their longer sides. The turned end would have allowed the tile to be hung on a horizontal

batten, while the ridges would have presumably directed rainwater down the tile, and helped reduce leakage. The tiles had a small central indented channel on the upper surface, and many had fractured along this line. The function of this indentation along the length of the tile is not clear. A comparison of the tiles found at Yon Hlut Kyun and the much smaller tiles excavated by the authors at Otein Taung, an earthenware production site within the Pagan archaeological zone, just east of the Sulamani pagoda, shows considerable difference in size, form and fabric (Figure 2.7). According to radiocarbon dates, the Otein Taung site was supplying Pagan with earthenware between AD 870 and 1350.[37] The tiles excavated there were made of a much finer paste than those at Yon Hlut Kyun, which is what one might expect from a long-term industry with highly refined and organised production methods. The key point about the tiles from the two locations is that they are as different as the bricks from Pagan and Yon Hlut Kyun are similar. While the bricks may be similar in size, at least, between the two sites, the variation in roofing tiles suggests different sources of supply, and what in effect are different builders' specifications.

Metals

Along with pottery, nails and other iron materials have been recorded as ritual burial inclusions in first millennium AD Burma.[38] Iron nails were the only metal items recovered at Yon Hlut Kyun. They were characteristically square in the shaft, and turned at the top (Figure 2.8). Nails have been excavated from the Pyu city of Sri Ksetra, or Hmawza, but in the absence of a formal typology or metallurgical study of nails in pre-modern Burma, it is not fruitful currently to do more than note that iron nails have long been in use. Early iron-working has been recorded in the Pagan area, including at some of the contenders for founding village status.[39]

Stone

There are several examples of worked stone at Yon Hlut Kyun. All are functional, and no decoration is evident. An augering programme, used to detect underground materials and record soil composition, located some pieces of sandstone near the centre of the site. Excavation of a one-metre square test pit uncovered one piece of stone that had been worked with a 22 mm chisel. There was a parallel row of dressed stones on the inner side of the north wall of the structure, in close proximity to some roof tiles. Our initial impressions are that the stones formed a drain or a path. A pivot stone, with an indentation to take a vertical wooden doorpost, similar to those seen in pagodas at Pagan, was found while excavating a section along the eastern wall. There was at least a centimetre of wear around the indentation in the pivot stone.

Bone and carbon

Fragments of animal bone and bovine teeth were found intermittently across the site. As the area is used for agriculture, and as none of the material was found under the brick structure, it must be assumed to have been introduced by natural processes. Carbon was found in relative abundance, but none was found in a context that would justify radiocarbon dating. Farmers annually burn off wood and straw in these fields, and charcoal from domestic cooking and sugar ovens could have been spread across the area.

Interpretation

The dating, and for that matter the function, of the building at Yon Hlut Kyun remains an open question. Augering of the site down to natural soil at ten metre intervals both inside and outside the wall failed to locate any central structure, which one might expect if the wall had enclosed a temple or monastery complex. The worn pivot stone, if it was original and not recycled, suggests use of the building over a considerable period of time. The bricks appear similar to those of the Pagan period, and dissimilar to those at Pyu sites. However, the roof tiles do not relate to the tiles observed or excavated at Pagan. Local people remain convinced that this is the palace of the first dynasties, but the conventional archaeologists' disclaimer, that 'further investigation is necessary', is in this case highly applicable.

Myegedwin (Mye-thintwin, Mye-thindwin).
Map 84 O/4, E 95.0024° N 21.1337°

The present site of Mye-thindwin is only 150 years old, but the area is claimed, both in chronicles and local folklore, to have been the birthplace of Pagan's first king, Thamoddarit. A local folk tale also tells how an old Pyu couple adopted and brought up Pyusawhti, who eventually married Thamoddarit's daughter after performing

Figure 2.9 An early stupa at Gu Gyaung, with relic chamber exposed. Photograph by the author.

many heroic deeds. Plots of land at Mye-thindwin retain names relating to these stories. A field (Map 84 O/4, E 95.0159° N 21.1215°) east of the village, said to have been uncultivated land only twenty years ago, is dense with potsherds, and smoking pipes and earthenware roof tiles have been recovered here by farmers. Augering and a small test pit uncovered a lens of potash, between 22 cm and 34 cm below the surface, which contained earthenware sherds, suggesting a site used for the open-field firing of pottery. More than one hundred abandoned furnaces for smelting iron have been located near the neighbouring village of Zi-O (Map 84 O/4, E 95.0411 N 21.1087).

Gu Gyaung Pagoda Map 84 K/16, E 94.9888°
N 21.1504°

The unrestored Gu Gyaung complex near Mye-thindwin features a stupa (Figure 2.9) sitting on the western side of a small temple. There is also a brick foundation of a third structure, eight by ten metres. The complex sits on a brick platform, 26 by 22 metres, and there is evidence of an enclosure wall. Temple doorways open to the east, north and south. The roof of the temple has collapsed and the structure is filled with rubble, but the temple appears to have had a vaulted chamber with no central pillars. A brick base that presumably supported a Buddha image abuts the western wall, indicating that the image faced east in the conventional manner. The stupa is 5.7 metres high, though the top is damaged. A sandstone spire about a metre high, with seven multi-tiered umbrellas was found here, and is now in the Bagan Archaeological Museum. The relic chamber in the stupa, broken open in times beyond the memory of the local people, is lined with stone, and has a capacity of more than one cubic metre. As discussed earlier, the bricks at Gu Gyaung when subjected to mathematical analysis cluster with bricks from Yon Hlut Kyun and twelfth- to fourteenth-century Pagan.

Kokko (Kote-ko, Kote-koo). Map 84 O/4, E 95.0195° N 21.0989°

Kokko was abandoned, according to local records, in 1878 and families transferred to neighbouring villages, including Mye-thindwin. Locals believe that Myin-kwe-min, said to have become king at Pagan in AD 716, was the son of a wealthy man from Kokko. On an unexcavated mound of potsherds up to two metres high remains from the Pagan and Ava periods have been recovered. In this general area near Shenme (Map 84 K/16, E 94.9841° N 21.0944°), the authors recorded two mounds (Map 84 K/16, E 94.9868° N 21.0795°), each about twenty metres in diameter, containing bricks as well as pieces of shaped and pecked sandstone. There are two other groups of apparently early pagoda ruins southeast of Shenme. These include a pair of mounds about eight metres in diameter (Map 84 K/16, E 94.9947° N 21.0848°), and a small monument known as the Shwe Anadaw Paya (Map 84 K/16, E 95.0006° N 21.0888°). Restored in 1973, the Shwe Anadaw Paya has a ruined pagoda mound which is nine metres in diameter beside it, containing dressed sandstone reminiscent of the capping of a medieval relic chamber. The presence of *sima* stones, which customarily mark the site of ordination halls, around the Shwe Anadaw Paya suggests that it may have been the site of an earlier monastery.

Tuti (Htu-te, Hton-kyauk, Tutain, Sate, Suti, Sade). Map 84 P/1, E 95.0163° N 20.9850°

Modern Suti reputedly has three fields nearby which contain old potsherds. An ash lens at forty centimetres deep in one of these (Map 84 P/1, E 95.0159° N 20.9993°), apparently an earthenware production site, produced a radiocarbon date that could sit anywhere between AD 1680 and 1960 (sample OZE 766: 70±40 BP). There was material below this that we did not have time to sample, so this does not necessarily represent the earliest possible date for the site. The ash was densely packed with potsherds which had a coarse, red fabric resembling the material from Taungba and Mye-thindwin. Another field on the eastern edge of Suti had potsherds scattered over an area of 170 by 100 metres. Further dating would be necessary to determine whether this is exclusively a recent site, or one that has continued since early times. A hint of antiquity is contained in the name of the village monastery, Than-bo, or 'iron smelting'. There are old iron furnaces nearby, and local people report digging up bronze bowls with lids.

Nyaungwun (Tetma, Nyaung-bin). Map 84 L/13, E 94.9905° N 20.9597°

The present Tetma village is near the southernmost tip of the Tuyin mountain range. Its older name was Nyaung Bin or Banyan Tree village, on account of big banyan trees that once surrounded it. Around the village are old and ruined furnaces for smelting iron. A *mu-htaw*, or small pagoda, supposedly dating from ancient times, stands about 800 metres southeast of the village.

Ywamon (Ywamone, Ywapon, Ywapu, Ywamo, Shapote, Ywahmine). Map 84 O/3, E 95.0707° N 21.2861°

This abandoned settlement known today as Shwetaung Ywahmain is near Letpanchibaw (Map 84 O/3, E 95.0627° N 21.2828°). Parts of a circular brick wall can be seen here, somewhat eroded by the river. In 1978, excavations by the Archaeology Department revealed evidence of Neolithic, Bronze, and Iron (Pyu) Age activity. Artefacts found included potsherds, domestic utensils, stone and bronze weapons, beads, ear plugs and stone rings. The evidence suggests continuous occupation, or regular re-occupation, from prehistoric times through to the Pagan and Konbaung periods. According to a local story collected during a visit by one of the authors (Win Maung), a thousand Ari monks, accused in some texts of being a heretical and profligate sect, came to stay here during the Pagan period.

Onmya (Ohnmyar, Okmya, Ngasintku, Ngasingu, Sinku, Sintku, Sintku Ohnmyar, Sint-ku-ohn)

There is disagreement in the *Great Chronicle*, the *New Chronicle* and the *Glass Palace Chronicle* as to whether the name Onmya, which appears on map 84 I/13 as Okmya (E 94.8675° N 20.9065°), or the name Singu (E 94.8675° N 20.9065°) should be in the canonical list of nineteen villages.[40] Conveniently for the purposes of regional settlement analysis, at least, both are in the same geographical area in relation to Pagan.

Village names with dubious or unknown locations
Magyigyi
According to local informants, this name appeared in a stone inscription which had been removed from a pagoda that was washed away by the river, a fate hypoth-

esised for the entire western part of the walled complex at Pagan.[41] The inscription supposedly placed the village to the northwest of the pagoda, which means the village must also have been washed away. On the strength of this, we have tentatively assigned Magyigyi to a hypothetical spot in the Irrawaddy River, at E 94.8562° N 21.1808°. However, unless the inscription can be located and studied, Magyigyi heads the 'dubious' list.

Tazaunggun

The *New Pagan Chronicle* estimated that this village was near Myingyan, a considerable distance upriver from Pagan. Tazaung (Map 84 O/3, E 95.3291° N 21.4426°) may be the place the chronicle's author had in mind, but our field survey has so far found no apparent link with antiquity.

Kokkethein and Tharekya

These villages were described as 'not existing now' in the *New Chronicle,* and no claimants have so far been found in our survey.

DISCUSSION AND CONCLUSION

Several issues come to the fore in the light of this investigation of whether the nineteen founding villages of Pagan are mythological, historical, or something between the two. The activity in Pagan's eastern hinterland is intriguing. Ritual buildings at Gu Gyaung, Taungba and Shenme appear to date from some part of the Pagan monument construction period, and further investigation might find them a more clearly defined place in the timescale. The geographical location of this cluster of villages would also fit Stargardt's model of first millennium settlements being located along secondary streams, rather than major rivers, to enable more efficient control of water resources.[42] The structure found at Yon Hlut Kyun remains a puzzle. The mytho-historical view is that it should be the palace of King Thamoddarit, as described in the *Glass Palace Chronicle*, although it does not immediately appear to be related in terms of its layout to palaces of the historical era, or for that matter to other buildings of the Pagan period. If this hinterland area was, as the chronicles say, the early administrative core of a confederation of villages, then what we see today are just the remnants.

The role of peripheral villages such as Onmya and Ywamon is unclear, though Ywamon is well situated for defence from any up river incursions. However, it might also be suggested that villages up or down the river would only assume strategic significance after the centre of government moved from the eastern side of Mount Tuyin to a location where control of the river as a permanent mode of transport for goods or armies became valuable.

A key aim of this project has been to investigate the settlement patterns at Pagan that later left their mark so

notably in Buddhist monuments. Six of the putative founding villages are within the monument zone. In the eleventh century, according to the dates for the city's buildings recorded or estimated in the *Inventory of Monuments at Pagan*, the riverside villages from Nyaung-u down to Kyaussaga all had monuments built nearby.[43] The city did not expand beyond this vertical limit, but instead increased in density at the centre, and eventually pushed eastward in the thirteenth century to the largely monastic centres at Minnanthu, just past the Otein Taung earthenware mounds, and Ywasaik.[44] The growth and eventual contraction of Pagan, and the movement of the locus of power up the river to Ava, Sagaing, Amarapura and Mandalay, have been studied in detail, but the origins of the city are much less clear.[45] We know that there was a dramatic change in settlement behaviour in first millennium Burma, from the walled habitations of the Pyu, big enough for the whole community to live inside, to the low-density, monument-rich city of Pagan, with most of its activity taking place outside the walled, elite core.[46] We hope that our survey data can contribute to a broad spectrum of enquiry and debate, from textual analysis to the application of archaeological and geographical theories of the human use of space, to help provide a clearer picture of the lives, times and behaviour of the founders of Pagan.

ACKNOWLEDGMENTS

We would like to thank the abbots and monks, village elders, friends from the 'nineteen villages' and the architects' group (Mandalay) who helped on several field trips. The archaeological side of the research was made possible by the Carlyle Greenwell Bequest, the Australian Institute of Nuclear Science and Engineering (Grants 00/180S, 01/150), the James Kentley Memorial Scholarship, and a gift from Roma Wilson. The work has been encouraged and facilitated by U Nyunt Han, Director General of Archaeology, and U Aung Kyaing, Assistant Director General. Thanks for data and ongoing academic input go to Pierre Pichard, Roland Fletcher, Mike Barbetti, Michael Aung-Thwin, Andrew Wilson, Ian Johnston and Pamela Gutman. At the Yon Hlut Kyun excavation, we would like to acknowledge the contributions of Tessa Boermah, Emma Hetherington, Shah Alam Zaini, Don Tindale, Ted Robinson, Jordan Robinson and our excavators, U San Ke, U Nyunt Aung, U Kan Myint, U Bo Kyin, U Aung-Nine, U Shwe-oo and U Myint-oo.

NOTES

1 Hundreds of these buildings have recently been repaired or substantially reconstructed. See Bob Hudson, 'The Merits of Rebuilding Bagan', *Orientations*, vol. 31, no. 5, 2000, pp. 85–6.
2 The data for 86 epigraphically dated buildings was gathered from Pierre Pichard, *Inventory of Monuments at Pagan*, vols.

1–7, Paris: UNESCO, 1992–9. Also, vol. 8 (unpublished proofs), supplied by the author (copy retained at Rare Books Dept, Fisher Library, University of Sydney). The dates are presented as a graph in Bob Hudson, Nyein Lwin, and Win Maung (Tanpawady), 'The Origins of Bagan; New Dates and Old Inhabitants', *Asian Perspectives*, vol. 40, no. 1, 2001, pp. 48–74.

3 Two Australian Nuclear Science and Technology Organisation radiocarbon dates from the Otein Taung pottery production site suggest activity involving burning wood or charcoal as fuel possibly as early as AD 650–830 (sample OZE 770, 1290±40 BP, which is probably redeposited material 1.2 metres from the top of a 7-metre mound of debris, which has earlier dates in its lower levels) and more certainly between AD 760–980 (sample OZE 769, 1190±40 BP, from an ash lens 1.5 metres below modern ground level).

4 Pe Maung Tin and G.H. Luce (trans.), *The Glass Palace Chronicle of the Kings of Burma*, Rangoon: Rangoon University Press, 1923 (reprinted 1960), pp. 28–9.

5 This refers to manuscripts. A good outline of the history of chronicle compilation can be found in the introduction to the *Glass Palace Chronicle* (Pe Maung Tin, 1960), pp. ix-xxii. G.H. Luce, 'A Century of Progress in Burmese History and Archaeology', *Journal of the Burma Research Society*, vol. 32, no. 1, 1948, pp. 79–94. Than Tun, *Essays on the History and Buddhism of Burma*, Whiting Bay, Arran, Scotland: Kiscadale, 1988.

6 As outlined in Eric Hobsbawm, 'Introduction: Inventing Traditions' in *The Invention of Tradition*, Eric Hobsbawm and Terence Ranger (eds), Cambridge: Cambridge University Press, 1983, pp. 1–14.

7 Pe Maung Tin, 1923, p. ix.

8 *Ibid.*

9 *Ibid.*, pp. 28–36.

10 *Ibid.*, p. 28.

11 Maung Hla, 'The Chronological Dates of the Kings of Burma who reigned at Thayekhittaya (ancient Prome) and at Pagan', *Journal of the Burma Research Society*, vol. 13, no. 2, 1923, p. 82.

12 Aung Thaw, *Report on the Excavations at Beikthano*, Rangoon: Ministry of Union Culture, 1968. Myint Aung, 'The Excavations at Halin', *Journal of the Burma Research Society*, vol. 53, no. 2, 1970, pp. 55–62. U Sein Maung U, 'Mongmao, a Forgotten City', *The Working People's Daily*, Jan. 21 and 23, and Feb. 3, 1981. There is no equivalent monograph in English for Sri Ksetra, as for Beikthano and Halin, but research dating back to the early twentieth century (such as in 'Excavations at Hmawza near Prome', *Archaeological Survey of India, Annual Report*, 1909–10, Delhi) is neatly summarised in Aung Thaw, *Historical Sites in Burma*, Rangoon, 1972, pp. 16–33. The scientific evidence for Pyu chronology is discussed in detail in Hudson, Nyein Lwin, and Win Maung, 2001.

13 Aung Myint, *Ancient Myanmar Cities in Aerial Photos* (in Burmese), Yangon: Ministry of Culture, 1999.

14 Michael Aung-Thwin, 'Burma before Pagan: The Status of Archaeology Today', *Asian Perspectives*, vol. 25, no. 2, 1983, pp. 1–21.

15 D.G. Donovan, Hayao Fukui, and Toshikatsu Itoh, 'Perspective on the Pyu Landscape', *Southeast Asian Studies*, vol. 36, no. 1, 1998, pp. 19–126. Janice Stargardt, *The Ancient Pyu of Burma: Early Pyu Cities in a Man-Made Landscape*, Cambridge: PACSCA, 1990.

16 G.H. Luce, 'Old Kyaukse and the Coming of the Burmans.' *Journal of the Burma Research Society*, vol. 42, no. 1, 1959, pp. 75–110.

17 Pe Maung Tin, 1923, p. 29.

18 The *Great Chronicle*, or *Mahayazawingyi*, by U Kala, compiled in 1714–33, was published in two volumes (in Burmese), in 1926, by Pyigyimundaing Pitakat Press, Rangoon. Three undated palm-leaf manuscripts, *Notes on Pagan*, *Royal Orders of King Nyaung Yan* and *Yazawin Choke*, in the possession of co-author Win Maung, or seen by him in other private collections, reproduce this list of nineteen villages, suggesting that the information was considered to be valid historical information by Burmese scholars from the time of U Kala onward.

19 Decimal degrees = degrees + (minutes/60) + (seconds/3600).

20 From a hand-written manuscript in a private collection, seen by Win Maung.

21 Pe Maung Tin, 1923, p. 45.

22 These beads are considered characteristic trade goods of the Pyu period. See Elizabeth Moore and Aung Myint, 'Beads of Myanmar (Burma)', *Journal of the Siam Society*, vol. 81, no. 1, 1993, pp. 55–81. See also, Aung Myint, 1999.

23 *Archaeological Survey of Burma*, Rangoon: Office of the Superintendent, 1907, p. 9 (referred to in subsequent notes as ASB).

24 Khin Maung Nyunt, *Hagiography of Maha Thera Shin Arahan and an Account of the Reconstruction of Shin Arahan's Brick Monastery*, Ministry of Culture, Myanmar, 1997.

25 AMS (Accelerator Mass Spectrometry) dating by ANSTO – the Australian Nuclear Science and Technology Organisation, Sydney. Calibration by OxCal, Version 3.5, a computer program by C. Bronk Ramsey, 2000.

26 ASB, 1915, p. 7.

27 Guy Lubeigt, *Pagan: Historie et Légendes*, Paris: Editions kailash, 1998.

28 ASB, 1906, p. 25.

29 Seen in a private collection by Win Maung.

30 Bob Hudson and U Nyein Lwin, *Archaeological Excavations and Survey, February-March, 1999, Yon Hlut Kyun, Bagan, Myanmar: A Preliminary Report*, unpublished report to the Director General of Archaeology, Yangon, Myanmar, 1999. Copy also held by authors.

31 See Myint Aung, 'The Contribution of Libation Jars to Defining Historical Periods', *Tetkatho Pyinnya Padetha*, vol. 4, no. 2, 1969, pp. 35–46 (in Burmese).

32 Virtually identical to one published in Barbara Harrisson, *Later Ceramics in Southeast Asia*, Kuala Lumpur: Oxford University Press, 1995, p. 78.

33 Measured and photographed in 1999, this brick had been removed by persons unknown by 2000.

34 R.V.S.Wright, *The MV-NUTSHELL Program for Multivariate Archaeology*, published by the author, Sydney, 1994. Also found at <http://www.archaeology.usyd.edu.au/resources/software/mvarch/mvnuts.html>

35 Hiram Cox, *Journal of a residence in the Burmhan Empire, and more particularly the court of Amarapoorah, by Capt. Hiram Cox, of the Honourable East India Company's Bengal Native Infantry*, London: Warren and Whittaker, 1821, p. 414.

36 Stargardt, 1990, p. 159. See numerous examples in Pichard, 1992–9.

37 Bob Hudson, U Nyein Lwin, and U Win Maung (Tanpawady), 2001.

38 *Archaeological Survey of India, Annual Report of the Director General* (ASI), 1923–4, p. 83; ASI, 1924–5, p. 106; ASI, 1926–7, pp. 166–7; ASI, 1929–30, p. 156.

39 ASI, 1909–10, p. 123.

40 The *New Chronicle*, according to Pe Maung Tin and Luce (1923, p. xvi), was compiled in the late eighteenth century by Twinthin Mahasithu, a minister who had access to inscriptions collected nationwide by King Bodawpaya, and who made the first serious attempt to check history by means of inscriptions. This argument is summarised in Pe Maung Tin, 1923, p. 29.

41 Daw Thin Kyi, 'The Old City of Pagan', *Essays Offered to G.H. Luce by his Colleagues and Friends in Honor of His Seventy-fifth Birthday*, vol. 2, Switzerland: Artibus Asiae Publishers, 1966, pp. 179–88. An undated palm-leaf manuscript in the possession of U Maung Maung Tin of the Myanmar Historical Research Commission also gives an intriguing description, including measurements comparable to the existing remnants of the city walls, of the now three-sided city as having four walls and twelve gates.

42 Stargardt, 1990, ch. 3.

43 Pichard, 1992–9.

44 Detailed spatial analysis appears in Bob Hudson, *Pagan and its Monasteries: Time, Space and Structure in Burma's Medieval Buddhist City*, unpublished BA (Honours) thesis, Archaeology Department, University of Sydney, 1997. A case study of the Otein Taung earthenware site and its relationship externally to the city, and internally to its residents, is presented in Hudson, Nyein Lwin and Win Maung (Tanpawady), 2001.

45 Notably in Michael Aung-Thwin, *Pagan: The Origins of Modern Burma*, Hawaii, University of Hawaii Press, 1985. Michael Aung-Thwin, *Myth and History in the Historiography of Early Burma*, Athens, Ohio: Ohio University Center for International Studies, 1998.

46 These issues are canvassed in Bob Hudson, 'The Nyaungyan "Goddesses": Some Unusual Bronze Grave Goods from Upper Burma', *TAASA Review*, vol. 10, no. 2, 2001, pp. 4–7. Bob Hudson, 'An Archaeological Settlement Database for Burma/Myanmar', conference presentation: Towards an Electronic Cultural Atlas: e-Publishing and Knowledge Management in the Humanities, Sydney, June 12–13, 2001. Also found at http://www.archaeology.usyd.edu.au/~hudson/Burma_Myanmar_database.pdf

3 Offering up a rare jewel: Buddhist merit-making and votive tablets in early Burma

John Guy

In 1892, Major Richard Temple undertook a tour of lower Burma with the objective of investigating the caves of the Moulmein and Thaton regions, which had been retreats for Buddhist monks and places of pilgrimage for the Mon and Burmese faithful for many centuries. Numerous caves were visited, many of which were filled with Buddha images, miniature stupas and manuscripts. Temple reported that he visited 'at least 40 caves in the Amherst District alone, of which at least 21 contain [Buddhist] antiquities of value'.[1] One of the largest and most spectacular of these limestone caves was Kaw-gun. The most prevalent 'antiquity' which Temple noted at these cave retreats were moulded clay votive tablets, used in great numbers to adorn the interior surfaces of the caves. He rightly noted that they appeared to represent the labour of devotees over many centuries. Of those he illustrates in his 1894 report, one from Kaw-gun Cave can now be identified as being the product of the Mon tradition and dated to circa the eighth century, and it may be compared to examples found in peninsular Thailand.[2] Others illustrated in his report are of later dates, the majority being associated with the Pegu kingdom of the fifteenth century and later.

Temple was among the first to recognise the archaeological value of these cave sites, regarding them as important for 'tracing the evolution of Buddhistic art' in the region.[3] Similar investigations of cave sites have been undertaken in the Thai and Malay peninsula, and an abundance of clay Buddhist votive tablets recovered, confirming the widespread distribution of these Buddhist devotional images. Georges Coedès was the first to undertake a systematic study of Buddhist votive tablets in Siam, and H.G. Quaritch Wales and Alastair Lamb undertook similar studies for the Malay peninsula.[4]

A shared feature of all these sites was their relative inaccessibility: they were often located high up cliff faces, reached by tortuous jungle paths and bamboo ladders. The very inaccessibility of these caves no doubt contributed to their value as places of meditation and retreat. It appears that these caves had been frequented over extended periods by Buddhist practitioners who presumably created the clay votive tablets that have been recovered in such large numbers from these sites. It is unclear whether members of the Buddhist lay community frequented them, or whether they were the preserve of monks. Burma had a long tradition of 'forest monks' (*arañ*) who chose such remote places for meditation and spiritual fulfilment. Inscriptions from Pagan indicate that a faction of the *saṅgha*, referred to as *taw kloṅ* (forest monastery), flourished, and that they received significant royal endowments in the late Pagan period (thirteenth century).[5] Could it be that members of these forest monasteries frequented the remote caves as places of retreat, and that the clay votive tablets are a legacy of their meditative activities? The later Thai tradition of forest monasteries presumably derives from this Burmese practice, and both ultimately stem from the early Indian practice of the retreat (*vāsāvāsa*) in the Buddhist *saṅgha*. Among those places listed in the Pali Vinaya as fit for a retreat is a cave.[6]

Clay votive tablets of the Buddha, quotes from Buddhist texts, and divine figures represent a significant element of the archaeological record of early Buddhist sites in Southeast Asia. They are most prevalent in Burma, Thailand and peninsular Malaysia, but have also been recorded in Laos, southern Vietnam and Champa.

The majority of the Burmese-provenanced impressions can be located stylistically; eastern Indian-style tablets are readily distinguished from Pyu or Mon types for example, but with those of the Pagan period, the differences become altogether less clear. Regrettably the votive tablets under discussion are notoriously difficult to secure in terms of place and date of manufacture, with the notable exception of those bearing donor inscriptions. These restraints are twofold, determined by the intrinsic mobility of both the votive tablet and the metal mould. The impression could have been made from the mould in one location and then taken by pilgrims to another location, where it was recovered. Alternatively, the mould may have travelled and been used to make the impressions local to where they were found. The archaeological record suggests that both practices occurred, but only geological analysis of clay-types can settle the issue of place of manufacture definitively.

These humble objects were produced, as acts of devotion, from the most inexpensive material, clay. They were simply made by pressing clay into a reverse-mould, usually metal, to produce a 'positive' casting or impression. The use of metal moulds achieved a sharpness of detail and a fineness of definition not achieved with the use of fired ceramic moulds.[7] Examples of metal moulds have been found throughout Southeast Asia, most notably in Thailand, Cambodia and Java. The clay images were either sun-dried or fired, the latter either in an open straw-fuelled fire or in a kiln. These sun-dried examples are typically a beige-buff colour, soft in texture, and fragile. Fired votive tablets tend to be a deep reddish colour, and are more robust, resembling fired brick in density and body. Burmese votive tablets are typically impressed deeply into the clay, which is displaced to form a pronounced surround, so that the impression is 'framed', adding to its presence as a devotional icon.

The metal moulds were lost-wax cast, and probably manufactured in foundry workshops under monastic supervision. Indian votive moulds were probably cast at monastic metal foundries, such as were known to operate within the larger monasteries of eastern India. Excavations at the great monastic centre of Nalanda in Bihar, for example, have revealed evidence of metal furnaces and smelting facilities, presumably for the casting of religious images. It is unknown if such practices were followed in Burmese monasteries, but given the scale of the temple-building programmes at Śri Kṣetra and Pagan, it would seem most likely that archaeology will provide the evidence in due course.

The abundance of clay votive tablets confirms the popularity of the practice of making such impressions, and the archaeological record from Burma establishes that their manufacture was not confined to the poor laity and to possessionless monks; several types recovered in Burma state in their donor inscription that they were made 'by the hand' of a king of Pagan or other members of the royal households.

The universality of this practice brings us directly to the issue of motive: what was the religious motivation which lay behind the prolific production of such modest expressions of devotion? Central to all Buddhist practice is merit-making. The fabrication of the clay devotional images was within the grasp of all devotees. It is perhaps as a result of the universality of the act of making such images that they acquired such potency in Buddhist Southeast Asia. But we must not lose sight of the fact that this form of merit-making was textually inspired and sanctioned. Buddhist texts are clear in expounding the meritorious benefits of the *act of making* such objects, explicitly rejecting the necessity for a high monetary value to be associated with such giving. As the *Sūtra on the Merit of Bathing the Buddha* explains, '. . . if someone writes the dharma-verse and installs it inside

the stūpa, it would be like doing homage by offering up a rare jewel'.[8]

Merit-making can take many forms, from acts of giving, piety and selflessness, to undertaking pilgrimage to sites deemed sacred in Buddhist geography. Places directly associated with major events in the Buddha's life feature prominently, most famously Lumbini (Birth), Bodhgaya (Enlightenment), Sarnath (First Sermon), and Kusinagara (Death). Whilst these sites are assumed to have always had a place in the pilgrimage system, in the medieval period they also assumed a place in Mahayana texts which in turn found expression in new and elaborate iconographic programmes for religious sculpture.

Votive tablets have always had a place in Buddhist devotion, but assumed an increasingly prominent role with the widespread adoption of Mahayana teachings in India in the second half of the first millennium. These theological and sectarian developments were reflected in devotional practices in regions of Southeast Asia sympathetic to Buddhism, most particularly Burma, which received the teachings of the Buddha earlier than elsewhere.

Buddhist worship is prescribed in a variety of texts written to guide both monks and laity in the pursuit of correct practice. Many of these texts are concerned with the correct ways in which the Buddha's example should be understood; others focus on the mechanics of veneration. All place great emphasis on the paramount importance of the Buddha's teachings, and on the veneration of his relics.

Early Burmese Buddhism has left no descriptions of ritual practices, beyond what can be deduced from the choice of *dharma* verses used in votive inscriptions. India is served a little better, thanks to the diaries of the Chinese pilgrims who recorded their observations of Buddhist life in India from the early fifth century onwards. The pilgrim-scholar Yijing (I-tsing, AD 635–713) has provided the most complete descriptions of Buddhist worship in seventh century India, observed during his pilgrimage which spanned the years AD 671 to 689. Yijing not only translated many texts into Chinese, but also left his unique diary account of what he saw. Both his translations of the sutras and his writings make it clear that the veneration of the Buddha's teachings, images and relics were all central to the Buddhist practice that he witnessed. Of key interest here is his description of the making of votive objects.

> [Buddhists in India] make . . . paste caityas . . . [i.e., miniature stupas/stūpikas] and paste images from rubbings . . . [which they] impress . . . on silk or paper . . . Among the monks and laity of India, they all take this as their practice. Furthermore, whether they build images or make caityas, be they of gold, silver, bronze, iron, paste, lacquer, brick, or stone . . . they

place inside [them] two kinds of relics. One is called the bodily relic of the Great Teacher; the second is called the dharma-verse relic on causation. This verse goes as follows:

> All things arise from a cause
> The Tathāgata has explained their cause
> And the cessation of the cause of these things
> This the great ascetic has explained

If one installs these two [relics], then one's blessings will be extremely abundant.[9]

The writings of Yijing reflect a development within Buddhist theology in which emphasis was moving from veneration of the Buddha's physical remains (the authenticated 'true relics', which by this period must have been exceedingly scare) to a focus on his teachings as the true embodiment of the Buddha. It is in the light of these developments that the circulation in Burma of clay votive tablets bearing verses of the Buddhist creed, images of stupas, and Buddha figures must be seen.

SACRED WORD VOTIVE TABLETS

Among the earliest clay votive items are those simply bearing lines of the Buddhist creed. It is known that these were produced in vast quantities at major pilgrimage centres, such as Bodhgaya, and circulated widely in the Buddhist world, no doubt reaching Burma. Among the earliest securely identifiable votive tablets from Burma are those which combine texts and the stupa as its principal motifs (Figure 3.1). Such objects reflect the prevailing influence of those texts describing the funerary ceremony appropriate for the Buddha's remains and the associated cult of relic veneration which grew up around this. Texts, such as the *Mahāparinibbānasutta*, deal with such matters and employ the term *śarira-pūjā*, later interpreted as "worship of relics" but which may well have begun as a reference to the original funeral rites of the Buddha.[10] Early in the history of Buddhism, Buddha-relics came to be symbolised by the stupa-mounds in which they had been interred. This practice is verified in the time of Aśoka (fourth century BC), when eight great stupas were erected at the sacred sites across India expressly to contain original Buddha relics. Later commentaries, such as the fifth-century AD Sri Lankan recension of the *Milindapañha*, expound the importance of the cult of relics. 'Venerate that relic of him who is to be venerated; by doing so you go from here to heaven.'[11]

STŪPIKA VOTIVE OBJECTS AND THEIR MANUFACTURE

Excavations at Bodhgaya have revealed moulded, three-dimensional, miniature clay stupas (*stūpika*) in vast quantities, the majority having been heaped up and

Figure 3.1 Clay votive tablet with decorated stupa and four lines of *nāgarī* script. Reportedly found in Burma, *c.* seventh–eighth century. Ht 5.3 cm. Private collection.

ultimately buried near the innumerable small stone stupas erected around the Mahabodhi temple.[12] It seems apparent that these stone miniature stupas served as memorials, presumably incorporating ashes of the deceased, just as portable metal and ivory stupa models continue to do so even today among the *saṅgha* of Sri Lanka. The *stūpikas* became an important sub-group of the multiple clay votive objects being produced in Buddhist India.[13] The seventh-century Chinese pilgrim Xuanzang (Hsuen Tsang) provides the explanation of their spiritual importance. 'It is the custom in India [for the devout Buddhist] to make little stūpas . . . [W]ith his hands he constructed these stūpas. Thus he acquired the highest and most excellent religious merit.'[14]

The clay stupas are typically of unadorned form, with a plain or lotus platform, drum, railing (*vedikā*) and umbrella finial (*chattrāvalī*), which was often detached. It is now clear that similar clay stupas circulated in Southeast Asia, and examples have been recorded in the Malay peninsula, Sumatra, Java, and Bali.[15] The funerary aspect of the stupa appears to have been widely understood in Southeast Asia, particularly by the Buddhist *saṅgha*, who often incorporated the cremation ash of revered monks in the clay employed in the making of such stupas.[16]

An important discovery was made in 1997 which adds further to our understanding of the circulation of such moulds in Buddhist Asia. An early- to mid-tenth-century shipwreck in the Java Sea, the Intan, was excavated in 1997 by Michael Flecker. Its cargo included an assortment of metal moulds and ritual utensils associated with Mahayana Buddhism. Three metal stupa moulds were

Figure 3.2 A copper-alloy bodhisattva mould, early tenth century. Recovered from the Intan shipwreck, Java Sea, 1997. Ht 5.5 cm. Photograph courtesy of M. Flecker.

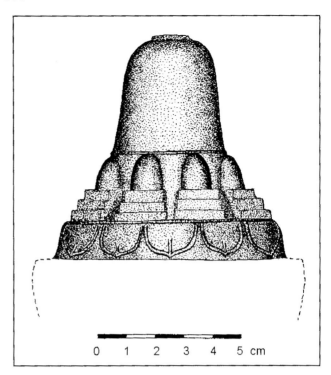

Figure 3.3 A copper-alloy *stūpika* mould, early tenth century. Recovered from the Intan shipwreck, Java Sea, 1997. Ht 8 cm. Line drawing courtesy of M. Flecker.

found, the first hoard of such moulds ever to be recovered in Southeast Asia, thus representing an important addition to our knowledge in this field. The only previously recorded example came from the peninsula region, though undoubtedly belonging to the same cultural sphere.[17] The same cargo produced five copper-alloy moulds for the making of bodhisattva votive tablets (Figure 3.2), of a type already known from Java, and one for the moulding of a stupa votive tablet.[18] In all probability the moulds were imported from eastern India, but could have been made in Sumatran Srivijaya, a major international centre for Buddhist studies in the tenth century. Srivijaya was described as such a centre as early as the seventh century by Yijing, and is known to have supported *vihāras* at two of the greatest Buddhist monasteries in medieval India, Nalanda in Bihar and Nagapattinam in Tamilnadu. The form of the *stūpika* moulds from the Intan do not mimic those found at Bodhgaya, which are simple and unadorned; those from the wreck are more elaborate, with a pronounced lotus foot and eight subsidiary stupas partially projecting from the lower drum (Figure 3.3). In the use of the multiple appearances of the secondary stupas, they hint at the iconographic complexity seen at Borobudur, known to have been inspired by a variety of Mahayana textual sources. Impressions from this type of stupa mould have also been found in Phattalung Province in peninsular Thailand.[19]

BUDDHA-RELIC VOTIVE ITEMS

In Burma the earliest known stupas were built at Śri Kṣetra and Beikthano. Several of those at Śri Kṣetra (near modern Prome) are still maintained and, judging from those depicted on Pyu-period reliefs, can be regarded as largely authentic in their overall form.[20] An elliptical votive tablet attributable to the later Pyu period (eighth–tenth century) with a stupa motif displays the characteristic Pyu-style stupa, with a tall cylinder supported on a high 'lotus'-base, clearly defined *vedikā*-railing and a three-tier umbrella finial, from which banners stream (Figure 3.1). This style of stupa is also identifiable with Indian types and the possibility cannot be ruled out that this votive (or the mould from which it was made) was imported from India. The sealing has four lines of text in *nāgarī* script below the stupa.

Stupas appear on late Pyu-period votive tablets depicting Buddha images. An example excavated at Śri Kṣetra provides one of the finest examples of a sealing clearly in the Pyu-style (Figure 3.4).[21] It depicts two stupas supported by lotus flowers and stems, richly festooned in garlands and surmounted by a tasselled umbrella, flanking an enthroned Buddha seated in the earth-touching posture. A variant design, with two stupas supported by kneeling elephants, is also recorded from excavations at Śri Kṣetra.[22]

These votive tablets served to evoke the Buddha's doctrine through the use of symbols and sacred verse.

Figure 3.4 Clay votive tablet depicting enthroned Buddha in *Māravijaya*, flanked by adorned stupas on lotus supports. Pyu period, Burma *c*. eighth–ninth century. The Buddhist creed in *nāgarī* script in Pali with an inscribed Pyu name on the reverse, probably identifying the donor. Archaeology Department, Burma.

Not only did image and text serve as vehicles for the Buddha's teachings, they became synonymous and interchangeable. The *ye dharma* verse ('He who sees the *dharma*, sees me; he who sees me, sees the *dharma*') became accepted as the essence of the Buddha's message and appears widely on votive tablets in Burma and elsewhere in Southeast Asia.[23] It was even ascribed magical properties, including the power to convert the non-believer by its mere utterance.

BUDDHA AND BODHISATTVA IMAGE TABLETS

While sacred texts or sacred texts combined with relic–stupa imagery were important categories of votive tablet design, those which included the Buddha himself were by far the most prevalent. Of these, the Buddha seated calling

the earth to witness his victory over Māra (*Māravijaya*), was the most popular form in Burma. Initially, the Buddha teaching the First Sermon occurs on a number of Pyu votive tablets, but this disappears from the iconographic repertoire as the earth-touching gesture gained ascendancy in the Pagan period. The consolidation of this Buddha-type was stimulated by the renewed Burmese contacts with Bodhgaya, which are recorded in a number of inscriptions of the period.[24]

During the late first millennium, Mahayana Buddhism became predominant. This important theological development found its ultimate expression in the cult of the Bodhisattva Avalokiteśvara, popularly referred to in Burma as Lokanātha. The Chinese pilgrim Xuanzang witnessed this development in eastern India in the early seventh century. He wrote that the Mahabodhi Sangharam, one of the four great monasteries at Bodhgaya, built by a former king of Ceylon, was populated by over a thousand monks, 'all Mahāyānists of the Sthavira school and all perfect in Vinaya observances'. He also noted that at the nearby monastic university of Nalanda was a brick shrine housing a large image of Tārā P'usa.[25] All this amounts to compelling evidence of the widespread popularity of Mahayana Buddhism at this time. Its mass appeal was rooted in a promise of salvation within one's lifetime through divine intercession, rather than the lengthy (and tedious) accumulation of merit through successive rebirths. Buddhas-to-be, in the form of bodhisattvas and Tārās, were widely venerated, and the making of their images in clay votive tablets became common, both in eastern India and in Burma.

By the eighth century this new trend was visible in Burma, and indigenous style votive tablets began appearing alongside the Indian imports. Direct imports from India progressively diminished, displaced by locally made examples using moulds reflecting local styles. Both Mon and Pyu examples reflect this localisation trend, but enough examples continued to appear in Indian style to suggest that this external source did not disappear altogether.

Clay votive tablets appear both with the Buddha being attended by bodhisattvas, and with images of a bodhisattva or Tārā alone. As noted at the outset, Temple published one of this type from his cave investigations in peninsular Burma. A similar tablet depicts the Buddha and two bodhisattvas with three previous Buddhas seated above him (Figure 3.5). It is Mon in style, of a type known most frequently from sites in the Burmese and Thai peninsula, and may be attributed to the eighth century.[26] Two key centres for the Buddhism of the Mon of the Dvaravati polity were Nakhon Pathom and the region around Nakhon Si Thammarat, both of which have yielded examples of these votive types. Those recovered in lower Burma had, in all probability, circulated through the movement of monks in this early period.

Figure 3.5 Clay votive tablet depicting the Buddha seated in *pralambapādāsana* and with hands in *vitarkamudrā*, and flanked by two bodhisattvas with previous Buddhas above. Mon period, lower Thailand/Burma, eighth century. Ht 6 cm. Private collection.

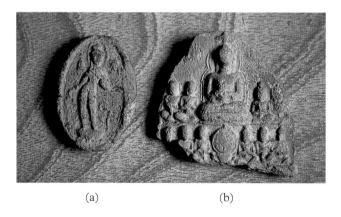

(a)   (b)

Figure 3.6 (a) Clay votive tablet depicting the Bodhisattva Avalokiteśvara. Pyu period, Burma. Reportedly recovered from Śri Kṣetra. Archaeology Department, Burma. (b) Clay votive tablet depicting the Buddha preaching his first sermon at Sarnath. Pyu period, Burma, eighth–ninth century. Reportedly recovered from Śri Kṣetra. Archaeology Department, Burma.

Figure 3.7 Clay votive tablet depicting the seated Buddha in *dharmacakra mudrā*, flanked by a previous Buddha and the Bodhisattva Maitreya, Pyu period, Burma, *c.* eighth–tenth century. Ht 8.3 cm. Private collection.

A clay votive tablet depicting a standing bodhisttva recovered at Śri Kṣetra appears to be in an Indian style, but as few bodhisattva votive items are known from India, the mould may have been made locally, as were sculptures of the period (Figure 3.6a). A bronze sculpture of a four-armed Avalokiteśvara, standing in a flexed posture, was discovered in the vicinity of the Bawbaw-gyi Pagoda at Śri Kṣetra.[27] Such figures typically formed part of a triad, with two bodhisattvas flanking a central figure of the Buddha. When a bodhisattva was represented on its own, it was usually shown with frontal symmetry, as seen in a newly discovered metal mould of a four-armed bodhisattva from the Intan cargo (Figure 3.2). This figure holds what appear to be a rosary and a lotus, attributes of Avalokiteśvara, and was found with other Mahayana image moulds and ritual paraphernalia.

A rare composition from Śri Kṣetra depicts the Buddha preaching to an assembly of followers, all seated with their hands raised in *añjalimudrā* (Figure 3.6b). In the foreground is the symbol of his teachings, the *dharmacakra*, a motif rarely encountered in Pyu art but elevated to a central position in the Buddhist iconography of the neighbouring Mon of the Dvaravati kingdom.[28] The lower section of this plaque is missing, but judging from a complete example excavated at Śri Kṣetra, it probably included two kneeling deer, emblematic of the forest at Sarnath where the First Sermon took place.[29] Variants of this composition occur; one version of this subject, also recovered from Śri Kṣetra, depicts the Buddha preaching the First Sermon, flanked by two stupas supported on

Figure 3.8 Clay votive tablet depicting the enthroned Buddha in *Māravijaya*, flanked by verses of Buddhist creed. Pyu period, Burma, eighth–tenth century. Ht *c.* 6 cm. Private collection.

Figure 3.9 Clay votive tablet depicting the Buddha seated beneath the Bodhi tree in *Māravijaya*, and flanked by stupas. Pagan period, Burma, *c.* eleventh–twelfth century. Ht 15.2 cm. Victoria and Albert Museum, 658–1883.

lotus flowers, the stem of each being held in the trunk of a kneeling elephant. The throne back has elaborate *makara* terminals, which frame the Buddha's head.[30] Other versions of this subject, representing the Buddha delivering his First Sermon, seated on a simple throne with *makara*-crossbar and flanked by two stupas, are in the Victoria and Albert Museum and the British Museum, both in London.

A favoured configuration in Pyu Buddhist sculpture was the triad, a group of three figures represented either singly or on a single stele. Such triads are typical of Buddha imagery at Śri Kṣetra.[31] A number of votive tablets associated with Pyu sites are of this type, with a central seated figure of the Buddha flanked by an earth-touching Buddha and the saviour-bodhisattva Maitreya (Figure 3.7).[32] Each figure is enthroned on its own lotus cushion and displays a different *mudrā*; the Buddha is unusually represented in the gesture of preaching the First Sermon. An indecipherable inscription, in a cursive script suggestive of Pyu, can just be detected on the panel directly beneath the central figure. A number of these votive items have been recorded at Pagan, which supports the view that the Burman capital drew on the earlier Buddhist traditions of the Pyu and Mon of Lower Burma, importing objects and artisans to their service. Two examples in the British Museum, of unclear provenance but clearly in the Pyu style, show variant

types (Figure 3.8). A copper-alloy mould which closely approximates Figure 3.11 was recovered at Thaungbyegon at Śri Kṣetra and published by Luce.[33]

Votive tablets depicting the enthroned Buddha with stupas typically represent him with his right hand touching the earth in *bhūmisparśamudrā* (Figure 3.4). It is a sophisticated and complex composition; the Buddha is represented with flames issuing from his aureole, enthroned on a lotus cushion which is in turn supported by an architectural dais. From this platform emerge the two lotus stems whose flowers support the stupas described above. This representation of the Buddha is both place and time specific; the event, indicated by the Buddha's *mudrā*, took place immediately before he experienced Enlightenment at the site marked today by the Mahabodhi temple and the Bodhi tree. The reference to place is made explicit by the depiction of the foliage of the tree seen behind the Buddha's nimbus and umbrella. Three lines of the *ye dharma* text in *nāgarī* script fill the voids above the stupas, and a Pyu inscription is incised on the reverse.

The vast majority of Burmese tablets belong to the Pagan period, and these typically carry at least one line of Buddhist scripture, most often the *ye dharma* verse. The classic Pagan-period Buddha votive tablet which typifies the production of this period is the seated Buddha, hands in *bhūmisparśamudrā*, variously surrounded by previous Buddhas, *caityas*, and with an architectural setting intending to evoke the Mahabodhi temple at Bodhgaya (Figure 3.9). This is the classic Bodhgaya-type, well recorded from the site of the Mahabodhi temple itself. In all probability the Pagan examples were made from imported Indian metal moulds.

Variant types depict the Buddha flanked by two standing Buddhas, one gesturing protection (*abhayamudrā*), the other teaching (*vitarkamudrā*) in a scene depicting the Twin Miracles (Figure 3.10). Another type depicts the Buddha preaching the First Sermon, as seen in Pyu examples, but having assumed the *pralambapādāsana* posture (Figure 3.11). The combination of this *mudrā* and this *āsana* follows established Mon conventions, and

Figure 3.11 Clay votive tablet depicting the Buddha preaching the First Sermon, flanked by multiple stupas with five broken lines of inscription at base. Pagan period, Burma, eleventh–twelfth century. Ht 16 cm. Victoria and Albert Museum, IM 357–1924. Given by the Royal Asiatic Society.

Figure 3.10 Clay votive tablet depicting the scene of the 'Twin Miracles', with the Buddha in *Māravijaya*, flanked by two standing previous Buddhas with the single line 'ye dharma hetuprabhava' in *nāgarī* script. Pagan period, Burma, eleventh–twelfth century. Reportedly found at Tagaung, upper Burma. Ht 18.5 cm. Victoria and Albert Museum, IM 305–1921.

may be taken to reflect the element of ongoing Mon influence at Pagan.

A more highly elaborated version is the design which depicts the Eight Great Events of the Buddha's life, reflecting the *Aṣṭamahāprātihārya*, a text which celebrates the veneration of holy sites and appears to have become popular around the eighth century.[34] Although this subject is elaborated in stone sculptures in eastern India, most spectacularly in the famous stele at Jagdispur, near Nalanda in Bihar, and in the portable *andagu* stones known from eastern India, Burma and Tibet, it is uncommon in clay votive tablets. A rare complete example, recovered from Pagan, was published by Luce.[35]

A comparison of the Pyu and Pagan versions (Figures 3.8 and 3.9) vividly illustrates the radical shift in style which occurred as a result of the influx of eastern Indian Pala influences linked to the revival of Burmese interest in Bodhgaya as a pilgrimage centre. These differences are self-evident. For example, compare the treatment of the Buddha's physiognomy, the different elaboration of the architectural setting (including the use of a dais rendered in perspective on the Pyu type), the treatment of the foliage, and the re-location of the lines of text from the background to beneath the main subject.

THE ROLE OF INSCRIPTIONS

A considerable number of the votive tablets recovered at Pagan bear donor inscriptions, some of which have royal associations. They typically record that the image of the Buddha was made by the named donor 'with his own hands', for the 'sake of deliverance'. Amongst the simplest of messages is the one inscribed in Pali which reads *namo buddhāya* (Honour to the Buddha) inscribed on a votive tablet with the enthroned Buddha, venerated by the two kneeling figures of his disciples Sariputta and Moggallana.

The most complete published series of inscribed Burmese votive tablets with translations appeared in G.H. Luce's *Old Burma – Early Pagan*, with a supplement of Pyu examples, largely from Śrī Kṣetra, appearing in his *Phases of Pre-Pagan Burma*, published posthumously. The royal inscriptions are particularly significant in the Burmese context, demonstrating very clearly that this pious act was performed across society, irrespective of rank.

> This is the pious gift of . . . the great king Śrī Aniruddha the divine. . . .
>
> This Blessed One was made by the great queen, Trilokavataṁsakā, with her own hands, for the sake of Deliverance.[36]

In a particularly important unpublished paper, the Burmese historian Nai Pan Hla recorded the discovery of five inscribed votive tablets in the years following Luce's 1970 publication, which add further evidence of royal donations of this kind. They record the making of clay votive tablets by the following members of the Pagan royal family:

> King Anawrahta (Aniruddha *deva*), written in Mon (two plaques).
>
> Prince Trilokasinghavijaya, the Mon prince Nakasa-man, son-in-law of King Kyanzittha.
>
> Princess Trilokaculamanidevi, daughter of King Kyanzittha.
>
> Queen Mother Mahadeviculamani, mother of Prince Trilokasinghavijaya.[37]

In addition to royalty, monks, nuns and members of the laity are recorded in votive tablet inscriptions.[38] They are variously written in Pali and Mon, and sometimes Pali in Mon script, indicating that the Mon language continued to exert influence at Pagan. A short selection of these inscriptions, all on votive tablets recovered from Pagan, give the flavour, and contain the key to under-standing the motivation behind this devout activity, 'deliverance' or spiritual liberation:

> This Blessed One [Buddha image] was made by the *sambeṅ Jesalya* with his own hands, for the sake of Deliverance.
>
> This image of the Buddha was created by the Teacher *Muggaliputta*.
>
> This tablet was made by Mahasalini [Prince Yasa?] [Mon], with his own hands [Pali].[39]

Donor inscriptions do not form part of the mould's impression, but are incised into the reverse side of the clay tablet before it is dried or fired. Thus they reveal no inherent information as to where the mould originated from but do confirm that the impression in question was made in Burma.

CONCLUSION

The following anecdote serves to underscore the inherent problems in establishing the true origin of many of Burma's votive tablets. Rajendralala Mitra, the leading Indian historian of the Mahabodhi temple and advocate for its restoration as a site of Buddhist worship, wrote in 1876 of the discovery of innumerable votive tablets at the Mahabodhi temple site:

> Thousands of them have been taken away from this place. From a small area cleared by a Burmese gentleman, 2000 . . . [were] recovered. I saw, in a godown adjoining the dwelling of the Burmese, 500 small ones, evidently picked up with a view to be carried to Burmah.[40]

Mitra's observation should serve to remind us that many of the Buddhist clay votive plaques circulating in Burma over the past century are indeed of Indian manufacture, *and were not necessarily* transported there in the Pagan or earlier periods. Their presence in modern Burma will undoubtedly continue to confuse the archaeological record.

NOTES

1 R.C. Temple, 'Notes on Antiquities in Ramannadesa (The Talaing Country of Burma)', *Indian Antiquary*, vol. XXIII, 1894, p. 3.

2 Temple, 1894, pl. XVI, upper right. S.J. O'Connor, 'Buddhist Votive Tablets and Caves in Peninsular Thailand', *Art and Archaeology of Thailand*, Bangkok: Department of Fine Arts, 1974, fig. 16, found in Khao Ok Dalu and Phattalung. P. Krairiksh, *Art in Peninsular Thailand Prior to the Fourteenth Century A.D.*, Department of Fine Arts, Bangkok, 1980, pl. 23, found in Khao Khanab cave, Krabi. M.L.P. Chirapravati, *Votive Tablets in Thailand: Origins, Styles and Uses*, Kuala Lumpur: Oxford University Press, 1997, fig. 7, found in Chula Pathom Chedi, Nakhom Pathom Province.

3 Temple, 1894, p. 3.

4 G. Coedès, 'Siamese Votive Tablets', *Journal of the Siam Society*, vol. XX, 1926, pp. 1–24. H.G. Quaritch Wales, 'A Newly-Explored Route of Ancient Indian Cultural Expansion', *Indian Art & Letters*, vol. IX, 1935, pp. 1–31. A. Lamb, 'Mahayanist Buddhist Votive Tablets in Perlis', *Journal of the Malaysian Branch of the Royal Asiatic Society*, vol. 37, pt. 2, 1964, pp. 47–59.

5 Than Tun, 'Mahakassapa and His Tradition', *Journal of the Burma Research Society*, vol. XLII, pt. ii, 1959, pp. 99–118 (reprinted in Than Tun, *Essays on the History and Buddhism of Burma*, Arran: Kiscadale Publications, 1988).

6 Monastic rules specify the appropriate periods for retreat, all during the rainy season, suggesting that its origins may be in a practical response to the difficulties of travel during the wet months. See N. K. Prasad, *Studies in Buddhist and Jain Monachism*, Vaishali: Research Institute of Prakrit, Jainology and Ahimsa, 1972, pp. 169–90.

7 Ceramic moulds have been recovered from Cambodia. It is probable that indigenous moulds were also made from stone and wood, though examples have not been recorded to date.

8 Quoted in D. Boucher, 'Sūtra on the Merit of Bathing the Buddha', *Buddhism in Practice*, Donald S. Lopez, Jr. (ed.) Princeton: Princeton University Press, 1995, p. 65. See also, I-Tsing, *A Record of the Buddhist Religion as Practised in India and the Malay Archipelago (A.D. 671–695)*, J. Takakusu (trans.), Delhi: Munshiram Manoharlal, 1966.

9 Boucher, 1995, p. 61.

10 G. Schopen, 'Monks and the Relic Cult in the *Mahāparinibbānasutta*: an Old Understanding in Regard to Monastic Buddhism', *From Benares to Beijing: Essays on Buddhism and Chinese Religion in Honour of Prof. Jan Yun-Hua*, K. Shinohara and G. Schopen (eds), Oakville: Mosaic Press, 1991, p. 189.

11 *Ibid.*, p. 195.

12 A. Cunningham, *Mahabodhi or the Great Buddhist Temple under the Bodhi Tree at Buddha-Gaya*, London: India Office, 1892. Examples of clay *stūpikas* from Bodhgaya are held in the British Museum, Department of Oriental Antiquities (W. 405 among others).

13 The term *stūpika* has acquired popularity in vernacular literature, but the term has no historical validity, and is not used in Sanskrit or Pali Buddhist sources.

14 S. Beal (trans.), *Si-Yu-Ki: Buddhist Records of the Western World Translated from the Chinese of Hiuen Tsiang (AD 629)*, 2 vols., London: Kegan Paul, Trench, Trubner, 1884 (reprint Delhi, 1981), pp. 146–7.

15 A group of *stupikas* was recovered early this century around Palembang, Sumatra, the probable site of the maritime entrepôt of Srivijaya, and near Pejeng, Bali; see Lamb, 1964, pls 45–6 and O'Connor, 1974, fig. 13 respectively.

16 This was presumably also well understood by the Thai monks living at a *wat* near Kampong Kurong Batang in the Malay state of Perlis, who removed many Buddhist votive tablets from a cave site before archaeologists could record them, and *ground them up* for use in a new Buddha image. No doubt they were motivated by a desire to acquire the spiritual power and accumulated merit embodied in these ancient relics, but they may also have been aware that such objects often contained the ashes of highly revered monks, so further adding to the efficacy of the new image; see Lamb, 1964, p. 48.

17 S.J. O'Connor, 'A Metal Mold for the Manufacture of Clay Buddhist Stupas', *Journal of the Malaysian Branch of the Royal Asiatic Society*, vol. 47, no. 2, 1975, pp. 60–3.

18 M. Flecker, *The Archaeological Excavation of the 10th Century Intan Shipwreck*, unpublished PhD thesis, University of Singapore, 2001; personal communication, April 2001.

19 The clay stupas are in the collection of the National Museum, Wat Machimawas, Phattalung. M.L.P. Chirapravati, 'Development of Buddhist Traditions in Peninsular Thailand', *Studies in Southeast Asian Art: Essays in Honor of Stanley J. O'Connor*, N.A. Taylor (ed.), Ithaca: Cornell University Southeast Asia Program, 2000, p. 187.

20 See J. Guy, 'The Art of the Pyu and Mon', *The Art of Burma: New Studies*, Donald Stadtner (ed.), Bombay: Marg, vol. 50, no. 4, 1999, figs 1–2.

21 *Archaeological Survey of India, Annual Report, 1927–8*, (ASIAR), pl. LV (5), pp. 130–31. See also, G.H. Luce, *Phases of Pre-Pagan Burma: Languages and History*, 2 vols, Oxford: Oxford University Press, 1985, vol. 2, pl. 60.

22 Compare Luce, 1985, vol. 2, pls 58a and 58d.

23 P. Skilling, 'A Buddhist inscription from Go Xoai, Southern Vietnam and notes towards a classification of *ye dharma* inscriptions', *80 pi sastrachan dr. prasert na nagara: ruam bot khwam vicchakan dan charuek lae ekasanboran* [80 Years: A collection of articles on epigraphy and ancient documents published on the occasion of the celebration of the 80th birthday of Prof. Dr. Prasert Na Nagara], Bangkok, 21 March 2542 [1999], pp. 171–87.

24 J. Guy, 'The Mahabodhi Temple: Pilgrim Souvenirs of Buddhist India', *The Burlington Magazine*, vol. CXXXIII, 1991, pp. 364–5.

25 T. Watters (trans.), *On Yuan Chwang's Travels in India (A.D. 629–645)*, T.W. Rhys Davids and S.W. Bushell (eds), London: Royal Asiatic Society, 1904 (reprint Delhi 1961), book 2, pp. 136, 171.

26 For examples from peninsular Thailand, see National Museum collections at Nakhon Si Thammarat, Songkla, Surat Thani, and the University of Southern Thailand. Few of these are published. Published examples can be found in Krairiksh, 1980, pl. 23 (from Krabi), and Chirapravati, 1997, fig. 7 (from Chula Pathom Cedi, Nakhon Pathom).

27 Illustrated in Guy, 1999, p. 24.

28 For a study of the Mon *dharmacakra*, see R.L. Brown, *The Dvaravati Wheels of the Law and the Indianization of South East Asia*, Leiden: Brill, 1996.

29 ASIAR, 1909–10, pl. XLIX, no. 8.

30 There is an example in the Rijksmuseum voor Volkenkunde, Leiden (B79–205) that was acquired by J.P. Vogel and reportedly collected at Śri Kṣetra.

31 See Guy, 1999, p. 17.

32 For examples of this triad votive tablet type recovered from sites at Pagan, see G.H. Luce, *Old Burma – Early Pagan*, 3 vols, Locust Valley, NY: J.J. Augustin, 1969–1970, vol. 3, pl. 55.

33 Luce, 1985, vol. 2, pls 55a and 55b.

34 This text is only known from a tenth century Chinese version. J. C. Huntington, 'Pilgrimage as Image: The Cult of the *Aṣṭamahāprātihārya*, Part I', *Orientations*, vol. XVIII, no. 4, 1987, pp. 55–63; and Part II, vol. XVIII, no. 8, 1987, pp. 56–68.

35 Luce, 1970, vol. 3, pl. 71. Other complete, but un-provenanced, examples are in the National Museum, Bangkok; the Museum of Fine Arts, Boston; and an incomplete version in the Victoria and Albert Museum, London, IM 366–1914.

36 Luce, 1970, vol. 2, pls 8a and 8c, and vol. 3, pls 8a and 8c.

37 Nai Pan Hla, 'Old Terracotta Votive Tablets and New Theories on History of Old Burma', unpublished paper, nd.

38 See Luce, 1970, vol. 2 and vol. 3, pl. 53. This tablet was donated by a lay couple, presumably a husband and wife.

39 Luce, 1970, vol. 2 and vol. 3, pls 57b, 57c and 61c; *ASIAR*, 1930–4, p. 186.

40 R. Mitra, *Buddha-Gaya, the Great Buddhist Temple, the Hermitage of Sakya Muni*, Calcutta, 1878 (reprinted Delhi: Indological Book House, 1972), p. 12.

4   A Burma origin for the Sukhothai walking Buddha

Pamela Gutman

The origins of the unique Sukhothai icon, the walking Buddha, have often been discussed.[1] Most recently, Woodward has established that the earliest examples appeared in the pre-Sukhothai period, and has illustrated a walking Buddha, probably from Lopburi, which he has dated to the thirteenth or fourteenth century.[2] This chapter seeks to trace the origin of the icon to Pa-an, upriver from Martaban, where a distinctive image type evolved in the eleventh century, influenced by Pala, Mon-Khmer and Srivijayan sculpture.

THE DESCENT FROM TAVATIMSA HEAVEN AND THE WALKING BUDDHA

Robert Brown has traced the depiction of the walking Buddha from aniconic depictions at Bodh Gaya. After the Buddha achieved Enlightenment there, he spent a week walking in meditation on a jewelled promenade, the *ratna cankrama*. At Sukhothai, the walking Buddha was known as *chongkrom* or *cankrama* ('walking back and forth'), referring to this event, although the Buddha walking also appears in a depiction of an event in the Buddha's life, the Descent from Tavatimsa Heaven, where he had preached to his mother during the three-month rainy season retreat. While the Buddha walking in meditation is never depicted in the iconic art of India, or indeed of Southeast Asia, apart from Thailand from around the thirteenth century, the Descent from Tavatimsa Heaven has a long and interesting iconographic history.

The Descent is one of the oldest subjects of Buddhist narrative art, and illustrates the Buddha's descent to earth from Indra's Heaven down the celestial staircase. This refers to the time when after his Enlightenment, the Buddha ascended to the Heaven of the Thirty-three Gods (Tavatimsa Heaven), to preach to them and to his mother Maya (who after her early death had been reborn there). After converting his mother and the gods who dwelled there, he descended again to earth. He is nearly always depicted as being flanked by Indra on the right and Brahma to the left, the two gods who accompanied him on his descent. The descent of this triad symbolises the incorporation and subjugation of Hindu traditions by Buddhism. Indra, king of the gods, resided with them on the summit of Mount Meru, the mountain at the centre of the universe. Brahma, the supreme creator, is paired with Indra to emphasise the submission of the whole universe to the Buddha. The Buddha is thus seen to be a *cakravartin* or Universal Ruler, on earth and in the heavens. This can clearly be seen in a third century Gandharan relief where the artist relies on continuous narration to emphasise the fact that the Buddha is walking, showing the Buddha three times, at the top, centre and bottom of the ladder.[3] Brahma and Indra, the same size as the Buddha, are depicted in attitudes of devotion, while the figure of the walking Buddha is an adaptation of the more usual standing Buddha figure, the right hand held up to the right shoulder and the left hanging down to his side.

Chinese Buddhist texts translated about a century after the Gandhara image was made refer to a cult which emerged at the supposed site of the Descent. Alexander Soper has shown that interpolations to the original Pali *Anguttaranikaya* relate that after the Buddha's absence from earth became known, one of his royal converts, King Udayana, had a sandalwood statue made.[4] This image was taken to Sakyamuni when the Buddha eventually returned to earth, who then promised its maker that he would enjoy a life of health and strength and in the end would be reborn as a *lokapala* (guardians of the four directions). Fa-Hsien, the Chinese traveller, visited Jetavana in AD 400 and found a sandalwood image there. He recorded that this statue was the very first of all images, and had served as a model for posterity.

Whatever the origin, the 'Udayana' image type, standing, with the left arm bent and holding a corner of the monastic garment, and the right raised, was regarded as the first true likeness of the Buddha and copied again and again in India and beyond. Some of the earliest Buddha images in Sri Lanka and Southeast Asia have the right arm raised and the left holding the robe, recalling the image revered as the one first made.[5] The iconographic type, with few changes, is found in India as late as tenth century Pala Bengal, as is seen in an image depicting the Descent recovered from the site of Kurkihar and now in the Indian Museum in Calcutta.[6] Here, the figures of Indra and Brahma have been reduced to a more appropriately subservient size. The Buddha, who stands rigidly, holds his robe with the left hand while his right is lowered, not raised, with the palm outwards.

Figure 4.1 Descent from Tavatimsa Heaven. Kaw-gun caves, Karen state. Sandstone, ht 136 cm, w. 84 cm, d. 18 cm. Photograph by Luke Hardy.

David Wyatt has recently drawn attention to a series of images depicting the Descent from Tavatimsa Heaven found in Thailand at Nakhon Pathom, Dong Mae Nang Muang, and Muang Fa Daed and dating from around the eleventh century.[7] He has suggested that these illustrate the replacement of state-patronised Hinduism of the Angkorean empire by Theravada Buddhism. A resurgence of the Theravada religion was fuelled, he says, both by visiting monks from Sri Lanka and by Buddhist monks returning to Burma and the Malay peninsula from study and, sometimes, reordination in Sri Lanka. From the tenth and eleventh centuries these monks built thriving intellectual communities on their 'beachheads' in Martaban and Nakhon Si Thammarat from whence Theravada Buddhism spread. Wyatt cites the introductory passage of the Tai Wat Bang Sanuk inscription, now dated by Penth to 1219, which states, 'I raise my hands to salute the Three Gems, which are more excellent than Indra and B[rahma]', and which refers to the author as, '. . . the ruler of Muang Trok Salop and Chae Ngun, who has diffused the love of earning merit and [observing the] Dharma', and who, 'persuaded

nobles, officials, *mun nay* [chieftans] and the populace, as well as many princes and princesses, to stamp images of the Buddha in tin or clay. . .'.[8] Wyatt asks whether 'the whole inscription is a counter-argument to those who are adherents of the Indic Brahmanical religion that for centuries had been present in this region and was associated particularly with the Angkorean empire?'[9] He suggests, and this author accepts, that the inscription's emphasis on the idea of merit implies that individuals may already have greater or lesser amounts of 'merit'; this includes kings, who had a great deal of merit as proven by their worldly status. Individuals and societies might improve their status and prospects by making merit here and now.

The Descent from Tavatimsa Heaven is illustrated in at least one, but probably two images now installed in the Kaw-gun caves, in Karen state, west of Pagat village across the Salween River from Pa-an, twenty-six miles upriver from Moulmein.[10] While these caves were explored by Sir Richard Carnac Temple over a century ago, and later by Taw Sein Ko, the images of the Descent were not noticed until Gordon Luce and Ba Shin visited the caves during their tour in 1958.[11] The caves had been in use since around the seventh century, as is evidenced by a partly deciphered inscription on the wall, although most of the Buddhist remains appear to date from the fifteenth century and later. A third sculpture in a related style and apparently contemporary with the Descent images, but depicting the reclining Vishnu, was found at the same time.

The first of the sculptures depicts, in high relief, the Buddha, his face and headdress mutilated, standing with the right knee raised and the leg flexed, the torso bent towards the left hip in an exaggerated *tribhanga* movement, suggesting that he is walking (Figure 4.1). His right arm bends to the right shoulder, palm facing outwards, suggestive of the *vitarka mudra*, while the left is held out by his side, the hand again facing out. Two long garments hang open with pointed ends conspicuous near the ankles, the folds on the left side, which are meticulously depicted, foreshadow the style adopted in Pagan and at Sukhothai. A modesty panel falls between the legs. He wears royal ornaments: a wide necklace, armlets and an ornate belt. On either side stands a much smaller figure. A haloed Indra on his right stands in a pose similar to the central figure and wears similar garments and carries an unidentifiable object in his upraised inner hand. The four-faced Brahma, who also has a halo, stands to the Buddha's left, wearing a tall ornate headdress, large ear ornaments, and a *dhoti*-like lower garment held with a decorative belt. Both the attendant gods, while smaller than the Buddha, come to navel height, in contrast to the Pala prototype, where they merely reach mid-thigh, perhaps reflecting a greater importance placed on them in Lower Burma. The series from Thailand mentioned above gives similar prominence to the attendant gods. At Kaw-gun, above Brahma and Indra, on the upper section of the back-slab and in low relief, are crowned figures in the attitude of obeisance seated on triple-lotus thrones mounted on pillars. Similar smaller figures sit on either side of them. These are inhabitants in the *Brahmaloka* and *Devaloka* Heavens from which the Buddha descends. Their pillar-mounted thrones recall similar renditions on late Dvaravati steles, later Mon sculpture in Lower Burma, and the Sukhothai *prasada*.

The second of the sculptures is inscribed with twenty-three lines in Old Mon script on the inside of the hem of the robe under the left armpit, and a few lines under the right armpit (Figure 4.2). The script has been dated to the tenth or eleventh centuries AD, Luce and Shorto suggesting the eleventh, which is acceptable.[12] The inscription appears to claim that this image of the Buddha (*yo bodhirukkham)* and other Buddha images were made by the Queen of *Muhtahma'*, resident at Du'wop, although Luce notes that the readings and identifications are uncertain. He suggested that *Muhtahma'* might denote Martaban, *Matma* in Old Mon. The place-name Du'wop has a close resemblance to the Mon-Khmer Trok Salop of the Tai Wat Bang Sanuk inscription.[13] It is interesting, too, that both inscriptions refer to the making of Buddha images at the ruler's instigation.

The image in Figure 4.2 has been broken at the base, around the ankles, and at the neck. The right side, including the arm, is completely lost and the left is

Figure 4.2 Inscribed Descent from Tavatimsa Heaven. Kaw-gun caves, Karen state. Sandstone, ht 135 cm, w. 82.5 cm. Photograph by Luke Hardy.

damaged. It is apparent, however, that the identical event is intended. Brahma holds the pole of an umbrella, now lost. The Buddha figure, interestingly, has the left leg raised, in contrast to the first image. His garments and ornaments are better preserved and more ornate. He wears a wide necklace which falls into a point between the breasts, a waistband above navel height, and a wide belt around the hips clasped in front. A wide band, similar to that worn by some Srivijayan bodhisattvas, falls over his left shoulder and around the right thigh. A decorated panel falls softly between the thighs. A third identical sculpture, even more damaged than the second, has been recorded at Thaton, at the Dhammayon northeast of the Shwezayan pagoda.[14] An Old Mon inscription around the hem of the robe is a duplicate of that of the second. In these images the main figure appears to be springing vigorously from the stone. The composition is dynamic, and displays an energy often found in Southeast Asian art when it is exposed to new influences and ideas.

The acceptance of the Tavatimsa iconography by the Mons and later by the Thai probably has its roots in pre-Buddhist beliefs and ceremonial. Gao Xingjian in his novel *Soul Mountain* describes the performance of a Miao ancestral sacrifice in the Miao Autonomous District in Southern China where, after an ox is ritually slain, God in Heaven is happy and lets down the Heavenly Ladder on which father and mother descend, the rains fall, and the people are assured of wealth.[15] Similar traditions persist today throughout Southeast Asia. The story of the Buddha ascending to Heaven to convert his mother and the gods who lived there, and then descending with the gods subservient to him, would be readily received by people holding such beliefs. The continued popularity of the story is attested by a folk art example from Moulmein in the Victoria and Albert Museum and a ceremony described by Guillon, also performed at Moulmein, in which the Descent is recreated with a Buddha image.[16]

Also found together with the Kaw-gun Buddha images and apparently contemporary with them is a large, rectangular relief, flat-pointed at the top, showing the sleeping Vishnu sleeping cross-legged on the serpent Shesha. While the subject of this image is not that of this chapter, it appears to have been connected with a royal cult, and the influences on its iconography are similar. These aspects are described in the Appendix at the end of this chapter.

THE HISTORICAL CONTEXT

Before attempting to explain how these sculptures relate to the art of Sukhothai, it is necessary to examine the influences on their style and significance in the context of the history of the period. There is little or no evidence of the Mon in Lower Burma much before the eleventh century, despite the fact that chronicles and inscriptions written several centuries later give them a much greater antiquity. Michael Aung-Thwin has recently proposed that Mons were migrating into the Lower Burma region after the decline of Dvaravati in the tenth and eleventh centuries, perhaps partly as a result of Tai and Khmer pressure from its north and east. A large number of people migrated southwestward into what was then sparsely populated Lower Burma as a result of a cholera epidemic in the Mon city of Haripunjaya (Lamphun) during the eleventh century. Angkor had been growing since at least the ninth century, and continued to do so during the eleventh century, which may have put a longer and more sustained pressure on the Mons of the declining Dvaravati entity to move northwestward into the Three Pagodas Pass area. At the same time, the Pagan Empire had also begun to expand southward, into the very area where the Mons had been migrating, squeezing them between the Khmers and the Burmans.[17]

Wyatt has added an economic dimension to this, the east–west seaborne trade which had begun to use land porterage between the Gulf of Siam and the Gulf of Martaban.[18] By the eleventh century a strengthening maritime connection linked the Burma coast and the western side of the Malay peninsula to the east coast of India and Sri Lanka. This was aided by the fact that the sea power of the Cholas waned towards the end of the twelfth century. The peoples of Lower Burma and Thailand were linked by three routes: the riverine route between Martaban and Haripunjaya, another from the Gulf of Martaban through Tak and Mae Sot, and a route over the Three Pagodas Pass to Kanchanaburi, Ratnaburi and Phetburi in Thailand. By the twelfth century, the Khmer garrison towns in northwest Thailand, Si Satchanalai, Sukhothai, Phitsanulok and Kamphaeng Phet, were becoming centres of silk and ceramic manufacture which were to find an outlet in Martaban. Luce has suggested that Khmer attempts to invade Lower Burma probably encouraged King Anawrahta to absorb the region in the mid-eleventh century.[19] Ram Khamhaeng's claimed suzereinty over Martaban at the end of the thirteenth century, while probably nominal, illustrates its importance to Sukhothai's trade at that time.

These convoluted historical events were to have their impact on Old Mon art, and in particular on the Kaw-gun sculptors. The Buddhism practised at Martaban in the eleventh century was subject to influences from both east and west, from north and south India and from Cambodia and its provinces in northwest Thailand. Indeed, the fifteenth-century Kalyani inscription mentions sects originating in south India (Kanchipuram), Bengal and Cambodia living in Martaban in the second half of the twelfth century.[20] In addition, Lower Burma was in contact with Nakhon Si Thammarat on the Thai peninsula and with the Mons of Haripunjaya, and from the mid-eleventh century exercised an important influence on the religion and art of Pagan. It was not until the end of the eleventh century and the end of the Chola occupancy of Sri Lanka that the conservative Theravada Buddhism practised in that country enjoyed a resurgence in mainland Southeast Asia.

INFLUENCES ON THE KAW-GUN IMAGES

It would appear that in their depiction of the Descent from Tavatimsa Heaven the Kaw-gun sculptors adapted Pala and Pagan iconography, but also used other Southeast Asian models for their rendition of the Buddha image. In Pala and Pagan sculptures of this period the figure stands erect, devoid of movement. The left hand holds the robe nearly to shoulder height, while the right is outstretched in the manner of the first Kaw-gun image (Figure 4.1). In the second Kaw-gun image (Figure 4.2), the position of the arms is reversed, and the left leg is flexed.

The depiction of the Buddha standing in an exaggerated *tribhanga* pose, one leg flexed with the foot in front of the other, is found in the art of Srivijaya of around the ninth century.[21] The same posture is characteristic of the art of Si Thep, also dating to around the ninth century, which Boisselier has described as a synthesis of the sculptural styles of Dvaravati, Srivijaya and Lopburi, notable for their exceptional freedom of movement and the boldness of their execution.[22] Brown regards Si Thep as a site connecting various areas and cultures, particularly central, eastern, and northeastern Thailand and Cambodia.[23] The Si Thep images, both Buddhist and Brahmanical, are remarkable in that they depict the *tribhanga* without resorting to any support or prop. While the Kaw-gun Buddhas do rely on a back-slab for support, they are conceived almost in the round. Their wide shoulders, pronounced breasts, long narrow waists and well-formed thighs also reflect the impressive Si Thep style. It is probable therefore that the Kaw-gun *tribhanga* derives from Si Thep, and reflects Martaban's place as an outlet for Thailand's trade.

The ornaments of the Buddhas at Kaw-gun have greater affinity with Khmer art than with Pala India. The wide necklace and lower belt with a diamond-shaped belt in front, most clearly seen in the second image, are paralleled in the Khmer-influenced sculpture of Lopburi and Haripunjaya.[24] At Lopburi the crown of the Buddha is the Khmer type, while at Haripunjaya the five-pointed Pala type common at Pagan is more usual. (The Kaw-gun Vishnu, however, wears a Pala-type crown.) There are also similarities in the Buddhas' robes: the outer hems ending in sharply defined points, while a decorated band falls between the legs, illustrated in a more naturalistic manner at Kaw-gun.

In Lower Burma, the appearance in the eleventh century of the Buddha wearing royal ornaments and (presumably) a crown coincides with its appearance in Pala, Pagan and Khmer art.[25] In most contexts the adorned Buddha is regarded as a Mahayanist icon, illustrating the *sambhogakaya* aspect of the Buddha where he is regarded as a king in whom the transcendental form is made manifest.[26] Woodward recently drew attention to the proliferation around Bodh Gaya in the eleventh century of the garment and diadem initiation rites of the Mantrayana, during which the Bodhisatta undergoes the *mukuta-abhiseka* in preparation to his becoming a Manifest Complete Buddha as Mahavairocana, the *sambhogakaya*.[27] He also illustrates one of the giant stone sculptures at Bodh Gaya, a crowned Buddha standing, as at Kaw-gun, left hand holding the garment and right raised in *abhaya mudra* which, he suggests, in the context of the Tantric sect present there, portrays a manifestation of one the Buddhas of the past. Given the existence of both Bengali and Cambodian monks in Martaban it might be assumed that the queen who had the Kaw-gun images made was influenced by this sect.

It is probable that the sect followed in Lower Burma in the eleventh century was a precursor of Ariya Buddhism about which we know little as it has left no texts or inscriptions. Woodward has suggested that the roots of Ariya Buddhism as practised in Thailand lay principally in Burma, and that key features of its iconography were the standing Buddha with his hand on his chest and the crowns inspired by eleventh-century images of Pala India.[28] These features symbolised the achievement of supreme Buddhahood and commemorated what was believed to have been the true Enlightenment, when the Buddha Sakyamuni ascended into the air and was crowned by Buddhas who had gathered from different galaxies.[29] The sect started to challenge the dominant Mahayana of Cambodia towards the end of the twelfth century and persisted in Thailand until it was overtaken by a new wave of Sri Lankan Buddhism in the fourteenth century. While it is beyond the scope of this chapter to explore the connection of Ariya Buddhism with the Aris of Burma and with Buddhist sects which emerged in Cambodia, common features appear to be the incorporation of a *naga* cult, as evidenced by the preponderance of images of the Buddha protected by the *naga*, and practices such as the ritual deflowering of virgins by the clergy.[30]

There are certain similarities between the Kaw-gun sculptures and others around the Thaton area and the art of early Pagan. The Buddha image type is found again in a sculpture depicting the Taming of the Nalagiri Elephant from Nagawun Thein, which is five miles south of Pegu.[31] The Buddha in bold relief stands in *tribhanga* pose on an ornate double-lotus throne, with a carved oval halo behind him; his garments are rendered in the Kaw-gun manner. The legs and arms are thick and solid; the feet and knees, placed together, turn to the left suggesting that the image might be of a later date. The Buddha with his left hand held at the shoulder and the right arm stretched down with the hand facing forward became a dominant motif in later Mon art.[32] Several uncrowned wooden images, twice or three times life-size, now in the Mon Museum at Moulmein, stand erect with the right hand on the chest and the left outstretched. Luce has suggested that a series of life-size wooden crowned Buddha images found with hands in this position at the Kyaukku Ohnmin at Pagan and in some other temples might be portrait statues of Pagan royalty, now gods in *devaloka*.[33]

LOWER BURMA AND SUKHOTHAI

How then, did the Kaw-gun Buddha type reach Sukhothai? The Mons of Lower Burma are known to have been in contact with the Mons of Haripunjaya, which was conquered by Sukhothai in 1281. There would have been considerable intercourse between the *sangha* of Lower Burma and central and northern Thailand throughout the twelfth and thirteenth centuries, and this was paralleled by the laity as the ceramics trade developed. The originality and energy of the Kaw-gun type would have thus become known. Woodward has identified two further prototypes from Lopburi and Chiang Sen as dating to the thirteenth to fourteenth centuries. Krairiksh has placed the metal repoussé walking Buddha images at Phra Maha That at Haripunjaya to the end of the thirteenth century, although Woodward prefers a date in the fourteenth century.[34] These have certain important characteristics in common with the Kaw-gun Buddhas, particularly the placement of the hands and the rendering of the robes.

A single plaque, probably from a Buddhist shrine in Lower Burma, exhibits some remarkable similarities with Sukhothai art. Now in a private collection, the terracotta plaque, measuring 46 by 33 cm, illustrates a pair of women who might represent the daughters of Mara seeking to thwart the Enlightenment of the Buddha (Figure 4.3). Such pairs of figures have long been known in the Mon-inspired art of early Pagan and in the later Mon art of the south.[35] The two figures have been built up with stucco. The background has been covered with a pale green glaze, the figures with a paler white-green glaze, while their garments, ornaments and hair have been picked out with a dark chocolate-coloured glaze. All of these colours are typical of glazes associated with kiln sites in Lower Burma.[36]

The two figures stride arrogantly across the plaque, their bodies elongated and sinuous. Both have one foot on the ground shown in profile, and the other merely brushing the surface with the toes. Each carries a lotus bud behind the shoulder, while the left hand is held to the side. Their faces wear a disdainful expression, the eyes almost hooded, the nose long and the lips pursed, while the bodies demonstrate a command of stylisation rarely

Figure 4.3 Plaque. Terracotta and stucco, pale green and chocolate glaze, ht 46 cm, w. 33 cm, d. 3.5 cm. Photograph by Luke Hardy.

found in the sculpture of Burma, with their long necks, wide shoulders shown frontally, and long thighs. The connection, on the one hand, between the Si Thep-inspired bodies of Kaw-gun and, on the other, the Sukhothai walking Buddhas with their unearthly anatomy and bearing, is apparent. The impression of movement is accentuated by their out-thrust breasts and the draping of their lower garments, which swish between their legs. The garments and the ornaments have parallels at both Pagan and Sukhothai. The women's headdresses comprise pointed diadems on top of a wide, decorated base surmounted by a tall, elongated crown, from behind which their long and elaborately coiffed hair extrudes. These elements have Sukhothai counterparts.[37] Their bustiers are similar to those in the paintings of early Pagan. Around their waists are double belts, caught at the sides through loops, somewhat in the manner of the costumes of Brahma and Indra in the Descent from Tavatimsa Heaven relief at the Wat Trapang Thong Lang in Sukhothai. An early fourteenth-century date is therefore suggested.

The impact of Lower Burma on Sukhothai art is convincingly documented by the Thai chronicles, notably the *Jinakalamalini* and the *Mulasana*.[38] These recount how an orthodox forest-dwelling Sri Lankan sect came to be established in Thailand in the fourteenth century. In the 1320s a number of monks from the Mon kingdom in Lower Burma went to Sri Lanka to study at the Udumbaragiri monastery. In 1331, at the request of the Mon king, they returned and established a branch of the Udumbaragiri in Pan, near Martaban. This must be modern Pa-an, across the river from the Kaw-gun caves. The order's leader attracted pupils to Pan, including monks from Sukhothai, who in 1341 were sent to establish the Sinhalabhikku or Singhalese order in Sukhothai at the request of King Lo Tai. The Sukhothai monks may have become familiar with images of the Kaw-gun type during their stay.

Walking Buddhas first appear at Sukhothai around the end of the fourteenth century, notably in the depiction of the Descent from Tavatimsa Heaven at the Wat Traphang Thong Lam. Here again we have Brahma holding the umbrella over the Buddha's head, and the *devas* behind. The physiognomy of the Sukhothai walking Buddha has been described as owing something to Sri Lanka but more to local genius. While Brown suggested a possible wooden prototype, we can now trace a development through Si Thep to the Mon country of Lower Burma. The royal ornaments of Kaw-gun have been discarded in accordance with the more orthodox form of the religion introduced from Sri Lanka via Pa-an by Lo Tai. The physiognomy and the placement of the robes, worn in the open mode, however, can be ultimately connected to the Kaw-gun type, and the feet no longer tentatively step out from the background – they are walking.

APPENDIX
Vishnu at Kaw-gun (Figure 4.4)

This is one of six images of the reclining Vishnu described by Luce found in Lower Burma.[39] Vishnu holds his attributes, the conch, mace, wheel and, probably, lotus. At his feet is a four-armed Ganesha. Behind him rear seven crowned serpent heads, their faces rendered in the Khmer manner. Above, rise three double-lotuses on stalks, on which a four-armed Vishnu sits in the centre, with Brahma to his right and Shiva to his left. At the side, adjacent to Brahma, is a small figure of a man on a horse, while next to Shiva is a small *linga*. There are three niches at the base of the image. To the left is a kneeling female figure with a high headdress, in the centre are two seated figures, one apparently male with a flower at his left shoulder, the other defaced, while another damaged figure is in the right-hand niche. These may represent worshippers or donors.

This complex composition depicts the moment of creation of the universe at the beginning of each world era as described in the myth. Vishnu in human form sleeps on a *naga*, either Ananta (Endless) or Shesha (Remainder), symbolising the cosmic fluid of creation.

A lotus springs from Vishnu's navel, upon which is seated the god-creator Brahma, his four faces illustrating the moment when, as the lotus opens, he expands space in all directions. This scene was formulated in Indian sculpture of the Gupta period, and is found at the eighth-century Cave 15 at Ellora, in association with images of Shiva. Vishnu's feet here are crossed in the same way as at Kaw-gun.

The sleeping Vishnu became popular in the art of mainland Southeast Asia, where it resonated with earlier *naga* cults and creation myths. A remarkable eleventh-century equivalent is found at Angkor, at Kbal Spean, near the source of one of the tributaries of the Siem Reap River.[40] The river-bed itself has been engraved with the sleeping Vishnu who has, at his right, a figure on a horse, as does the Kaw-gun sculpture, as well as what appear to be three courtiers carrying fans.[41] Below the image platform is a row of *lingas*. The site appears to symbolise a royal connection with the act of creation, as did the massive main image from the West Mebon temple, which according to the Chinese envoy Zhou Daguan originally had a fountain of water flowing through his navel. Vishnu's ornaments at Kaw-gun and at the West Mebon

Figure 4.4 Vishnu reclining on the *Naga* Ananta. Sandstone, ht 134 cm, w. 79 cm, d. 23 cm. Photograph by Luke Hardy.

are identical. There are other connections with Khmer art: the crowned *naga* heads, for instance, first appear in Cambodia and in the Khmer art of northeast Thailand at about this time.

In the Kaw-gun sculpture, as in others from southern Burma, particularly those from around the Thaton area, Brahma has been given an almost secondary role; it is Vishnu who emerges from the central lotus, and Shiva, the other member of the Hindu trinity, is also given a place equivalent to Brahma's. Shiva's function is stressed by the *linga*, placed like a god on a lotus throne at his side. Lakshmi, Vishnu's consort, is absent here, her place at his feet taken by the elephant-headed Ganesha.

Vishnu played an important role in the kingship of early Burma and Thailand where various Vaishnava rituals were incorporated into a cult of kingship.[42] In the early Vaishnava cult, Vishnu was considered to enter the king at the time of his consecration. By identifying himself with Vishnu the king would be able to conquer the three worlds. All *cakravartins* or paramount sovereigns were regarded as bearing a portion of Vishnu's personality. The role of the king was to guarantee the furtherance of vegetation and thus the fertility of the land. It was the king's duty to ensure rain fell and to cause the crops to thrive, and the same functions are attributed to Vishnu who is always concerned with generation and fertility, most obviously in his Anantashayanin mode.

Vishnu was associated with kingship and with the foundation of urban centres in Thailand and in Burma. The *Jinakalamalini* and the *Camadevivamsa* relate that the *rishi* Vasudeva (an epithet of Vishnu) was associated with the foundation of the Mon city of Haripunjaya.[43] Similarly, only a few years after the Kaw-gun sculptures were installed, King Kyanzittha of Pagan described his ascension of the throne as the fulfillment of a prophecy of the Lord Buddha. In what is obviously a legitimisation of Kyanzittha's rule, the Buddha tells his disciple Ananda, Gawampati (who has been described as the patron saint of the Mons), Indra (the King of the Gods), and the sage Bisnu (Vishnu), that Bisnu will be reincarnated and will rule first at Shri Kshetra, the last of the Pyu cities, and later at Pagan as Kyanzittha. Minor personages destined to assist are a *naga* king named Katakarmma, Bissukarmma, and Vishvakarman, the celestial architect.[44] Moreover, it is forecast that the people of Pagan (Arimaddanapur) will be disciples of the Buddha, the Law, and the *sangha*, rain will fall and great prosperity will be enjoyed. Kyanzittha is described as a mighty *cakravartin* king and a bodhisattva who will become a Buddha. Here, the Vaishnava cult is acknowledged but made subservient to Buddhism, a process which may have begun in Lower Burma as illustrated by the Kaw-gun images. Later, King Lo Tai is recorded as having established a pair of images representing Vishnu and Shiva at Sukhothai.

It is apparent that both Buddhism and Vaishnava Hinduism with some Shaiva accretions were practised concurrently in Lower Burma in the eleventh century. All three had been patronized by the same king at Angkor. A Khmer inscription of the tenth century mentions the Buddha and the Hindu Trinity in juxtaposition.[45] The present author would suggest that in Lower Burma both were associated with a royal cult in which the *cakravartin* ruler was given the power to regulate the celestial and terrestrial forces in order to control the coming of the rains which would ensure the fertility of the country. The *cakravartin* king, as we have seen, was considered to embody the qualities of Vishnu in the royal consecration ceremony. The sleeping Vishnu is intimately associated with terrestrial forces, and the Descent from Tavatimsa Heaven illustrates the Buddha's subjugation of the heavens and the gods who dwelt there.

NOTES

1 A.B. Griswold, in Theodore Bowie (ed.), *The Arts of Thailand*, Bloomington: Indiana University Press, 1960. A.B. Griswold, *Towards a History of Sukhodaya Art*, Bangkok: National Museum, 1967. A.B. Griswold, 'Buddhas of Sukhodaya', *Archives of the Chinese Art Society of America*, vol. 7, 1953, pp. 23–9. Piriya Krairiksh, 'The Repoussé Buddha Images of the Mahā Thāt, Lamphun', *Artibus Asiae*, vol. XLIX, pts 1/2, 1989, pp. 169–83. Robert L. Brown, 'God on Earth: The Walking Buddha in the Art of Southeast Asia', *Artibus Asiae*, vol. L, pts 1/2, 1990, pp. 73–8.

2 Hiram W. Woodward, Jr., *The Sacred Sculpture of Thailand*, London: Thames and Hudson, 1997, repr. 1999, p. 123, 158–60 and fig. 140.

3 Brown, 1990, fig. 6.

4 Alexander Coburn Soper, 'Literary Evidence for Early Buddhist Art in China', *Artibus Asiae*, vol. 21, 1959, pp. 259–65.

5 These include images found at Dong Duong (Vietnam), Pong Tuk (Thailand), Sulawesi and East Java. A South Indian or Sri Lankan derivation is often attributed to this group. An example from Thaton is illustrated in G.H. Luce, *Phases of Pre-Pagan Burma: Languages and History*, vol. 2, Oxford: Oxford University Press, 1985, pl. 96a. In his discussion of the type, A.J. Bernet Kempers refers to Krom's identification of certain of these as Dipankara, patron of sailors, but concludes that the *mudras* and the position of the hand holding the robe do not form a foundation for identification. A.J. Bernet Kempers, *The Bronzes of Nalanda and Hindu-Javanese Art*, Leiden: Brill, 1933, p. 18, repr. from *Bijdragen Tot de Taal-, Land- en Volkenkunde van Ned. Indie*, vol. 90, fasc. 1.

6 Brown, 1990, fig. 3.

7 David K. Wyatt, 'Relics, Oaths and Politics in Thirteenth Century Siam', *Journal of Southeast Asian Studies*, vol. 32, no. 1, 2001, pp. 3–66.

8 Wyatt, 2001, p. 28, referring to Hans Penth, 'The Date of the Wat Ban Sanuk Inscription', *Proceedings of the 6th International Conference on Thai Studies; Theme VI, Chiang Mai 1296–1996* (Chiang Mai, 1996), pp. 19–29. A.B. Griswold and Prasaert na Nagara, 'The Second Oldest Writing in Siamese', *Journal of the Siam Society*, vol. 67, no. 1, 1979, pp. 179–228.

9 Wyatt, 2001, p. 28.

10 The Kaw-gun images have been described by Luce and Ba Shin in the 'Report of the Director', *Archaeological Survey, Burma*, Rangoon: Superintendent of Government Printing, 1957–8, pp. 14–15; Luce, 1985, vol. 1, pp. 176–7 and vol. 2, pls 99–100. E. Guillon, 'Notes sur l'ancienne région de Thatön (Basse-Birmanie)', *Artibus Asiae*, vol. XXXVI, pt. 4, 1974, pp. 273–86.

11 Taw Sein Ko, 'Archaeological Tour through Ramannadesa (1891–2)', *The Indian Antiquary*, vol. XXI, 1892, pp. 377–86. Richard Carnac Temple, 'Notes on Antiquities in Ramannadesa', *The Indian Antiquary*, vol. XXII, Nov.-Dec. 1893, pp. 327–66. While none of these sources refers to the provenance of the sculptures under discussion, the former headmaster of Pagat school, U Maung Maung Kyi, relates (personal communication, 17 May 2001) that in 1997 a former head of Kaw-gun village, U Chit Tin, told him that in 1958 three foreigners (one female) escorted by a group of government soldiers visited the caves and that the villagers, under the supervision of a white man, had to dig out the three sculptures 'in different places'. U Maung Maung Kyi speculated that Luce was the white supervisor.

12 G.H. Luce, 'Mons of the Pagan Dynasty', *Journal of the Burma Research Society*, vol. XXXVI, pt. 1, 1953, p. 5, 6. Luce, 1985, vol. 1, pp. 175–7 and vol. 2, pl. 98. H.L. Shorto, *A Dictionary of the Mon Inscriptions from the Sixth to the Sixteenth Centuries*, Oxford: Oxford University Press, 1971, p. xxviii. Guillon, 1974, pp. 283–5.

13 Wyatt, 2001, p. 29.

14 *Archaeological Survey of India, Annual Report*, 1930–4, pt. 1, p. 196 and pt. 2, pl. CXII (a). *Inscriptions of Burma*, Rangoon: Superintendent of Government Printing, pl. IV, 360b.

15 Gao Xingjian, *Soul Mountain* (Mabel Lee, trans.), Flamingo, Sydney, 2000, pp. 238–43. Gao Xingjian states that he referred to a copy of Drum Sacrifice Songs written down and translated into Chinese by a Miao acquaintance.

16 John Lowry, *Burmese Art*, London: HMSO, 1974, pl. 14. E. Guillon, *The Mons: A Civilization of Southeast Asia* (James Di Crocco, ed. and trans.), Bangkok: Siam Society, 1999, p. 44.

17 Michael Aung-Thwin, 'Lower Burma and Pegu in the History of Burma' in Jos Gommens and Jacques Leider (eds), *The Maritime Frontier of Burma: Exploring Political, Cultural and Commercial Interaction in the Indian Ocean World, 1200–1800*, Koninklijke Nederlandse Akademie van Wetenschappen, Amsterdam, Leiden: KITLV Press, 2002, pp. 44–6. His account of the history of Lower Burma is paraphrased here.

18 Wyatt, 2001, pp. 21ff.

19 G.H. Luce, *Old Burma – Early Pagan*, vol. 1, Locust Valley, New York: J.J. Augustin, 1969, pp. 21–3.

20 Kanai Lal Hazra, *History of Theravada Buddhism in South-East Asia*, New Delhi, 1982, pp. 92ff. E. Guillon, 1999, p. 154.

21 Piriya Krairiksh, *Art Styles of Thailand: A Selection from National Provincial Museums*, Bangkok: Fine Arts Department, 1977, pl. 19.

22 J. Boisselier, *The Heritage of Thai Sculpture*, New York: Weatherhill, 1975, p. 104 and pl. 69.

23 Robert L. Brown, *The Dvaravati Wheels of the Law and the Indianisation of Southeast Asia*, Leiden: Brill, 1996, p. 36.

24 For example, see Boisselier, 1975, pl. 79. Also, Pisit Charoenwongsa and M.C. Subhadradis Diskul, *Thailand*, Archaeologia Mundi Series, Bangkok: Nagel, 1978.

25 Pamela Gutman, 'Crowned Buddha Images of Arakan', *Art and Archaeology Research Papers*, vol. 15, London, 1979, pp. 48–56.

26 Paul Mus, 'Le Buddha Paré. Son Origine Indienne. Çākyamuni dans Le Mahāyānisme Moyen', *BEFEO*, vol. 28, 1928, p. 197.

27 Hiram W. Woodward, Jr., 'The Life of the Buddha in the Pala Monastic Environment', *The Journal of the Walters Art Gallery*, vol. 48, 1990, pp. 13–27.

28 Woodward, 1997, pp. 115–16. Also, Hiram W. Woodward, Jr., 'Ram Khamhaeng's Inscription: the Search for Context', *The Ram Khamhaeng Controversy*, James R. Chamberlain (ed.), the Siam Society, Bangkok, 1991, p. 424.

29 Woodward, 1997, p. 138 and figs 140–1.

30 A terracotta plaque in the Mon Museum at Moulmein depicts an earth-touching Buddha seated above and between two stupas placed over a giant *naga*. On either side are a monk and a crowned figure. See also Charles Duroiselle, 'The Ari of Burma and Tantric Buddhism', *Archaeological Survey of India, Annual Report*, 1915–16, pp. 82ff. and L.P. Briggs, 'The Ancient Khmer Empire', *Transactions of the American Philosophical Society*, New Series, vol. 41, pt. 1, 1951, p. 246.

31 Luce, 1985, vol. 1, p. 168 and vol. 2, pls 82–3.

32 *Ibid.*, vol. 1, p. 174 and vol. 2, pls 96 c, e, f. Several of these later Mon images have a goose perched above each shoulder. This is a reference to the foundation legend of Pegu which records that a goose, the vehicle of Brahma, the creator of space, alighted on a small patch of ground in the shallow sea, and in time the ground expanded to become dry land to which people migrated. Brahma is also the dominant motif at the Nanpaya temple, reputed to have been built by the Mon king captured by King Anawrahta when he conquered Thaton in 1057.

33 Luce, 1969, vol. 1, p. 291; vol. 2, p. 187; vol. 3, pls 421–2.

34 Krairiksh, 1989, p. 181 and figs 10,11. Woodward, 1997, pp. 116–19; 151–3; 138–9; and figs 140 and 141.

35 Luce, 1969, vol. 1, p. 241; vol. 3, pls 329–34. R. Carnac Temple, 1893, pp. 353–4 and pls IX and IXa. Lowry, 1974, pl. 21.

36 Myo Thant Tyn and Dawn F. Rooney, 'Ancient Celadon in Myanmar: A New Ceramic Discovery', *Orientations*, vol. 32, no. 4, April 2001, pp. 57–61.

37 Boisselier, 1975, pl. 95.

38 Georges Coedès, 'Document sur l'histoire politique et religieuse du Laos Occidental', *BEFEO*, vol. 25, pts 1–2, 1925, pp. 1–3. Griswold, 1967, pp. 15–16.

39 Luce, 1969, vol. 1, pp. 217–18. Luce, 1985, vol. 1, pp. 176–7. Guillon, 1974, was of the opinion that this image was inscribed by the same queen who had the Descent from Tavatimsa Heaven images made. U Maung Maung Kyi has confirmed that the image is not inscribed, and has suggested that Guillon followed Nai Pan Hla who in 1960 had confused it with the five-headed Anantashayin from Thaton (personal communication, 17 May 2001).

40 Claude Jacques, *Angkor*, Cologne: Könemann, 1999, p. 11.

41 A royal ritual involving a figure on a horse is also found illustrated at the altar of the Cham Buddhist Dong Duong shrine.

42 Pamela Gutman, 'Vishnu in Burma', *The Art of Burma – New Researches*, Donald Stadtner (ed.), Mumbai: Marg Publications, 1999, pp. 29–36. Virginia Dofflemeyer, 'Visnu Images from Ancient Thailand and the Concept of Kingship', *Art from Thailand*, Robert L. Brown (ed.), Mumbai: Marg Publications, 1999, pp. 34–48.

43 Coedès, 1925.

44 *Epigraphia Birmanica being Lithic and Other Inscriptions of Burma*, vol. 1, pt. 2, repr. Rangoon: Superintendent of Government Printing, 1960, *passim*.

45 Kamaleswar Bhattacharya, 'The Religions of Ancient Cambodia', *Sculpture of Angkor and Ancient Cambodia – Millennium of Glory*, Helen Ibbitson Jessop and Thierry Zephir (eds), New York: Thames and Hudson, 1997, pp. 47, 51.

5 Relationships between Buddhist texts and images of the Enlightenment during the early Pagan period

Charlotte Galloway

The Enlightenment is the most important event of the life of Gotama Buddha, the Buddha of the present era. It signifies the transition between his life as a mortal, one who suffers the continual cycle of death and rebirth, and his life as a Buddha, an Enlightened one who has overcome all earthly attachments, is now all knowing and will attain *nibbāna*. Imagery of the Enlightenment is associated with the story of Māra and his army, and the Buddha's calling of the Earth as witness to his past deeds. Māra attempts to deter the Bodhisatta from continuing along the path to Buddhahood, but Earth testifies to his worthiness to obtain Enlightenment.

While this story is now an integral part of Burmese Theravada lore, its current form is a synthesis of events drawn from many different versions of the Buddha's life story. A review of depictions of the Enlightenment made during the early Pagan period (*c.* AD 1050–1287) reveals a remarkable richness of visual expression. However, explanations regarding the details of these images are glossed over in existing art historical writings. Even though there is substantial epigraphic and physical evidence which confirms strong Mahayana and Brahmanical practices in Pagan prior to Anawrahta's reign (*c.* AD 1044–1077), when interpreting imagery Mahayana influences are overlooked in these writings. The study of Southeast Asian art history by Western scholars has developed in an environment dominated by the Theravada tradition. The polarisation of Buddhism into two distinct schools, the Theravada and the Mahayana, has become a fixed concept in much of the art historian's subsequent interpretations of iconography. There is no such clear cut division between the two streams and viewing Southeast Asia through such a narrow interpretation of Theravada Buddhism is no longer sustainable.

The focus on the current Theravada dominance of Southeast Asian Buddhism has discouraged the study of other textual accounts that can provide further insight into the meanings of Enlightenment imagery. The reading of these texts which are rich in visual narrative in conjunction with the images, can be shown to expand our interpretation of the iconographic details contained within them. This chapter highlights some of the iconographic features and their relationship to texts that have gained prominence in both the Mahayana and Theravada traditions. The presence of imagery that can be shown to draw clearly on material from both streams provides further insight into the nature of Buddhist practice in early Burma, namely that it was a syncretic mix of traditions superimposed on a pre-existing culture of *nat* worship and Brahmanism.[1]

The widespread depiction of the Enlightenment, particularly in Southeast Asia, is due to its importance to Buddhist teachings. The discourse relating to the event is one that reinforces the importance of *kamma*.[2] The recollection of past good deeds which have led to the final rebirth is the crucial event, and explicitly infers that accumulation of good *kamma*, through life cycles of good deeds, is the essence of achieving Buddhahood in a future life. *Kammatic* Buddhist practice focuses on the present and the future, hence in Burma, imagery of the current Buddha is paramount. The appearance in the art record of Metteya, the future Buddha, also reflects an overriding concern with what lies ahead rather than with the past.[3] Metteya and Gotama appear in a particularly Burmese-style dyad from about the twelfth century onwards.

Accounts of the Enlightenment occur in numerous texts that can be divided into two categories: those incorporated into the Buddhist scriptural canons and those that are independent of them. There are elements of the Buddha's life story scattered throughout the Theravada canon, the *Tipiṭaka*.[4] The Pāli canon is concerned primarily with the teachings of the Buddha and rules for the behaviour of its *saṅgha*, and therefore the absence of a complete account of the Buddha's last earthly life in the *Tipiṭaka* should not be considered unusual. One of the more expansive accounts of Gotama's life can be found in the *Khuddaka Nikāya* of the *Sutta Piṭaka*. Written in dialogue form, as is much of the *Tipiṭaka*, in the exchange of words between Māra and Gotama during his meditation under the Bodhi tree near the river Nerañjarā, the Buddha says:

'Seeing the surrounding army ready and Māra mounted on his elephant, I am going out to fight so that he may not shift me from my position. This army of yours which the world together with the devas is unable to subdue, that I will destroy with wisdom, like an unbaked clay bowl with a stone. Having mastered the mind and firmly established mindfulness I shall wander from country to country guiding many disciples. And they will be diligent and energetic in practising my teaching, the teaching of one without sensual desire, and they will go where, having gone, one does not grieve.'

Māra: 'For seven years I followed the Lord step by step but did not find an opportunity to defeat that mindful Awakened one. A crow flew around a stone having the colour of fat: "Can we find even here something tender? May it be something to eat?"

'Not finding anything edible the crow left that place. As the crow and the stone, we leave Gotama, having approached and become disheartened.'

Overcome by sorrow his lute fell from his arm and thereupon the unhappy spirit disappeared from that place.[5]

The *Mahāsaccaka Sutta* of the *Majjhima Nikāya* also refers to the moment of Enlightenment. The Buddha recounts to Saccaka, the wandering ascetic, the process by which he came to attain his Awakening. He describes his privileged background, his renunciation and the six years spent as an ascetic. This account makes no mention of Māra or his armies, nor even the Bodhi tree, two elements which are generally considered synonymous with imagery of the Enlightenment.[6]

These examples are typical of the references to Gotama's life found in the *Tipiṭaka*. It is difficult to see how the *Tipiṭaka* could be the source of the expansive imagery that has arisen within the Buddhist world. The *Tipiṭaka* was the exclusive domain of the monks, written in a liturgical language, Pāli. It then became the role of the monks to deliver oral recitations of the Buddha's teachings. This set the scene for later commentators and writers who composed a number of texts which were narrative and amenable to public recitation; a tradition of oral transmission of Buddhist teachings had been in place for centuries, while a popular written version only developed well after the Buddha's lifetime.

The popular narratives, which form the second source for information regarding the life of the Buddha, are rarely mentioned when discussing Buddhist iconography, even though they are vividly descriptive. While imagery of the Enlightenment has been present from as early as the reign of king Aśoka (*r.c.* 272–231 BC), the earliest known accounts dedicated to the Buddha's life story are the *Lalitavistara* and the *Buddhacarita*, both dating from about the first century AD.[7] These texts can be seen to have their origins in legends that have existed from at least the second or first centuries BC, as evidenced by the

imagery that appears on the great stupa at Sanchi in India. The extensive carvings include scenes of the Enlightenment episode, such as the Buddha represented in aniconic form surrounded by Māra's armies.

The author of the *Lalitavistara* is unknown but the text, which was written in Sanskrit, is believed to have its origins in the Mahayana school, and the text is certainly known today in Tibet. The *Buddhacarita* was the work of one of the greatest Buddhist poets, Aśvaghoṣa, and was also written in classical Sanskrit. While this would suggest the work was that of a Mahayana follower, Sanskrit generally being associated with Northern Buddhism, with Pāli the language of the Theravadins, scholars generally agree that Aśvaghoṣa was a follower of the Theravada school.[8] Between AD 671 and 695 the Chinese pilgrim I-Tsing wrote that the *Buddhacarita* was 'widely read or sung' throughout India and the countries of the Southern Sea.[9]

The next extant complete account of the Buddha's life is the later sixth-century AD work called the *Nidānakathā*, attributed to the Pāli commentator Buddhaghosa.[10] It was written as an introduction to the final part of the *Sutta Piṭaka*, the *Khuddaka Nikāya* which contains the Jātaka stories, and was not part of the original Pāli canon. The first cohesive version of the Buddha's life story to be written in Pāli, the *Nidānakathā*, could be expected to relate most closely to the imagery of Burmese Buddhism since Buddhaghosa became renowned in Burma. He is the compiler of a large number of Buddhist texts and is believed by the Burmese to have lived in Thaton around AD 400.[11] Buddhaghosa is said to have travelled to Sri Lanka and brought back to the mainland Theravada Buddhist texts which helped consolidate the religion's foothold in the country.[12] His account is positioned as a link between the canon and a more public audience, and its language is much less poetic than that of the *Lalitavistara* and the *Buddhacarita*.

There are numerous other texts that refer to Gotama's last earthly existence. The vast Tibetan collections, the *bKa'-'gyur* and *bsTan-'gyur*, while agreeing in general terms with the previously mentioned versions, contain many small but interesting differences regarding specific moments.[13] There is also mention of the Enlightenment in Aśvaghoṣa's other famous poem, the *Saundarananda* or Nanda the Fair, which recounts the tale of Nanda, Gotama's cousin, his renunciation of earthly delights and conversion to a follower of the 'true path'.[14] A text purporting to represent a Burmese version of the Buddha's life is the *Tathāgatha'oudana*.[15] It provides a specific insight into the complexities of the Burmese version of Gotama Buddha's life story and is particularly interesting as it demonstrates the seamless incorporation of the indigenous Burmese *nats* into the legend. This supports the commonly held belief that their presence was very strong and important to the indigenous populations when Buddhism arrived in Burma. While the date of its compilation is not known, it is unlikely to have been written before the fourteenth century AD.

Another account which could reasonably be assumed to have influenced Burmese Buddhist imagery is the *Jinacarita,* which was written in Sri Lanka in the twelfth century.[16] However, it does not provide any new insights into Gotama's life. A final source of information regarding the Buddha's life story is the Mon inscriptions. The translations of the medieval inscriptions, which date from the eleventh to fifteenth centuries, reveal that the events surrounding the Enlightenment were very prominent, particularly in the later writings.[17] These texts could be expected to show the closest links to the visual images made during the same period. Unfortunately they are rather fragmentary and as such will not be specifically referred to. There are other more recent publications relating to the Buddha's life but this chapter is concerned with accounts that are known to have been in existence prior to the Pagan period. Therefore the texts discussed here are the *Lalitavistara,* the *Buddhacarita* and the *Nidānakathā.*

While little is known of the arrival of Buddhism into Burma, the physical evidence available so far indicates that at the Pyu city of Sri Kshetra a highly developed level of understanding of Buddhism existed by the fifth century AD. From this period until around the tenth century there are few known Buddhist remains. Then a more narrative type of imagery appeared, as can be seen on the many votive tablets discovered throughout Burma. These tablets were used to spread the religion and as such had an educational role. It has long been held that votive tablets heralded the rise of Theravada Buddhism in the region.[18] However, there exists a marked contrast between the imagery evoked by the orthodox Theravada tradition and the often elaborate and complex imagery which appears on these plaques. If we look to Buddhaghosa's *Nidānakathā,* a Theravada text, which is indeed wonderfully descriptive, it still fails to conjure up the many captivating scenes found on artwork of this era.

What, then, are possible sources for this visually complex imagery? If we look to the northern texts of the *Lalitavistara* and *Buddhacarita,* we find them full of rich descriptions concerning the Enlightenment. These stories of the Buddha's life would no doubt have captured the imagination of the Burmese. Full of magical events, miracles and supernatural beings, these legends would have provided a convincing link between Buddhism and their nature spirits, the *nats.* These were successfully integrated into the Burmese belief system alongside Buddhism, and the Buddhist *devas.*

With such complex imagery in mind, the votive tablets of King Anawrahta's reign (*c.* 1044–1077) are open to further interpretation. The purpose of the tablets was without doubt a missionary one, aimed at spreading the

teachings of the Buddha throughout Burma. The imagery is fairly consistent, with a central image of the Buddha surrounded by various decorative elements and more recognisable symbols of Buddhism such as stupas. Anawrahta's votive tablets almost exclusively depict the central Buddha in *bhūmisparśa mudrā,* signifying the importance of the moment of Enlightenment when teaching the doctrine. There is usually an inscription, often referring to the *ye dhamma* stanza which was a symbol of conversion and the power of the *saṅgha.*[19]

The elements shown on these votive tablets dating from the eleventh century are particularly interesting (Figure 5.1). The Buddha is flanked by the Bodhisatta Lokeśvara on his right and Metteya to the left, which immediately suggests a Mahayana influence, *bodhisattas* playing a leading role in Mahayana imagery. Luce comments on this link with the Mahayana but only describes the imagery in relation to similar images from other sites and countries.[20] However, Lokeśvara is not just a *bodhisatta* but is meant to be pre-eminent after the death of Gotama, until the arrival of Metteya. Therefore, his presence is also consistent with the practice of *kammatic* Buddhism mentioned earlier: that is, they reinforce a focus on future rebirths and act as guides along the path to Enlightenment. The Buddha, depicted at the moment of Enlightenment, is seated on a double-lotus throne raised on a pedestal. He is framed by a niche draped with beads. There are stupas above the central image interspersed with flowers. The leaves of the Bodhi tree under which the Buddha sits are prominent, the tree symbol being an important motif in Buddhism since early times when it was an aniconic symbol for the Enlightenment of the Buddha. Lotuses spring from the ground and support Lokeśvara and Metteya.

When viewed in parallel with the various life stories of the Buddha, the selection of elements included in this work suggests a strong link with the *Lalitavistara,* which makes particular mention of the displays occurring at the site of the Enlightenment. Once Gotama was seated under the Bodhi tree, he was approached by the *bodhisattas* of the ten directions who were attracted by the light emanating from the Buddha-to-be. Mahāsatta, from the south, 'gave shelter to the entire assembly with a single jeweled parasol' (other votive tablets have a definite parasol shape at the top of the stupa).[21] From the west came Indrajāli 'who gave shelter to the whole assembly with a single jewelled net'. From the southwest came Ratnasambhava who 'manifested within the circle of the assembly immeasurable and innumerable celestial temples'. Hemajālālamkāta 'caused figures of *bodhisattas* completely adorned with the thirty-two signs to appear in all of the storied palaces and temples, each figure holding garlands of divine and human flowers'. From the lower region, Mahāsatta Ratnagarbha caused 'golden lotuses which grows [sic] in the water of Jambu to appear within

Figure 5.1 Votive tablets with King Anawrahta's seal, *c.* 1050, terracotta, ht 13.3, w. 9.4 cm. Courtesy of Artibus Asiae Supplementum 25, *Old Burma – Early Pagan*, 1970, Plate 8a.

the circle of lapis lazuli'.[22] Other gifts are not so readily converted into imagery, such as the manifestation of a cloud of balm and sandalwood dust.

With these descriptive images in mind, the visual elements on the tablets become more than merely decorative. Each can be seen as representing part of the narrative of the Enlightenment as told in the *Lalitavistara*. Buildings in the form of the temple at Bodh Gaya, a place very few if any of the local Burmese artisans would have seen, symbolise not only the Enlightenment, but also the ideal form for any buildings mentioned in the context of this important event. The lightly incised wavy line surrounding the structure is not just for decoration but takes on a particular meaning, namely it becomes Indrajāli's jewelled net. The flowers under the *bodhisattas'* seats are not only symbolic lotuses, but part of the greater narrative. The strings of pearls on the columns and the flowers are also part of the *Lalitavistara* story. Similarly the other elements, such as the leaves of the Bodhi tree, are not random, put into the image to make it more pleasing, but deliberately included to represent this particular narrative.

The more distinctly Burmese artistic style which evolved from the time of King Kyanzittha (*r.* AD 1084–1113) corresponds to a period when Buddhism was also taking on a particularly Burmese form. Kyanzittha

oversaw the building of the Ananda Temple, completed around AD 1105. The dominance of the Ananda Temple even today can readily lead us to believe that it embodies the contemporary ideals of Buddhist thought during the time of its construction. The depictions of the Jātaka stories on tiles decorating the exterior, which correspond to those of the Buddhaghosa tradition, imply that the *Nidānakathā* story was well known.[23] Therefore, the imagery of the period would be expected to adhere to this account most closely. Thanks to Luce, we have a wonderful record of the images that were placed inside the Ananda Temple. However, when we examine these images carefully, we can see that this was still a transitional period in the development of Burmese Buddhism with a mix of influences and traditions.

Luce's series of images from niches seventy-three to eighty at the Ananda Temple provides a chronological account that is said to represent the period immediately prior to the Enlightenment until the end of the following seven weeks. A standing image shows the Bodhisatta carrying the grass bundles that he will place at the base of the Bodhi tree. The next image shows Sujātā's offering of milk rice. The Buddha is already in the Enlightenment position, *bhūmisparśa mudrā*, even though he has not yet attained Enlightenment. This is an iconographic device that helps us place the scene into the correct context.

The third image clearly depicts Sakka and Brahmā in a scene which parallels the text of the *Nidānakathā* when, after the Buddha-to-be seats himself under the Bodhi tree prior to the arrival of Māra's armies, Sakka blows his conch, and Brahmā holds the white parasol (Figure 5.2). This is not conclusive though, as the *Buddhacarita* narrates how Sakka and Brahmā, the 'two chiefs of the heavenly dwellings' approached the Buddha once they became aware of the Buddha's decision to teach the *dhamma*, an event placed at the end of the seven weeks after Enlightenment.[24] The *Lalitavistara* also mentions that Sakka and Brahmā are present when Gotama seats himself under the Bodhi tree prior to Enlightenment. Therefore it is possible that this image could represent a scene from any of these texts. Whether this series of images still remains in its original position is also open to debate.

The next image shows the Buddha seated alone. This should represent the moment prior to the arrival of Māra's armies, when all of the other gods have fled in

Figure 5.3 Gotama with Māra, Ananda Temple, Pagan. Photograph by the author.

Figure 5.2 Gotama flanked by Brahmā holding the parasol and Sakka holding the conch shell, Ananda Temple, Pagan. Photograph by the author.

terror. The soon-to-be Buddha is now shown with an *ūrṇā*, and this follows the text of the *Lalitavistara* more closely. The *Lalitavistara* is the only text of those discussed here which specifically mentions the *ūrṇā*. The Buddha-to-be calls Māra by emitting a ray of light 'from the tuft of hair between his eyebrows, a ray called Sarvamāra-maṇḍalavidhvamsanakar, 'That Which Destroys All the Domains of the Demon'.[25] The *ūrṇā* is present in three of the next four images. While the *ūrṇā* is absent in the next scene, which depicts Gotama and Māra, it is possible that this sculpture has been moved and was not one of the original images associated with this group (Figure 5.3).[26] The scene represents Māra's attempts to make Gotama move from his seat under the Bodhi tree.

The following figure depicts the temptation by Māra's daughters (Figure 5.4). The *Nidānakathā* specifically refers to Māra's three daughters as does the *Lalitavistara*, but they are present at different times in each narrative. Duroiselle described this scene in 1913 as a depiction of Māra's three daughters who, during the period after

Figure 5.4 Gotama with Māra's daughters, Ananda Temple, Pagan. Photograph by the author.

However, the Buddha blesses them and they turn into old women, which is not apparent in this depiction. Therefore it is most likely that this image is not drawn from the *Nidānakathā*, but represents the initial onslaught of Māra and his armies prior to the attainment of Enlightenment.

The next scene supports the above conclusion as the base shows a number of *devas*, or gods, making obeisance to the Buddha (Figure 5.5). This event is recounted in both the *Nidānakathā* and the *Lalitavistara*, the latter telling that after the defeat of Māra 'the gods of the earth joined their palms and bowed respectfully to the Bodhisattva'.[29] The positioning of this event does not make sense in the context of the *Nidānakathā*, however, as it should precede the image of Māra's daughters. The next scene at the Ananda shows the solitary Buddha after the Enlightenment, which corresponds to the *Lalitavistara* story when the gods, having paid their respects, stepped to one side.

In summary, this series of images can be interpreted in two ways. Firstly, if it is accepted that the scene with the three daughters represents their appearance during the period after Enlightenment, then the images draw on the

Enlightenment, try to distract the Buddha, followed by an image of two of them representing the next moment when they return defeated and bow down to the Buddha.[27] Although difficult to determine conclusively, these two women appear to be stroking their hair, not bowing, Duroiselle provided no explanation why the three women were not shown twice. Also, he drew only on the *Nidānakathā* for an explanation of the imagery.

If we look to the *Lalitavistara*, we find that Māra calls his daughters on two occasions. The first is prior to the Buddha's attainment of Enlightenment, as part of the onslaught to distract him. They appear in great numbers, 'and manifested the thirty-two kinds of feminine wiles', 'some were dancing and singing, . . . some flirted shamelessly, some were moving their hips like palm trees shaken in the wind, some were displaying their arms, rubbed with perfumed ointments . . .'.[28] On the second occasion Māra specifically calls three of his daughters during the fourth week after the Enlightenment and, in the guise of young beauties, they try to distract the Buddha.

Figure 5.5 Gotama with the *devas*, Ananda Temple, Pagan. Photograph by the author.

Nidānakathā. While being an easy conclusion to reach as the exterior Jātaka friezes on the Ananda do follow this tradition, this interpretation does not fit well with the other images. If we look to the *Lalitavistara,* then all of these scenes relate to the moments prior to and including the Enlightenment, rather than the period afterwards. This is a more convincing interpretation. The differing appearance of other series that depict the narrative of the Enlightenment suggests that there were teams of artisans at Pagan, perhaps with differing knowledge of Buddhism, and with more than one tradition active at this time. The review of other series, comparing the imagery to the various narratives, is part of ongoing research.

As a final example, a wooden image dating from the late Pagan period, around AD 1250, demonstrates the move towards a distinctly Burmese interpretation of the Enlightenment (Figure 5.6). It is still a transitional piece,

Figure 5.6 Buddha sheltered by the *nāga* hoods, Pagan period, *c.* thirteenth century, wood, lacquer, gilt, 115 × 47 × 25 cm. Courtesy of National Gallery of Australia Collection, Canberra, 1979.81.

encapsulating the Enlightenment narrative. The contraction of the narrative becomes more obvious in Burmese art as Buddhism establishes itself as the common religion. The Buddha is in *bhūmisparśa mudrā* as expected, but is also sheltered by the *nāga.* It is very unusual to see the Buddha in the earth-touching *mudrā* while surrounded by the *nāga.* However, a possible origin for this lies in the *Buddhacarita.* This text, which recounts in great detail Māra's assault and his armies states '. . . the earth-bearing *Nāgas,* devoted to *dharma,* did not brook obstruction to the great sage and, turning their eyes wrathfully on Māra, they hissed and unwound their coils'.[30] In other accounts, all beings were terrified and fled on Māra's arrival. Also, the rear of the image clearly shows separated snake tails rather than the heads belonging to a single serpent. This differs specifically from the moment after Enlightenment when the *nāga* king surrounds the Buddha to shelter him from a storm. The gruesome face under the central image may symbolise Māra and his terrifying army, '. . . the hordes of fiends who stood encompassing the root of the Bodhi tree on all sides . . .'.[31]

Therefore, if we follow the story as told in the *Buddhacarita,* the *nāgas* and Māra represent the time immediately prior to Enlightenment while the central image represents the period of Enlightenment and the time spent afterwards under the Bodhi tree. In this context, the two figures on either side of the Buddha would represent Tapussa and Bhallika, the two merchants who were the first to give alms to the Buddha and hear his words after the Buddha decided he would preach the *dhamma.* The medieval Mon inscriptions often refer to the Enlightenment and this moment.[32] In the case of the *Buddhacarita,* the period between attaining Enlightenment and leaving the Bodhi tree is given very little emphasis, the Buddha spending seven days meditating before taking alms. The other accounts give quite specific details about the seven weeks Gotama spends at the site. These companion figures are often said to be Mogallana and Sariputta, the two disciples who were converted on hearing the *ye dhamma* stanza mentioned earlier. While they are indeed present in later images, their presence in this Enlightenment scene is difficult to substantiate, as they are not mentioned in the *Buddhacarita.*

There are many aspects of the iconography of the Enlightenment which have not been mentioned, including Māra's armies and his elephant, the double-pedestal throne, the Buddha's golden glow, all of which are treated differently in each text. However, by comparing the imagery with specific texts the interpretation of the iconography and its origins can be expanded.

While this chapter has focused on a small part of one event of the Buddha's life represented in Buddhist art, the following preliminary remarks are offered. It is surprising to find that the imagery appears to draw strongly on the *Lalitavistara* narrative. At a time when the

Theravada canon was being promoted, it is logical to expect the work of Buddhaghosa to dominate as a source for imagery. Even the *Tathāgatha'oudana*, which is distinctly Burmese, owes more to the *Lalitavistara* than to any other account of the life story of the Buddha. Knowledge of the *Nidānakathā* during the Pagan period is supported by the Jātaka friezes at the Ananda Temple but it should not be assumed it was the only tradition followed at Pagan.

Since King Kyanzittha's time, Burmese Buddhism has consolidated as a Theravada tradition, and the iconography has become standardised and far less variable. To the casual viewer, the apparent sterility of later images, primarily in the earth-touching *mudrā* and devoid of any subtleties of design, is misleading in the extreme. Buddhism in Burma remains a complex entity laid, as it has been, on a strong and elaborate tradition of *nat* worship and animist beliefs. The fusion of these traditions has resulted in a repertoire of imagery which is bold and vibrant, the Buddha image itself standing out against a luminous backdrop which evokes the elaborate poetic language found in the texts written by the great Buddhist scholars of the past. The apparent contradiction between the orthodoxy of Burma's Theravada Buddhism and this elaborate imagery must surely be explained by the willing acceptance of the accounts of the Buddha's life story over one thousand years ago. These great stories provided the bridge that linked the Buddhist tradition with the deep-rooted and long-standing spiritual beliefs of the Burmese.

NOTES

1 Than Tun, 'Religion in Burma', *Journal of the Burma Research Society*, vol. 42, no. 2, 1959, pp. 47–69.
2 For details of *kammatic* Buddhism at Pagan, see Michael Aung-Thwin, *The Nature of State and Society in Pagan: An Institutional History of 12th and 13th Century Burma*, PhD thesis, University of Michigan, Ann Arbor, 1975, pp. 70–82.
3 *Ibid.*, p. 75.
4 The Pāli canon is divided into three sections, the *Vinaya Piṭaka*, which is primarily a book of rules for the monastic order; the *Sutta Piṭaka*, the collection of discourses; and the *Abhidhamma Piṭaka*, the collection of higher knowledge. For a summary of the Pāli Canon see *Guide to the Tipiṭaka: Introduction to the Buddhist Canon*, Bangkok: White Lotus, 1993.
5 John D. Ireland, *The Discourse Collection: Selected Texts from the Sutta Nipāta (WH 82)*, Kandy: Buddhist Publication Society, 1983, vv. 425–49.
6 Edward J. Thomas, *The Life of Buddha as Legend and History*, London: Kegan Paul, Trench, Trubner, 1931, pp. 66–8. Thomas states that the absence of Māra in the account indicates it was not part of the original story and such events were added later in different places 'according to individual ideas of fitness' (p. 68). As imagery of Māra was strongly present from the reign of Aśoka, any absence of these events in texts should not be interpreted as being later additions. Rather, they indicate the importance of an event in relation to the Buddha's discourses.
7 The translations of the texts used in this paper are E.H. Johnston (trans.), *Aśvaghoṣa's Buddhacarita or Acts of the Buddha*, Delhi: Motilal Banarsidass, 1934 (reprint 1998), and Gwendolyn Bays (trans.), *Lalitavistara: The Voice of the Buddha*, Berkeley: Dharma Publishing, 1983. When citing these texts, the abbreviations Lv and Bc are used. The page number is given for the Lv and the canto and verse number for the Bc. The Lv is also part of the Mongolian Buddhist literature. See Nicholas Poppe, *The Twelve Deeds of the Buddha*, Wiesbaden: Asiatische Forschungen Band 23, 1967.
8 In Johnston's introduction, he discusses the evidence which would place Aśvaghoṣa within the Theravada tradition (pp. xxiv–xxxiv).
9 I-Tsing, *A Record of the Buddhist Religion as Practised in India and the Malay Archipelago (AD 671–695)*, J. Takakusu (trans.), Delhi: Munshiram Manoharlal, 1966, p. 166.
10 N.A. Jayawickrama (trans.), *The Story of Gotama Buddha (Jātaka-nidāna)*, Oxford: The Pāli Text Society, 1990, p. xiv.
11 G. Luce and Pe Maung Tin (trans.), *The Glass Palace Chronicle of the Kings of Burma*, London: Oxford University Press, 1923, pp. 46–50.
12 Niharranjan Ray, *An Introduction to the Study of Theravada Buddhism in Burma: A Study in Indo-Burmese Historical and Cultural Relations from the Earliest Times to the British Canquert*, Calcutta: University of Calcutta, 1946, reprinted 1977, pp. 24–6. Note, however, that the legend says that Buddhaghosa translated a copy of the Pāli grammar and a commentary on this into Burmese. This is obviously a later attempt to further the claim of Buddhaghosa's Burmese origins but must be false as the Burmese language did not appear until the eleventh century. The local languages of the Mon and Pyu were written in scripts which were similar to the Magadha and Kadamba scripts of India.
13 W. Woodville Rockhill, *The Life of the Buddha and the Early History of His Order*, London: Kegan Paul, Trench, Trubner, 1884 (reprint 1907). Rockhill does compare this text with the works compiled by other eminent authors such as Rhys Davids, Bigandet and Beal. However, these comparisons do not extend to comments on imagery.
14 E.H. Johnston (trans.), *The Saundarananda or Nanda the Fair*, Kyoto: Rinsen Book Co, 1931 (reprint 1971).
15 Rev. P. Bigandet, *The Life or Legend of Gaudama the Buddha of the Burmese*, London: Kegan Paul, Trench, Trubner, 1866 (4th ed, 1911).
16 Charles Duroiselle (trans.), *Jinacarita or 'The Career of the Conqueror'*, Delhi: Parimal Publications, 1906 (reprint 1982). In the introduction he places the writing of this poem in the late twelfth century, during the reign of Vijayabāhu II who ascended the throne in AD 1186. It lacks the free flowing poetry of earlier works.
17 U Mya (ed.), *Epigraphia Birmanica being Lithic and Other Inscriptions of Burma*, vol. 4, part 1, Rangoon: Superintendent Govt. Printing and Stationery Office, 1934. Some of these inscriptions recall the Buddha's life particularly the events that occurred around the time of Enlightenment. They are tentatively dated to the fifteenth century.
18 D.G.E. Hall, *A History of South-East Asia*, London: Macmillan Press, p. 158. Hall refers to the tradition that King Anawrahta brought the Theravada Mon court from Thaton, and the monk Shin Arahan to Pagan with the aim of 'converting the Burmese to Hinayana Buddhism'.
19 The 'ye dhamma' stanza is translated as, 'Of all those things that from a cause arise, Tathāgatha the cause thereof has told, And how they cease to be, that too he tells, This is the doctrine of the great Recluse.' After hearing this phrase spoken by the Elder Assaji, both Sāriputta and Moggallana

passed through the stage of stream-enterers and became stream-winners. The phrase became a symbol of conversion and the power of the *dhamma*. See Nyanaponika Thera, 'The Life of Sāriputta', *The Wheel Publication*, vol. 5, no. 90–2, 1996, pp. 1–112.

20 G.H. Luce, *Old Burma – Early Pagan*, Locust Valley, New York: J.J. Augustin, for *Artibus Asiae Supplementum* 25 (3 vols), 1969–70, vol.1, pp. 16–17.

21 *Ibid.*, vol. 3, pl. 8b. In this example the parasol shape is very obvious.

22 Lv. 444–451.

23 Charles Duroiselle, 'The Talaing Plaques on the Ananda', *Epigraphia Burmanica being Lithic and other Inscriptions of Burma*, Rangoon: Superintendent, Government Printing, Burma, vol. 2, pt. 1, 1921, p. 1.

24 Bc. xiv. 98.

25 Lv. 458.

26 Luce (1969–70, vol. 2, p.134) comments that the position of the image with Sujātā appears out of sequence and may have been moved. There is no guarantee that all the images are in their original place.

27 Charles Duroiselle, 'The Stone Sculptures in the Ananda Temple at Pagan', *Archaeological Survey of India, Annual Report*, Calcutta: Superintendent, Government Printing, India 1913–14, pp. 63–97 and pls XXXI–XXXIX.

28 Lv. 484.

29 Lv. 555.

30 Bc. xiii. 30.

31 Bc. xiii. 27.

32 C.O. Blagden, 'Mōn Inscriptions Section II – The Mediaeval Mōn Records Nos. XIII-XVIII', *Epigraphia Birmanica being Lithic and Other Inscriptions of Burma*, Rangoon: Superintendent, Government Printing and Stationery, Burma, 1934, vol. IV, part 1.

6 Burmese bronze sculpture in the British Museum

T. Richard Blurton

This chapter is an introduction to a part of the Burmese collections in the British Museum, in London.[1] These collections are divided amongst three different departments, those of Coins and Medals, Ethnography, and Oriental Antiquities. It is the holdings of Burmese sculpture of the latter department which are the subject of this chapter. What follows is a brief presentation of the great variety of Burmese material in the collection, followed by a detailed discussion of five bronze sculptures. Finally, other bronze sculptures also in the collection are mentioned to guide future researchers.

By far the majority of the Burmese material in the Department of Oriental Antiquities is of sculpture – of many different types, and in a variety of media. However, the gift in 1998 of the Ralph and Ruth Isaacs Collection of Burmese Lacquer has greatly increased the representation of lacquered items (mostly vessels),[2] and there is also a large group of terracotta plaques dating from the Pagan period up to the nineteenth century, and including examples of the celebrated late fifteenth century glazed plaques from Pegu and the nineteenth century ones from Mingun.[3] Other areas well-represented include market weights – there are over 300 examples in the important collection assembled by Donald and Joan Gear, which was presented to the British Museum in 1993[4] – and the material culture of prehistory (the latter has mostly, and unfortunately, been gathered as a result of surface collection, rather than from archaeological excavation; its scientific use is therefore limited). Smaller collections of silver, and of textiles, including several fine *kalaga*, are also housed here.[5] The collections are large, and this chapter will therefore concentrate only on sculpture, and within that category, sculpture made of bronze.

By far the majority of the sculptures in the collection are of the Buddha, usually seated, but standing, reclining and walking images also exist. Most are made of bronze or of other copper alloys and were produced using the lost-wax process. However, other materials include wood (sometimes sheathed in silver sheet, or sometimes gilded and/or lacquered), dry-lacquer, ivory, and the distinctive white marble used so widely from the eighteenth century onwards. Concentrating on the bronze images, the earliest are of Pagan date for there is none in the collection which has yet been identified as of the Pyu or Mon period.[6]

1 BRONZE IMAGE OF THE BUDDHA, in *bhūmisparśamudrā* (Figure 6.1)[7]

This is the most important, and the earliest, of the Pagan images in the Museum collection and has been previously published.[8] Comparing this with Buddha images from Pagan, both in bronze and in stone, a date of *c*.1100 has been realistically suggested for it. The Buddha is shown with the *mudrā* which later becomes the standard in Burmese depictions, *bhūmisparśamudrā*, and the face displays the somewhat triangular shape associated with Pagan developments of the eastern Indian style. The *uṣṇīṣa* rises from the top of the head without a break in contour, and culminates in a point which was originally set with a jewel, though this is now lost. The robe clings tightly to the body and is only clearly differentiated at the ankles and where it spills away from the ankles on to the base,[9] as well as where it crosses from the covered left shoulder (the right shoulder is uncovered) across the chest and under the right armpit. Lying parallel to this line across the chest is the robe end, which is folded in a zig-zag pattern. The hands and feet are elegantly positioned so that the viewer is conscious of the individual toes and fingers; the toes of the right foot are clearly splayed and visible because of the *padmāsana* position of the seated image. There is evidence on the reverse for a now lost back-plate. The sculpture was made using the lost-wax process, a technique presumably introduced from India along with Buddhism, and still in use today to produce Buddha images.[10]

Demonstrating the eastern Indian connection of this Pagan image is a magnificent bronze sculpture of the seated Buddha that was discovered at Fatehpur, in Bihar (Gaya District), and which was once in the museum at Bodh Gaya (it was stolen some time between 1979 and 1986).[11] The simple lines indicating the robe, the splaying of the toes, the upturned fingers of the left hand held in the lap, the plumpness of the right hand held in *bhūmisparśamudrā*, the fan-shaped 'spill' of the robe below the ankles and on to the base, and the pointed *uṣṇīṣa* with a place for a jewel at the very top – all of these

Figure 6.1 The Buddha seated in *bhūmisparśamudrā*. Pagan period. Ht 34 cm. Museum registration number OA.1971.7–27. Brooke Sewell Fund.

features are also seen in this Pagan bronze. The main difference is in the shape of the face – the Pagan image has a more triangular shape and the eyes have a more obviously downward gaze; the Fatehpur image has a face of more sub-rectangular shape and the eyes look out more obviously to the viewer. The Fatehpur image has been discussed in further detail by Huntington, who interestingly notes its similarity to Burmese images, suggesting that the influence is from India to Burma, though also noting the Burmese presence at Bodh Gaya in the late eleventh century, and thus flagging up the possibility of influence in the opposite direction.[12] She also suggests a date in the twelfth century for the Fatehpur sculpture (closer to the suggested date for the British Museum Pagan image), while the Indian scholars place it earlier, in the late tenth century (see note 11).

2   BRONZE IMAGE OF THE BUDDHA AKṢOBHYA, in *bhūmisparśamudrā* (Figure 6.2a and b)[13]

From later in the Pagan period comes an intriguing Buddha image set on an elaborate base. The main element

of the base is rectangular and is stepped back at the sides. It is also made of two vertical elements, with a waisted section between them. Such an arrangement of a stepped and waisted base is well-known from eastern Indian bronzes of the Pala period.[14] Above this is a pearled band and then a double-lotus base; this in its turn is surmounted by a smaller pearled band, all of which is very much in the eastern Indian style. On the top of this, and prominently displayed, is a *vajra* (thunderbolt) lying in front of the seated Buddha (Figure 6.2b). The presence of the *vajra* must suggest that this image is Akṣobhya, an interesting further indication of the presence of Mahayana ideas in Burma during the late Pagan period. The Buddha image is depicted with his right hand in *bhūmisparśamudrā* as is canonically correct for Akṣobhya,[15] and with his left held flat in his lap holding the end of his monastic robe. The other end of the robe is depicted not across the chest as is common, but lying on the shoulder (indeed, perhaps indicating that the image was never to be seen from behind, the robe-end just sits, like a separate, rectangular pile of cloth, on the top of the shoulder and is not indicated falling down the back of the

Figure 6.2a Akṣobhya Buddha seated with a *vajra* on the throne. Pagan period. Ht 16.5 cm. Museum registration number OA. 1971.1–25.1. Brooke Sewell Fund.

Figure 6.2b Detail of the Akṣobhya Buddha showing the *vajra* lying in front of the seated Buddha.

image). The presence of a (now lost) back-plate for this image is suggested by stubs of bronze which stick out at the side of the throne. A bronze image recovered from the Pahtothamya temple at Pagan which is illustrated and also dated by Luce (*c.* AD 1080) offers an interesting comparison.[16] Here the Buddha is crowned, unlike the British Museum example, and it is this, along with the other royal accoutrements, upon which Luce concen-

trates in his comment. Indeed, he makes no mention of the presence of a *vajra* which is, however, clear in the photograph.[17] Is this a crowned Akṣobhya? At least one other example, in stone, is illustrated by Luce in the same publication – again without comment on the presence of the *vajra*; there may be other examples.[18] Both of the sculptures illustrated by Luce share with the British Museum example the double-lotus base, while the two bronzes (one in Luce and one in the Museum) show the pearled band separating the lotus base from the surface on which the Buddha sits. This is yet another element which links these magnificent bronze images with eastern Indian prototypes.

3 GILT BRONZE IMAGE OF THE CROWNED BUDDHA (Figure 6.3)

From the post-Pagan period is a remarkable gilded bronze sculpture of the crowned and seated Buddha, depicted in *bhūmisparśamudrā*. This sculpture has never previously been published but was purchased by the Museum as long ago as 1894, in London, from a Miss Granger about whom nothing further is known.[19] This sculpture presents a more specifically Burmese depiction of the Buddha. Despite the persistence of one or two elements still harking back to the Indian prototype, the overall impression is quite different from an Indian image, especially on account of the tall flanges decorating the sides of the crown. The crown itself is made up of seven pointed, leaf-like elements which rise up vertically from a beaded band around the forehead of the Buddha image.[20] These leaf-like elements are based on eastern Indian prototypes, though they are taller and thinner than most Indian examples. The bronze images from Kurkihar in Bihar provide the clearest *comparanda*, reminding us of the primacy of conventions from that part of Bihar so closely linked with the ministry of the Buddha – and of Burmese involvement there in the medieval period.[21] More startlingly different from the eastern Indian prototypes, however, are the massive appendages which appear on each side of the crown. These two elements are a Burmese development of the ribbon seen in eastern Indian sculpture which ties the crown to the Buddha's head.[22] Within the crown, this Buddha image probably once had a high *jaṭā* with distinctively shouldered profile; this would have been extended in the form of a tall spire. Both these elements are now lost, but an idea of how it might have looked can be seen from an example in a private American collection and another published in a London sale catalogue in 1981.[23] The British Museum example still displays the scar where the *jaṭā* has been broken within the crown.

The Buddha wears large plug earrings with tassles which hang down over his upper chest. These are distinctive Burmese features not seen on Indian crowned images of the Buddha. He also wears two necklaces which

Figure 6.3 Crowned Buddha image. Post-Pagan period, perhaps seventeenth century. Ht 36 cm. Museum registration number OA.94.6–22.1.

Examples of this type of Buddha image have been illustrated in the literature, but few are of the quality of this example in the British Museum, despite the missing *jaṭā*. The example in the American private collection mentioned above, lacks the double-lotus base and merely sports a simple stepped arrangement; it is dated to the eighteenth century.[26] The use of the double-lotus throne in the British Museum example, with its links back to eastern India, probably indicates an earlier date, perhaps some time in the seventeenth century. Other examples published by Karow[27] and in the already-mentioned London sale catalogue of 1981,[28] also support a seventeenth or eighteenth-century date for the British Museum example (at the latest), though on what basis these previously published dates were arrived at, is not known.

The gilded decoration of the image has probably been fixed to the surface using lacquer; a reddish undercoat beneath the gilding can be seen in various places. Finally, the reverse side of the throne is flat and undecorated, so that an inscription could be added by a donor.

4 BRONZE IMAGE OF THE CROWNED BUDDHA (Figure 6.4)[29]

In this image, the Buddha is shown seated in *padmāsana*, with his right hand in *varadamudrā* (though also holding a small fruit), while the left hand, in the lap, holds a lidded pot. This image is related to, though clearly not the same as, the one described above. The base, although waisted, has no lotus petal decoration cast in relief; petals are merely engraved on the equivalent areas of the base. The upper and lower elements of the waisted base are visually linked by small stubs at each extremity; these either hang down (from the upper element) or stick up (from the lower one). Again, the reverse side of the base is flattened for an inscription. The sculpture is slightly damaged, but the eight leaf-shaped elements of the crown, rising from a thickly beaded band are clear. Also clearly visible is the central projecting *jaṭā*, with its distinctively shouldered shape; even here though the thinner uppermost part is broken (the scar is, however, visible). Also now broken, but nevertheless recognisable, are the remains of wing-like appendages attached to the side of the crown. Although of the same general type, they are not identical to those seen in sculpture no. 3, being more solid in construction. Tassles, perhaps part of the appendage to the crown, hang along the shoulders, rather than hanging from the earrings over the chest, as in no. 3. The Buddha is again depicted as a king, not only crowned, but also decked with jewellery. This includes disk earrings in the lower lobe as well as rich necklaces and bracelets (with cuffs). Just visible from the front, but very clear behind, is a cape over the shoulders. A sash with triangular ends falls over both upper forearms, but does not continue across the back (the image was presumably not intended to be seen from behind). The

hang down over his chest – one curving round above the nipples, and the other dipping down between them – as well as several bracelets at each wrist. The Buddha is depicted here as a royal personage, suitably clothed and decorated – the so-called Jambupati type of Buddha image.[24] Recent cleaning of this fine image has brought to light shallowly engraved lines on the cushion-like top of the throne indicating the falling ends of the Buddha's robe. Other than this, the robe is not articulated, a feature which perhaps links it to earlier, Pagan, and ultimately eastern Indian prototypes.

The double-lotus base has here developed from the eastern Indian type where the upper and lower bands of lotus petals meet in the centre, to a Burmese version where a vertical band separates the two lotus petal elements; further, each band of petals is more steeply raked. In silhouette the base now has an hourglass shape. An example of this very Burmese style of base for a Buddha image now in the Victoria and Albert Museum, in London, has been dated to, 'probably 17th century'.[25]

Figure 6.4 Crowned Buddha image. Post-Pagan period, seventeenth or eighteenth century. Ht 24.5 cm. Museum registration number OA.FB Ind.16. Bequeathed by Sir Augustus Wollaston Franks.

folds of the lower garment where it is rolled at the waist, are clearly indicated, and the folds of this lower garment over the crossed legs are quite distinctly articulated. Especially noticeable are the creases of the robe over the knees, shown by means of concentric oval ridges. The lower part of the robe falls down in front of the crossed legs in mirror-image folds. This more elaborate way of treating the drapery places this image in a different category from that of no. 3, where the drapery is practically unarticulated, other than the very faintly engraved lines on the top of the base. Sculpture no. 3 in this respect (but not as far as the crown appendages are concerned) is close to Indian prototypes, while no. 4 has moved away from those prototypes, and is thus either from a centre within Burma with less substantial links with India, or is of different – probably later – date.

The question of date is complicated by the existence of an image, similar to this one, published by Luce.[30] Following Duroiselle,[31] he records its provenance as from a '*sima* at Aungbintha village, "a few miles to the south of Sameikshé"'. Hsameikshé is in Thazi township, in Meiktila district. Luce is in some doubt as to the date of the sculpture, feeling that the eleventh/early twelfth-century date suggested by Duroiselle is too early; however, he does not definitely vouchsafe another date.[32] Certainly the similarity between the Hsameikshé image and image no. 4 is considerable: both have waisted but undecorated bases with upward- and downward-pointing stubs (the Thazi image also has a small central outward step); both have similar crowns with the distinctive shouldered *jaṭā* within it, and lack the elaborate side flanges, as seen in image no. 3 (they have flaps above the ears, instead); both have tassles down the shoulder rather than over the chest, and elaborate though not identical jewellery on the chest; both have sashes over the inner side of the elbows; and finally both display the same configuration of drapery on the knees, illustrating volume in a way unlike that seen on Buddha images from Pagan. A further relevant image is the one published in the London 1981 sale catalogue.[33] In this example the different elements are few, but include the plug earrings made up of large disks, the necklaces which are closer to the Mahamuni type seen on images from Arakan and the throne which is of the *pañcaratha* type. However, in almost every other way – as far as can be compared from the catalogue photograph (the current whereabouts of the image are unknown) – it appears to be close to image no. 4. The *jaṭā*, crown, tassles on the shoulders, delineation of the drapery over the knees, and the *mudrās* in both hands (*varada* with fruit in his right, and holding a pot in his left) – all of these features appear in both images. The image in the 1981 sale catalogue is said to be from Arakan and said to be of fifteenth or sixteenth-century date, a date which is substantiated in the catalogue not only by reference to Luce (as here), but also to a published image which can be dated, apparently, to 1602.[34] Given this wide range of *comparanda*, a date several centuries removed from the Pagan period would seem likely, though the precise chronology cannot yet be determined.

Given the presence of the pot held by the Buddha in this British Museum example, it may be legitimate to suggest that this is an image of Maitreya who can also be shown in royal garb, for he currently rules as a king in the Tāvatiṁsa Heaven.[35] Or should this be taken to be Bethinsaguru (Sanskrit: Bhaiṣajyaguru), the Buddha of healing, on account of the medicinal fruit held in his right hand, offered as benediction to the supplicant?[36] The present author has not yet found further information on the cult of a healing Buddha image in Burma.

Other examples of crowned Buddha images made of bronze exist in the Museum's collection, two of which are on public display in the Sir Joseph Hotung Gallery (Room 33); one of these has previously been published.[37] A further, but unpublished example is discussed below.

5 GILDED BRONZE IMAGE OF THE CROWNED BUDDHA (Figure 6.5)[38]

Here the Buddha wears an elaborate crown, made up of eight leaf-like elements rising from a band around the forehead. To the sides of the crown are the same substantial flanges, close in style though not the same as those described for nos. 3 and 4. Different from the flanges described in no. 3 is the way in which the upper part is solid (seen only on the right side as viewed; the left side is broken). Whether this is a diagnostic feature as far as date and/or region are concerned, is unknown. From the centre of the crown rises a shouldered *jaṭā*; here, as with the previous examples, the final spire-like extension of this is now broken. The Buddha also wears massive ear-plugs in the lower lobe with large 'S'-shaped tassles spilling from them down over his chest. As well as these tassles which are part of the ear-plugs, he also sports tassles hanging down along his shoulders, similar to those recorded on no. 4. The chest is covered in jewellery and includes a necklace with further strands hanging down over the middle of the chest to the waist. Again there are bracelets with cuffs. He is seated in *padmāsana* and in *bhūmisparśamudrā*, with the left hand held in the lap, palm upwards. The fingers on both hands are all of the same length. The base is a development of the waisted and engraved base seen above. Here it is almost lenticular in shape (though the back is squared off to allow for an inscription) and is marked with stubs along the bottom of the upper part (hanging down) and along the bottom part (pointing up). Lightly engraved lotus petals are depicted on the upward and downward facing elements of the base. The central, vertical element of this hour-glass profile is decorated with a lightly engraved design of lozenges. The gilding of the image is almost completely intact, though in places the brilliant red lacquer coating can be seen beneath the layer of gold. Some spaces, such as the back of the base, the inside of the crown and the bottom-most moulding of the base, have been left ungilded, and remain scarlet.

Different from all the other images so far discussed, however, are the two additional figures seen at the side of

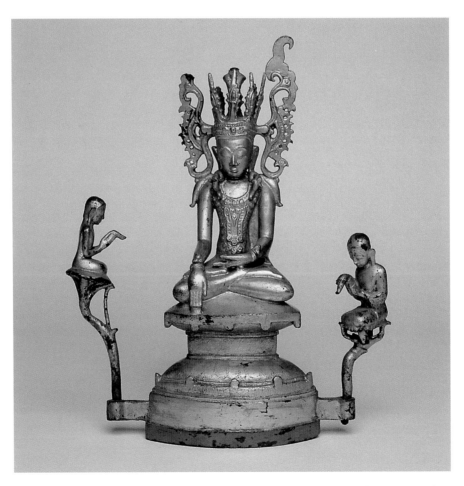

Figure 6.5 Crowned Buddha image attended by adorants. Post-Pagan period, eighteenth or nineteenth century, ht 35 cm. Museum registration number OA.1939.1–20.1.

the image. These are attached to the central image by lugs which are part of the main casting. These lugs end in rings in which are loosely set separate castings made up of stalks on which sit figures which are probably to be taken for the two foremost of the disciples of the Buddha, Sariputra and Maudgalyayana. The two stalks are of different height and construction, a fact which reinforces the identification above. Sariputra is canonically shown on the right and, as the right is the auspicious side, always slightly higher than the figure on the left; he is, after all, the foremost of the all the disciples and this requires him to be shown higher than all others, except the Buddha. This higher position is in keeping with his perceived embodiment of wisdom and intellect, while the slightly lower position is reserved for the second-most favoured disciple, Maudgalyayana, who is the perceived embodiment of action.[39] The figure to the right of the Buddha is on the taller, thinner stalk which seems to end in a lotus seed pod; the figure to his left is on the shorter stalk which ends in some sort of vegetal motif, though what precisely is intended here is unclear. Both diminutive figures make offerings to the Buddha – these are probably to be taken as lotus blossoms. While this sculpture is the only example here described of this distinctive 'Buddha with adorant' iconography, it is by no means uncommon, appearing frequently in sculpture.[40]

6 OTHER IMAGES IN THE BRITISH MUSEUM COLLECTION

There is considerable variety in the remaining bronze images in the Museum collection, and the brief notes which follow provide nothing more than an introduction to them. Of great interest, but requiring study in more detail than is possible here, is a seated Buddha image, depicted crowned and jewelled, of the well-known Arakan type. This was collected in the late nineteenth century in Sri Lanka, and is presumably to be viewed as the opposite end of the exchange system to the many Sri Lanka images to be found in Arakan.[41] An example of this type, published in London in 1981, provides one of the very few scientifically-determined dates in this corpus of sculpture – a range of AD 1430–1630 based on a thermoluminescence test.[42]

Another interesting image is set on a stepped *palin*-style wooden base which has been gilded and lacquered. (Figure 6.6). The Buddha is again shown seated in *padmāsana* with the toes all the same length; the right hand is displaying the gesture of *bhūmisparśamudrā*. One of the fingers of the left hand lying in the lap points upwards slightly, while the fingers of the right hand are clearly all of the same length, though the thumb still remains shorter than the fingers. The robe is depicted with the right-hand shoulder exposed while the left-hand one is covered with the end fold of the robe separately delineated down the middle of the chest. It also displays

Figure 6.6 The Buddha seated in *bhūmisparśamudrā*. Post-Pagan period, perhaps eighteenth century, ht 22 cm (with *palin* 29.2 cm). Museum registration number OA.1992.2–7.1. Brooke Sewell Fund.

a comparatively short *uṣṇīṣa* with a small flame or jewel at the top reminiscent of the similar feature of the Pagan sculpture, no. 1. The individual curls of the hair are distinct and separate, though only in low relief. It lacks, however, the graceful and supple quality of the earlier work. It has been gilded and is perhaps eighteenth century in date. On the back of the wooden base are fragments of a label, in English, as follows, '[br]onz . . . of Buddha, 17th Century, from . . . The . . . palace at Mandalay'.

Mandalay is represented in the collection by a large number of bronze images – either made in the environs of the city itself or during the period in which it flourished. Sculptures of this type follow a standard pattern, which includes the small, domed *uṣṇīṣa*, the cap-like hair separated from the forehead by a thick band, the elegant arrangement of the robes with pleats and folds delineated, often with projecting 'tails' to the robe edges, the body covered except for the right shoulder and arm, and the Buddha shown in *bhūmisparśamudrā* (Figure 6.7)

Some examples also have inset coloured glass spangles – sure indications of the Mandalay aesthetic.

A category of sculpture also represented with many examples in the Museum's collection are small narrative bronzes. These invariably illustrate scenes from the Life of the Buddha. Technically, they are both cast and wrought, with the figures usually set on openwork bases. A large number of these have been published as many survive – they are deposits from pagoda relic chambers (Figure 6.8).[43] They invariably illustrate scenes from the Life of the Buddha. Other than the narrative aspect, they all share a somewhat crude but lively style, and are frequently made up of several parts which fit together using tangs and loops. Scenes found in the Museum's collection of this type include the following: the Birth, the Great Departure, the Cutting of the Hair, the Enlightenment, the Jewel Tower, the First Sermon and the Mahāparinirvana. One unusually large example of the Great Departure is associated in the Museum records with Mogok, though whether it was actually made there is unknown.[44] Other small sculptures probably also made as pagoda deposits include double-sided lead plaques, of which there are several examples in the Museum's collection. On one side is an image of the Buddha seated in *bhūmisparśamudrā* and attended by Sariputra and Maudgalyayana; the leafy scroll above and on either side of the image is presumably to be taken as the Bodhi tree. On the reverse is a stupa.[45]

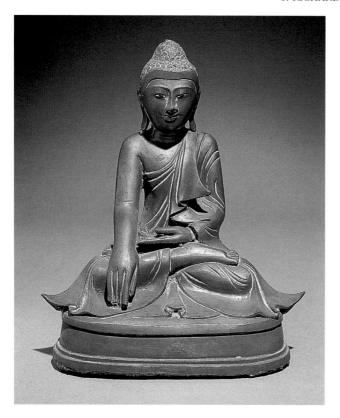

Figure 6.7 The Buddha seated in *bhūmisparśamudrā*. Nineteenth century. Ht 24 cm. Museum registration number OA.1932.7-14.1. Gift of Mrs E. L. Passman.

Figure 6.8 Three narrative bronzes depicting scenes from the Life of the Buddha (left to right, the Enlightenment, the Jewel Tower and the Cutting of the Hair). Height of Jewel Tower 20.6 cm. Museum registration numbers OA.1995.11-7.8, 2 and 6. Brooke Sewell Fund.

CONCLUSION

This description of some of the other types of Burmese sculpture within the collections can only provide a suggestion of the variety of the whole. However, it is hoped that through this and the previous more detailed analysis of a handful of important sculptures – most of which have not previously been published – scholars will be encouraged to look closer at this large assemblage of Burmese art which has been gathered together since the mid-eighteenth century.[46]

Finally, it is important to emphasise the paucity of our knowledge concerning all traditions of sculpture in Burma. This study can only seriously advance once all available sources are utilised. These include the study and careful assessment of archival data, the collection through field-work in Burma of *comparanda* which are securely dated and provenanced through inscriptions, and the setting up of programmes of scientific analysis of sculptures, such as thermoluminescence dating, whereby runs of secure dates can be ascertained. All too often scholars – including the present writer – have only been able to give a provenance no more exact than 'Burma' and dates covering several centuries. The study of Burmese sculpture can only be taken forward decisively when all these elements are addressed.

NOTES

1 Until the recent catalogue of the Isaacs Collection (see note 2) items from the Burmese collections had been published only in volumes dealing with other subjects, most notably in the catalogue for the joint British Museum/British Library exhibition in 1985, *Buddhism: Art and Faith*, W. Zwalf (ed.), London: British Museum Press. See pp. 157–74 for the section dealing with Burma (further manuscripts are found elsewhere in the volume). The division of the British Library from the British Museum in 1973 means that Burmese material held in what was then the British Museum's Department of Oriental Manuscripts and Printed Books is now held in a different institution, the British Library (Oriental and India Office Collections). The recently retired curator of these British Library collections, Patricia Herbert (see this volume), has published some of these holdings. See Patricia Herbert, 'The Sir Arthur Phayre Collection of Burmese Manuscripts', in *The British Library Journal*, vol. 1, pp. 62–70, 1975; 'The Making of a Collection: Burmese Manuscripts in the British Library', *The British Library Journal*, vol. 15, no. 1, pp. 59–70, Spring 1989; *The Life of the Buddha*, London: British Library, 1993; and 'An Illustrated Record of Royal Donations', *Études birmanes en hommage à Denise Bernot*, Réunies par Pierre Pichard et François Robinne, Paris: École française d'Extrême-Orient, 1998, pp. 90–100.

   All photographs in this chapter are courtesy of the Trustees of the British Museum.

2 See Ralph Isaacs and T. Richard Blurton, *Visions from the Golden Land: Burma and the Art of Lacquer*, London: British Museum Press, 2000. The Isaacs Collection is located under the Museum registration numbers 1998.7–23.1–269.

3 Examples include: from Pagan, OA.1899.10–16.1 (Gift of Lt. Dobson) and OA.1947.2–8.1 and 2 (Gift of Cdr.

Rundle); from Pegu, OA.1892.11–8. 1 and 2 (Gift of Major R.C. Temple) and OA.1965.12–17.1 (Gift of Cyril Newman); from Mingun, OA.1896.3–14.12, 13 and 14 (Gift of Sir A.W. Franks) and OA.1894.7–19. 4.

4 Museum registration numbers OA.1993.7–31.1–323. Some examples, including the rare non-representational examples made of white marble, are exhibited in the Sir Joseph Hotung Gallery (Room 33), Case 45.

5 For these *kalaga*, see, '"Looking very gay and bright": Burmese textiles in the British Museum' by T. Richard Blurton in *Apollo*, vol. CL, no. 453, November 1999, pp. 38–42. Museum registration numbers OA.1996.4–30.01; OA.1998.4–29.01; OA.1999.11–3. 01 and 02. The first two, Brooke Sewell Fund; the last two, Gift of Dr Henry Ginsburg.

6 Numismatic material of the Pyu period is located in the Department of Coins and Medals in the British Museum; some is displayed in the Sir Joseph Hotung Gallery (Room 33), Case 48.

7 On public display in the Sir Joseph Hotung Gallery (Room 33), Case 45.

8 See Zwalf, 1985, cat. no. 222, p. 161. As this is a well-known image, the discussion of it in this chapter is restricted. See also *Exhibition: Indian Influence on Art in South-East Asia*, London: Spink, 1970, Cat. no. 45, pp. 32 and 33.

9 This fan-shaped 'spill' of the robe on to the base is a distinctive feature also of eastern Indian bronze images of the seated Buddha.

10 All the other bronze sculptures described in detail (nos. 2 to 5 inclusive) have been made using the same technique of lost-wax production; it is therefore not mentioned again. The author has on several occasions visited foundries in the Tampawady suburb of Mandalay where Buddha images are still made using this technique. Similar foundries have been recorded by Sylvia Fraser-Lu in her *Burmese Arts and Crafts, Past and Present*, Kuala Lumpur: Oxford University Press, 1994, pp. 128ff.

11 See Nihar Ranjan Ray, Karl Khandalavala and Sadashiv Gorakshkar, *Eastern Indian Bronzes*, New Delhi: Lalit Kala, 1986, pl. 232a.

12 Susan L. Huntington, 'Some Bronzes from Fatehpur, Gaya', *Oriental Art*, new series, Summer 1979, vol. XXV, no. 2, pp. 240–7. See note 21 for further discussion of the links between Burma and Bodh Gaya.

13 On public display in the Sir Joseph Hotung Gallery (Room 33), Case 45.

14 Bronze images set on stepped and waisted bases are recorded from all over eastern India from the tenth to the twelfth centuries. Many examples are recorded in Nihar Ranjan Ray, *et al.*, 1986, pls 138, 211, 233a and b, 242, 251a, 255a, 261, 268, 269, 272, 273, 275, 276. Also see, U. von Schroeder, *Indo-Tibetan Bronzes*, Hong Kong: Visual Dharma Publications, 1981, pp. 66–71. For the link between this form of base and architectural forms, see Susan L. Huntington, and John C. Huntington, *Leaves from the Bodhi Tree: The Art of Pala India (8th–12th centuries) and its International Legacy*, Seattle and London: University of Washington Press, 1990, Cat. no. 48, p. 175 and black and white plate.

15 The identificatory elements of the Buddhas of the *maṇḍala* are listed in Gordon H. Luce, Artibus Asiae Supplementum 25, *Old Burma – Early Pagan*, vol. I, 1969, New York: J.J. Augustin, p. 196.

16 Luce 1969–70, vol. I, pp. 84–5 (for the architecture and the painting sequence of the Pahtothamya temple, see p. 303); vol. II, p. 200; vol. III, pl. 439. NB the date of publication for vols II and III is 1970, one year later than vol. I.

17 Luce, 1969, vol. I, p. 309, describes this temple as '. . . this Mother of Theravada temples . . . .' but makes no comment on the discovery there of this bronze image with its *vajra* on the throne, which must indicate some Mahayana context for it. He merely describes the image as depicting the Buddha in *vajrāsana*, a term with a number of meanings – it can refer both to the position in which the Buddha sits, as well as to the presence of a *vajra* on the throne. See, Gösta Liebert, *Iconographic Dictionary of the Indian Religions*, Leiden: Brill, 1976, p. 323. Even if this is a reference by Luce to the presence of the *vajra*, he, surprisingly, passes no comment on its presence there. The recovery of this sculpture from a context which Luce considers so over-whelmingly Theravada is perhaps a warning to scholars not to take as rigid the distinctions apparent in the twenty-first century between Theravada and Mahayana Buddhism. Certainly the evidence from India as surviving in the accounts of the Chinese pilgrims allows of monks dwelling in the same monastery following very different cults. There was less exclusivity than one might expect, and this may also have been the case in Pagan.

18 Luce, 1970, vol. II p. 180, vol. III, pl. 411.

19 The acquisition is recorded in the ledger, *Register of Antiquities, British and Mediaeval*, vol. 7, April 1893 to July 1898, p. 88. This volume is now housed in the Department of Medieval and Modern Europe, in the British Museum. Also acquired from the same source was a smaller, but also fine image of the Buddha, Museum registration number OA.1894.6–22.2. Ht 17.50 cm. The Buddha is shown seated on a double-lotus throne of a similar type as 1894. 6–22. 1, is uncrowned and is depicted in *bhūmisparśamudrā*; the *uṣṇīṣa* is topped by a bulbous and spired finial. There is a flat back for an inscription and there are still remains of gilding and red lacquer evident. It is believed to be of seventeenth or eighteenth century date.

20 One of the leaf-like elements of the crown, back left as viewed, is broken.

21 See von Schroeder, 1981, p. 279 for illustrations of two typically grand eleventh-century examples from Kurkihar with tall crowns made up of leaf-like elements. In Nihar Ranjan Ray, *et al.*, 1986, p. 102, there is the suggestion of specific links between Kurkihar (via Bodh Gaya) and Pagan – 'It is not unlikely that such images [crowned Buddha images] were fashioned at Kurkihar and thereafter taken elsewhere. So far as [Bodh] Gaya is concerned, it seems that the Pagan kings had close ties with the temple [i.e. these easily-portable images were taken from Kurkihar to Gaya and thence to Burma].' On the previous page, stylistic links in the eleventh century between Kurkihar and specifically the Apanaka Mahavihara at that site are linked to Pagan bronze images of the Buddha. For Burmese involvement in the restoration of the temple at Bodh Gaya, see Zwalf, 1985, p. 115, Cat. no. 154; and ultimately for the relevant inscription of Kyanzittha, see Luce, 1969, vol. I, p. 62.

A further record of the link between Bodh Gaya and Burma is demonstrated by a once-gilded bronze image of the seated Buddha (Museum registration number OA. 1894.7–27.46. Ht 15 cm.) which belonged to Sir Alexander Cunningham, the excavator of Bodh Gaya. It is clearly of Burmese origin, though almost certainly comes from Bodh Gaya. It, along with other elements of Cunningham's collection, were acquired from his estate by Sir Augustus Wollaston Franks who in turn gave them to the Museum. The image, which is set on a simple waisted base lacking any lotus petal decoration, is in *bhūmisparśamudrā*, the *uṣṇīṣa* is short and pointed and the robe is merely hinted at

by a small number of engraved lines, after the casting. The shape of the face certainly suggests a date in the late Pagan period which is credible given its provenance.

22 For examples of the Indian prototype, see von Schroeder, 1981, p. 262, pl. 59A. An intermediary form of this elaborate crown is found in the late Pagan wooden sculptures of the standing Buddha. These have been interpreted variously as Bodhisattva-Kings (Luce, 1969–70, vol. I, p. 291; vol. II, p. 187; vol. III, pls 421 and 422) or crowned Buddhas (Zwalf, 1985, p. 164, Cat. no. 225. Museum registration number 1981.6–11.1. Brooke Sewell Fund). In these wooden sculptures, the origin in the ribbon-ends of the crown seen on eastern Indian Buddha images can still be discerned. The Burmese term for these highly developed appendages is *nha-gin*, or ear-ornament (information courtesy of U Kyaw Zan Tha, London).

23 Pratapaditya Pal (ed.), *Light of Asia: Buddha Sakyamuni in Asian Art*, Los Angeles: Los Angeles County Museum of Art, 1984, Cat. no. 184, p. 241. This sculpture was pre-viously published in *The Sensuous Immortals: A Selection of Sculptures from the Pan-Asian Collection*, Los Angeles, Los Angeles County Museum of Art, 1977, Cat. no. 92, p. 157. The example in the London sale catalogue is illustrated in *Burmese Art and its Influences*, exhibition catalogue of Beurdeley, Matthews and Co. Ltd, London, 1981, Cat. no. 38. It is described as being 'Shan Style, 17th/18th century'. Whether the word 'Shan' refers to the region (i.e. eastern Burma) or the period (i.e. post-Pagan) is unclear.

24 See Zwalf, 1985, p. 165, Cat. 228. See also Maung Mya, 'Notes and Reviews: Our Museum', *Journal of the Burma Research Society*, vol. IV, part III, 1914, p. 219, Here both Burmese and Talaing versions of the Jambupati story are mentioned. For a more recent discussion of the Jambupati story in neighbouring Thailand, see Hiram W. Woodward, *The Sacred Sculpture of Thailand: The Alexander B. Griswold Collection*, Baltimore and London: the Walters Art Gallery and Thames and Hudson, p. 79, fn. 7 and index references.

25 John Lowry, *Burmese Art*, London: HMSO, 1974, p. 13.

26 See note 23.

27 See Otto Karow, *Burmese Buddhist Sculpture: The Johan Möger Collection*, Bangkok: White Lotus, 1991. See especially Cat. no. 48 (dated seventeenth–eighteenth century), with side appendages and stepped but not lotus base; Cat. no. 51 with same date, side appendages and double-lotus base, but with *varadamudrā*, not *bhūmisparśamudrā*, and Cat. no. 56 with same dates and attributes and *bhūmisparśamudrā* and a double-lotus and hourglass base. These examples are all in bronze, but a beautiful example in carved wood is seen in Cat. no. 47; it is dated eighteenth–nineteenth century by Karow.

28 Beurdeley, Matthews and Co. Ltd., 1981, Cat. no. 38, p. 35.

29 Sir Augustus Wollaston Franks, who bequeathed this Buddha image to the Museum, died in 1897. The Museum records indicate that it was found in Thailand, at Phra Sek-tai, not in Burma.

30 Luce, 1970, vol. II, p. 201; vol. III, pl. 439, c and d.

31 Duroiselle in his *Report of the Superintendent, Archaeological Survey of Burma* for 1920 (pp. 23–4) and 1922 (pp. 9–10), both Rangoon, mentions at least two bronze sculptures recovered from Hsameikshé. One of them, which Luce identifies with the image he illustrates, he dates to the eleventh or early twelfth century.

32 Luce, 1970, vol. II, p. 201, says 'Such "Crowned Buddhas" become common in Central Burma during the early Ava period; but they were certainly known at Pagan . . . One

hesitates, I admit, to date the Thazi image as early as Duroiselle does, but most of his other finds in this neighbourhood confirm this date.'

33 Beurdeley, Matthews and Co. Ltd, 1981, Cat. no. 36, p. 33.

34 Jean Terry Bailey, *A Syllabus for a Course in Burmese Art*, no. 124. This publication has not been seen by the present author, but the date quoted in the sale catalogue apparently comes from this publication.

35 Karow, 1991, p. 3. Also, Luce, 1969, vol. I, p. 188.

36 Personal communication from U Kyaw Zan Tha. See also, Zwalf, 1985, Cat. no. 228, p. 165 for a similar interpretation (though for a different image) – '. . . this [crowned] Buddha has a bowl and, in his right hand, the myrobalan which has medicinal properties. The Buddha as healer is an old and widespread concept . . .'

37 (1) Museum registration number OA.1969.2–11.1. Brooke Sewell Fund. Ht 53 cm. Published in Zwalf, 1985, p. 165, Cat. no. 228 with a date of eighteenth–nineteenth century; (2) Museum registration number OA.1894.7–27. 47. Gift of Sir Augustus Wollaston Franks. Ht 14 cm. Also on public display is an ivory example of the crowned Buddha image – 1993. 7–24. 1. Brooke Sewell Fund.

38 The Museum records mention that this image was acquired, along with five other examples of Burmese bronze sculpture, from the well-known London store, Harrods.

39 Are these distinctions perhaps to be viewed in the same way as other India-derived distinctions of action (female) and contemplation (male); right as auspicious (and male) and left as inauspicious (and female)? I am grateful to U Kyaw Zan Tha for helping me to understand better the positions and meaning of Sariputra and Maudgalyayana.

40 See, Lowry, 1974, p. 2: 'The group of three figures comprising the Buddha Shakyamuni in the centre, with Moggallana on his left and Sariputta on his right has a long history in Burmese art. They are shown on terracotta plaques . . . belonging to the early 12th century AD . . . .'

41 Museum registration number OA.1880–4070 (Nevill Collection). Ht 24.70 cm. For the range of crowned Buddha images from Arakan, including this type, see San Tha Aung, *The Buddhist Art of Ancient Rakhine*, 2nd edition, Rangoon: U Ye Myint, Insein, 1997, chapter XV, pp. 48–56

and pls 31–52 and 75–6. For Sri Lanka images found in Arakan see pl. 74. For a more recent discussion of the crowned Buddha image type from Arakan, see Pamela Gutman, *Burma's Lost Kingdoms: Splendours of Arakan*, Bangkok: Orchid Press, 2001, pp. 146–53, and for Sri Lanka images in Arakan, pp. 153–8.

42 Beurdeley Matthews and Co. Ltd, 1981, cat. no. 34.

43 For a large published group, see Karow, 1991, pp. 5–44. For archaeological recovery of images of this type, see Maung Mya, 1914, p. 221: 'Sets of such figures illustrating the life of the Buddha generally form the contents of relic chambers of the Buddhist shrines in Burma.'

44 Museum registration number OA.1981.10.-23.1. Ht 23 cm. Gift of Mrs Florence Macdonald. The donor of this sculpture to the Museum's collection recorded that it had had a special usage in Mogok where it was set up at the entrance to the ruby diggings. Burmese workers passing it on their to way to dangerous work in the mines, paid homage before it; the donor's husband had been a manager at the Mogok ruby mines before Independence in 1948. There is no reason to doubt the explanation of this specific secondary use, though its original function must also have been as a votive in a pagoda relic chamber.

45 Examples include (1) OA.94.7–27.50, gift of Sir Augustus Wollaston Franks. Ht 9.70 cm. (2) OA.1930.4–8.1. Ht 11.30 cm. The second example was found in a cave halfway between Hsenwi and Bhamo, perhaps suggesting that these small sculptures were votives for deposition not only in pagoda relic chambers, but in shrines generally.

46 The Museum was founded in 1753. There was at that time already a Burmese manuscript in the Sloane Collection (the Foundation Collection), see Herbert, 1989, p. 59. For the history of the Sloane Collection, see Arthur MacGregor (ed.), *Sir Hans Sloane: Collector, Antiquary, Founding Father of the British Museum*, London: British Museum Press, 1994. For the history of the Museum, see Marjorie Caygill, *The Story of the British Museum*, London: British Museum Press, 2nd edition, 1992. Sir David Wilson, Director of the British Museum from 1977–92, is currently preparing a new history for publication in 2003 to mark the 250th anniversary of the foundation of the Museum.

7 Narrative modes in late seventeenth- to early nineteenth-century Burmese wall paintings

Alexandra Green

The analysis of visual narrative modes reveals the construction of space and time in the depictions of stories. These compositional devices are the means by which the artist communicates the narratives to his or her audience, and renders the information comprehensible to the viewers.[1] Several scholars have addressed the issue of visual narrative modes in their writings. One of the most recent is Vidya Dehejia who has developed a clear set of modes and applied them to Indian narrative painting and sculpture.[2] According to Dehejia there are eight primary modes: the monoscenic (both active and static), the synoptic, the conflated, the sequential, the *in medias res*, and the continuous modes, and also the narrative network.

Although only some of Dehejia's modes are used in Burma, a variety is still used to represent the Jātaka stories, primarily the last ten tales, scenes from the life of Gotama Buddha, and the twenty-eight previous Buddhas. By examining this variety, the importance of the modes in identifying the role that each part of the mural depiction plays in the construction of meaning becomes evident. The purpose of this chapter is to define the main narrative mode types used between the seventeenth and early nineteenth centuries, to note the apparent prioritisation of space, to question the importance of narrative modes as a classificatory method of Burmese murals, and to suggest new methods of analysis through the presentation of alternative interpretive paradigms.

THE ORGANISATION OF BURMESE MURALS

The general organisation of the Burmese wall paintings consists of the twenty-eight previous Buddhas seated in *bhūmisparśamudrā* under their trees of Enlightenment along the tops of walls. Underneath these images are usually scenes from the life of Gotama Buddha; most commonly the emphasis of these narratives is upon events prior to and including Gotama's Enlightenment. The *Mahānipāta*, or the last ten Jātaka stories, follows Gotama's life events. Moving from the bottom of walls upwards, the order of these stories is usually as follows: Mūgapakkha (Temiya), Mahājanaka, Sāma, Nemi, Mahā-ummaga (Mahosadha), Bhūridatta, Khaṇḍahāla, Mahānāradakassapa, Vidhurapaṇḍita, and Vessantara

Jātakas. The narratives are organised into registers, generally about 30–45 cm high. Sometimes, but not very frequently, hell scenes are included at the bases of walls. Whether the limited number of hell scenes is due to the fact that the lowest few feet of plaster has often been whitewashed or has fallen away, or whether the hell scenes were never included in the mural programme initially, is unclear. Floral bands frame the previous Buddhas, separate the Jātaka stories from the hell scenes, and comprise a last row under the hell scenes or the last ten Jātaka stories. The ceiling is usually covered with repetitive floral and/or geometric motifs with lotus pools as the most common form of decoration. While this organisation does not apply to all mural paintings produced during the seventeenth to nineteenth centuries, it is fairly standard, and exact copies or variations exist at most sites in Burma.

THE ACTIVE MONOSCENIC MODE

The active monoscenic mode is characterised by a single event, taken from a narrative tale, that has been selected to represent the whole. Generally the moment chosen is not only an instance of action, but is also the one that demonstrates the moral point of the tale. As a single action within the limits of a single scene, the monoscenic method is unified in time and place.[3]

Although popular in the eleventh to thirteenth centuries, the active monoscenic mode was used very infrequently between the seventeenth and nineteenth centuries. Only a few sites dating to the eighteenth century have examples of the active monoscenic mode. Use of this mode occurs mainly when the story is very short, and extending the narrative beyond one or two scenes would be difficult, as can be seen in the murals at the Ananda Ok-kyaung (c. 1785) in Pagan and at Tilokaguru cave-temple (c. 1700) on Sagaing Hill.

An example occurs in the Ananda Ok-kyaung, where, sandwiched between two longer depictions of Jātaka stories, is a single-scene depiction of the Nalapāna Jātaka (no. 20)[4] (Figure 7.1). Separated from the preceding and succeeding Jātaka paintings by highly stylised mountain-like lines,[5] the main action of the narrative occurs on

Figure 7.1 Naḷapāna Jātaka (no. 20), Ananda Ok-kyaung, Pagan. Photograph by the author.

the right side of the approximately rectangular space in which it is located. Although the story tells how a monkey troop is slowly being eaten by an ogre when members go to the pond to quench their thirst, and how the monkey leader (the Bodhisatta) saves his flock by proposing that they use hollow grass blades to suck up water, here only monkeys drinking through reed straws are shown. Deer, stylised trees and mountains, and red and turquoise patches comprise the left side of the picture, while the water tank with a centrally located, crouching figure with extended arms is on the right. The beige monkeys, swinging from the trees or dipping their straws into the water of the tank (the water is not depicted) are not only small and obscure in comparison to the rest of the painting, but are at the very edge of the painting. The action has been subtly reproduced, and the detail of the background has been given equal space with the event depicted, or even, arguably, foregrounded. The story has been incorporated into its surroundings, rather than singled out.

The paucity of examples of the active monoscenic mode in the seventeenth to nineteenth centuries demonstrates that extended forms of narration were preferred at the time. This may in part be due to the types of stories which were selected for portrayal: these were primarily the lengthy narratives of the last ten Jātaka tales and scenes from the life of Gotama Buddha. Corroborating this hypothesis is the fact that the examples of the active monoscenic mode occur in the two temples of this period

with narrative material which do not depict the last ten Jātakas.

THE STATIC MONOSCENIC MODE

The static monoscenic mode consists of a single scene which has no action or in which the action is reduced. These static images depict scenes from the Buddhas' lives where the supremacy of a Buddha is the main emphasis. The action itself is not the most important part of the painting. Whatever is depicted, the objective is to elicit from the viewer a sense of awe towards the Buddha's wisdom and abilities. The static monoscenic mode needs a strong focal point, and the majority of these images are therefore presented in a frontal pose, not in a three-quarter or profile one.[6]

Use of the static monoscenic narrative mode creates an icon. These are generally produced in comprehensible patterns and are repeated to enhance reception.[7] Repetition is emphasised in the seventeenth- to nineteenth-century mural paintings as the static monoscenic scenes look virtually identical. This lack of variation makes the images instantly recognisable. Though the captions underneath the images indicate that a specific action is occurring, the repetition of the images suggests that it is the Buddha's knowledge and supremacy that are emphasised, not the action itself.

In the seventeenth century the static monoscenic mode was most commonly represented by rows of the twenty-eight previous Buddhas seated in *bhūmisparśa mudrā* under their respective trees of Enlightenment at the tops of walls (Figure 7.2). Other images shown in the static monoscenic mode include the previous Buddhas making the Renunciation on horseback (not in a frontal pose) and scenes of Gotama Buddha preaching during his residencies at various monasteries in the rainy season. These figures are produced in repetitive sequences of virtually identical images. The Eight Great Events of Gotama's life are also portrayed, but in conjunction with, and often in a long sequence with, other scenes from the Buddha's life. Whether or not they are shown in the static monoscenic mode entirely depends upon how the images are integrated with the sequence in which they are located. The Jātaka stories are not depicted in this mode.

THE CONFLATED MODE

The conflated mode is distinguished by one of the characters (usually the protagonist or another important figure) being presented only once despite their involvement in several closely clustered scenes. Several moments in the tale are depicted in a single scene without the repetition of the participants essential for the sequential and continuous modes (see next section). By placing several scenes within a single frame the unity of time is destroyed.[8] Use of this mode forces attention upon the major character. Spatial limitations or the importance of the protagonist may have been the reasons why this type of mode was utilised in Burma.

In the seventeenth to nineteenth centuries, the conflated mode was very rarely employed, and like the continuous one is only found within the sequential mode. It does not stand alone. The main example, a depiction of the Vessantara Jātaka, is found at Laung U Hmaw in Ywa Thit Gyi village, Sagaing Division (Figure 7.3). Here, Jūjaka is asleep in a treetop with Vessantara's children chained to the base of the tree. On each side of this scene is a *deva* holding a child. Representing the incident where the gods disguise themselves as Maddī and Vessantara and come to comfort the children, this mural changes from a sequential mode of narration to a conflated one. If the sequential mode had been employed, then the tree with Jūjaka would have been depicted twice, once when the children are tied to it and once when the *devas* comfort the children. Instead, the same tree with Jūjaka asleep in its boughs has been used for both events. All of the previous scenes have occurred in different places, but here two incidents happening in the same location result in the conflation of that space, emphasising space over time. The infrequent use of this mode, and the fact that it is only seen combined with other modes, suggests that the distinction between it and the sequential and continuous modes was unimportant to the Burmese. In

Figure 7.2 The twenty-eight previous Buddhas, Zedi Daw Taik, Anein village. Photograph by the author.

69

other words, the conflated mode appears to be merely a device for conserving space.

EXTENDED NARRATIVE MODES

The broad category of extended narrative modes comprises the sequential, continuous and *in medias res* modes. These three modes have can be grouped together because they have some features in common. Dehejia describes sequential and continuous narratives as multiple appearances of the characters in successive states of action within a single overall frame, extending through units that are related by proximity and organisation so as to suggest association and compatibility.[9] This results in a linear construction for both modes, which are generally organised from left to right.[10] The difference between the two types lies in the use (or non-use) of spatial dividers. The sequential mode divides space using extrinsic criteria, such as landscape elements, while intrinsic criteria divide space in the continuous mode, such as figures facing in different directions. The *in medias res* mode's main characteristic is temporal, with the story being laid out in an achronological fashion. Generally, the depiction begins with a scene from the middle of the story, but eventually reverts to the beginning scenes. Because the story is presented in segments, ultimately like the sequential and continuous modes, linearity is a prerequisite for the *in medias res* one.[11]

The continuous, sequential, and *in medias res* modes form the primary means of representing the Jātaka stories and the life of Gotama Buddha during the seventeenth to early nineteenth centuries, though the sequential mode with clearly demarcated space cells comprises the bulk of all painted pictorial narration. The increasing amount of detail portrayed in the paintings, including specific architectural forms and extensive foliage, which locates the action of the episode in a specific place and separates it from other events, causes the sequential mode of narration to be paramount. Because little background detail, which divides scenes, can be included in depictions in the continuous mode, it is possible that the sequential mode is the most common due to the level of detail utilised in the murals during the seventeenth to nineteenth centuries.

The sequential mode

Sequential narratives are presented with divisions composed of architectural features, trees, the positioning of figures, the use of different backgrounds, and wavy lines following the outline of the action. For instance, in Laung U Hmaw library, which dates to the eighteenth century, most of the wall paintings are depicted in the sequential mode. The layout of the murals is linear with occasional serpentine sections, usually found where a series of small scenes are depicted, and the narrative moves from left to right. Scenes are clearly framed by green and white wavy lines, which follow the outlines of the scene. If a scene does not fill the entire height of the narrative register then it is framed by a wavy line and additional detail in the form of figures or landscape imagery is added above that line. Often figures are placed above the line as observers to the action occurring below. Occasionally, a change in background colour thinly outlined by a single black line acts as a divider between the actors and observers. Finally, when multiple incidents of a single episode in a story

Figure 7.3 Vessantara Jātaka (no. 547), Laung U Hmaw, Ywa Thit Gyi village. Photograph by the author.

70

Figure 7.4 Vessantara giving away his children, Vessantara Jātaka (no. 547), Laung U Hmaw, Ywa Thit Gyi village. Photograph by the author.

need to be shown, scenes are piled up on top of each other with a zigzag or serpentine effect; the complexity of this layout can vary considerably, depending on the number of scenes portrayed.

All of these elements are found in the depiction of the Vessantara Jātaka at Laung U Hmaw. The story is located on the third row from the ceiling and begins on the east side of the south wall and continues to the north side of the west wall, moving in a clockwise direction. The first scene is of a palace with male and female attendants on each side of the royal couple; a wavy line separates this scene from a double layer of soldiers, this double layer itself being indicated by the coloured double line. These soldiers are observing Vessantara giving away the precious white elephant to the eight Brahmins kneeling before him. Soldiers, some of whom are watching events, are located above the kneeling Brahmins and are against a black rather than the standard red background. Only a thin black line and the colour of the background separate them from the Brahmins. The scene is followed by another wavy dividing line. The subsequent scenes depicting the Brahmins riding away on the white elephant, Vessantara in a carriage with his family giving the horses to another Brahmin, Vessantara in a carriage drawn by deer giving the carriage away to yet another Brahmin, and a hermit indicating the way to Vessantara and his wife who are carrying their children, are all framed by a more or less vertical green and white wavy line.

With the depiction of Vessantara giving away his children to the Brahmin Jūjaka, a slightly different format is utilised (Figure 7.4). Scenes are still demarcated by the green and white wavy line, but the amount of space given to each scene is small with the result that events no longer follow a linear format, but are piled up with a zigzag effect on the narrative order. At the left side of the

picture Vessantara is giving the children to Jūjaka. To the right of this action, Jātaka drives the crying children forward. They escape when he falls down and return to the lotus pond at the monastery where the family is residing. The positioning of the children's flight in a diagonal line pointing to the left takes the viewer's eye to a space almost directly above the original giving scene. Here the scenes of Vessantara admonishing the children, who are hiding in the pond, and then returning them to Jūjaka, once again move in a linear, left-to-right fashion. This zig-zag organisation not only permits multiple scenes to be shown in a small space, but also emphasises the repetitive nature of the events.

During the seventeenth and eighteenth centuries this serpentine method was a standard way of depicting this series of scenes from the Vessantara Jātaka. Temples located as disparately as Po Win Daung, Zedi Daw Taik and other temples at Anein village near Monywa, the Upali Thein, Hman Si Paya and the Taungbi Ok-kyaung at Pagan, and Tilokaguru and Loka-hman-gin cave-temples at Sagaing, all dating to the late seventeenth or eighteenth century and painted in the same or similar style as Laung U Hmaw, also exhibit the same division of space and time.

During the late eighteenth century another method for dividing space and time in a sequential fashion is utilised in visual narratives. Here, instead of using trees, architecture, or wavy lines to divide scenes, the visual texture and/or colour of the background is altered. For example, in the depiction of the Sāma Jātaka at the Shwe Kyaung U at Pagan, the first scene, which shows Sāma's parents dressed as ascetics in a building and Sāma with his deer, has the building and a grey-blue area with brown lines suggestive of a rocky landscape formation as a background (Figure 7.5). The scene where Sāma is shot near

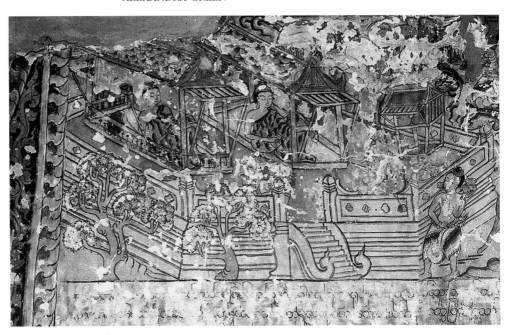

Figure 7.5 Sāma Jātaka (no. 540), Shwe Kyaung U temple, Pagan. Photograph by the author.

a lake is set against a pink rocky landscape with the watching deer set on a red ground. The remorseful king leads Sāma's parents to Sāma's body against a red background, and the final scene, where Sāma's parents cry over his body and make asseverations of truth to bring Sāma to life again, occurs on the grey-blue rocky ground with blue lines.

This latter form of the sequential mode is considerably more subtle than the use of landscape, buildings, or lines in the division of space and time. Of course, foliage and the one building in the scene can also be viewed as dividers, but the irregular use of these indicates that without the changes in background creating discrete space cells, the narrative mode depicted here would undoubtedly be continuous (i.e. spatial dividers are intrinsic), rather than sequential.

The continuous mode

Narratives portrayed without the use of spatial dividers are rare in paintings from the seventeenth to early nineteenth centuries. The continuous mode is less common than the sequential one, and the two are often combined within a single narrative. Examples of short sequences of the continuous mode within an overall sequentially organised narrative occur at most temples from the seventeenth- to early nineteenth-century period. Here stories are primarily laid out in a sequential fashion with segments depicted in a continuous mode. For example, in the first half of the Kumbha Jātaka (no. 512) at Tilokaguru cave-temple, no space cells or lines break the space into recognisably separate units (Figure 7.6). Only

the repetition of the characters, the hermit Varuṇa and the hunter Sura, indicates the alteration of time and place. The remainder of the narrative is constructed in a sequential format with buildings acting as spatial dividers. The frequent combination of continuous and sequential modes in late seventeenth- to eighteenth-century mural paintings, and the fact that without knowing the artist's intentions, separating sequential and continuous modes is often problematic, suggests that Burmese artists did not distinguish between the two modes, or at least did not see the difference as significant.

In medias res

Stories are sometimes portrayed in such a way that the narrative begins with scenes other than the first one in the order of the tale. The *in medias res* mode, while maintaining a generally linear progress, reverses itself part of the way through the depiction.[12] If the achronological layout of this mode were rearranged chronologically, however, the result would be either a sequential or continuous narrative, depending on the subtlety of the space cells. The *in medias res* mode can therefore be considered an achronological form of the sequential and continuous modes.

Examples of achronological narration are uncommon in Burmese wall paintings and occur primarily at the Ananda Ok-kyaung and at Tilokaguru cave-temple. The Ananda Ok-kyaung has two examples of the *in medias res* mode (the Kaṭṭhahāri Jātaka [no. 7] and the Kukkura Jātaka [no. 22]) out of thirteen identified depictions of Jātaka tales. In the Kukkura Jātaka, the order of the scenes is 4, 5, 1, 2, 3 (Figure 7.7). The final episode where the

Bodhisatta in the form of a dog talks to the king is presented in a palace scene first; then the Bodhisatta is honoured. The beginning of the story where the palace dogs chew the chariot harness, the slaughter of the common dogs, and a depiction of the dogs discussing how to resolve the situation follows. The narrative line in the Kukkura Jātaka travels from left to right. While the overall organisation of the paintings begins in the middle, time and space are still in accord within the segments. Scenes four and five are in sequential order, as are scenes one to three, and the division of space within these episodes of events replicates that found in the sequential and/or continuous modes. The organisation of this story may be due to the use of space within the murals. Many of the Ananda Ok-kyaung murals begin with a palace scene; these scenes utilise a larger space than other scenes, and therefore combining the beginning palace scene with the palace scene or scenes occurring later in the story conserves space. Only one palace is depicted in each tale, and events that occur within it are all placed in the single building.

Five stories, located at various points in Tilokaguru, are depicted in the *in medias res* mode; these include the Alambusā (no. 523), Saṁkhapāla (no. 524), Gaṇḍatindu (no. 520), Rohanta-miga (no. 501), and Citta-Sambhūta (no. 498) Jātakas. In these, the most frequent occurrence is the reversal of the first two or the last two scenes. In three of the stories, the rearranged order produces scenes of luxury or scenes set within buildings at the end of the tale. In the remaining two stories (the Rohanta-miga and the Gaṇḍatindu), the reversal of the scenes means that the tale has been rearranged so that the story imagery

begins with a palace scene. Most of the stories depicted at Tilokaguru begin with a palace scene or a scene that occurs within a building; only three stories out of thirty do not, and the rearrangement of narrative order may be because it was preferable to have architectural backgrounds at the beginning or at the end. Having these types of scenes at either the beginning or end of the depiction seems to be part of a standard formula, and the use of the *in medias res* mode results from this use of space.

An explanation for the use of the *in medias res* mode at both sites thus derives from the organisation of scenes within the stories. The use of this mode further corroborates the Burmese emphasis upon space rather than time in the mural depictions.

THE ROLE OF NARRATIVE MODES IN BURMA

Frequently, visual narratives are constructed from a variety of modes. These include combinations of the sequential and continuous, the sequential and conflated, and the *in medias res* and sequential modes. This organisation probably derives from an emphasis on spatial conservation and particular themes denoted in the paintings, rather than a deliberate emphasis upon narrative modes.[13] It is this fact that calls into question the importance of narrative modes as a classificatory method for Burmese murals.

Dehejia's mode system does not function well in Burmese wall paintings, revealing ambiguities in the narrative structure and suggesting alternative systems.[14] What do the ambiguities tell us? First, the mode categories

Figure 7.6 Kumbha Jātaka (no. 512), Tilokaguru temple, Sagaing. Photograph by the author.

Figure 7.7 Kukkura Jātaka (no. 22), Ananda Ok-kyaung, Pagan. Photograph by the author.

are not set totally, creating an overlap between modes; more than one mode can be represented at a time. Second, although combinations exist, often one mode is privileged over the other. Third, emphasis in the murals is periodically on space rather than time, and thus the relationship between time and space is sometimes unclear. Fourth, sometimes this ambiguity derives from the nature of the story itself. Fifth, the use of more than one mode at a time suggests that the Burmese artists were not necessarily concerned with the relationship between time and space. Spatial sequence is usually tied to temporal diachrony, but in instances of insufficient room on the wall to depict events occurring in the same narrative space and where the repetition of substantial background scenery is essential for narrative understanding, the co-ordination between space and time dissolves.

If minor variations in narrative mode types do not seem particularly important in Burmese murals, perhaps other, broader categories should be considered instead. The narrative modes discussed here can be separated into two main types: monoscenic and extended. The monoscenic depictions are shown as a single scene, while the extended ones are in a strip format. In general, Burmese murals of the seventeenth and eighteenth centuries depict two main topics: the twenty-eight previous Buddhas, and the Jātaka stories and the life of Gotama Buddha. The monoscenic mode is primarily used for depictions of the previous Buddhas and Gotama after he

has reached Enlightenment, while the extended mode is used for the Jātaka stories and the life of Gotama Buddha prior to his Enlightenment. The use of virtually only these two modes for specific topics suggests that they may be meaningful in their own right.

According to Michael Aung-Thwin, the Burmese Buddhist cosmos exists in a physically represented space with a precisely formulated network of time. Time and space establish context and limits by which humans exist, and with such a system it is pointless to 'capture' or 'conquer' time even in concept. One must instead escape time through *nibbāna*.[15] The Buddhist conceptual world can thus be divided into two parts. *Lokiya* is the Buddhist concept of this world. All levels and forms of existence,

including the heavens, earth, hells, gods, men, beasts, and demons are included. Merit is a part of *lokiya*, as it keeps individuals within the world through samsaric life-cycles. *Lokuttara*, on the other hand, is the other world, associated with *nibbāna*, the extinction from rebirth and existence. It is the liberation from sentient existence.[16] Juliane Schober states that *lokuttara* derives from reflection and contemplation (i.e. meditation or concentration) but is not immediately available. The benefits of *lokuttara* promote the quest for enlightenment beyond the acquisition of merit.[17]

These concepts may explain why so few variations in the relationship between time and space are actually seen in the wall paintings. I would like to suggest that an accord between time and space produces an extended mode of narration that most clearly reflects the cause and effect cycles of *saṃsāra* that occur in *lokiya*. Furthermore, the monoscenic mode, represented primarily by the twenty-eight previous Buddhas, is used to depict scenes associated with *nibbāna* and enlightenment, since it is in these representations that there is a cessation of cause and effect and time. While the artists may not have had distinct narrative themes in mind, it is possible that the Burmese wall paintings of this era are characterised by the dichotomy between *saṃsāra*, expressed by the extended format, and *nibbāna*, exemplified by the monoscenic mode in the form of the twenty-eight previous Buddhas. Therefore, the static monoscenic mode is primarily used to depict the previous Buddhas reaching Enlightenment,[18] indicating the cessation of time and the rounds of *saṃsāra*. Alternatively, scenes where cause and effect, change, and events still occur, including scenes of the Buddha's life, scenes from the lives of the previous Buddhas, and the Jātaka stories, are depicted in the extended narrative mode. Thus, the monoscenic mode can be equated with the concept of *lokuttara*, and the extended format with that of *lokiya*.

To sum up, the extended mode is used to portray the Jātaka stories and pre-enlightenment life events of Gotama Buddha because they are concerned with the cause and effect results of *kamma*, the samsaric cycle, and ways to escape the suffering encountered in life. An accord between time and space producing an extended mode of narration most clearly reflects cause and effect processes. The single scenes of the monoscenic mode are used to depict scenes associated with *nibbāna* and enlightenment, since it is in these representations that there is a cessation of cause and effect and temporal considerations. The extended mode thus explicates the process of reaching enlightenment, and the monoscenic provides an image of the goal.

ACKNOWLEDGEMENTS

The research for this paper was supported by the Henry James Green Trust, The Central Research Fund, University of London, and a fieldwork grant, SOAS. Thanks are also due to my mother, Joy Schochet, for her encouragement and assistance.

NOTES

1 Kirsti Evans, *Epic Narratives in the Hoysaḷa Temples: The Rāmāyaṇa, Mahābhārata and Bhāgavata Purāṇa in Haḷebīd, Belūr and Amṛtapura*, Leiden: E.J. Brill, 1997, p. 13.

2 Vidya Dehejia, 'On Modes of Visual Narration in Early Buddhist Art', *Art Bulletin*, vol. 72, no. 3, 1990, pp. 374–92. Vidya Dehejia, 'Narrative Modes in Ajanta Cave 17: A Preliminary Study', *South Asian Studies*, vol. 7, 1991, pp. 45–57. Vidya Dehejia, *Discourse in Early Buddhist Art: Visual Narratives of India*, New Delhi: Munshiram Manoharlal Publishers, 1997. Vidya Dehejia, 'India's Visual Narratives: The Dominance of Space Over Time', *Paradigms of Indian Architecture: Space and Time in Representation and Design*, Giles Tillotson (ed.), Collected Papers on South Asia no. 13, Richmond, Surrey: Curzon, 1998, pp. 80–106.

3 Dehejia, 1997, pp. 10–12. Richard Brilliant, *Visual Narratives: Storytelling in Etruscan and Roman Art*, London: Cornell University Press, 1984, pp. 51–2. Kurt Weitzmann, *Illustrations in Roll and Codex: A Study of the Origin and Method of Text Illustration*, Princeton, NJ: Princeton University Press, 1947, pp. 14–15.

4 This numbering system is derived from E. Cowell's edition of the Jātaka stories. E.B. Cowell (ed.), *The Jātaka or Stories of the Buddha's Former Births*, vols 1–6, Cambridge: Cambridge University Press, 1897.

5 Interestingly, these seem to reflect Chinese painting styles used to portray mountains.

6 Dehejia, 1997, pp. 12–15

7 Brilliant, p. 116. This particularly occurs between the eleventh and thirteenth centuries, where the way the Jātaka stories are presented and the repetition of that pattern ensures the reception of the message. The necessity of viewing each story or image is then negated.

8 Weitzmann, pp. 13–14.

9 Dehejia, 1997, pp. 15–21. See also, Brilliant, pp. 29–30.

10 *Ibid.*

11 Dehejia, 1997, pp. 18–19. See also, Brilliant, p. 19.

12 *Ibid.*

13 It is for this reason that the occasional use of the active monoscenic mode is irrelevant and does not affect this argument. The use of this mode is merely a space saving device.

14 Helmut Bonheim, 'Theory of Narrative Modes', *Semiotica*, vol. 14, no. 4, 1975, p. 341. Bonheim discusses how identifying modes shows how a sense of reality is constructed. It is where the system fails that ambiguities are identifiable, and thus other or additional meanings emerge.

15 Michael Aung-Thwin, *Pagan: The Origins of Modern Burma*, Honolulu: University of Hawaii Press, 1985, p. 40.

16 S.J. Tambiah, *Buddhism and the Spirit Cults in North-East Thailand*, Cambridge: Cambridge University Press, 1970, pp. 40–1.

17 Juliane Schober, *Paths to Enlightenment: Theravada Buddhism in Upper Burma*, PhD dissertation, University of Illinois, Champaign-Urbana, 1989, p. 178. See Spiro's book on Buddhism and society for a discussion on Burmese ideas relating to the merit path and meditation paths to enlightenment. Melford E. Spiro, *Buddhism and Society: A Great Tradition and its Burmese Vicissitudes*, Berkeley: University of California Press, 1982, chapters 3–5.

18 It may be pointed out that the monoscenic Jātaka stories, particularly from the eleventh to thirteenth centuries do not accord with this theory. Examined with the concept of a pragmatic use of space by the artists, it appears that the use of the generally single-scene squares is not associated with the cessation of time. Corroboration comes in two forms: one is that the scene depicted is active. Emphasis is not exclusively upon the wisdom of the Buddha (or Bodhisatta). Secondly, the organisation of the stories implies cause and effect, leading ultimately to enlightenment. The events of the Buddha's life, on the other hand, are not as emphatically demonstrating cause and effect, but are presenting the Buddha teaching the Law.

8 Burmese cosmological manuscripts

Patricia Herbert

Although the Buddha discouraged speculation on the nature of the universe (cosmology) and its origins (cosmogony), this did not inhibit Buddhists from seeking to accommodate not only the known face of the earth and the heavenly bodies but also other realms, those of the dead and of deities and other beings, which form part of their mythology and beliefs. Buddhist cosmology was to a large extent based on ancient Indian texts and classical Hindu cosmology, modified to accord with Buddhist teachings and, as Buddhism spread from India to other countries, adapted to incorporate local beliefs and divinities.[1] This chapter is not primarily concerned with the textual sources and systematisation of cosmological information that developed over time, but focuses on the representations of Buddhist cosmology that are found in Burmese art and, in particular, in Burmese manuscript art.

The ways in which Buddhist cosmology and symbolism are represented in art and architecture and underlie ritual and ceremony are well-known and it is only necessary to outline these and to cite some Burmese examples.[2] The supreme representation of the Buddhist cosmos in architecture is the stupa or Buddhist temple, each element of which has symbolic and often multiple significance.[3] The world of humanity parallels the universe, and man's life and that of the state has to be in harmony with the gods and cosmic forces. The layout of royal palaces and the rituals and responsibilities of kingship reflect in microcosm the kingdom of the gods. Among the many elements of Buddhist cosmology that are found in a range of Burmese art and architectural forms, that of Mount Meru is strikingly predominant.[4] Most unusual is the monumental (over ten metres high) cross-sectional representation of Mount Meru carved into the rock face of the remote Po-win-daung cave complex (in Lower Chindwin District).[5] Near Mingun, in Upper Burma, is the Mya-thein-dan (or Hsin-byu-me) temple built by Bagyidaw in 1816.[6] Designed as an earthly replica of the Sulamani temple in the heaven that crowns the summit of Mount Meru, it is circular in plan with seven concentric terraces (representing the seven mountain ranges around Mount Meru) with wave-like balustrades (to represent the seven surrounding seas), interspersed with niches containing images of Mount Meru's supernatural guardians. Cosmological scenes are found in many temple wall paintings and bas reliefs from the Pagan period onwards, and in early reliefs at Mrauk-U (capital of Arakan from 1430).[7] Hell scenes were represented on temple walls, but were also vividly depicted on the elaborate catafalques of olden-day funerals. At grand funerals, especially those of monks, the catafalque (placed on a platform on wheels) that bears the coffin was surmounted by a huge multi-tiered finial *pyathat*, often accompanied by subsidiary carriages topped with *pyathat* and sometimes bearing giant paper and bamboo models of a white elephant or, most commonly, of Mount Meru and its denizens.[8] Models of Mount Meru also feature at the annual Thadingyut festival celebrating the Buddha's descent from heaven after preaching the Abhidhamma to his mother and assembled deities.[9] Many cosmological principles and motifs that once found expression in the rituals of the Burmese royal court have survived and continue to inform aspects of contemporary practice. In 1980, the site-marking ceremony for the construction of the Maha Vijaya temple in Rangoon was conducted in accordance with tradition: the stakes for marking the site were passed through the hands of the gods of the Buddhist heavens and the supernatural guardians of the cosmic axis (all represented by men dressed in appropriate costumes), who offered them to the presiding most senior monk (*hsayadaw*) by whom they were handed to distinguished laymen to be driven into the ground simultaneously at the most auspicious moment.[10] Linking such varied manifestations of cosmological elements is the central concept of an endless cosmic cycle of creation and destruction, within which all sentient beings die, only to be reborn in one of thirty-one levels of existence, an individual's rebirth into a particular level being determined by the effects of past merit (or demerit) accumulated in previous lives (the law of *kamma*[11]) and, at the highest levels, by meditational attainments (*jhāna*).[12]

For a pictorial representation of the Buddhist universe in its entirety we must turn to Burmese manuscript sources. Burmese illustrated cosmology manuscripts constitute a rare and little-studied category of manuscripts and, unusually, occur in both palm-leaf (*pei-za)* and

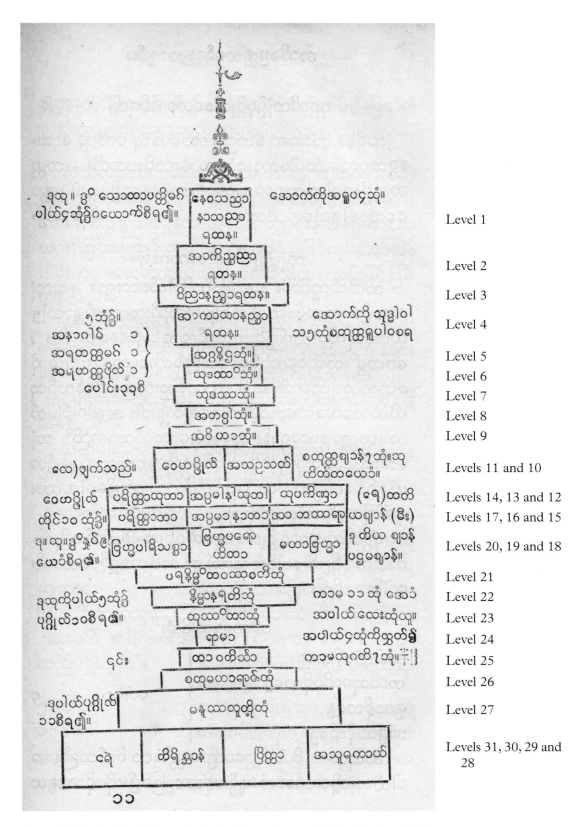

Figure 8.1 Chart of the thirty-one levels of existence from an 1883 publication (British Library, OIOC: VT 116/1, p. 81). See note 16. By permission of the British Library.

paper folding-book (*parabaik*) formats. I categorise as cosmological (or cosmographic) manuscripts those that combine text and a sequence of illustrations of the three realms of the Buddhist cosmos extending from the highest heavens to the multiple hells.[13] Given the complexity of the subject matter, its reduction or translation into a predominantly visual representation is an artistic *tour de force*. Yet, we know virtually nothing about the authorship and production of these manuscripts. Unlike most other Burmese manuscripts, which identify the text and contain a colophon with the date of composition and copying (and sometimes also the names of the scribe and the commissioner and donor of the manuscript), Burmese cosmological manuscripts do not include this information. To incise so elaborately a palm-leaf cosmology text and illustrations must have required special skills on the scribe's part and commanded higher fees. In the case of folding-book cosmologies, there are some which are quite crudely painted in a limited colour palette, while the sumptuous gilding and rich colours of others indicate that they are the work of artists at the royal court. Many manuscripts show considerable signs of wear and tear, and it is possible to surmise that they were frequently consulted and appreciated, both as a stunning visual representation of the Buddhist cosmos and as a reference guide to the path to enlightenment and ultimate release from the cycle of rebirth (Pali, *saṃsāra*).

The schematic appeal and arrangement of cosmological scenes into a top downwards vertical presentation of the highest to the lowest realms of existence has given rise to some specific conventions. The narrow, oblong format of the palm-leaf does not lend itself to illustration. Indeed palm leaf manuscripts from Burma with incised decorations are (apart from single-leaf half-length horoscopes still produced today) comparatively rare. Unlike other palm-leaf manuscript texts (which are incised on both sides of each leaf so that the text is read in the order of upper and reverse sides of each leaf), cosmology palm-leaf manuscripts have the text and illustrations running continuously on one side only of each leaf which is, however, doubled up on its blank side to another blank-sided leaf which continues the sequence of incised text and illustrations on the reverse side. The back-to-back leaves are strung (or stitched) together allowing a small gap or loop between each leaf so as to permit the leaves to be viewed as linked scenes when suspended vertically (rather like the slats of an open venetian blind) first on one side and then on the other. The foliation sequence used in these manuscripts also differs from other palm leaf manuscripts in that the reverse leaves are (usually, but not always) numbered kya, kyā, kyi etc., presumably as a way of matching them to the front side leaf sequence of ka, kā, ki, etc. The complete sequence of the heavens, the worlds and the hells, and interspersed text and captions occupies, from manuscript to manuscript, a varying

amount of space which must require careful calculation on the scribe's part as to where the front sequence ends and the reverse starts, so that an even number of decorated leaves is ensured. Over time, some manuscripts have been split up, while even those with a full sequence very often have leaves strung in the wrong sequence. Paper folding-book cosmologies also follow a vertical presentation with the manuscript opening vertically (instead of opening sideways from left to right as do most other illustrated *parabaik*) with the text and scenes painted in a vertical sequence down one side of the *parabaik*, and continued on the reverse side (although not necessarily for a matching number of folds). Folding-book cosmologies are known in Burmese as *bhon-zin parabaik*.[14]

The following description of scenes depicted in Burmese cosmological manuscripts is based on three palm-leaf manuscripts (Add. 17699A, Or. 12168 and Or. 15283) and five folding-book manuscripts (Or. 3591, Or. 14004, Or. 14550, Or. 14965 and Or. 15284) in the Oriental and India Office Collections of the British Library, and on four fine palm-leaf manuscripts in a private collection.[15] In order to provide a simple reference framework, a Burmese chart of the thirty-one planes/levels of existence is reproduced here, together with a list of the Pali names and meanings of each (Figure 8.1). A number of such charts exist in late nineteenth-century printed editions of works compiled by Burmese monk-scholars.[16] These present the structure of the Buddhist universe in a compressed and diagrammatic form, each level of existence listed by name in a tier of boxes which, with symbolic significance, assume a stupa-like shape; the charts also give brief supplementary information on dimensions, life spans and correlating meditation levels (*jhāna*).

Realm of Non-Form (Pali, *arūpaloka*)
1) Nevasaññā-nāsaññāyatana – neither perception nor non-perception.
2) Ākiñcaññāyatana – nothingness.
3) Viññānañ̄cāyatana – infinity of consciousness/intellect.
4) Ākāsānañcāyatana – infinity of space.

Realm of Form (Pali, *rūpaloka*)
5) Akaniṭṭha – highest/supreme.[17]
6) Sudassī – seeing well/clear-sighted.
7) Sudassā – beautiful/easily seen.
8) Atappā – non-tormentors/serene.[18]
9) Avihā – not falling from prosperity [or effortless].[19]
10) Asaññasatta – unconscious/without perception.
11) Vehapphala – abundant fruit/richly rewarded.
12) Subhakiṇṇā – entirely lustrous/radiant.
13) Appamāṇasubha – unlimited beauty/radiance.
14) Parittasubha – of limited beauty/goodness.

15) Ābhassarā – radiant.
16) Appamāṇabhā – unlimited splendour.
17) Parittābhā – limited splendour.
18) Mahābrahmā – great Brahmās.
19) Brahmaparohita – Brahmā priests/ministers to the Mahābrahmā
20) Brahmapārisajja – Brahmā assembly/retinue of the Mahābrahmā.

Realm of Desire/Sensuous Universe
(Pali, *kāmaloka*)

21) Paranimmita-vasavattī – beings who indulge in pleasure created by others.
22) Nimmānarati – those who have pleasure in creation.
23) Tusita – blissful/satisfied.
24) Yāmā – happiness attaining/inhabited by Yāmā deva
25) Tāvatiṁsa – world of the thirty-three gods.
26) Cātummahārājika – four great kings
27) Manussa – world of human beings/earthly plane
28) Asura – demons/fallen gods
29) Peta – departed/the world of ghosts/spirits
30) Tiracchāna – world of animals
31) Niraya – the hells/world of the damned

GENERAL FEATURES OF BURMESE ILLUSTRATED COSMOLOGIES

Cosmological manuscripts all represent and describe the Buddhist universe beginning with the heavens of the world without form (levels 1–4) and descending level by level to the world's cosmic axis, Mount Meru, and its metaphysical geography, the terrestrial abodes and on to the hells below the earth. In palm-leaf cosmologies, the illustrations of the uppermost heavens occupy only the central portion of a palm leaf – typically two leaves are allocated to each level – but widen out by level 25 (Tāvatiṁsa Heaven) to occupy the entire surface of the leaf. The depiction of Mount Meru from its summit to its ocean-submerged base occupies several leaves and is full of intricate and lively decoration. A striking feature of the cosmology manuscripts is the changing perspectives employed, whereby the vertical axis of Mount Meru is shown with seven diminishing pillars on both sides (in vertical cross-section), followed by a horizontal presentation of the metaphysical world which includes scenes of the forests, lakes and mountains of Himavanta, and of the source of the world's great rivers, and an aerial view of the circular outer walls of the universe and the four great island continents that face Mount Meru.[20] The sequence then reverts to a vertical presentation of hell scenes. Lastly (in most manuscript sequences), comes a feature unique to Burmese cosmology manuscripts: a depiction of the Buddha seated under the Bodhi tree, surrounded

by spokes radiating outwards in different compass directions, ending in captioned boxes containing geographical names and distances of journeys to them. The illustrative material takes precedence over the textual in the sense that the text is written in an indifferent hand and often crammed into the space on either side of illustrations, although sometimes longer passages of uninterrupted text occur. The accompanying text primarily catalogues the names of the abodes, measurements, modes of conception, life spans of inhabitants, with longer, more descriptive passages reserved for the terrestial worlds and the sufferings in hell, and draws on canonical sources and commentaries.

The following presentation of the sequence of the thirty-one levels (or planes) of existence gives, firstly, basic information of the context derived from the accompanying manuscript text and captions, and secondly, a description of the scenes represented, and variations found from manuscript to manuscript.

FRONT SIDE OF MANUSCRIPTS
Levels 1–4 (Nevasaññā-nāsaññāyatana, Ākiñcaññāyatana, Viññānaññcāyatana, and Ākāsānaññcāyatana Heavens)

Levels 1 to 4 are the four highest heavens of the world without form (called in Burmese, *ayupa bhon lei-pa*), also known as the world of formless *Brahmā* (Pali, *arūpabrahmāloka)*. Existence in this realm has no physical components and is gained by mastery of the four formless meditations, the highest level of mental attainment this side of *nibbāna*. Life span in level 1 is 84,000 *mahākappa*; in level 2 it is 60,000; in level 3 it is 40,000; and in level 4 it has reduced to 20,000. The distance between the last level (Ākāsānaññcāyatana) and level 5 (Akaniṭṭha) is 558,000 *yojana*.[21]

Each heavenly realm or plane of existence is depicted, one above the other (each occupying two palm leaves or one folding-book opening), in the centre portion of the leaf (or folding-book opening) and is represented as a central three-tier roofed pavilion surmounted by an elaborate tiered spire-like roof (Burmese, *pyathat*; Pali, *pāsāda)*, flanked by single-storey open-sided pavilions, supported on columns. In royal palaces the multi-tiered central spire rises above the throne room of the audience hall and, in microcosmic replication, symbolises the position of the king at the centre of the universe.[22] The celestial pavilions are consistently depicted as a royal palace, usually with flanking pavilions shown in frontal elevation.[23] In the four upper heavens of the world without form, the central pavilion is usually shown with an empty throne or a lotus emblem inside (often differing in design from one level to another). Or. 14004 has a triple-roofed palace, with a gilded seven tier *pyathat*, set against a background of swirling rocks; inside is a large empty gilded throne, backed by closed doors (as in the throne halls of Mandalay palace). The colour of the background mountain and the wood-panelled palace interior change at every level. Or. 15283 and Or. 15284 feature a large stemmed lotus inside each pavilion; in some it is a half-open lotus, in others fully open. Or. 15284 also depicts stemmed lotuses and three-leaved stalks floating to the left and right above the ornate gables and high upturned roof eaves (at all levels) and incorporates many other floral motifs.

PC MS 2 has a triple-roofed central pavilion, with long finial poles rising from the roof eaves (which each have separate up- and down-turned decorative elements, collectively called *su-lit* in Burmese), and reaching to the level of the topmost roof tier. PC MS 3 has an enormous bird looking down from the roof of one pavilion. The *pyathat* in PC MSS 2 and 3, and Or. 15284 (but only for levels 1–20), although topped with finials, appear in the form of an elongated front gable, shaped like a high, steep mountain with curved sides, rather than as clearly differentiated levels. In Or. 15284 the side pavilions are sometimes depicted at an angle to the central pavilion, thereby adding depth to the scene; and the roofs are shown with overlapping fish scale shaped tiles, although sometimes other tile shapes occur. The same fish scale tiles are also distinguishable in some of the palm-leaf cosmologies.

From this point on, the sixteen heavenly abodes of the world of form (called in Burmese *yupa bhon ta-hse-chauk-pa*) are depicted with a *Brahmā* deity, seated in bliss, inside each palace.[24] The inhabitants of these worlds are free from sensual desires and have gained rebirth there as the result of great virtue and meditation.

The great variation found in the depiction of the deities (their faces, ornaments, such as crowns and diadems, etc., and style and pattern of costume) and of their heavenly abodes invites a closer comparison with Buddha images and architecture, as well as mural paintings. Many of the gods have large side flanges to their headdresses, and at either shoulder- or waist-level, long upward or sideways pointing winged or flame-like extensions.[25] PC MS 1 has crown flanges and immense shoulder flanges; PC MS 3 has feathery side flanges rising vertically from hip level to the height of the flanged crown; PC MS 4 has elaborate flame-like side flanges to the crown and large flared ends to the sideways projecting waist sash.

Levels 5–9 (Akaniṭṭha, Sudassī, Sudassā, Atappā, and Avihā Heavens)

Levels 5 to 9 are the five upper heavenly domains, known as the pure abodes (Pali, *Suddhāvāsa*). In these are reborn the *anāgāmī* (non-returners), those who will not be reborn again in the world of men or world of *devas*, but only in a *Brahmā* world, having entered the third of the four paths (*magga*) to *nibbāna*. The Suddhāvāsa *Brahmās*

provide the four omens – an old man, a sick man, a corpse and a monk – which led the Bodhisatta (Buddha-to-be) to renounce worldly pleasures and to embark on his search for enlightenment. Life span in level 5 is 16,000 *mahākappa*; in level 6 it is 8,000; in level 7 it is only 4,000; in level 8 it is 2,000; and in level 9 it has reduced to only 1,000.

Each heaven's central pavilion contains a seated *Brahmā*, dressed in full, long-sleeved robes and wearing a tiered headdress. In the left panel of the first heaven appear two splendid pagoda flag staffs (*tagun-daing*) with cylindrical pennants/streamers. In some manuscripts the streamers swirl round the flag staff; in others they appear as straight, geometrical shapes; the *tagun-daing* are sometimes topped with a *haṃsa* bird.[26] Between these is a stupa, named Dussacetiya (Burmese, *Tok-tha ze-di-daw*). This stupa, according to legend, was built by the *Brahmā*, Ghaṭīkāra, to enshrine the garments discarded by Prince Siddhattha when he renounced the world, donned the robes of a monk and embarked on his quest for enlightenment. Or. 14004 depicts the gods of these heavens holding a royal fly whisk. PC MS 3 has on either side of each pavilion a large stand with a fringed white umbrella, almost as high as the pavilion's spire.

Levels 10–11 (Asaññasatta and Vehapphala Heavens)

Levels 10 to 11 are the two upper heavenly *Brahmā* domains, where those gods and men who have attained the fourth *jhāna* are reborn. Their lifespan is 500 *mahākappa*.

The heavens are (usually) depicted as twin, linked pavilions, each with a seated *Brahmā* figure. Or. 3591, unusually, depicts the right hand deity in red/orange robes of a monk, reclining on a low couch (perhaps a literal interpretation of this heaven whose name means 'unconscious'!). Or. 15284 has no flanking pavilions, and the tiered roof eaves have high finial poles (similar to PC MS 2).

Levels 12–20 (Subhakiṇṇā, Appamāṇasubhā, Parittasubhā, Ābhassarā, Appamāṇabhā, Parittābhā, Mahābrahmā, Brahmaparohita, and Brahmapārisajja Heavens)

Levels 12 to 20 are the nine upper heavenly domains, grouped into threes; in these are born those who have attained the third, the second and the first *jhāna*. Life spans decrease by halves from 64 *mahākappa* in level 12 to 2 in level 17, and then from 1 *asaṅkheyya-kappa* in level 18, to one half in level 19, to one third in level 20.[27]

Each group of three is depicted on two palm leaves, as triple, linked pavilions, each with a seated *Brahmā* figure. Some manuscripts show the deities with the central figure facing forwards, and the outer ones facing towards the central god.

Next come eleven levels of the sensual realm (levels 21–31), or world of sense enjoyment (Pali, *kāmarūpa*; Burmese, *kama bhon*) which include six worlds (levels 21–26) or lower heavens of the gods (Pali, *devaloka*) and the human plane (level 27). The sensual realm actually extends right to the bottom-most hell levels.[28] The gods of these lower heavens are superhuman beings, living a life of happiness, exempt from the ills of human existence, but are inferior to the *Brahmā*, being subject to *kāma*. Life in these heavens is much longer than human life and is filled with the bliss of supreme sense enjoyment. The heavens of the *devas* are magnificent. Some Burmese manuscripts depict these heavens most lavishly and in increasing detail for those nearest the human plane, while the deities associated with each heaven take on more varied forms.

Or. 14004 gives the heavens of the sensual realm most lavish treatment. Inside each palace sits a deity in white triple-tiered robes, flanked by a queen on either side, with other deities kneeling before them, all enjoying the performance of a dancer and a harpist. Add. 17699A, Or. 12168 and PC MS 2 have gods with large hands, with long fingers and thumbs. PC MS 3 shows many different patterns on the gods' robes including checks, circles with an inner circle, spangles, and flowers.

Levels 21–22 (Paranimmita-vasavattī and Nimmānarati Heavens)

Paranimmita-vasavattī and Nimmānarati Heavens are each depicted on two palm leaves, with a single deity seated inside. Māra, known in Burmese as Man Nat, who challenged and tempted the Buddha on different occasions, is said in some accounts to reign over Paranimmita-vasavattī.

Level 23 (Tusita Heaven)

Tusita is the heaven in which all future Buddhas (*bodhisatta*) are born before their penultimate human existence. It is the most beautiful of the celestial worlds and its king (chief *deva*) is Santusita. Four hundred years of human life equal one day in Tusita and the term of life for a *deva* born in Tusita is 4,000 years.

In the left hand panel, beside the central palace wherein sits Santusita, is a separate, elaborate open pavilion, captioned in Burmese *Thu-dama zayat* (Pali, Sudhammā). This is a rest house named after Sudhammā, a wife of Magha (name born by the god Sakka in a previous birth) who contributed a seasoned wood pinnacle to Magha's construction of a rest house for travellers. As well as the central palace scene of the deity entertained by a harpist and dancer, Or. 14004 depicts, uniquely, a white-robed deity seated in the gilded rest house surrounded by ten other deities paying reverence.

Level 24 (Yāmā Heaven)

Level 24 shows the seated figure of Suyāma, king of the gods of Yāmā Heaven, within the central palace. Or. 14004 includes the figures of two queens, a dancer and a musician.

Level 25 (Tāvatiṁsa Heaven)

Level 25 is the lowest heaven but one of the *devaloka*, and is always depicted in the most splendid detail. It is situated at the top of Mount Meru and is the abode of the god Sakka (*Thagya-min* in Burmese), the first of the thirty-three gods of this heaven.[29] Sakka is guardian of moral law in the world and plays an important part in Buddhist cosmology, aiding the Bodhisatta in many of his existences. In this heaven are numerous parks, ponds and gardens enclosed by walls, with entrances through splendid gateways. Burmese manuscript scenes of this heaven contain different features relating to mythology and events in the previous lives of the Buddha.[30] The depiction of Tāvatiṁsa Heaven itself usually occupies three or four palm leaves, and is followed in unbroken succession by 10 to 15 leaves (or 2 to 4 folding-book pages) that show the cosmic pillar, Mount Meru, with its guardian figures and the great ocean in which it is submerged.

The central scene is of Sakka's palace, called Vejayanta, an elaborate structure with tiered roofs, surmounted by a soaring *pyathat*.[31] Seated inside is Sakka, flanked by two consorts on either side. The queens' names are (usually) given as Sudhammā, Sujātā, Sujita, and Sunandā (not always captioned in the same order).[32] They have elaborate hairstyles and headdresses, and beautiful costumes, and are usually depicted seated with a forearm bent facing outwards.[33] They are most exquisitely depicted in PC MS 2. Add. 17699A depicts the four queens (named as Sudhammā, Sujātā, Sucittā and Sunandā) in a row with Sakka at the end, all with hands raised in devotion and turned to face a seated enthroned Buddha (on this scene, see below). Each figure is seated in a pillared chamber, of which four are surmounted by particularly elaborate and unusual finials, each of a different shape and decoration, and taking up a whole leaf. PC MS 4 also shows the queens with hands joined in reverence, one is holding flowers between her clasped hands, another a palm fan. Or. 3591, singularly, shows Sakka, but no queens.

All depictions of Tāvatiṁsa Heaven also include, usually in the left panel, a stupa, with adjacent magnificent *tagun-daing* and streamers. This is the Cūlāmaṇicetiya (Burmese, *Sulamani zedi*) where the Buddha's topknot of hair, which he had cut off and thrown skywards before donning the robes of a monk and embarking on his quest for enlightenment, was deposited by Sakka. Another structure depicted (usually beside, above or below the stupa) is a large highly orna-

Figure 8.2 Tāvatiṁsa Heaven. Burmese palm-leaf manuscript, early eighteenth century. British Library, Or. 12168, fol. 3–7. By permission of the British Library.

mented pavilion surmounted by a *pyathat* and captioned *Thu-dama zayat*. This is the Sudhammā-sabhā or hall (built for Sudhammā who was reborn in Tāvatiṁsa Heaven) wherein the gods of this heaven assemble on the eighth day of every month.[34]

The Cūḷāmaṇi stupa varies in form from manuscript to manuscript. In some it is very narrow, with high steep square terraces, and an elongated, ringed and conical spire; in others, it is a bell-shaped stupa.[35] The palm-leaf manuscript depictions differ from the pattern of most Burmese stupas in that the terraced bases are not graduated and receding, but stepped in and out, rather in the manner of some throne pedestals. An exception is PC MS 4 which shows the stupa with seven receding terraces, flanked by *tagun-daing* with two long cylindrical streamers flowing from each.

Burmese manuscripts always depict in Tāvatiṁsa Heaven a tree, the *padesa* tree (Burmese, *padei-tha bin*) which bears exotic fruits and flowers and is said to produce whatever an applicant might desire.[36] Some manuscripts include figures of male and female *nats*. The *padesa* tree supplies their wants and the *nats* are sometimes shown plucking items from it. Or. 14965 (Burmese side) has a particularly elaborate *padesa* tree hung with garments and objects. PC MS 4 has a large *padesa* tree hung with scarves (*pawa*), with a male and female *nat* on either side. Or. 15283 has a *padesa* tree on both the left and the right hand side of this scene, each attended by male and female *nats*.

Also included are one or two high-roofed gateways. One, usually shown in the left panel, is Cittakūṭa, the entrance to Tāvatiṁsa Heaven. Another gateway on the far right is Suvaññacitta gate, a golden gateway leading to the garden named Cittalatā where, on the full moon day of the month of *Kason* (May), all the great spirits of the earth, forests and skies gather.

Another tree is sometimes also depicted. This is the sea coral tree, one of five celestial trees, captioned in Burmese *pin-le kathit-pin*.[37] PC MS 2 depicts both trees, with the unusual, and fanciful, addition of a rat in the coral tree and a parrot landing in the *padesa* tree.

Some manuscripts include Sakka's chariot and charioteer, Mātali, who is sent to fetch distinguished humans to Tāvatiṁsa Heaven, among them King Nimi (the story of whose visit to the heavens and hells is told in the Nimi Jātaka).[38]

Or. 12168 has the finest of all palm-leaf manuscript representations of Tāvatiṁsa Heaven, and incorporates the most elements (Figure 8.2). Birds perch on the tops of the soaring eaves of the roofs and *pyathat* tiers of Sakka's palace. The elongated Cūḷāmaṇi stupa is flanked by a *tagun-daing* topped by a *haṁsa* holding in its beak a

Figure 8.3 Tāvatimsa Heaven. Nineteenth-century Burmese *parabaik*. British Library, Or. 15284, fol. 10. By permission of the British Library.

flowing cylindrical cloth pennant. To the right the Buddha is seated cross-legged with his right hand touching the earth (but, unusually, holding in his left hand a circular fan), flanked by a kneeling figure, hands raised in reverence, and a tree in bloom. The tree, although very similar to the *padesa* tree, is the Pāricchattaka which is associated with this heaven and grows at the foot of the Paṇḍukambala, the stone seat of Sakka.[39] The Buddha in this scene is pictured within a surrounding trefoil background border and seated on a throne with intertwining vegetal scrolls. This scene represents the Buddha's preaching of the Abhidhamma to his mother and assembled deities for three months in this heaven. Below, a smaller Buddha figure in earth-touching posture is seated on a low throne (with upward curving sides) beneath the celestial *mandārava* (*pin-le kathit-pin*) tree. Below this is Sakka's chariot (with solid wheels and protruding axles, and drawn by two horses) bearing King Nimi, seated under a tiered (white) umbrella, an insignia of royalty. PC MS 3 includes a large kneeling figure of the Buddha's mother in the scene of the Buddha preaching the Abhidhamma.

Or. 12168 has unusual additional scenes on either side of Mount Meru, before level 26 is depicted. These show in the left-hand panel a second scene of Mātali in a horse-drawn chariot bearing King Nimi, with Mātali pointing towards a pavilion in which is seated a *devadhūtā* (female goddess) named Bīraṇi.[40] In the right hand panel is another pavilion in which is seated a *devaputta* (god) named Soṇadinna.[41]

Or. 14004 depicts Sakka's queens with hands joined in reverential homage, while before them perform musicians and dancers. The central palace is depicted within crenel-

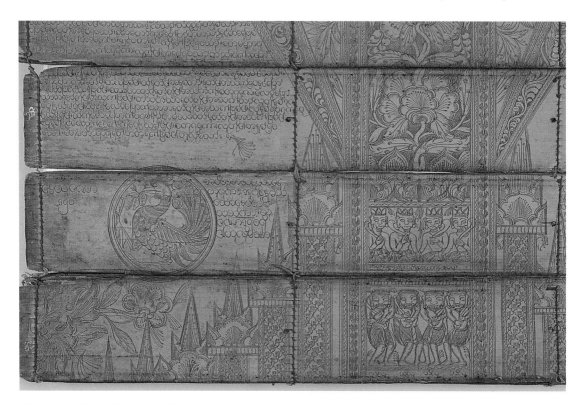

Figure 8.4 Mount Meru (detail of upper axis and solar orb). Burmese palm-leaf manuscript, late eighteenth century. British Library, Or. 15283, fol. 28–30. By permission of the British Library.

lated palace walls and city gateways are topped with a seven-tier *pyathat*. The identification of the Burmese king in the throne room of Mandalay palace with Sakka in his heaven is explicit in this (and other) scenes. Or. 14004 also includes other elements associated with this heaven: the Cūḷāmaṇi stupa, Sakka's stone seat at the foot of the celestial tree and the Sudhammā hall. Or 15283 has a fine representation of Sakka's palace, with male and female *nat* figures beside the *padesa* tree in the left panel and the Cittakūṭa gate; in the right panel appears another *padesa* tree with *nats* and another gateway called Sugandacitta. Or. 15284 shows Sakka's palace (with five-tier *pyathat*) set inside crenellated zigzag brick walls; other features (including a *padesa* tree and female *nat* and a celestial tree) are depicted outside the walls (Figure 8.3).

Beneath Tāvatiṃsa Heaven descends the cosmic pillar which extends vertically through ten or more manuscript leaves and plunges into an immense ocean. Mount Meru forms the centre of the world and is stated to rise 84,000 *yojana* above the sea and to descend by the same depth into it. On either side of the central cosmic pillar are seven narrow pillars of graduated heights, sometimes topped with *tazaung* and *pyathat*, which are the seven mountain ranges that surround Mount Meru. These are named Yugandhara, Īsadhara, Karavīka, Sudassana, Nemindhara, Vinataka, and Assakaṇṇa. Some manuscripts also include a border on either side at the extreme edge of the manuscript leaf or page to indicate the outermost iron mountain wall that encompasses the universe (Cakkavāḷa) and within whose limits the sun and moon and celestial orbs move round the central axis. In palm leaf manuscripts the cosmic pillar is incised with a wealth of cross-hatching, geometric and floral patterns. Or. 15283 in particular has superb floral and geometric motifs (Figure 8.4). Or. 14004 depicts the cosmic axis in three colours (red, green and gold), representing three of the four sides of Mount Meru which reflect onto and give colour to the four islands that face them.

Level 26 (Cātummahārājika Heaven)

Cātummahārājika, the lowest of the *deva* worlds, is usually depicted about a third of the way down the cosmic axis (although texts state that it is halfway down). This is the heaven of the four regent kings who guard the four quarters, namely: Dhataraṭṭha of the East, Virūḷaka of the South, Virūpakkha of the West and Vessaraṇa of the North. They report to the assembly of gods in Tāvatiṃsa Heaven on how much righteousness and virtue has (or has not) been cultivated in the world of men.

This heaven is depicted on or within the cosmic pillar, and usually only one of the four kings is portrayed, seated as in the other heavens, beneath tiered palace roofs and *pyathat*. Or. 12168 includes all four kings, standing. Or. 14965 (reverse, Shan, side) has one regent king, with a queen kneeling on either side. PC MS 4 depicts all four

Figure 8.5 Mount Meru, its guardians and encircling giant fish. Burmese court *parabaik*, late nineteenth century. British Library, Or. 14004, fol. 22–23. By permission of the British Library.

regent kings. Or. 14004 is the only manuscript that shows this heaven outside the cosmic pillar, immediately below and to the left of its summit, floating beneath the pavilion of the sun (which houses a green peacock). A single regent king, with a queen either side, is depicted. Or. 14004 does not depict the guardian figures in tiers, but disposed on rocky crags and ledges at the base of the pillar which is encircled by an immense, characterful giant fish (Figure 8.5).

Most manuscripts include, on either side of the central Mount Meru pillar, a large roundel with a peacock in one and a rabbit (or hare) in the other, representing the sun and the moon which are believed to revolve around the earth at the level of Yugandhara mountain.[42] Usually the peacock is in the left panel and the rabbit in the right. Sometimes small circles labelled 'gyo' (Burmese, meaning celestial orbs) are placed near the sun and moon symbols to indicate the other planetary orbs.[43] The sun is stated to be fifty *yojana* and the moon forty-nine *yojana* in diameter. Or. 12168 has, perched on top of the sun and moon roundels, an unusual variation: a small pavilion with only the top half of a figure inside and the caption: 'sun [or moon] mansion'.[44]

Inserted on the cosmic pillar in separate tiers are its guardian figures who form part of the retinue of the four regent kings, arranged (and listed by their Burmese name) in the order of *bilu* (ogres), *kon-bhan* (monsters/demons), *galon* (mythical birds) and *naga* (dragon-headed serpents).[45] Usually the ogres and the monsters are holding clubs or short double-edged swords, and sometimes the *galon* hold a circular snare, or noose.[46] Some manuscripts have a single figure of each, but mostly four of each are shown (to indicate the four cardinal directions guarded), with the *naga* often intricately intertwined, or standing on their tails in pairs, facing each other. PC MS 1 has two each of the four guardian figures; PC MS 4 has four. PC MS 2 has a single figure of each, and all, except the *naga*, are brandishing weapons. Or. 14550 has an additional upper tier of four *gan-daba*, followed by four each of the other guardian retinues.[47] Or. 3591 also has a fifth upper tier of *gan-daba*, with a single figure of each guardian.

The great ocean into which Mount Meru descends is full of giant fish and other sea creatures (which can include elephant-headed fish or sea elephants, crabs, squid, eels, jellyfish, and turtles). The names and life spans of the giant fish are often given.[48] Dominating this scene is a giant fish who is conventionally shown encircling the cosmic pillar with his body and biting his own tail. He is called Ānanda, the king of the ocean fish, and the story of his greedily mistaking his own tail for another fish and biting it is told in the Mahā-Sutasoma Jātaka.[49] The Burmese have transposed this story into their cosmology as an overlay to ancient Indian cosmogonic myths. In some manuscripts this fish is more elongated and serpent-like and indeed must relate to the *naga* of Indian (and Khmer) tradition that, wrapped around Mount Meru, churns the ocean; those manuscripts which have an encircling serpent often include and name Ānanda among the fish swimming in the ocean. Add. 17699A shows the giant fish biting his tail, but not encircling the axis. PC MS 2 has a wonderful array of sea creatures, but, singularly, no encircling giant fish. Or. 15284 includes in the sea a scaly crocodile/lizard-like creature, with a crest along its head, back and long tail.[50]

Level 27 (Manussa Realm)

Level 27 is discussed below as it is principally depicted on the reverse side of the palm-leaf cosmologies.

Level 28 (Asura Realm)

The Asura level is shown next and is stated to be situated 'a hair's breadth from Mount Meru'. These words and the accompanying depiction of Asura (a palace with a seated king and a queen either side) are usually upside-down, a device used in the manuscripts to mark the beginning of the four realms of punishment and, perhaps, also to accord with the belief that the Asura once dwelt with the gods in Tāvatiṁsa Heaven, but were cast out to live at the very base of Mount Meru.[51] It was, according to some accounts, to prevent the Asura returning to Tāvatiṁsa Heaven, that Sakka charged the Four Great Kings and their respective retinues with guarding Mount Meru.

The palace is that of the Asura king or chief, Asurinda and is sometimes captioned in Burmese *athu-yein myauk*.[52] Also labelled are two great lakes (Pali, Mahāsara) as being to the east and the west. Or. 14004 has a sumptuously gilded palace in which is seated the Asura king, a queen on either side, palace ladies and gods all paying reverence. In front of the king are arranged a gilded *haṁsa*-shaped betel box and four other gilded containers. Or. 14004, Or. 15283, Or. 15284 and PC MS 4 do not invert the Asura scene. Or. 15284 has, on the right-hand side, a side pavilion from which peep the heads of a man and a woman; beside is an enormous and beautiful tree, labelled *thahkut pin*.[53] This tree is also depicted in PC MS 4 which states that it grows in Asura country and is 100 *yojana* high. PC MS 3 has the most unusual of the Asura scenes (Figure 8.6). The Asura king and a single queen are shown upside down, enclosed in an oval banded frame. On the right-hand side and the right way up is an uncrowned female figure, captioned *Athura-ke* seated in a three-tiered roof pavilion;[54] to the right is a bare-breasted female figure, with a dog biting her shoulder. We are told that this is a punishment for deceiving her husband.

Most manuscripts have (either just above or just below the Asura palace and its ruler) three circles, with the word *sela* (Pali, stone/rocky/crystal mountain) written three times, sometimes within each circle. The circles represent the three rocks (some sources say ruby carbuncles) that support the base of Mount Meru and also serve as an introductory link into the world of men (level 27) that is presented later, on the reverse side of the manuscripts. In PC MS 2 the circles occupy a whole palm leaf. Or. 14965 (reverse side) has, instead of circles, three humps at the base of the cosmic pillar, immediately beneath the encircling tail of the giant fish, followed by the inverted scene of the Asura palace.

To the right of the Asura scene appear the first hell scenes (except in Or. 14004, which depicts the hells on its reverse side only). These are the right way up in contrast to the upside-down Asura scene on the same leaf. They present a summary of the eight hells, leaving a full depiction of level 31 (Niraya) to a later sequence. In palm-leaf manuscripts, the hells are shown only in the right-hand panel of a single leaf as a large circle, representing the hell cauldron or pot (Burmese, *ngaye-o*). The circle is shown crammed full of faces, except in PC

MS 4 which shows within the cauldron four standing figures, one balanced upside-down on the head of another, flanked by an upright and an inverted figure.

These brief hell scenes end the first side of the cosmology manuscripts. Or. 14004 follows (as already stated) a different sequence, depicting after the Asura scenes of the four island continents, the Buddha and the radiating spokes scenes (which in most other manuscripts appear on the reverse side). Both scenes are far less detailed than in other manuscripts, and are painted in subdued colours, in striking contrast to the vividly coloured and gilded scenes in the rest of this manuscript.[55]

REVERSE SIDE OF MANUSCRIPTS

At this point occur scenes that merge the world of mythical geography with the known terrestial world. The first scene, which is common to all the cosmology manuscripts, is preceded by a text describing Himavanta or Himavā (equated with the Himālaya), a land of fabulous creatures, mountain peaks and great lakes.

This scene depicts the origins of the world's great rivers which flow from an immense lake in Himavanta out of four rocky outlets shaped like animal heads (an elephant, a horse, an ox and a lion/*chin-thei*) (Figure 8.7).[56] This lake (named *Nawa-dat-aing* in Burmese, but in Pali sources, Anotatta) is surrounded by five great mountain ranges. In palm-leaf manuscripts this scene

can extend across several leaves; in folding-books it occupies only one opening. Some include more detail, both visual and textual, than others. A combination of aerial and linear perspectives is used.

Topmost (left panel) is the mountain range called Gandhamādana and its three caves (depicted as doorways with *pyathat* and labelled in Burmese as gold, silver and ruby caves).[57] The caves are the dwelling place of Pacceka Buddhas.[58] In the top right-hand panel is the range called Kelāsa which is stated to be silver in colour. Between these is seated the Buddha, in earth-touching posture, and, to the right, kneeling devotee gods, clasping flowers. It is stated that the Buddha, after receiving alms in Uttarakuru, would go to Anotatta lake to bathe, and would take his meal on its banks.[59]

The style of the Buddha and the throne on which he is seated and the number of devotees varies from manuscript to manuscript. PC MS 1 shows the Buddha seated on a high, waisted throne. PC MS 2 depicts the Buddha with his almsbowl placed on a stand to his right, and the devotees wear patterned robes and carry large offerings of flowers. Or. 14004 shows the Buddha holding his almsbowl in his lap, with one hand dipping into it. PC MS 4, has to the left of the Buddha, large birds holding in their beaks lotus flowers; one bird is captioned 'parrot king' (although all the birds look more like partridges) and near them are shown two monkeys, one eating fruit; one

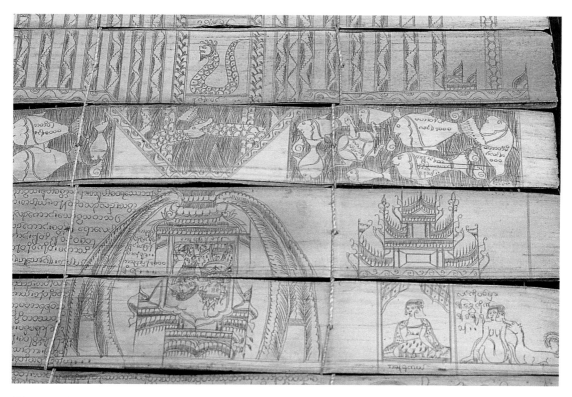

Figure 8.6 Asura realm and base of Mount Meru (detail). Burmese palm-leaf manuscript, late seventeenth/early eighteenth century. Private collection (PC MS 3). Photograph by the author.

Figure 8.7 Origins of the four great rivers. Burmese palm-leaf manuscript, late eighteenth century. British Library, Or. 15283, fol. 9a–12a. By permission of the British Library.

is captioned 'monkey king' and both (unreverentially) have their backs to the Buddha who is depicted with one hand in his almsbowl, while to one side kneel three gods in spangled and multi-patterned robes, holding offerings of large lotus sprays. PC MS 3 includes in this scene on either side of the Buddha a monkey bearing a wild honeycomb and a caparisoned elephant holding a vase in its trunk, while to the right of the elephant the god Sakka is shown holding between clasped hands a small pennant which the caption states is made from scented wood.[60] Or. 15283 (Figure 8.7) also includes a parrot, a monkey and an elephant and depicts the Buddha touching the earth with his left hand; the right holds an almsbowl.[61]

In the left panel below the caves is a Mañjūsaka tree (a celestial tree, 100 *yojana* high, that grows at the entrance to the ruby cave and bears all the flowers that grow on land and in water, on earth and in heaven).[62] It is depicted naturalistically and upright in folding-book scenes and in some palm-leaf manuscripts, but in others it is stylised and projecting sideways from a mountain range. Below (left panel) is the Kālakūṭa mountain range. Opposite in the right panel is the Sudassana mountain range that is stated to be gold in colour and is the first range surrounding the lake. The fifth mountain range, Cittakūṭa, is depicted centrally below the lake.

The great Anotatta lake itself occupies most of the central portion of this scene and is circular in shape with three surrounding concentric rings (in accordance with the text that states that the rivers flow initially three times round the lake) interspersed with more solid rings (representing the mountains?), from the outermost of which swirl wavy crests, filled (usually) with overlapping scale patterns, and seemingly representing both the mountain peaks and the rivers' outlets.[63] PC MS 1 manuscript does not show the river outlets as animal-headed spouts, but instead on a following leaf each of the animals, a horse, a *chin-thei* (mythical griffin-lion), an elephant and an ox, are depicted amidst foliage. PC MS 2 has similar crest-shaped wavy peaks, but the names of the mountain ranges are written in a band cutting through the crests. In PC MS 3 the disposition of the mountains is different and their names are written in triangular frames. Or. 15284 has, dispersed among the mountain swirls, large decorative circles with a fish inside an inner circle (which represent the other great lakes of Himavanta, each lake associated with a particular mountain) and also includes figures of elephants, a horse, an ox and *chin-thei*.[64] PC MS 4 has two decorative leaves incised with spirited figures of an ox, horse, elephant and *chin-thei* amidst foliage.

One river, shown flowing to the right, emerges from a channel, dashes against a rock named Tiyaggala, spurts high in the air and falls back to earth and runs underground to a horizontal rock, named Vijja, from which it re-emerges and divides into five rivers that flow through Buddhist lands.[65] PC MS 4 shows this river with fish swimming along it.

The disposition of the mountains, lakes, and animal-headed water outlets differs from manuscript to manuscript. Or. 14004 depicts the outer mountain range of Sudassana at the very top of the page, in diminishing perspective, and the three rocky caves of Gandhamādana are depicted naturalistically. Four *chin-thei* appear on the slopes of Cittakūṭa mountain range.[66]

Or. 14004 next includes several magnificent and colourful scenes that are not found so extensively depicted in other Burmese cosmologies. Two openings are devoted to the main forest, lake and elephants – all three bearing the name Chaddanta – of Himavanta as well as its other lakes frequented by maned lions (not depicted as *chin-thei*), tigers, monkeys, deer, one-horned rhinos, herons, *karavika* and *kinnara* who are shown frolicking and picking lotuses.[67] The brightly-coloured (red, blue, green, white or gold) elephants, accompanied by baby elephants, are particularly skilfully depicted – some bathing in the lakes, others plucking branches from trees. In Himavanta grow, according to the accompanying text, groves of bananas, mangoes, jackfruits and betel trees whose fruits are immensely rich and satisfying. The trees and their fruits and other plants, such as red bamboo, are botanically identifiable in this manuscript.[68]

Or. 14004 follows this scene with a unique one of level 27, captioned *manok-tha bhon* (the world or abode of men), which depicts this world solely in terms of a Mandalay palace scene of the king receiving homage from his chief queen, four chief ministers, and courtiers. On either side of the king are two furled gold umbrellas and two white umbrellas, with other royal regalia set out before him.

In all the other manuscripts, it is to be understood that level 27, the abode of man, includes the whole universe (its metaphysical and terrestial geography) as encompassed and depicted in the scenes of Mount Meru and the giant ocean, the Himavanta, the origins of the four great rivers, and the four great islands, each one of a different shape, colour and type of inhabitant. Of these, ours is the southern continent, Jambudīpa, and it is only here that Buddhas are born to teach the law of deliverance from the cycle of rebirth.

Or. 14004's royal palace scene (level 27), is followed by another opening that is captioned *tareit-hsan bhon* (the abode of animals; that is, level 30) and depicts disproportionately-sized tigers, monkeys, water buffalo, cattle, deer, rabbits and junglefowl amidst forests and mountains, and with pairs of crested, red birds perching in trees.

In the palm-leaf cosmologies, the Himavanta scenes are reduced, if they appear at all, to depicting some animals (PC MS 3 has an elephant and a deer at the bottom of the preceding origins of rivers scene) and, on

a single leaf, six circles each with a large fish inside, representing six of the seven great lakes (Mahāsarā) of Himavanta (the seventh lake, Anotatta, having already been depicted in the centre of the preceding scene of the origins of the four great rivers).

PC MS 1 includes one leaf entirely decorated with plants, immediately preceding a scene which, as in all the palm leaf cosmologies, is most striking and skilfully executed, requiring the matching of a huge circular representation of the Cakkavāḷa and the four island continents across six to eight leaves. It combines an aerial perspective and cross-sectional plan of the islands with linear representations of fish and other creatures in the sea.[69]

In the very centre is Mount Meru, represented as a small circle, surrounded by seven concentric rings of mountain ranges and seas. Beyond in the great ocean plane of the universe in each of the four cardinal directions are set the four island continents. The abode of man is the southern continent, called Jambudīpa; the western continent is Aparagoyāna, the northern, Uttarakuru and the eastern, Pubbavideha. Each continent is a different shape (southern: wedge or lozenge shaped; western: square; northern: circular; and eastern: three-quarter moon, or half-moon or semi-circular) and each is surrounded by three to seven small tributary islands of matching shape. A sacred tree that is associated with, and gives its name to, each island is depicted therein; for example, the rose-apple tree (Burmese, *zabu-thabye*) is associated with Jambudīpa.[70] Associated with the northern island is the *padesa* tree, with the western one is the *htein* tree, and with the eastern island, the *kot-ko* tree.[71] Usually, the eastern continent is situated at the top (of the page) with Jambudīpa on the right.[72] The Buddha appears seated, in earth-touching posture, within the southern island shape (Figure 8.8). The sun and moon are also depicted (in symbolic form of a peacock and a hare within a circle) in the great ocean which (in some manuscripts) is bursting with wonderful sea creatures. The sea itself in the palm-leaf manuscripts is not shown as wavy lines, but as straight or cross-hatched lines. Or. 15283 and PC MS 4 place the southern island at the top; Or. 15284 has the northern island at the top. PC MS 1 does not include a Buddha figure within the southern island shape. PC MS 4 is the only manuscript to depict, outside the outer circular wall of the universe, an array of dancing figures. At the top are *galon*, *kinnari* and *kinnara*, *chin-thei* and birds with flowers in their beaks; below are more birds, including the *karavika*, and *manok-thiha* figures.[73] Or. 14965 has, on the Shan reverse side, a unique scene of golden fruits falling from the rose-apple tree into water where giant fish swallow them.[74]

This horizontal, more cosmographic, depiction of the four islands concludes what could be classified as the human plane (Manussa). Burmese cosmological manu-

Figure 8.8 The Buddha on Jambudīpa, the southern continent (detail). Burmese palm-leaf manuscript, late eighteenth century. Private collection (PC MS 2). Photograph by the author.

scripts do not include a separate representation of level 29 (Peta), the world of departed spirits, nor of the animal realm (with the exception of Or. 14004), although the text always cites these as belonging to the four realms of punishment.[75]

Level 31 (Niraya Hells)

In depictions of level 31 the hells occupy most of the reverse of all the double-sided palm-leaf manuscripts. They are depicted in more detail than in the short hells sequence that appears immediately after the Asura level on the front side of the manuscripts. The names of the principal hells as successively depicted are:

1　Sañjīva. Beings born in this hell (its name means 'alive') survive numerous tortures.
2　Kāḷasutta. Beings born here are placed on a heated iron floor, marked with red hot black thread and cut into pieces along the markings.
3　Saṅghāta. Here huge rocks of heated iron crush the victims.
4　Roruva, the screaming hell. Beings born here have cast aspersions on the *dhamma*, been miserly, or committed adultery. They are tormented by flames.
5　Mahāroruva (or, in some manuscripts, Jālaroruva), great screaming hell.
6　Tapana, the hell of burning fire.[76] Beings born here are pierced and transfixed by heated stakes.
7　Mahātapana, the great, excessively hot hell of fire.
8　Avīci. The lowest hell of suffering without respite wherein suffer those who have committed the gravest crimes. Devadatta, who plotted to kill the Buddha, is tormented there.

The length of time that beings born into each hell live doubles from one hell to another for the first seven levels of hells: from 500 hell years in Sañjīva to 16,000 in Mahātapana, while the length of time beings spend in the lowest hell, Avīci, is an incalculable number of *kappa*.[77]

Each principal hell has four sides with gates, and each has four sub-hells which in turn are surrounded by smaller hells. The sub-hells are called Ussada-nirayā (protruding hells). The principal hells together with the sub-hells number 136. Surrounding the hells is the domain of the Yama king (Burmese, *Yama min*) who pronounces judgement on how much merit and demerit beings have accumulated and assigns each to the appropriate heaven or hell, having received from the *devatā* a record, on dog skin, of the individual's deeds. There are guardians, known as *yama*, who stay in the auxiliary hells. There is another series of terrible cold and dark hells, called Lokantaranirayā, which are each bounded by three *cakkavāḷa*, and are 8,000 *yojana* in extent. Here are reborn those who have harmed parents, monks and teachers.

Palm-leaf manuscripts show the second sequence of hells in a series of scenes, each occupying three palm leaves, illustrating the torments of the inferior (sub) hells. To the left and right are the pavilions and servants of the guardian kings of the hells; each pavilion and king is named. The servants are sometimes shown as a dog-headed figure named Thirikuṭha, but are usually portrayed as fierce and ugly, bare-chested demons, with huge teeth and bulging eyes, and occasionally as buffalo-horned figures. They drag victims before the guardian king or stuff them into a circular hell pot which, labelled with the name of the principal hell, occupies the central portion of the leaf. Below the main pot is a vertical column of small circular pots each labelled with the particular form of torment endured successively in the inferior hells. The order of the listing of these torments changes from scene to scene, and are given as follows: fire (or flaming) water, (molten) iron, hot ashes, silk-cotton tree, hot water, copper, cane net, ordure.[78]

Figure 8.9 Avīci Hell. Burmese court *parabaik*, late nineteenth century. British Library, Or. 14004, fol. 53. By permission of the British Library.

Or. 14004 devotes several spacious pages to the eight major hells, and in some shows (in different permutations) scenes of the eight different torments suffered (Figure 8.9). Figures are shown entangled in cane nets, wading through cotton-wool-like hot ashes, having red molten metal poured down their throats, climbing the spiny silk-cotton tree, struggling in flaming waves, and so on. The hell guardians have dark skin and they, and their victims, have tattooed thighs. In Avīci, the lowest hell, Devadatta appears, transfixed by metal stakes.

There is great variation in the hell scenes with victims speared, chopped up, mangled, sawn, transfixed by stakes, pecked at by giant birds and bitten by huge dogs. Names given for the guardian kings of the hells in the manuscripts vary, but in PC MS 4 are given as Kāla (of Kālasutta Hell), Vemadika (of Rularo), Yamaka (of Jalaro) Yamaha (of Tapana), Yamato (of Mahātapana) and Yamala (unspecified hell). Other names of guardian kings appearing in manuscripts are Somavanna, Vassavanna and Vemavadhaka. Or. 12168 shows the hell guardian seated in a pavilion with his consort.[79] PC MS 4 also depicts the hell lord accompanied by a fierce consort who, like him, sometimes holds a sword. In the Mahātapana hell scene, beneath the large central hell cauldron, a huge thorny

tree (the *let-pan*, silk-cotton tree) is depicted with nude figures suspended from its branches, being pecked at by giant birds or bitten by dogs. To the right are beings who, like those condemned to climb the tree, have deceived their spouses and are shown being ground in a mangle while huge birds pull at their long topknots of hair. In another scene, over which Yamahla presides, those who are said to have killed pigs and cattle and sold the meat are shown being attacked by demons with swords and pickaxes; below is a large irregularly shaped hell cauldron crammed with faces and mounted on three wheels. Tears trickle from the eyes of the sufferers in the hell pots of PC MS 2. PC MS 4 instead of showing the eight kinds of torment as a vertical set of eight circles, arrays them in vertical and zigzag columns. Or. 14965 (Shan sequence) has delicately shaded scenes of the hells, and includes the device found in palm-leaf scenes of vertical columns of eight circles to indicate the eight kinds of torments (Figure 8.10). Or. 15824 is the only manuscript to depict the hells as four-sided, with the sub-hells projecting from them on each side – a representation which comes closest to textual descriptions.

Anyone viewing these terrible scenes must be reinforced in their resolution to lead a meritorious life and

Figure 8.10 Tapana Hell. Shan paper folding-book, eighteenth/nineteenth century. British Library, Or. 14965, fol. 33. By permission of the British Library.

to achieve a better rebirth. The aspirational message of the manuscripts parallels that of temple murals where the hells are depicted at the lowest levels, followed by the abode of men, of the *devas*, and the *brahmās*, with the uppermost levels reserved for Jātaka stories and the life of the Buddha.[80]

Lastly at the end of (most of) the cosmology manuscripts comes a diagrammatic picture of the Buddha seated (in earth-touching posture) under the Bodhi tree from which radiate twelve spokes, terminating in panels labelled with place-names and journey times.[81] The orientation of the scene is to the east (indicated at the top). This scene, we are told, represents the sixteen Buddhist countries and their location in relation to the Buddha's place of enlightenment, Bodh Gaya. The manuscripts all explicitly state that this picture is included so that those who are lacking in knowledge may know where the Buddhist lands, near and far, lie. The places/cities named (with journey times) as given in Or. 14004 are (reading from the east at the top, clockwise): Mithilā (one month), Saṅkassa (five days) and Jetuttara (one month), Takkasilā (one month), Sāvatthi (eight months), Kosambi (five months) and Kāliṅga (2 months), Mudu [?] (one month) and Koliyā (one month), Kapilavatthu (five days), Campā (one month), Bārāṇasī (fifty days), Rājagaha (three days), Vesāli (three days), Pāṭaliputta (eleven days) and Pāvā (one month).[82]

The central figure of the Buddha under the tree of Enlightenment is often shown within a bodhi (pipal tree) leaf shape, while the leaves and branches of the tree are beautifully delineated and intertwined. PC MS 4 includes on either side of the Buddha a (partridge-like) bird, with downward pointing stemmed lotuses held in its beak. Or. 15284 presents the scene quite differently: the Buddha seated on a double-lotus throne, is flanked by two reddish-orange robed disciples (Moggallāna and Sāriputta) seated on lotuses, at the centre of a maze-like diagram (Figure 8.11).

It remains to pose the question of the relationship of Burmese illustrated cosmologies and texts to the celebrated Thai Buddhist cosmology, the *Trai Phum* or *Traibhumikatha* (Three Worlds), compiled from more than thirty Buddhist sources in the form of a royal sermon by Phya Lithai in AD 1345.[83] This work commences with a description of the hells and then proceeds upwards through the realms of animals, ghosts, *asuras*, men, and the gods of the upper heavens, ending with an account of *nibbāna*. This textual sequence is the reverse of that followed in illustrated cosmologies, both Thai and Burmese, which contain only a limited amount of accompanying text that matches the top downwards sequence (heavens to hells) of the illustrations.[84] No complete surviving illustrated recension of the *Trai Phum* predates the eighteenth century, although earlier incomplete manu-

Figure 8.11 Diagram of the sixteen Buddhist lands. Nineteenth-century Burmese *parabaik*. British Library, Or. 15284, fol. 27. By permission of the British Library.

scripts exist.[85] It is known that Thai artists and craftsmen were brought back to Burma following the Burmese conquests of Ayutthaya in 1569 and in 1767, and while it would be easy to assume that the Burmese were influenced by Thai cosmological manuscripts and illustrations, it is not possible to make a definite link.[86] Many of the artistic conventions found in manuscript illustrations (for instance, the representation as vertical pillars of the seven mountains that surround Mount Meru) can be seen in early mural paintings at Pagan (in the twelfth-century Lokahteikpan). A study of textual variations and sources is outside the scope of this chapter, but no Burmese translation of the Thai *Trai Phum* appears to exist, and parallels found in Burmese cosmologies must derive, not from direct borrowing, but from shared elements of Buddhist cosmology as expounded in canonical texts and commentaries. Stylistically, the two remain quite distinctive. Significant differences between illustrated Thai and Burmese cosmologies include the following: in Burmese manuscripts there is no attempt to depict the undepictable state that is *nibbāna*, whereas in some Thai manuscripts it appears as a city and palace; in scenes of Tāvatiṁsa Heaven only the Thai portray Indra's mount, the mighty elephant Eravan; the pavilions that crown the vertical pillars surrounding the cosmic axis in Thai manuscripts are shown with deities inside them; the giant fish, Ānanda, that in Burmese manuscripts encircles the base of Mount Meru features less prominently (if at all) in Thai scenes; the inversion of the Asura realm occurs only in Burmese manuscripts; Thai manuscripts have

extensive scenes of Himavanta; Burmese manuscripts omit the realm of Peta; the circular hell pot columns of Burmese palm-leaf manuscripts do not appear in Thai versions; nor does the Buddhist lands diagram. Above all, the production of palm-leaf illustrated cosmologies appears to be unique to Burma. The merit gained by the artistic achievement of incising these scenes in elaborate and intricate detail onto palm leaves must rest with the unknown Burmese scribes and artists who so skilfully depicted the Buddhist universe in its entirety.

BRIEF DESCRIPTION OF MANUSCRIPTS DESCRIBED IN THIS STUDY (DATINGS PROVISIONAL)

British Library, Oriental and India Office Collections

Add. 17699A. Palm leaf, 50.5 by 6.5 cm, 114 leaves (edges gilded with red lacquer band in centre); wooden cover boards, 50 by 6.2 cm, lacquered red with gold patterns of interlocking roundels and lotuses. Complete sequence (with Buddha lands before main hells sequence). Late-eighteenth century. Acquired 1849.

Or. 3591. Shan paper folding-book, wooden covers with incised designs; 43 by 14 cm, 22 folds. Cosmology scenes (in red, green and yellow palette) on one side, and Burmese cabalistic squares and calculations in red and black on reverse. Damaged condition, pages torn and badly stained. Mid/late nineteenth century. Acquired 1888 from Lt. Col. P.D. Jeffreys (Connaught Rangers, and formerly Brigade Major 3rd Brigade Burma Field Force) who provides the following interesting note: 'This book was found by me in the Laywun hut at Thatwe which is about 20 miles S.E. of Yamethin in Upper Burmah. Thatwe was occupied on the 10th December 1886 by a column of the 3rd Brigade under the command of Brig. Gen. W.S.A. Lockhart. The Burmese Interpreter informed me that the pictorial side represents the progress of a saintly man from the nethermost regions to the acme of all goodness. One man shown upside down is supposed after reaching an exalted position to have led an immoral life from which he was sent down. The tables on the reverse are those from which the Horoscopes are worked out – every Burman always carries a Horoscope.'

Or. 12168. Palm leaf, 50 by 7 cm, 38 folios. Incomplete, with levels 24–31 on first side, and more detailed hells scenes on reverse. Early eighteenth century.

Or. 14004. Paper folding-book, 53 by 20 cm, 59 folds, brightly painted and lavishly gilded court manuscript, Burmese text in black ink; red leather covers with tooled floral patterns and pasted labels, inscribed in English (upper cover): 'The Bliss of the Country of the Nats, Buddhist Religion' and (lower cover): 'The Horrors of Hell acording to the Buddhist Religion'. Late nineteenth century. Acquired Mandalay, 1886.

Or. 14550. Paper folding-book, 39 by 13 cm, 81 folds, with crudely painted colour illustrations (fols 9–32; fol. 34; fols 36–38), brief Burmese text and captions in ink, some corrections and English notes in fainter ink. Inscribed in ink on the cover is: 'To Dr Ryland for the Museum of the Baptist College Bristol presented by John Lawson' and 'Representation of the Burmah Heaven'.[87] Early nineteenth century.

Or. 14965. Paper folding-book, 48.5 by 16.5 cm, 46 folds, with on one side Burmese text in black ink and crude illustrations (predominantly in red and yellow) of the heavens and hells on one side (fols 1–23), and on reverse side (fols 24–46) a much worn but more accomplished depiction of the heavens and hells in a different palette (predominantly red, blue and green), with Shan text in black ink. The illustrations on the first side begin with depictions of the twin pavilions (levels 10–11) and end at the level of the Tapana Hell. The illustrations on the reverse (Shan) side of the manuscript begin with the triple pavilions of levels 12–14 and end with a depiction of the Tapana Hell. Late eighteenth/early nineteenth century (Shan sequence); nineteenth century (Burmese sequence).

Or. 15283. Palm leaf, 53.5 by 6.5 cm, 86 leaves (stitched with four rows of stitching); with cotton-backed yellow silk cloth wrapper, 57 by 73 cm, printed in red and black with floral and leaf motifs and border. Superbly incised with distinctive geometric and floral designs. Late eighteenth century.

Or. 15284. Paper folding-book, 38.5 by 16 cm, 32 folds, Burmese text with unusual illustrations in black ink and red colour; plain black lacquered covers. Northern Burma, early/mid-nineteenth century.

Private collection palm-leaf cosmologies

PC MS 1. Palm leaf, 52.8 by 6.2 cm, 118 leaves threaded with string. The first side covers from highest heaven to short hells sequence (but lacks folios 27–28 [gi-gī] which should depict levels 18–20); the reverse has scenes of Himavanta, the origins of rivers, a cross-section of the four islands, hell scenes, and ends with Buddhist lands. Early eighteenth century.

PC MS 2. Palm leaf, 52.5 by 6 cm, 120 leaves, threaded with string and nylon in the wrong sequence. The first side (if put in correct sequence) covers from the highest heaven to a short hells sequence; the reverse has the origins of rivers, the four islands, and then sets of triple leaves each with one of the eight hells. It ends with a Buddhist lands diagram, beside which appears the cryptic inscription: 'Maung Yin San Ta, novice scribe'. This manuscript is particularly finely incised and has many distinctive embellishments. Late eighteenth century.

PC MS 3. Palm leaf, 49.5 by 5.5 cm, 126 leaves, threaded with string in the wrong sequence; the leaves are damaged at the edges. The first side (if put in the correct

sequence) covers from the highest heaven to a short hells sequence; the reverse depicts the origins of rivers, a cross-section of the four islands, the Buddhist lands, and detailed hells. Late seventeenth/early eighteenth century.

PC MS 4. Palm leaf, 51 by 6 cm, 138 leaves, stitched at the sides and through string holes; very worn and damaged. The first side covers from the highest heaven to a short hells sequence; the reverse depicts the origins of rivers, a cross-section of the four islands, hells, and the Buddhist lands. With cloth wrapper stiffened with split cane, and with (red and white, green edged) woven manuscript ribbon bearing donor's name (Ma Ma Hla of Ywama) and the Burmese Era date 1262 (AD 1900). Late nineteenth century.

NOTES

1 For an analysis of Hindu and Buddhist cosmologies, see Richard Gombrich, 'Ancient Indian Cosmology', Carmen Blacker and Michael Loewe (eds), *Ancient Cosmologies*, London: George Allen & Unwin, 1975, pp. 110–42. See also R. Kloetzli, *Buddhist Cosmology from Single World System to Pure Land: Science and Theology in the Images of Motion and Light*, Delhi: Motilal Banarsidass, 1983, pp. 23–50. For an invaluable account compiled from (unspecified) Burmese sources by an Italian Barnabite missionary resident in Burma from 1783–1808, see Vincentius Sangermano, *The Burmese Empire a Hundred Years Ago*, Bangkok: White Orchid Press, 1995 reprint; 1st published 1833, pp. 2–46. Sangermano's cosmography first appeared in print in Francis Buchanan, 'On the religion and literature of the Burmas', *Asiatick Researches*, vol. 6, 1801, pp. 167–94.

2 For a wide-ranging survey, see H.G. Quaritch Wales, *The Universe Around Them: Cosmology and Cosmic Renewal in Indianized South-east Asia*, London: Arthur Probsthain, 1977.

3 See Adrian Snodgrass, *The Symbolism of the Stupa*, Ithaca, NY: Cornell University Southeast Asia Program, 1985.

4 Mount Meru is the cosmic mountain and axis of the world. In Burmese it is called *Myin-mo*; in Pali, *Sineru* or *Sumeru*.

5 The Po-win-daung caves are illustrated and described in Charles Duroiselle, 'The rock-cut temples of Powun-daung', *Archaeological Survey of India Annual Report*, 1914–15, Calcutta: Superintendent, Government Printing 1920, pp. 42–55. See also, R. R. Langham-Carter, *The Powundaung Caves*, Rangoon: Rangoon Times Press, 1939, pp. 46–50.

6 Built by King Bagyidaw (1819–38) three years before his accession to the throne, in commemoration of the death of his senior wife, the Hsin-byu-me princess.

7 I am grateful to Dr Pamela Gutman for her observation that the representation of cosmological elements found on reliefs at the Maha-Bodhi Shwe-gu and Shit-thaung temples appears to be a development from that described by the Pali *Lokapaññati* text, and merits further research.

8 See, for example, the description and illustrations of late nineteenth-century funeral ceremonies in Max and Bertha Ferrars, *Burma*, London: Sampson Low, Marston, 1900, pp. 193–9. Also, Shwe Yoe (J. G. Scott), *The Burman: His Life and Notions*, London: Macmillan, 1906, pp. 578–89.

9 See Tha Myat, *The Twelve Festivals of Burma*, Rangoon: Student Press, 1973, pp. 20–1.

10 For photos and a report of this ceremony, see *Forward*, vol. 19, no. 1, October 1980, pp. 3–7. Although a state-spon-

sored grand ceremony (the temple was constructed under the patronage of President Ne Win and enshrines sacred gifts from the kingdom of Nepal), its symbolic elements may be found in much smaller scale ceremonies.

11 This is the Pali term; in Burmese, *kan*; Sanskrit, *karma*.

12 Burmese, *zan*. There are different jhanic states and levels which are correlated with the higher heavens or abodes of the thirty-one planes of existence. For an exposition of cosmological concepts and meditational routes to enlightenment, see Winston L. King, *A Thousand Lives Away: Buddhism in Contemporary Burma*, Oxford: Bruno Cassirer, 1964, pp. 85–112; pp. 221–3.

13 Terminology as used by Joseph Schwartzberg in his innovative study 'Cosmography in Southeast Asia', in J. B. Harley and David Woodward (eds), *The History of Cartography*, vol. 2, book 2: *Cartography in the Traditional East and Southeast Asian Societies*, Chicago: University of Chicago Press, 1994, pp. 701–40. Schwartzberg examines cosmographic conceptions, graphic cosmographies and cosmographic artefacts, with illustrations from a remarkable range of Southeast Asian sources (including some of the British Library manuscripts featured in this article, which owes much to Schwartzberg's detailed and unsurpassed survey). The three realms of the Buddhist cosmos are often misconstrued as heaven, earth and hell. They are in fact formlessness, form and sensual desire.

14 This can be translated as 'disposition of the planes/abodes [of existence] parabaik'. Logically, a parallel term for Burmese palm-leaf cosmologies should be *bhon-zin pei-za*, but this term does not appear to be used.

15 Basic details of these manuscripts, which vary greatly in quality and style and are difficult to date with any precision, are given at the end of this chapter. I am greatly indebted to the owner (who prefers to remain anonymous) of the four palm-leaf manuscripts (hereafter referred to as PC MS 1, 2, 3 and 4) for allowing me the opportunity to study and photograph them.

16 The chart reproduced here was compiled by U So Pon in 1875 as part of an abridgement or abstract of King Anawrahta's *Abhidhammatthasaṅgaha* compiled by the Bagaya Hsaya-daw and published under the title *Abhidham matthasaṅkhepanaya saṅgaha akauk-kyan*, Rangoon: Burmah Herald Steam Press, 1883. A similar, much larger chart, was compiled in 1882 by U Kalyana and was printed as a large single sheet (60 x 48 cm) under the title *Hbon zin*, Rangoon: Bengalee Job Printing Press.

17 Usually written Agganiṭha in Burmese manuscripts.

18 This definition is given in G. P. Malalasekera, *Dictionary of Pali Proper Names*, London: Luzac, 1960, vol. 1, p. 51. Ātabba or Ātabbha appear as variants.

19 *Ibid.*, p. 199.

20 This is associated with a physical counterpart, the middle region (Pali, *majjhima-desa)* of India that was the birthplace of Buddhism.

21 A *mahākappa* is the vast cycle of time which elapses from the commencement of the destruction of a a single world system (*cakkavāḷa*) to its complete renewal. A *yojana* (Burmese, *yuzana)* is a unit of measurement, approximately equivalent to 12 miles and often translated as 'leagues'.

22 Some *pyathat* of Mandalay palace (1857) are of seven tiers, but three- and five-tiered spires also exist. *Pyathat* are depicted in wall paintings and reliefs from as early as the Pagan period, while nineteenth-century illustrated manuscripts contain the best examples of palace scenes and architecture. The defining characteristic of the *pyathat* is its square-shaped, graduating tiered structure, topped by a

htupika (Pali, *dupika*) (bulging pinnacle) and *hti* (umbrella shaped finial). *Pyathat* crown not only the throne halls (and some other structures) of royal palaces, but also the shrine room of monasteries, and the *tazaung* (pavilion sheltering sacred objects) of temples and palace and city gateways. For descriptions and illustrations of different architectural forms, see Irene Moilanen and Sergey S. Ozhegov, *Mirrored in Wood: Burmese Art and Architecture*, Bangkok: White Lotus, 1999.

23 Accordingly, I use the term pavilion and palace interchangeably in descriptions of these heavenly levels.

24 Also known as the world of (corporeal) *Brahmās* (Pali, *Brahmaloka*). Depicted in a posture of legs crossed (concealed under robes) and hands resting on the knees (modified *sukhāsana*).

25 As seen in early depictions of the *nats* (Burmese spirit guardians) and royal costume; the projections are the flaring ends of shoulder mantles or scarves and/or waist sashes. The flanges to the crowns are also found on crowned Buddha images.

26 Burmese, *hin-tha*; a mythical goose/duck, particularly associated with Pegu and the old Mon kingdom of Lower Burma.

27 *Asaṅkheyya* is usually rendered as an incalculably vast period of time and is a subdivision of a *mahākappa*.

28 *Devaloka* is also applied as a collective term for the six lower heavens and the twenty higher *brahmaloka* (i.e. levels 1–26) as well as meaning a single heaven in each of these 26 realms. Burmese sources tend to use *nat* interchangeably with *deva*. Hence the six lower heavens are known in Burmese as *nat-pye chauk-pa*, the six *nat* countries.

29 Sakka, the guardian god of Buddhism, was added by King Anawrahta (*r.* 1044–77) to the cult of the spirits (*nat*), making Thagya-min the head of a pantheon of thirty-seven nats. On this and the incorporation of other folk elements into Buddhism, see Htin Aung, *Folk Elements in Burmese Buddhism*, London: Oxford University Press, 1962.

30 Thai depictions include the mighty thirty-three headed elephant, named Erāvaṇa, the mount of Indra (Sakka), but this never features in Burmese cosmological manuscript scenes of Tāvatiṁsa Heaven.

31 Usually depicted as a three-tier roof and a three-tier *pyathat*. The late nineteenth-century court *parabaik*, Or. 14004, has seven tiers.

32 There are different versions of how each became a queen of Sakka (or part of his retinue). For instance, Sujita (but in some accounts, Sujātā) was the daughter of an Asura king who chose Sakka as her husband by putting a garland of flowers round his neck.

33 A posture first appearing in late seventeenth century wall paintings at Sagaing.

34 In 1862 King Mindon, in preparation for the convening of the Fifth Buddhist Council, had thirty-three *Thu-dama zayat* constructed at the foot of Mandalay Hill, together with a more elaborate golden *Thu-dama zayat* and an ordination hall (Burmese, *thein*; Pali, *sima*) at the entrance to the Kyauk-daw-gyi temple. Most were burnt down in 1889, but subsequently rebuilt. They are illustrated in Moilanen and Ozhegov, 1999, pp. 105–7.

35 Neither shape corresponds exactly to the two temples at Pagan, the Shwe-hsan-daw and the Sulamani, which were inspired by Sakka's celestial stupa. The Shwe-hsan-daw, built by King Anawrahta (*r.* 1044–77) to enshrine a sacred hair relic, has five receding steep square terraces and a superstructure, on an octagonal base, of a bell-shaped dome and conical finial. The Sulamani (Cūḷāmaṇi) built by King Narapatisithu (*r.* 1174–1211) is a square two-storey struc-

ture, each storey surmounted by receding terraces. A closer parallel may be found in the elongated conical spires of some Shan (and Thai) stupas.

36 This tree is associated with the northern island continent. It appears in Buddhist ceremonies as an artificial tree laden with religious offerings.

37 The sea coral tree is of the *Erythrina* family; it is sometimes identified with the fabulous tree known in Pali as the *mandārava* (botanical name, *Erythrina fulgens*).

38 Jātaka no. 541. See, E. B. Cowell (ed.), *The Jātaka or Stories of the Buddha's Former Births*, Oxford: Pali Text Society, vol. 6, 1995 [reprint], pp. 51–68. In Burma, Nimi is better known as Nemi.

39 This tree is also sometimes called *pārijāta* (Burmese, *pari-zat*). Botanical name, *Erythrina indica*, the red coral tree.

40 She had been a slave at the time of Kassapa Buddha and was rewarded for her devotion by rebirth in a heavenly mansion in the Cātummahārājika world. Mātali relates Bīraṇi's story to King Nimi on his visit to Tāvatiṃsa Heaven.

41 He had been a householder at the time of Kassapa Buddha and built seven hermitages for holy men; he was reborn, with seven golden mansions, in Tāvatiṃsa Heaven.

42 As well as symbolising the sun and moon, the peacock and the hare represent the ancient solar and lunar lineages to which Burmese monarchs laid claim and thereby sought to associate themselves with the Buddha's Sakya lineage.

43 These are the sun, the moon, Mars, Mercury, Jupiter, Venus, Saturn and Rahu (the eclipse), which together constitute the eight astrological compartments.

44 Mansion is written in older Burmese spelling as *peit-hman* which is equivalent to the Pali, *vimāna*.

45 *Bilu* is sometimes labelled as *yet-hka* or *ya-hkaik* (Pali, *yakkha*), a group that includes spirits and ogres. Monsters and demons are *kumbhaṇḍa* in Pali. *Galon* are known in Pali as *garula* (but are better known by their Sanskrit name, *garuda*). Sometimes they are also called *supaṇṇa*. In Pali, nagas are written *nāga*. They are depicted with a dragon-like head.

46 It is clearly not a discus, an emblem associated with Garuda as the vehicle of Vishnu in Hindu iconography.

47 Pali, *gandhabba* (celestial musicians who inhabit Cātumma-hārājika Heaven and are attendants of Dhataraṭṭha (regent king of the East).

48 Other named fish (as given in Add. 17699A) include Acchahā, Ativā, Mahātimila, and Mahātipiṇa.

49 Jātaka no. 537. See, Cowell, vol. 6, 1995 [reprint], pp. 250–1.

50 Possibly the mythical sea creature that in Burmese is called *magan* (Pali, *makara)*. This creature also occurs in the waters surrounding the four island continents in PC MS 4.

51 This inverted upside-down convention has often been mis-understood as a mis-strung sequence! The four realms of punishment (i.e. levels 28–31) are known in Burmese as *ape lei-bhon* (Pali, *apāya*).

52 Asurinda is really a collective term for an Asura chief; the most well-known Asura chiefs are Rāhu and Vepacitti.

53 Botanical name, *Dolichandrone spathacea* (trumpet flower). It is considered to be another celestial tree.

54 *Athura-ke* in Pali is *asurakāya*, meaning the body or assembly of asuras.

55 Schwartzberg (1994) includes a colour reproduction (plate 35) of the Or. 14004 four islands scene.

56 Each outlet opens in the direction of the four quarters and is named (and pictured) after the animals which abound on its mountainous slopes: Sīhamukha (lion), Hattimukha (elephant), Assamukha (horse) and Usabhamukha (ox/bull).

57 *Shwe gu, ngwei gu* and *nan-da mu-la patta-mya gu.* Mala-lasekera, vol. 2, 1960, pp. 22–3, gives *Nandamūlapabbhāra* as a collective name of the caves, and their separate names as *Suvaṇṇaguhā* (gold cave), *Maṇiguhā* (jewel cave) *and Rajataguhā* (silver cave).

58 A Pacceka Buddha is one who has attained supreme and perfect insight, but has not before dying proclaimed it to the world; sometimes called 'silent Buddhas'.

59 Uttarakuru is the north great island continent of the four continents (Mahādīpā) in the world.

60 The monkey with honeycomb and the elephant occur in Burmese manuscripts depicting the life of the Buddha. They are associated with the tenth year of the Buddha's ministry when he spent some time in Pārileyyaka forest and where they looked after his needs.

61 The presence of parrots, partridges(?), monkeys and ele-phants in some of the manuscript Himavanta scenes proba-bly derives from different Jātaka stories which refer to these creatures visiting this region.

62 Burmese, *myin-zu-thaka.*

63 Thai sources say the mountains are shaped like a crow's beak and some Thai depictions include a crow's head. The wavy crests of Burmese illustrations do not bear much resemblance to this imagery. The overlapping scale patterns are known in Burmese as *magan-gwet* (*makara* circles).

64 The names of the other lakes are Kaññamuṇḍa, Rathakāra, Chaddanta, Kuṇāla, Mandākinī, and Sihappapātaka.

65 Named Sarabhū, Mahī, Acirāvatī, Yamunā and Gaṅgā.

66 The entire Or. 14004 origins of the rivers scene is illustrated in black and white in Schwartzberg, 1994, p. 732 (fig. 17.20).

67 In Burmese, *karavika* are called *karaweik*. It is a crested bird, with down-curving beak and clawed feet, sometimes called an Indian cuckoo, possessed of pleasant tones that is said to sing and dance in delight in the heavens when a Buddha attains enlightenment. *Kinnara* (male) and *kinnari* (female) are winged half-human, half-bird, celestial creatures.

68 The Or. 14004 Himavanta scene is reproduced in colour in W. Zwalf (ed.), *Buddhism: Art and Faith*, London: British Museum Publications, 1985, p. 174.

69 PC MS 4 shows turtles viewed from underneath, swimming upwards to the surface.

70 Pali, *jambu*. Botanical name, *Eugenia jambos*.

71 The botanical name of the *htein* tree is *Nauclea* (or *Mitragyna*) *parviflora*, and for the *kot-ko* tree, *Albizzia lebbek*.

72 Schwartzberg (1994) includes illustrations of the four islands scenes from two British Library manuscripts (Add 17699A [fig. 17.14] and Or. 14004 [fig. 17.20]), but unfor-tunately the former, which does not differentiate the islands by shape, is reproduced upside-down and the latter is reproduced with the southern island at the top instead of turned 90° to the right, causing Schwartzberg to query the orientations.

73 A fabulous creature with a man's torso and a lion's hind-quarters, depicted in a squatting posture on forked haunches.

74 A Burmese folk tale tells of a king's journey to the rose-apple tree at the foot of Mount Meru and of the sound of the fruit dropping into the water and of the gulps of the giant fish. See Gerry Abbott and Khin Thant Han, *The Folk-tales of Burma*, Leiden: Brill, 2000, pp. 342–5.

75 In Burmese *petas* are *pei-ta* or *pyeitta*. Thai manuscripts depict *peta* as wraiths and as famished beings and in other tormented forms. Some illustrations of *peta* can be found in an early nineteenth-century album of Burmese paintings in the British Library (Bur. MS 203) and are reproduced in Richard C. Temple, *The Thirty-seven Nats*, London:

Kiscadale, 1991; fascimile reprint [with appended essay by Patricia Herbert] of original 1906 edition. The cosmological illustrations in this album include both Indian and Western elements, and I have excluded them from consideration here as they do not constitute a discrete cosmological manuscript.

76 Burmese manuscripts consistently spell this and the following hell as Tapanna and Mahātapanna.

77 One day and night in Sañjīva Hell is equal to 9,000,000 years in the human world.

78 The silk-cotton tree is *let-pan bin* in Burmese. Its botanical name is *Bombax insignie*.

79 A scene of Saṅghāta hell from this palm-leaf manuscript is reproduced in black and white in Patricia Herbert, 'Burmese court manuscripts', in Donald Stadtner (ed.), *The Art of Burma*, Mumbai: Marg Publications, 1999, p. 91.

80 See Than Tun, *Royal Orders of Burma*, vol. 1, p. 139 for instructions issued in 1649 prescribing the sequence to be followed in decorating the Rājamaṇicūḷā temple.

81 A black and white reproduction of this scene from Add. 17699A appears in Heinz Bechert and Richard Gombrich (eds), *The World of Buddhism*, London: Thames and Hudson, 1984, p. 155.

82 The spelling of the place-names varies considerably; where two names are given together this indicates that they occur on the same compass direction 'spoke' in two separate boxes. The journey times and compass directions of the places can vary from manuscript to manuscript. Some manuscripts say that the journey time to Sāvatthi is only two months.

83 See the translation and critical edition by Frank E. Reynolds and Mani B. Reynolds, *Three Worlds According to King Ruang: A Thai Buddhist Cosmology*, Berkeley, California: Asian Humanities Press, 1982.

84 Jean Boisselier, *La peinture en Thaïlande*, Paris: Bibliothèque des Arts, 1976, p. 239, fn. 36. He notes that illustrated Thai cosmologies draw on different recensions of the *Trai Phum* and also that other cosmological texts and commentaries exist. As far as I am aware, Boisselier and other scholars do not identify the shorter texts accompanying Thai illustrated cosmologies.

85 These are all in folding-book format and it would seem palm-leaf versions were unknown in Thailand. Schwartzberg (1994, p. 720, footnotes 57 and 58) lists surviving Thai cosmological manuscripts in Thai, German, British and American collections and cites published studies which include reproductions from them.

86 This is not to deny the influence of Thai culture and art forms on Burma, merely to observe that it is not that apparent in cosmological manuscripts. Certainly the subject of Thai and Burmese cross-fertilisation in art deserves further investigation, and should take into consideration Shan and Ahom art.

87 Dr John Ryland was principal of the Bristol Baptist College from 1792 to 1825. John Lawson was a printer and engraver who arrived at William Carey's Serampore mission in 1814, and later moved to Calcutta. The circumstances of his acquisition of the manuscript are not known.

9 'Royal images' in their 'palaces': the place of the statues in the cult of the 37 *nats*

Bénédicte Brac de la Perrière

This chapter is a contribution to the knowledge of one specific kind of Burmese artefact, namely the statues of the *nats*. The purpose is not to analyse the iconography of the *nat* representations but to discuss their place in the cult of the 37 *nats*. This type of artefact has mostly been ignored by specialists of Burmese art, the exception being Sir Richard Carnac Temple with his famous book, recently republished with a helpful essay by Patricia Herbert.[1] The reason for this ignorance may well be linked to the symbolic status of *nat* worship in Burmese culture, or more specifically in the Burmese politico-religious hierarchy. Without going over what I have discussed elsewhere, it is worth noticing here that the *nat* cult is conceived as submissive to Buddhist kingship whose symbolic authority over the *nats* was based on ideas of Buddhist legitimacy.[2] In other words, it means that the *nats* are supposed to be kept potentially benevolent through their worship which is embedded in Buddhist society.

When speaking in this chapter of the cult of the *nats*, I am of course referring to the pantheon known as 'the 37 Lords'. The category 'nat' is highly inclusive in Burmese, encompassing various beings such as Hindu divinities (*deva*) or mere nature spirits. The *nats* belonging to the pantheon of the 37 are neither *devas*, nor nature spirits; they may be described as spirits resulting from the violent death of people, who have subsequently been the focus of an institutionalised cult on a regular basis.

The cult of the 37 *nats* permeates Burmese society, combining practices from all of the following levels – the global, national, regional, village, household and individual. The cult allows different kinds of rituals, among which the main ones are: the ceremonies offered directly to the 37 *nats* or *nat kana*, such as *pwe* (organised for private individuals or families by ritual specialists who are spirit-mediums), *nat kadaw*, and the festivals which honour each *nat* in the sanctuary (the *nat nan* or *nat* 'palace') in which that cult is supposed to have been founded. These are named according to the place where they are located (e.g. the Taungbyon *pwe*).

At both of these types of festival, it is expected that ritual specialists or devotees of the *nat* will be possessed by the *nat*. They believe also that the *nat* are represented by statues, called *pon-daw*, inside the ritual setting, either the *kana* or the *nat nan*. A *kana* is a temporary ceremonial building in which the spirit-medium in charge of the ceremony brings his own collection of statues and these stand for the whole of the pantheon of the 37 *nats*. However, a *nat nan* (*nat* 'palace') is a permanent temple, located in Central Burma in the case of the most important examples, where the image of the enshrined *nat* is considered to be at the very origin of the cult. Eventually images of some members of the *nat's* family also came to be found there.[3]

This chapter actually focuses on these so-called original images which are supposed to be the model for the statues belonging to the spirit-mediums. However, I will first quickly underline the related ritual positions of both kinds of representation.

The representations held by the spirit-mediums need to be ritually linked with their owner through a ceremony known as 'introducing the butterfly-spirit' (*leikpya thwin*); this is an animation ritual.[4] The images are then usually worshipped by the spirit-mediums at home where they are kept in private shrines. Each time though that the spirit-mediums need the images of the *nats* professionally, they are moved to temporary ceremonial pavilions (*kana*) which are built next to the client's house.

By contrast, the representations of the *nats* in the *nat* palaces (*nat nan*) are kept by hereditary temple custodians, called *nan dein*; these shrines are located in the place of origin of each *nat*. The custodians are usually supposed to have been installed by the king and are not thought to be possessed by the *nat*. These statues remain in the same place except during annual festivals, when at the beginning, they are removed for ritual purposes. At this time they are taken for a parade around their domains in the ritual known as the 'royal shower' (*cho-ye-daw-thon*). When they are returned to their palace they are then offered reverential homage both by the local population and by spirit-mediums who have come from all over Burma.

Throughout the year, the 'original' representation of the *nat* is supposed to be the main manifestation in

Burma, and the numerous other statues of the same *nat* are secondary manifestations linked to particular spirit-mediums. During the annual festival, the main image is thought of as a concentration of all the other manifestations of the *nat*. One of the effects of the ritual is to renew its symbolic efficacy. The representations of the *nats* which belong to the spirit-mediums are brought close to the *nat* palace during the festival and are thus 'irradiated' by the 'original' image. In other words, it is possible for there to be as many statues of a *nat* in the hands of the spirit-mediums as there is need for them, while the *nat nan* statues are, by definition, unique.

It is therefore not surprising that nothing is recorded concerning any consecration ritual for the images of the *nat* in their permanent temple, for each one is considered to have appeared at the same time as the *nat* himself, as a part of the process of the making of the *nat*. However, most of the sculptures are known to date only from King Mindon's time (AD 1853–1878). While we have no report of any consecration rituals for these statues, we do, in some cases, have foundation stories telling how the images came to light.

The foundation story connected with the representations of the brother and sister 'Lords of the Great Mountain' is the best known. It tells how the spirits Maung Tinde and his sister caused Thinlidjaung, a legendary king of Pagan, to have a revelatory dream. In the dream they came down the Irrawaddy River from the Pyu kingdom of Tagaung, travelling in the trunk of a champak tree where they had taken refuge. Following the dream, the Burmese king ordered representations of the spirits to be made out of the tree-trunk and put in an appropriate place at Popa, to serve as a decent abode for the spirits.[5] This tale can be understood as the first account of the transformation of mere spirits (*nat sein*) into fully recognised tutelary spirits, or *nat*. Further, the story compares the Pyu king who forced the *nats* to go away, as they were potentially dangerous, with the Burmese king who enshrined them. This story also tells us that the spirits were felt to be fixed in one place through their representation, or in other words, the placing of their images in *nat* palaces is fundamental to the Burmese cult of the *nats*.

Nevertheless, we also have evidence that casts doubt on the historical truth of parts of the story, such as the carving of the statues at Popa, and also the presence of images in a *nat* palace in ancient times.[6] We learn from the *parabaik* written in 1856 by the Kawi Dewa Kyaw Thu, who was in charge of *nat* rituals at the court of King Mindon, that Thinlidjaung had the brother and sister installed in a pillar in his own palace in Pagan, and not at Popa, and also there is no indication of the sculptures being made out of a tree-trunk. We also learn from this source that in 1555 animal sacrifices were forbidden at the annual festival which was celebrated at Popa during the month of Nadaw (December).[7] We further also know that on two separate occasions, in 1785 and in 1812, King Bodawpaya (*r.* 1782–1819) commissioned gold heads of the *nats* which were presented to them.[8] These offerings were kept by the local official at his home and taken out for the annual festival (then celebrated in the month of Nayon [June] and not in Nadaw), in the presence of representatives of the Court. From these contradictory statements, both legendary and historical, the following questions arise: did the sculptures actually exist at the time of King Bodawpaya and in what kind of setting? If they did exist at this time, what was the ritual position of representations when celebrations were organised around sacrifices? What has become of the statues supposed to be at Popa before King Bodawpaya presented the golden heads?

This is complicated by Temple's reports that the golden heads presented by King Bodawpaya were taken to the Pagan Treasury during the First Anglo-Burmese War, and that the festival then disappeared.[9] However, despite this, Kawi Dewa Kyaw Thu describes the festival ceremonies as they were celebrated at Popa during his time (the middle of the nineteenth century).[10] Clearly the celebration had not completely disappeared, but was held during Tabaung (March), rather than in Nayon or Nadaw. Indeed, representations were actually taken to Popa from the royal palace where they were usually kept and where they had previously been animated by the ritual of *leikpya theik*, a synonym for *leikpya thwin*. Were these representations brought to Popa to replace the golden heads presented by King Bodawpaya and how was *leikpya theik* celebrated in the royal palace? Was it, perhaps, comparable to the rituals celebrated today to consecrate the statues of the spirit-mediums? Festival organisation observed today differs from the ritual organisation of earlier periods in that there is no *leikpya theik* for the *nat* palace statues, though they are taken out for a 'royal shower' at the beginning of the ceremony to make their presence effective.

Today there is a *nat* festival celebrated at Popa during the Nadaw month, though the central figure that the spirit-mediums come to honour is not the pair, the 'Lords of the Great Mountain', but the 'Lady of Popa' (Popa *Medaw*) (Figure 9.1). The temple of the Lady, as well as her festival, were founded by the same monk who developed Popa as a famous religious and tourist complex during the Ne Win era (1962–88). The brother and sister 'Lords of the Great Mountain' have their own palaces located on the way out of Popa town and these are only slightly older. The main representations were carved by U Mya in the 1950s and donated by Prime Minister U Nu. There is a single pedestal in the sanctuary of the sister 'Lord of the Great Mountain', which is said to be part of the legendary trunk of the champak tree. Also during Nadaw month and 'according to tradition', the brother and sister are celebrated by the local population only, just before the Lady's festival.[11]

Figure 9.1 The Lords of the Great Mountain in the sister's temple at Popa. The two images of the sister are standing behind the brother; the smaller images in the front are those of other members of the *nat* family, Ma Hnemi and Ma Dwe Phyu (December 1995). Photograph by the author.

It is difficult to determine whether there were statues of the 'Lords of the Great Mountain' kept at Popa in some kind of sanctuary or custodian house before the presentation of the golden heads by Bodawpaya.[12] The lacunary and contradictory account of the history of the Popa *nat* festival shows, at the very least, that major changes have affected the role of statues in the ritual celebrations.

One of the main differences today seems to be the loss of the annual ceremony of animating the images (*leikpya theik*), when they were brought from the royal palace for the celebrations, and the settlement of permanent representations in the local ritual setting. Today, as already mentioned, the representations of the *nats* in the *nat* palaces are not animated. This is not necessary from a cognitive point of view, because the stories told about the first appearance of the statues make it explicit that they were already inhabited by the *nat*. For instance, in the case of the 'Lords of the Great Mountain', at their death, the brother and sister had taken refuge in the trunk of the champak tree that was thrown into the river on the order of the king of Tagaung. Thus they were already present in the very trunk which was later carved. In a way, the foundation story of these *nat* images stands for an animation ritual.

The same story of the 'Lords of the Great Mountain' is told in the small town of Sameikkon (Figure 9.2). Here the spirit-mediums come in Tabaung to honour the *nat* Ma Hnemi. At the place where the festival is celebrated there stand two separate buildings, dating from King Mindon's time. In the main one are located statues of the brother and sister 'Lords of the Great Mountain'. Ma Hnemi cannot be represented without them as she belongs to their *nat* family. Both of these palaces and the statues appear older and of a different style to those seen elsewhere in Central Burma. At this shrine, it is said that *three* tree trunks were thrown into the Irrawaddy at Tagaung, one of which landed at Sameikkon and it is from this that the statues were carved. Significantly, this version of the legend allows for ritual segmentation and explains why the 'Lords of the Great Mountain' are present here even though they are supposed to be already in Popa.

This motif of a trunk inhabited by spirits floating down the river is also present in a number of *nat* foundation stories. All of these concern *nats* whose festivals have recently emerged in the Mandalay area. One such example is the 'Golden Teak' brother and sister who have been celebrated at Mingun since the Second World War. They are spirits of Shans who took refuge in the trunk of

Figure 9.2 The 'Lords of the Great Mountain' in Ma Hnemi temple at Sameikkon; the sister stands on the left side of her brother. The statues have been recently gilded (March 2000). Photograph by the author.

Figure 9.3 Hlegyi, the 'Great Father' (December 1995). Photograph by the author.

Figure 9.4 Two representations of the Taungbyon brothers (late nineteenth century) standing beside Hlegyi, the 'Great Father' (December 1995). Photograph by the author.

a teak tree. Another example is of Hlegyi, the 'Great Father', who floated down a river on a trunk and became established by a minister of King Thibaw (*r.* 1878–1886) in his home village (Figures 9.3 and 9.4). This *nat* shrine was recently enlarged and new images were presented by the Mayor of Yangon who comes from the same village. A similar story of a spirit arriving on a floating tree-trunk is told of the 'Lady of the Golden Speech'. She is the mother of the 'Lord of the White Horse' recently established at Yegyibauk, the village close to Myitthu where he has his own *nat* palace.[13] In these cases the story of the coming of the miraculous tree-trunk legitimates the establishment of a new *nat* cult; most of these stories are less than 100 years old.

However, in the Mandalay area the main festival is at Taungbyon. The statues and the *nat* palace replacing the old modest shrine, *kwan thok*, are said to have been presented by King Mindon.[14] Although it is not widely reported, I have heard that these representations were also carved out of a tree-trunk. The tree-trunk that floated down the river to Taungbyon had been cut in such a way as to allow spirits to enter it. The motif of the inhabited tree-trunk reinforces the power of the *nat* images in this case, as it connects them with already well-known and respected *nats*.

The foundation story of the Pyu spirits of Tagaung played an important role in the evolution of the *nat* cult during the nineteenth and twentieth centuries. In the Mandalay region, such stories sustain the establishment of *nat* images within their own *nat* palaces. Another documented case is of Yadanagu at Amarapura, where

the 'Lady of Popa' is celebrated as the mother of the Taungbyon brothers. One of the sanctuaries here is said to date from the late eighteenth century and it could thus be the oldest *nat* palace of this area. According to the foundation stories, most of the *nat* cults started well before the eighteenth century, primarily during the

Figure 9.5 The 'Lady of the Running Water' in her Maundon Palace (March 1998). Photograph by the author.

Figure 9.6 A representation of four *nat*-ladies belonging to a local spirit-medium at Shweguni temple. The representation of the 'Lady of the Running Water' is shown sitting beside a buffalo and holding two serpents, with a third one emerging from her navel (March 1986). Photograph by the author.

Pagan period. However, the antiquity of the placing of 'original' *nat* images in *nat* palaces is still unclear.

In comparison, *nat* festivals in the area of the Chindwin–Irrawaddy confluence are considered to be ancient. For example, at the Shweguni temple, U Min Kyaw is celebrated, while at Maundon and Zidaw the 'Lady of the Running Water' is honoured (Figure 9.5). Similarly, at Alon, the 'Great Father of Alon' is commemorated, together with Ma Nwetaung. At Alon, the *nan dein* says openly that at the beginning of the century, no representation of the *nat* was placed in the palace. There is no miraculous origin now narrated for the currently existing statues. Moreover, an important part of the ritual programme which Langham Carter has called 'the migration of the *nat*' is performed in the absence of the *nat* statue.[15] The *nat* performs the annual parade around its domains by being summoned by the sound of a conch trumpet at various ritual places. He is then installed in the palace where the image was left during the parade. In this case it is clear that the *nat* image is a recent introduction.

At Maundon, local tradition records that four generations of *nan dein* ago, in a dream to a wood-cutter, the 'Lady of the Running Water' revealed that her image was hidden in a bamboo cluster. Because of this dream and the fact that the Lady was supposedly a witch during her lifetime, her image is believed to have particular powers by spirit-mediums. At Shweguni, one statue which was presented by King Mindon, is said to have been stolen by insurgents after the Second World War. The location of the palace where new statues are enshrined, was determined by the appearance of a giant snake (Figure 9.6).

To summarise, in the three cases located close to the Chindwin–Irrawaddy confluence, the establishment of *nat* images in their sanctuaries does not seem to be as ancient as the existence of the *nat* and its cult. This is also the case with the 'Lords of the Great Mountain' and the Taungbyon brothers as they have been introduced and established in *nat* palaces since the nineteenth century. In the Amarapura area they were not much older, with the late eighteenth century site of Yadanagu being the most ancient case documented. It therefore seems that the *nat* palaces are a comparatively recent development, having been considered a more proper place for 'royal *nat* images' (*pon-daw*) than local settings.

The introduction of *nat* images to specific *nat* shrines has been important in forming local rituals, and festivals today are structured according to this changed ritual practice. One aspect of this change has to be emphasised: *nat* images did exist before, probably as ritual objects to the royal cult of the 37 *nats*. Having been animated, these royal images were brought by officers to local annual festivals.[16] The establishment of these 'royal *nat* images' in local rituals seems to have eliminated the necessity of animating the *nat* representation because the *nat* spirit is

103

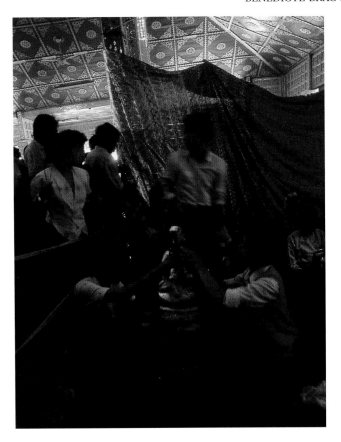

Figure 9.7 At the end of the festival, the statues (here the 'Royal Clerk') are regilded by Mandalay lacquer specialists who have come specially to the Taungbyon temple. The working area is ritually enclosed by white thread (August 1991). Photograph by the author.

believed to exist at its place of origin. Today, parts of the festival, such as the 'ritual shower', the cutting of the tree or the re-gilding of statues, ensure the presence of the *nat* during celebrations (Figure 9.7).[17] However, these activities did not replace the animation rite performed in the royal period for the images linked with the cult of the 37 *nats*. Today the animation rite is only performed for the numerous images owned by the spirit-mediums of the 37 *nats*. In a sense, the images held today by spirit-mediums are comparable to those previously linked with the royal cult of the 37 *nats*.

The circumstances of the establishment of permanent images in local cults need to be specified in a number of cases, but it seems that the general trend is a result of the intervention of concepts of kingship in local rituals. My hypothesis is that the legend of the 'Lords of the Great Mountain' was re-activated during the nineteenth century when a reformation of rituals occurred at Taungbyon. The actual *nat* palace was established there and the organisation of the festival focused on the sanctuary containing an 'original' representation and therefore main manifes-

tation of the *nat*. Court officials were instrumental in the elaboration of this model that then spread to other *nat* festivals. I do not mean that existing forms of cults have been completely erased, as one can recognise variant styles in different areas, but they still fit the ritual model. Although kingship has disappeared, the process described above is still active, with the ritual model now being conveyed primarily by the specialist community, namely the spirit-mediums.

NOTES

1 R.C. Temple, *The Thirty-Seven Nats: A Phase of Spirit-Worship Prevailing in Burma*, 1906, reprint, Arran: Kiscadale, 1991.

2 For further details, see Bénédicte Brac de la Perrière, *Les rituels de possession en Birmanie. Du culte d'Etat aux cérémonies privées*, Ed. Recherche sur les civilisations, Paris ADPF, 1989. See also, Bénédicte Brac de la Perrière, 'Les *naq* birmans entre autochtonie et souveraineté', *Diogène*, vol. 174, 1996, pp. 40–52.

3 For more information on *nat* 'palaces', see Bénédicte Brac de la Perrière, 'Temple: *naq* (Burma)' in P. Oliver (ed.), *Encyclopedia of Vernacular Architecture of the World*, vol. 1, Cambridge: Cambridge University Press, 1997, pp. 723–24.

4 *Leikpya* means butterfly. In this context, it is usually translated as butterfly-spirit, but it actually symbolises the vital and identificatory essence of being. See Brac de la Perrière, 1989, pp. 91–4.

5 Temple, 1991, pp. 42–3. He quotes Taw Sein Ko and Scott and Hardiman. J.G. Scott and J.P. Hardiman, *Gazetteer of Upper Burma and the Shan States*, Rangoon: Superintendent of Government Publishing, 1904, vol. 1, pt. 2, p. 19.

6 Bénédicte Brac de la Perrière, 'Le roulis de la Dame aux Flancs d'or. Analyse d'une fête de *naq* atypique en Birmanie centrale (Myanmar)', *L'Homme*, vol. 146, 1998(a), pp. 47–85. Also, Bénédicte Brac de la Perrière, 'Le cycle des fêtes de *naq* en Birmanie centrale: une circumambulation de l'espace birman' in P. Pichard and F. Robinne (eds), *Études birmanes en hommage à Denise Bernot*, Paris: École française d'Extrême-Orient, 1998(b), pp. 289–331.

7 Kyaw Thu (Kawi Dewa). *Parabaik* no. 960, National Library, Rangoon, 1856 (in Burmese).

8 Temple, 1991, p. 43.

9 *Ibid.*

10 Kyaw Thu, 1856.

11 The Burmese refer to the tradition in which kings celebrated the '*nats*' (here the word encompasses the Hindu divinities or *devas*) during Nadaw. This is corroborated by the name of the month, *nat daw*, meaning royal *nat*.

12 Brac de la Perrière, 1998a, p. 302, n. 31, and p. 303.

13 Brac de la Perrière, 1998b.

14 According to Judson's dictionary, *kwan thok* actually means a 'place of refreshment' for kings. In the *nat* cult, the term is used to refer to places where *nats*, or their representations, rest. Its use in the context of Taungbyon supports the possibility that at that time there were no permanent, settled statues in the Taungbyon shrine.

15 R.R. Langham Carter, 'Lower Chindwin Nats' [part 1], *Journal of the Burma Research Society*, vol. 23, no. 3, 1933, pp. 97–105. R. R. Langham Carter, 'Lower Chindwin Nats' [part 2], *Journal of the Burma Research Society*, vol. 24, no. 2, 1934, pp. 105–11.

16 Another instance of supposedly ancient *nat* statues is the collection of 37 *nat* representations gathered on the platform of the Shwezigon pagoda at Nyaung-U. According

to the foundation story of the 37 *nat* cult, this group was collected by King Anawrahta (*r.* 1044–1077) himself. Although this collection can indeed be considered as items of the royal cult of the 37 *nats*, it probably does not date

back to the eleventh century. Unfortunately, no thorough study of this collection has been produced to date the statues specifically.

17 Brac de la Perrière, 1998b.

10 Problems and prospects for the preservation of wooden monasteries in Burma

Sylvia Fraser-Lu

On the eve of colonisation, there were over fifteen thousand monasteries in Burma, the majority of which were of wood. This averaged approximately one monastery for every ninety-three houses or two per village. Such monasteries were built either by a single donor and his family or by the community at large. Erected according to ancient architectural practices and beliefs that harked back to a much earlier era and modelled on earthly perceptions of what the heavenly mansions of the gods might be like, no expense was spared in their construction and embellishment (Figure 10.1).

THE COLONIAL PERIOD

With the British conquest in 1885, the former Konbaung palace at Mandalay was renamed Fort Dufferin, after the then Viceroy of India, and was transformed into an exclusive European preserve. The former centre of the Burmese temporal universe, known as the Lion Throne Room, became the garrison church, while King Thibaw's (r. 1878–1885) monastery was converted into a Protestant chapel. Much of the area surrounding the former palace site, including Mandalay Hill, became a military cantonment. Monks were turned out of many of the larger monasteries which were temporarily commandeered for use by the British army.[1] For example, the Salin monastery, built by a daughter of King Mindon (r. 1853–1878), soon found itself surrounded by a racecourse, a rifle range, and the servants' quarters of the Burma Sapper Regiment, which later caused the travel writer Scott O'Connor to remark wryly that, with 'the patter of soldiers' bullets, and the rush of racing ponies under his windows . . . [the Abbot] has learned to be something of a man of the world' (Figure 10.2).[2]

Some six thousand houses near the former Konbaung palace were also dismantled, and relocated in the southern and western quarters of the new town being erected outside the city walls.[3] This action effectively isolated the majority of monasteries located in the eastern section, from the bulk of the Buddhist population on whom the monks depended for their daily necessities.[4]

A series of fires between 1885 and 1892 destroyed many of these monasteries in the eastern quarter. Casualties included a majority of the open-sided rest-houses for pilgrims on Mandalay Hill, the wood and stucco superstructure of the Atumashi Kyaung and other royal works of merit which had been moved from Amarapura with the construction of the Mandalay Palace around 1857.

With no one to look after them, the remaining royal monasteries that survived the fires of the late nineteenth century gradually fell victim to the ravages of time. Travel writer Walter Del Mar in his rambles around Mandalay in the early years of the twentieth century noted that the Taiktaw monastery's 'fine carvings have gone to ruin' and that 'the basement now shelters litters of pigs and flocks of rabbit-eared goats'.[5]

Lord Curzon, Viceroy of India, in contrast to his immediate predecessors, felt that the promotion of archaeological study and the preservation of relics of the past was a part of 'our imperial obligation to India'. On paying an official visit to Burma in 1901, he professed to be appalled at the state into which the Mandalay Palace and environs had fallen in the care of his underlings. He decreed that the Christian churches within the palace compound and the Upper Burma Club were to find new premises immediately. With respect to wooden monasteries, he sadly noted that 'there is none which is not in a state of delapidation', and he ordered the replacement of broken, rotting wood on Queen Su-hpaya-lat's Golden Monastery (Figure 10.3).[6] Feeling that these monasteries would all be gone within a few years, he did not advocate plans for their long-term preservation.[7]

The Viceroy, however, on his return to Delhi, had the Ancient Monuments Preservation Act passed in 1904, which required the newly resuscitated Archaeological Survey of India to compile a list of 'protected monuments' of historical, archaeological and/or artistic interest. Such monuments were to come under the jurisdiction of the Department of Archaeology in Burma. Its officials were charged with protecting them from desecration and decay. By 1916 nearly five hundred monuments and sites in Burma had been added to the 'protected' list. Unfortunately, only eight wooden monasteries and two wooden rest-houses were deemed worthy of preservation. All except one, were in the Mandalay area.[8]

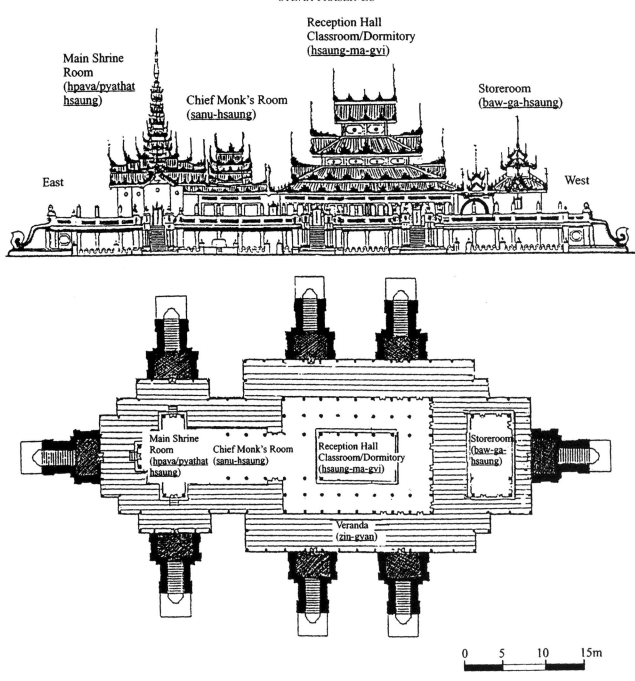

Figure 10.1 The Shwe-in-bin monastery, located in the Deiwun quarter of Mandalay, was built in 1895 by a wealthy Chinese merchant U Set Shwin and his wife Daw Bwa for U Javanadhaja, a monk venerated for his learning. Although constructed a decade after British annexation, the monastery is remarkable for its classic proportions and its elaborate, well-preserved relief carvings depicting scenes from Burmese and Buddhist folklore (after Myo Myint Sein *et al.* 1970a, figs 2b and 2c).

Throughout the colonial period Eurocentric views on conservation and repair generally prevailed over those of Burmese Buddhists. The antiquities of the Pyu (*c.* AD 400–900) and Pagan (*c.* AD 1044–1287) periods, being of greater age, were considered to be the most worthy of preservation, while the remains of the immediate Konbaung past tended to be regarded as inferior both in conception and form.[9] Burmese wooden monasteries

were described in rather derogatory terms by professional art historians of the colonial era, as may be seen in an influential standard work of the day, *The History of Indian and Eastern Architecture* by James Fergusson, which stated:

... the monasteries are ... generally less magnificent than the pagodas to which they are attached, and are

Figure 10.2 In 1876 the cruciform-shaped former *pyathat hsaung* apartment of the Salin Kyaung in Mandalay was built to the north of the palace by the eldest daughter of King Mindon and the Limbang Queen. The tiered spire and the fine woodcarving proclaim the sacred nature of the edifice. The writer Scott O'Connor noted in 1906 that its carving was, 'exceptionally fine' and that it was 'perhaps the most beautiful monastery in all of Burma' (photograph, after O'Connor, 1907, p. 63).

. . . built of wood – a practice . . . depriving them wholly of that monumental appearance of stability which is so essential to true architectural expression . . . [Their] real magnificence consists in the profusion of gilding and carving with which every part is covered . . . [but they suffer] all the defects arising from the use of so easily carved a material . . . carried to excess. If the colouring and gilding could be added it would represent a building such as the West never saw, and, let us hope never will see; for, however dazzling in its splendour, such barbaric magnificence is worthy only of a half-civilised race.[10]

Colonial architecture, as a potent and highly visible symbol of the imperial presence, was built to last, and naturally favoured large, imposing multi-storeyed brick and concrete structures in the then-prevailing Palladian, neo-Renaissance and neo-classical styles over wooden edifices for public buildings If 'eastern' touches were desired, colonial architects not unnaturally turned to India where they had been for close on two hundred years, rather than to the newly acquired outlying province of Burma.

Although on the 'protected monuments' list, the wooden monasteries built by former Konbaung royalty continued to be occupied and remained in the custody of their presiding abbots. Consequently, they could not be strictly classified as government property, which meant that the Archaeological Survey did not feel obligated to provide the necessary resources required for their systematic maintenance and restoration. Little help was also forthcoming from Burmese Buddhists in this task, for according to the way the merit system operates in Burma, with the exception of an especially sacred shrine, there is a widely held belief that it is an exercise in futility to refurbish the religious works of another, particularly monasteries.

By the 1930s the remaining Konbaung period wooden monasteries had fallen into a truly sorry state which so moved H.R.H. Prince Damrong, a son of King Chulalongkorn and founding father of the disciplines of art and archaeology in Thailand, when visiting the Salin monastery in 1936, that he noted:

I felt a sense of dismay, because the monastery had been left to fall to ruin. Some of its gable-finials have come loose and are dangling down. Even the surviving decorations (such as murals and carvings) have worn away, leaving only traces of the originals, because they are wooden objects and have been exposed to the sun and rain for a long time. On reflection, Salin Monastery might be compared to a once-beautiful woman whose body has shrivelled, whose hair has turned grey and whose teeth have broken off. One must rely on one's imagination to perceive which parts were once beautious [sic].[11]

The death knell for the Mandalay Palace and the remaining Konbaung royal monasteries came during the Allied and Japanese bombing in the Second World War. King Thibaw's monastery, Queen's Su-hpaya-lat's Golden Monastery and the Salin Kyaung were all burned to the ground. Miraculously, the Shwe-nan-daw Kyaung was the only former royal monastery to escape destruction (Figure 10.4).

POST-SECOND WORLD WAR

Following the Declaration of Independence in 1947, the devoutly religious prime minister U Nu readily assumed the mantle of a former Burmese monarch as defender

Queen's Golden Kyoung — Mandalay.

Figure 10.3 Mya-taung-kyaung located to the southwest of the Mandalay Palace was commissioned as a work of merit by Queen Su-hpaya-lat, consort to Thibaw, the last king of Burma (*r.* 1878–85). Popularly known as the Queen's Golden Monastery, due to the lavishness of the gold-leaf embellishment, it was designed on classical Konbaung lines by architect Hsaya Khin. It was erected between 1881 and 1885 using the profits of the state lottery. It was barely completed before the donor and her husband were exiled from Mandalay. Like the Salin Kyaung, it was destroyed by fire during the Second World War (postcard courtesy of Noel F. Singer).

and promoter of the Buddhist faith. A number of notable sacred war- and earthquake-damaged pagodas such as the Shwe-maw-daw at Pegu and the Botataung in Rangoon were repaired with government funding and private donations, and the Department of Archaeology, continued its exacavations at the Pyu site of Beikthano.[12] However, with its meagre allotments, which appeared to be little better than those granted during the colonial era, there was no surplus to spend on the preservation of wooden monasteries. Foreigners when visiting Mandalay in the 1950s expressed concern over the water and termite damage inflicted on a then very delapidated Shwe-nan-daw monastery.[13]

Ne Win, U Nu's successor, took a less 'activist' approach towards the preservation and propagation of the Buddhist faith. New works of merit continued to be constructed, but with private donations, rather than with state resources. Continuing insurgency problems and declining economic conditions following the 1962 *coup d'état*, meant that budgetary allocations to the Department of Archaeology had became positively miniscule. Only minimal repairs to monuments threatened with imminent collapse could be carried out, such as the erection of a make-shift protective veranda around the

balustrades of the tottering Yokson Kyaung in Sale to prevent the carvings from being stolen.

A devastating earthquake at Pagan in 1975 led the UNDP and UNESCO organizations to offer Burma the services of an architect-restorer to advise on restoration and conservation measures and to draw up an inventory of religious monuments.[14] Special training was given to Department of Archaeology personnel on the application of modern engineering and preservation techniques for the restoration of monuments, artefacts, and murals.

With the Pagan restoration programme well underway in the early 1980s, the UNESCO conservation project began to turn its attention to the preservation of other important monuments in Burma. In 1983 a widely respected architect, Jacques Dumarçay, with extensive experience in South-east Asia, was invited to Burma to compile an inventory of timber monasteries worthy of preservation. This month-long mission visited a number of monasteries, rest-houses, and pavilions, in the Central Burma and Mandalay areas. A list of twenty-three timber structures requiring attention was compiled.[15] The report also advocated that a number of 'technically or aesthetically harmful repairs' should be immediately dismantled and that close attention should be paid to water drainage.

Figure 10.4 Shwe-nan-daw Kyaung, Mandalay (photograph 1998). Photograph by the author.

These concerns included avoiding the use of termite-infested wood and expelling excess water run-off well away from the base of the building.

The report also recommended that a team of fifteen carpenters and woodcarvers be employed full time by the Department of Archaeology. Based in Mandalay, this team would acquire expertise by first dismantling and cleaning smaller structures with air compressors, and then reconstructing them on thirty centimetre-deep concrete slabs or blocks to stabilise the pillars and form a barrier against termites. At the same time, unique problems associated with each structure slated for renovation would be carefully studied to find solutions to aid in its conservation. During the 1980s, with a continuing paucity of funds at its disposal, the Department of Archaeology was unable to make much headway on implementing the conservation measures advocated in the UN report.

CHANGES IN THE 1990s

In 1990 there was a complete about-turn in policy. The State Law and Order Council (SLORC) (now known as the State Peace and Development Council or SPDC), which seized power after the disturbances of 1988, enthusiastically embraced the development of tourism as a catalyst to start the economy and bring in much-needed foreign exchange. This has meant not only the development of large modern joint-venture hotels and associated facilities, but has also led to the allocation of sizeable amounts of government money towards rebuilding and restoring ancient monuments, commissioning colossal Buddha images, and building new museums of national culture.

Under this new directive the former Konbaung palace at Mandalay and the Audience Hall of the Kanbawza Thadi at Pegu, reportedly a palace of King Bayinnaung (*r.* 1551–81) have been rebuilt as replicas of the originals.[16] Because there are no longer sufficient teak logs of suitable size available, the basic pillar and beam structures have been made of reinforced concrete and painted in yellow and red to resemble the original gilt and lacquer. In some cases stucco decoration has been used instead of the traditional woodcarving.

Coinciding with this change of policy, the leaders of the military junta have sought to portray themselves as 'guardians' of traditional 'Myanmar' culture, and in the same vein have assumed the role of meritorious Buddhist rulers on a most ambitious scale.[17] Many sacred pagodas throughout Burma including the Shwedagon and the Kaba Aye in Rangoon, have been extensively refurbished with government funds and public donations.[18] Critics of the regime have accused the government of 'appropriating the Buddhist religion for state objectives'.[19]

Under this 'Myanmafication' policy, there has also been a resurgence of interest in monastic education. A steady decline in academic standards and classroom

Figure 10.5 A monastery at Taungbi on the outskirts of old Pagan that was refurbished by the Department of Archaeology in 1991. Photograph by the author.

discipline, coupled with numerous school closures and increasing incidental expenses, have led to widespread disillusionment with public education. Some members of the junta who look on the Western-based state system of education as a breeding ground for dissidents are also more favourably disposed towards monastic education than previous administrations. Some cabinet members are known to sponsor children from minorities in monastic schools.[20]

During the latter part of the 1990s there has also been an upsurge in interest in domestic group travel amongst the Burmese themselves, in the form of Chaucerian-style pilgrimages to pagoda sites located near historical remains and popular scenic spots. An organisation or a large group of friends and relatives hire a bus and driver; petrol rations are pooled and food shared. Costs are kept low by putting up at local monasteries *en route* which are usually most willing to accommodate such pilgrims as their donations contribute to the upkeep of the establishment.[21]

The State Peace and Development Council has also decreed traditional monasteries to be ideal 'showcases of Burma's cultural heritage' from which to 'promote patriotism' and to revive the traditional art of fine Burmese woodcarving. A training school for abbots (Kyaunghtaing Hsayadaw-mya Thindan) has been established in Rangoon. As part of the general coursework, future monastic leaders are given lectures by architects and engineers on building maintenance and preservation.

Generous annual budget allocations have been granted to the Department of Archaeology to carry out restoration projects. At this juncture there does not seem to be a well-coordinated plan or blueprint to restore all monasteries cited as worthy of preservation on the UNDP/UNESCO list systematically. Many restorations appear to have emanated from the personal behest of individual SPDC members and powerful local military commanders rather than from the Department of Archaeology which has responsibility for the implementation of such projects.

In undertaking monastic restoration projects the current administration has been beset with some of the same problems that confronted their former colonial masters. The question of what should be restored and how it should be done remains a perennial one. Whether a restoration should be an exact replica of the original in terms of design, scale and materials used, or whether the restorer should be granted 'poetic license' to modify the basic structure and come up with a different work of art using modern materials and different floor plans and motifs from the original, remains a contentious issue. In general, members of the artistic community, the intelligentsia, and the Department of Archaeology advocate restorations faithful to the orginal plans, while members of the central government, local military leaders and many of the less educated amongst the faithful favour fanciful 'restorations' and the addition of 'new' elements to the basic plans.[22]

As in the colonial era the majority of monasteries remain in the custody of their presiding abbots, many of whom are very happy to have their buildings 'restored' to their former glory at government expense. There are others, however, who vehemently object to any government 'intrusion' on their authority and have refused to cooperate with the Department of Archaeology. Some abbots have even been known to sell woodcarvings to raise money to support the activities of the monastery.[23] Others have undertaken their own 'restorations' independent of the local authorities.[24]

Monasteries restored in the more remote areas often need armed protection to prevent their carvings being stolen. Ariyawuntha Kyaung and Minbu Kyaung, two meditation monasteries with fine woodcarvings in a remote part of the Sagaing Hills, were beautifully restored by the Department of Archaeology in the late 1970s, but fell prey to thieves some ten years later who stripped the monasteries of their fine woodcarvings, leaving behind disintegrating shells of rotting timbers.

Given these complex circumstances, it is not unnatural to expect that as far as monastic restoration is concerned the results to date have been mixed. The Taungbi monastery on the outskirts of old Pagan, which was

selected in 1991 as the flagship 'practice site' to be dismantled under the supervision of the Department of Archaeology to give fledgling restoration carpenters training in refurbishing a monastery, is still unoccupied. Monks in the area have declined to take up residence because they feel that there are not enough people in the vicinity to supply them with food on a regular basis (Figure 10.5).[25]

A number of edifices have been carefully restored to their former grandeur down to the last detail, such as the Shwe-nan-daw, which was originally the northern chamber of the Glass Palace. Deemed inauspicious because King Mindon had died in this building, Thibaw, his successor, had the building dismanted and refurbished as a monastery in the northeastern section of Mandalay in 1878. The building, supported by 150 teak pillars, rests on a 2-metre high platform. It consists of a 35-metre long by 21-metre wide main hall surrounded on all sides by a 2.5-metre wide veranda. During the 1960s, in an effort to preserve the building, the Department of Archaeology had the foundation pillars with their outward-facing effigies of rearing dragons and rock shoes of Sagyin marble anchored to concrete foundations. A full-scale refurbishment took place in 1996. The rotting timbers of the veranda and missing carvings were replaced with well-carved replicas. However, it is no longer a 'working' monastery. The monks who previously

Figure 10.6 The recently rebuilt Maha-wei-yan-bon-tha Kyaungtawgyi, Bagaya Kyaung at Amarapura is the fourth monastery to be built on exactly the same site (photograph 1996). Photograph by the author.

Figure 10.7a Yokson Kyaung (Sale) and U Pon Nya Museum of Sale Culture (photograph 1985). Photograph by the author.

Other monasteries have been carefully restored to become 'history museums' or museums of 'local culture'. The earliest building in the Shwegyin Kyaungdaik compound on Mandalay Hill, which was donated to the Order by King Mindon, has been competently restored on classic lines by Tanpawady U Win Maung and engineer Daw Tin Ohn, using the original carvings where they still existed. The western end of the monastery now houses effigies of the thirteen previous Shwegyin abbots of the monastery.

Using the 1848 Kyauktawgyi murals as a guide, the 105-metre long by 50-metre wide Maha-wei-yan-bontha Bagaya monastery of Amarapura (not to be confused with the Bagaya Kyaung at Ava) was rebuilt in 1993 by architect Myanmar Ah Lin. The balustrade is of brown and yellow moulded stucco rather than of wood. Traditional-style, brown-painted wooden relief-carving adorns the roof.[27] Built at a cost of 64.5 million kyat, from both public and private donations, the monastery now serves as a museum to house more than 400 Buddha images in the main hall and a library of 6,000 manuscripts in the enclosed basement below. The latter is to be air-conditioned through donations from Buddhists abroad (Figure 10.6).[28]

The Yokson Kyaung of Sale, built around 1882 at the behest of U Po Gyi, a local merchant, and his spouse Daw Shwe Thet, was famous for its beautiful wood-carvings. With the demise of its founders, the monastery gradually succumbed to the ravages of time. In an effort to prevent further deterioration and loss, the Department of Archaeology in the 1970s took what was left of the building and placed it on a conrete slab. The carvings were roofed over and placed behind bars to prevent what was left from being stolen. Under the direction of artist Tanpawady U Win Maung, in 1992 the monastery was restored to much of its former splendour with government funding (Figures 10.7a and 10.7b). It was designated a museum of local culture and given the additional name of U Pon Nya Museum, after a famous Burmese poet and native son of Sale. Important manuscripts and beautifully embellished scripture chests (to the chagrin of some of their previous owners) have been taken from neighbouring monasteries and housed here.

The Pakhangyi monastery north of Pakokku, famous for its over 20-metre high pillars, has also been rebuilt, but without the balustrades which had disintegrated with the passage of time. In 1998 the Shwe-in-bin monastery in Mandalay was undergoing similar repairs.

Such efforts to preserve for posterity the remnants of Burma's magnificent religious wooden architecture traditions after a century of neglect are indeed commendable, as are the government's efforts to sensitise future heads of monasteries to conservation issues. However, there has been concern expressed over the fact that a number of monks have had to vacate their quarters, which have then

resided there have been transferred to other establishments and the building has been transformed into a tourist site replete with a ticket kiosk and surrounded by the usual touts eager to peddle their wares. The unheralded charm when visiting this monastery in the past was to be graciously welcomed by the resident abbot and invited in to observe Buddhist monasticism first-hand; unfortunately, this is no longer possible.

The Atumashi monastery, originally built by Mindon in 1847 for the primate of the Buddhist religion in Burma, has been refurbished as an assembly hall in masonry replete with a glittering glass mosaic interior and marble floors (which according to some government sponsored publications is supposed to 'outshine the Hall of Mirrors at Versailles'). In this imaginative restoration the traditional supporting pillars have been replaced by flying buttress beams concealed behind the ceiling to provide a completely open space for a thousand delegates.[26] Predictably, response by SLORC/SPDC detractors to this restoration has been less than enthusiastic.

Figure 10.7b The original veranda woodcarving of the Yokson Kyaung, Sale, part of which may be seen here. It was cleaned, oiled and installed along the remains of a floral-carved balustrade in 1992 and depicts a variety of episodes from Buddhist and Burmese folklore in high relief (photograph 1998). Photograph by the author.

been converted into tourist sites and museums. Although in their case alternative accommodation is readily available, given the large number of monasteries in Burma, such action is not compatible with the tenets of Buddhism and is undoubtedly at cross-purposes with the aims of the original donor.[29]

To date, most restored monasteries have largely been former royal works of merit or those with notable wood-carvings.[30] Pre-colonial works of merit built by former famous ministers and eminent monks (with the exception of royal preceptors) have not so far been repaired. Many are in a deplorable state, such as the Pakhan-nge in Pakokku district, built at the behest of Maung Yan Wei, the Pakhangyi Myosa Wungyi, a former monk and tutor of King Mindon. All that remains of the latter are the foundation pillars and eight masonry staircases.[31]

Thakawun monastery in the Deiwun quarter of Mandalay, commissioned by the controversial former Kinwun Mingyi minister around 1879, is the result of the former minister's interest in Western architecture aroused by a trip to Europe as a Burmese envoy (Figure 10.8).[32] Upon his retirement he hired the services of Comotto, an Italian, and Bonvallein, a Frenchman, both architects formerly in the employ of King Mindon, to design a wooden monastery. The result is a unique multi-storeyed European building embellished with fine Euro-Burmese woodcarving. The administration of this monastery has been invested in a Board of Trustees, while the Department of Archaeology is responsible for preserving the building. It was formerly used for various religious events such as ecclesiastical examinations. It is currently unoccupied and not well maintained. Some of the rooms have been defiled with grafitti, and the fine carved open-work screens on the front doors have been

Figure 10.8 Thakawun Kyaung, Mandalay. Photograph by the author.

damaged. Conservation measures are urgently needed to preserve this monastery for posterity.

Some consideration perhaps should also be given to the preservation of works of merit donated to famous monks of the past such as the Thingaza monastery in Mandalay, built during the reign of King Mindon in honour of Thera Aggadhamma, a monk whose humorous down-to-earth anecdotal discourses on everyday problems inspired monks' tales to become a genre of literature.[33] Bhamo Kyaung in southeast Mandalay was built by a Manipuri princess, a minor consort of King Tharawadi (r. 1837–46). It was donated to U Pandita, a learned but controversial monk from Bhamo, noted for his searing wit and penchant for ridiculing some of the less edifying edicts of the temporal and ecclesiastical authorities in lively lyrics and ballads. Both these monasteries will be lost to posterity unless repaired soon.

A similar fate awaits other lesser-known gems of monastic architecture, such as the Taingtaya Kyaung-yi Kyaung of Lezin village in the Monywa district. It was built in 1892 for the Ledi Hsayadaw, a renowned Pali scholar who wrote widely on Burmese history and culture.[34] In this case the villagers themselves would like to repair the monastery, but they lack the needed half a million kyat (approximately US$15,000) to carry out the task.

A few informal workshops abroad which have focused attention on cultural preservation in Burma have expressed concern over the perilous condition of many lesser-known wooden monasteries. Given the present situation of conflict, contending priorities and scarce resources, these workshops have come to the conclusion that preservation efforts in this area might be best achieved piecemeal by working through religious groups and independent non-governmental organisations. International Buddhist groups could be encouraged to open links with local Burmese Buddhist Associations to co-operate on monastery restoration. Small grants could be made, through Buddhist organizations and expatriate Burmese to help preserve these buildings. Domestic tourism and pilgrimages in Burma could also be harnessed to assist in historic preservation.

To break down the widespread prejudice towards repairing the former meritorious works of another, UN cultural organisations have hopes of encouraging eminent local Buddhist patriarchs and charismatic international Buddhist leaders, such as the Dalai Lama, to proclaim the 'merit-making worthiness' of restoration and preservation work as far as religious monuments of historic significance are concerned.[35]

To discourage the wholesale theft of Burma's cultural heritage, a comprehensive photographic inventory of Burmese sculpture, including monastic woodcarvings, should be compiled to serve as a record. Photographs of stolen items could be made available on a computer web site as has been done with Cambodian and Nepalese art.

In conclusion, the demise of these little-known and under-appreciated gems of monastic architecture would represent an irreparable cultural loss not only to Burmese Buddhists, but to the art world in general, where only fragments of other formerly magnificent traditions of wooden architecure have survived the depredations of time, nature and man.

NOTES

1 Noel F. Singer, *Burmah: A Photographic Journey 1855–1925*, Gartmore, Stirling: Kiscadale, 1993, p. 72. Another interesting, related work by the same author is *Old Rangoon: City of the Shwedagon*, Arran: Kiscadale, 1995.

2 V.C. Scott O'Connor, *Mandalay and Other Cities of the Past in Burma*, London: Hutchison and Co., 1907, p. 60.

3 John Nisbet, *Burma Under British Rule and Before*, 2 vols, Westminster, England: Archibald Constable, 1901, p. 119.

4 Singer, 1993, p. 18.

5 Walter Del Mar, *The Romantic East, Burma, Assam & Kashmir*, London: Adam & Charles Black, 1906, p. 70.

6 Postscript quoted in O'Connor, 1907, from sections entitled 'Minute by the Viceroy on the Preservation of the Palace at Mandalay' and a 'Note by the Viceroy on Public Buildings (other than the Palace) in Mandalay', dated 2 December 1901, by Lord Curzon, pp. 418–22. See also Gwendolyn Trench Gascoigne, *Among Pagodas and Fair Ladies: An Account of a Tour Through Burma*, London: A.D. Innes, 1896, pp. 149–67, for her impressions of some of the Mandalay monasteries.

7 Taw Sein Ko, 'Some Conservation Works in Burma', *Archaeological Survey of India Annual Report*, Delhi, 1903–4, pp. 70–2.

8 According to the *List of Ancient Monuments in Burma*, Rangoon: Office of the Superintendent, Government Printing, 1916. The following wooden buildings were included: Shwe-nan-daw Kyaung, Thudhamma Kyaung, Thudhamma Zayat, Patan Zayat, Salin Kyaung, Mya-taung Kyaung (Queen Su-hpaya-lat's Golden Monastery), San-gyaung (Medaw and Thami-daw Kyaung) and the Taik-taw Kyaung. The other 'protected' monastery was the Lei-dat Kyaung at Yenan-gyaung in the Magwe district.

9 For an excellent account of the conflicting expectations and perceived responsibilities between Burmese Buddhists and the colonial administration, see Mark Woodward, 'When One Wheel Stops: Theravada Buddhism and the British Raj in Upper Burma', *Crossroads, An Interdisciplinary Journal of Southeast Asian Studies*, vol. 4, no. 1, Fall 1988, pp. 57–90.

10 James Fergusson, *History of Indian and Eastern Architecture*, vol. II, London: John Murray, 1910, pp. 366–7.

11 Damrong Rajanubhab, Prince of Thailand, *Journey Through Burma in 1936*, Bangkok: River Books (translated from Thai), 1991, p.110.

12 The Botataung pagoda was repaired in 1953 and the Shwe-maw-daw in 1954. Others refurbished under U Nu include the Shwe-san-daw at Taung-ngu, the Kyauk-daw-gyi at Amarapura, and the Ananda temple at Pagan which was re-gilded. New government-sponsored works of merit include the Kaba-Aye (World Peace) pagoda and a massive assembly hall (Maha Pasana Guha) resembling a cave, built for the convening of the Sixth Great Synod of Buddhism in 1954–6.

13 Hugh Tinker, *The Union of Burma: A Study of the First Years of Independence*, London: Oxford University Press, 1957,

p. 172. In Tinker's footnote 2, the building being described has been mistakenly written as Shwesandaw Kyaung, when obviously the edifice is the Shwe-nan-daw Kyaung in Mandalay. There is no monastery in Mandalay which bears the name of Shwesandaw Kyaung.

14 The person sent was a French archaeologist, Pierre Pichard, who has been working on the Pagan project in Burma for over twenty years. The fruit of his work may be seen in Pierre Pichard, *Inventory of Monuments at Pagan*, vols. 1–7, Gartmore, Stirling: Kiscadale, 1992–7. He was also the editor of the *Pagan Newsletter*, UNDP/UNESCO, Pondicherry, 1983–1989.

15 Jacques Dumarcay, 'Mission Report, March–April, 1983', Project BUR/78/023', 1983. A UN Report on the preservation of Burmese wooden monasteries. A list of monasteries worthy of conservation is appended to the report.

16 For information on the restored palace at Mandalay, see Elizabeth Moore, 'The Reconstruction of Mandalay Palace: An Interim Report on Aspects of Design', *Bulletin of the School of Oriental and African Studies*, University of London, vol. 56, pt. 2, 1993, pp. 335–50. Anon., *Mya Nan San Kyaw, The Royal Palace*, Mandalay: Central Command Security Printing Works Factory, *c.* 1996. For the palace at Pegu, see Thaw Kaung, 'Bago: Ancient City with Renewed Splendour', *Myanmar Perspectives*, vol. 3, pt. 6, 1996, pp. 66–9. Government sources have stated that there are also plans afoot to build a replica of the first Konbaung palace at Shwebo, and possibly a palace of King Kyanzittha's (*r.* 1084–1112) at Pagan. For an account of the traditional architecture of the Shwe-nan-daw, Shwe-in-bin of Mandalay and the Bagaya Monastery at Ava, see Myo Myint Sein *et al.*, *Burmese Monasteries during the Late Kon-baung Period*, Rangoon: Department of Archaeology, Rangoon Institute of Technology, 1970 (in Burmese). For an account of the architecture of monasteries of Lower Burma during the British annexation, see Lwin Aung, 'Architecture of Abbot's Monasteries During the Colonial Period', *Pinnya Padetha Journal*, series 2, vol. 4, November 1976, pp. 97–136 (in Burmese).

17 Such actions can also be interpreted as a time-hallowed means of seeking legitimacy for the regime in power. For a general background account to the current situation in Burma, see David I. Steinberg, *The Future of Burma: Crisis and Choice in Myanmar*, Lanham, New York and London: The Asia Society, University Press of America, 1990. Also by the same author, *Burma: The State of Myanmar*, Washington, DC: Georgetown University Press, 2000.

18 In a government-sponsored publication, the Burmese leadership has expressed great pride in its achievement in refurbishing the Shwedagon pagoda. 'The efforts of the State Law and Order Restoration Committee in this regard has set a high watermark in terms of financial, organizational and administrative assistance that succeeding generations will find hard to match, let alone surpass.' U Cho Aye, *Shwedagon: Symbol of Strength and Serenity*, Yangon: Yangon City Development Committee, 1997, p. 317.

19 This idea was discussed in an interesting, yet unpublished, paper by Janette Philp entitled, 'Nation Building and the Appropriation of Buddhism in Contemporary Burma: The State Peace and Development Council's Propaganda Campaigns', delivered at the Burma Studies Conference at Northern Illinois University, DeKalb, 14 October 2000.

20 In 1998 the writer observed a number of minority male children who were being sponsored by a leading member of the SPDC at a monastery attached to the Naga-lein pagoda just outside Rangoon.

21 For a delightful account of one such pilgrimage, see Ma Thanegi, *The Native Tourist in Search of Turtle Eggs*, Yangon: Daw Shwe Eine, Taing Lin Sapay, 2000.

22 Dr Than Tun, Burma's foremost historian, has been very critical of the government's renovation efforts at Pagan as may be seen in two articles published in Burmese: 'Defacing Old Pagan', *Nainwinba*, 1995, pp. 182–203 (mimeographed copy in Burmese), and 'Depreciation of Pagan Art', *Nainwinba*, 1995, pp. 205–67 (mimeographed copy in Burmese). The above two references have been cited in Anon., *Studies in Myanma History: Essays Given to Than Tun on his 75th Birthday*, vol. 1, 1999, p. xii. The government's viewpoint has been (tactfully) expounded by Dr Khin Maung Nyunt of the Myanmar Historical Commission in various articles. See 'The Great Incomparable Monastery', *Myanmar Perspectives*, vol. 2, no. 6, 1997a, pp. 78–81; 'Mandalay Palace Reconstructed', *Myanmar Perspectives*, vol. 2, no. 5, 1997b, pp. 26–30; and, 'Bakaya Monastery of Amarapura', *Myanmar Perspectives*, vol. 2, no. 5, 1997c, pp. 77–80.

23 Hman Kyaung in the Ananda temple compound at Pagan is a case in point where the Department of Archaeology has indicated a willingness to assist in the restoration of the monastery. The abbot has been suspicious of government assistance and has preferred to pursue his own solutions to the monastery's financial problems.

24 According to U Thanwura, the abbot of Na-taung Kyaung at Taungbi on the outskirts of Pagan, the monastery staircases were being renovated with donations from foreigners who had previously visited the monastery.

25 In 1991 the government forced the residents of the village of Pagan to move to a new site a few kilometres away, which is now known as 'New Pagan'.

26 Khin Maung Nyunt, 1977a, p. 81.

27 Min Thu, 'Maha-wei-yan-bontha Bagaya Kyaung', *Sa-Myet-na*, Rangoon, 9 September 1993 (in Burmese).

28 John F. Dean, 'The Preservation and Conservation Needs of the Upper Regions of Southeast Asia', *Libri*, vol. 47, no. 3, Sept. 1997, p. 127.

29 Some tourists too may well express concern if they were aware that some members of the religious community had been forced to move on their behalf.

30 For a description of some of these monasteries, see Myo Myint Sein, *et al.*, 1970. Also, Elizabeth Moore, 'Monasteries of Mandalay: Variations in Architecture and Patronage', paper presented at a conference on Myanmar and South-East Asian Studies, 15–17 November 1995, Yangon; and Elizabeth Moore, 'Monasteries of Mandalay: Changes in Patronage and Architecture', *SPAFA Journal* (SEAMEO Southeast Asian Ministers of Education Organization Project in Archaeology and Fine Arts), vol. 6, no. 3, September–December, 1996, pp. 5–34.

31 Maung Yan Wei is also known as the Min-kyaung Hsayadaw. For details of his life and service, see Ma Kyan, 'King Mindon's Councillors', *Journal of the Burma Research Society (JBRS)*, vol. XLIV, pt. 1, June 1964, pp. 43–60. According to the local inhabitants, U Saw Maung, a former member of SLORC, had previously visited the village on two or three occasions and was apparently enthusiastic about the possibilities of the monastery's restoration. Since his demise, there have been no plans to restore what would be the largest wooden monastery in Burma. The Department of Archaeology at Pagan, however, has stabilised its foundations in an effort to prevent further deterioration.

32 The Kinwun Mingyi was a leading minister of both King Mindon and King Thibaw. He is controversial because with

the demise of the Konbaung dynasty he also served as an adviser to the British Government. For further details see R. R. Langham-Carter, 'The Kinwun Mingyi at Home', *Journal of the Burma Research Society (JBRS)*, vol. XXV, pt. 3, 1935, pp. 121–8.

33 For a brief account of Thera Aggadhamma's life and a sampling of his discourses, see Maung Htin Aung, *Burmese Monk's Tales*, New York: Columbia University Press, 1966, pp. 31–3.

34 Joel M. Maring and Ester G. Maring, *Historical and Cultural Dictionary of Burma*, Metuchen, NJ: Scarecrow, 1973, p. 116. For a description of the monastery, see Sylvia Fraser-Lu, *Splendour in Wood: The Buddhist Monasteries of Burma*, Bangkok: Orchid Press, 2001, p. 212.

35 Open Society Institute Report, *Cultural Preservation in Burma*, Bellagio Conference Follow-up Workshop, 19 March 1999, New York.

11 The Kachin *manau* and *manau shadung*: the development of an ethno-cultural symbol in Burma

Mandy Sadan

INTRODUCTION

Most visitors to Kachin State in northern Burma will know of the *manau* festival as a one-day, secular community dance, performed around a set of painted wooden posts in a dancing circle. This kind of one-day festival, most commonly represented by the government-sponsored festival held each year on Kachin State Day, has become the pre-eminent symbol of the Kachin peoples of Burma, and the *manau* posts, or *manau shadung*, have become their emblem.[1] This chapter will suggest a possible historical narrative for the development of these symbols, as well as highlighting some contemporary local concerns relating to them. Constraints of space and the desire to maintain a lucid narrative have inevitably dictated that some points of difference in the evidence have become homogenised, and that some of the subtleties in the argument have been lost. However, it is hoped that the chapter will serve as a viable introduction to the subject in the absence of any other substantive literature.[2]

Despite the apparent consensus among Kachin peoples as to the popularity of the *manau* as a symbol, it is nonetheless a contentious subject. Many independent local researchers find it difficult to engage the Kachin community in support of more in-depth studies on the *manau* because of local political sensitivities. Many Kachin people doubt that the subject deserves serious interest and study, an attitude influenced by years of marginalisation from mainstream debates on 'Burmese culture' which have focused almost entirely upon the Burman political and cultural centre. As should become clear in the course of this chapter, if such encouragement is not given to locally instituted independent archiving and research, the chances of furthering our knowledge on this and related subjects in the future will be extremely slight.[3]

THE RITUAL AND SOCIAL MEANING OF A JINGHPAW ANIMIST *MANAU*

It is clear that the *manau* festival has long occupied a unique position as a cultural emblem for Jinghpaw people. This is born out by the extent to which the icon of the *manau* is embedded in the oral culture, folklore and traditions of this community as a whole. Because the

full rituals associated with the festival actually extended for a period of two years or more (to include the clearing of the dancing circle where the dance took place and the ritual dismantling of the posts), the festival provides the perfect dramatic backdrop for all the most popular Jinghpaw stories: plans hatched over many years reach their denouement at these events, truths are manifested, and concealed identities uncovered. Furthermore, the *manau* festival plays a key role in Jinghpaw historical tradition, being a point of historical periodisation at which lineages were deemed to have splintered into segments, or at which disparate communities came together to celebrate their kinship. It is clear from the broader narrative significance attached to the *manau* festival in Jinghpaw society that the symbol is deeply evocative culturally, and this continues to have an impact on the contemporary understandings of the symbol as an emblem of modern Kachin identity.

Yet a 'traditional' (i.e. animist) *manau* festival also functioned within a specific sphere of local power relations.[4] A 'traditional' *manau* was an animist ritual that was associated most strongly with Jinghpaw communities headed by chiefs and was one of the main ways by which chiefs of high status could ritually consolidate their socio-political position. Animist *manau* festivals took place over a period of four, and sometimes eight days, rather than one as is common at the secular festival today, and dancing in the *manau* arena, the *naura*, took place for many hours on each of those days. However, the dance itself was not the key ritual act of the animist festival, rather it was the complex structure of recitations and offerings to spirits that defined the animist *manau's* purpose, of which the dance was just one element. The most important of these recitations was performed by the spirit priest, *joiwa*, and was referred to sometimes as the Jinghpaw 'Creation Story', in which the genealogy of the host was recounted by detailing the names of ancestors who had also held *manau* festivals.[5] The recitation thus confirmed the right of the host to hold the festival and for the family line to benefit from the blessings that accrued as a result. This personalisation was important and it was emphasised in all the festival's key rituals. The most important recitations took place inside the host's house, with which the *manau* posts and the *naura* had to be aligned, and all the dances would begin and end within the house (Figure 11.1). The private aspects of the animist *manau* were, therefore, never far from the surface, and public participation, in contrast to the modern symbol, was not the animist festival's defining purpose.

The Jinghpaw claimed the *manau* as the right only of certain chiefs and those chiefs claimed an exclusive relationship with *Madai*, a spirit of great wealth who could bestow *sut* (wealth and fertility) on those who made offerings. Offerings did not have to be accompanied by a *manau* but, as *Madai* loved to dance, this spirit would be more generous when entertained in such fashion. The necessity of holding a *manau* festival was conceived as part of kinship obligations because one of the chiefs' mythological ancestors had married a daughter of *Madai*. The duty of the bride-taking family, the *dauma*, included paying its respects regularly to the bride-giving family, the *mayu*, who in return would grant their blessings. The kinship obligations between chief and spirit mirrored those of human relationships and a *manau* was also an opportunity for the chief's closest human kin groups to fulfil their obligations to him, as well as to benefit from certain rituals at the festival reserved for them alone.

There has probably been some overstatement in recent years of the role that the *manau* was traditionally supposed to have played as the key ritual of kinship affirmation, no doubt a consequence of the festival's modern political repositioning as a symbol of cross-group unity. An animist *manau* was in fact one of a number of major rituals, such as weddings and funerals, to which kin groups would be invited from considerable distances and in large numbers and at which kinship bonds were affirmed through the fulfilment of ritual obligations between families. What helped to distinguish the *manau* from other rituals, however, and which has pertinence to the principle of broadly defined community participation today, is that greater blessings of *sut* were bestowed by *Madai* when many stepped or danced in the dancing circle for his entertainment. *Nau ai*, from which the term *manau* is derived, means to step and stepping together

Figure 11.1 Hkahku manau shadows [*shadung*] and sacrificial posts. The exact date and location depicted in this photograph is unknown, but it was probably taken in the late 1920s. It shows the position of the *manau* posts in relation to the chief's house, which can be seen directly behind. This structure used four upright posts and shows the geometric and curvilinear designs that have been adapted for the modern standard *manau* post design. The three posts in the centre were used for sacrificial purposes. Today they are not used for this purpose and have been incorporated into the modern posts as part of the structure. (Photo courtesy the James Henry Green Collection, Royal Pavilion, Libraries and Museum, Brighton and Hove [A0195].)

was used in the language of the spirit priests as a metaphor of prosperity and social development.[6] In *manau* oral traditions, moments of unity stood in juxtaposition to the fragmented migratory patterns of family lines; unity brought prosperity, whilst separation brought hardship.[7] Today, the private rituals of the festival have been discarded and it is this broader connotation of kinship affiliation, writ large to extend to all six groups defined as 'Kachin', that has been incorporated into secular understandings of the modern event and has become the modern *manau* festival's defining characteristic.

INVESTIGATING THE ANIMIST ORIGINS OF THE *MANAU* AND *MANAU SHADUNG*

It is extremely difficult to pursue research on the origins and animist meanings of the *manau* and its posts, and these issues can be properly investigated only by studying the esoteric recitations of the spirit priests. Yet today the handful of people who still have this knowledge generally prefer not to engage with these practices lest their interest be misinterpreted by the local community.[8] Many Kachin people (who are today predominantly Christian inside Burma) associate animism with popular Buddhism and construe any expression of interest in animism as giving succour to the political and cultural processes perceived as 'Burmanisation'. Thus, what it is possible for us to learn on these matters currently exists within ever-decreasing and elusive circles of knowledge.

A number of myths are still recounted concerning the origins of the festival, yet these have become disconnected from their place in ritual oral culture and are usually presented as a dissociated form of folklore. Lacking all context they consequently teach us little about the animist meanings of the festival itself. However, this dislocation satisfies a contemporary desire for the expression of continuity of 'tradition' through the *manau* through the telling of 'ancient' tales, whilst simultaneously stripping that tradition of any uncomfortably overt references to animism.

The most commonly related myth tells how the dance was learned from a flock of birds celebrating at a banyan tree bearing an abundance of fruit. Some of the older printed versions of the story portray this tree as being a site of competition between different birds, some of whom wanted to keep their discovery secret. However, contemporary narratives emphasise the common unity of all the birds dancing in celebration together.[9] The hornbill's head, typically seen carved on the horizontal cross-beam of the *manau* posts, is today interpreted as a reference to this birds' *manau* as a symbol of unity. It was also commonly held that the hornbill was a symbol of the chief himself, who kept all the disparate segments of his lineage united and in order, just as the hornbill symbolically keeps the upright posts in position on the

manau shadung.[10] This kind of imagery is one aspect of the *manau* that can only be investigated satisfactorily by a study of its ritual recitations in context (Figure 11.2).

The upright *manau* posts are explained thus: an ancestor of the chiefs married a dragon lady who became homesick. Therefore, posts were painted for her depicting the swirling waters of the river so that she could look upon them whenever she missed her parents. For this reason, the uprights were distinguished as male and female by their convex and concave tips and the curvilinear designs represented the river, the latter replicated also in the dance. The geometric patterns often seen paired with this design represent the folded leaves that women dancers used to fan themselves. These curvilinear and geometric designs are today promoted as the two distinctive elements constituting a standard Kachin *manau* post design. Again, all of these elements have animist connotations, but current political and social concerns inhibit attempts to relocate them within their ritual context for purposes of research. Consequently, we cannot easily examine (1) possible connections between the *manau shadung* and other structures implanted in the ground for the fertility of the land, (2) associations made between the curvilinear design and the acquisition of *sut* or (3) the journeying towards the spiritual land of *Madai* possibly suggested by both the geometric design and by the imagery of the hornbill cited previously. Similarly, we cannot easily investigate clan, group or regional differences given legitimate local concerns that such research may be used to undermine expressions of political or cultural unity (Figure 11.3). It seems certain that within another twenty years any such study will prove nearly impossible. There are attempts to address these issues locally but, in the present situation, there is also a great deal of pressure to impose upon such research a sociopolitical agenda. Typically, this includes an effort to construct a generic 'Kachin' standard that can represent all groups, and research that may provide theological insights to assist the process of Christianising 'traditional' culture.

THE BRITISH ADMINISTRATION AND THE JINGHPAW *MANAU*

Between the First and Second World Wars the Jinghpaw *manau* festival seems to have emerged conspicuously as the key act of gathering together the administratively defined ethno-political community known as 'Kachin'. While the development of the festival in this period was not entirely an invention of the British administration, having involved a dialogue between British and 'native' administrators with Kachin chiefs and elders, the power relations of the colonial situation in which this cultural dialogue took place were inevitably unequal. After the First World War the nature of imperial responsibilities throughout India were in question and administrative policy towards potentially turbulent 'frontier' communi-

Figure 11.2 Carvings on a Kachin *nta pungum* or weatherboard. The weatherboard of a chief's house would be carved in a similar way to the horizontal beam of the *manau* posts. It would have a hornbill's head at one end and would also have carvings of bees, women's breasts, paddy and so forth. These were all symbols of the prosperity and fecundity of the chief. The weatherboard would be made of hardwood and could be re-used in successive houses. Dismantled *manau* posts could also sometimes be found on the front porch of a chief's house as they could be used on more than one occasion. (Photo courtesy the James Henry Green Collection, Royal Pavilion, Libraries and Museum, Brighton and Hove [1230].)

ties was under revision. For example, there had been an extensive Kachin uprising during 1914–15. It was believed that the cause of this was an impression created by the withdrawal of Gurhka troops from the Kachin hills that British military strength had declined, and that a British withdrawal from Burma was imminent.[11] The report into the uprising considered that this belief had arisen because government policy had not been clearly explained locally. Clearly new modes of administrative contact with Kachin communities were needed and the cross-border clan kinship relationships that could be called upon when a *manau* was held made the festival perfect for administrative purposes as the forum for an officer's durbar.[12]

Durbars had originally been part of the ritual of the Mughal court in India and were gatherings at which gifts were exchanged, and political hierarchies and loyalties between ruler and subordinates confirmed. In adapted form the durbar proved a useful tool for the Government of India when, towards the end of the nineteenth century, it sought to present itself as the just and rightful heir of the Mughal imperial entity. The definitive British imperial durbar was that of the Imperial Assemblage held at Delhi in January 1877. This celebrated the assumption of the title of Empress of India by Queen Victoria and brought together heads of state and local dignitaries from all over the Indian subcontinent who were invited to participate in the grand imperial vision. From this point, the durbar was used as a ritual of government whenever it was deemed desirable to mark key narrative moments appropriate to the myth of empire, such as the accession of a new monarch. However, at the peripheries of empire, such as at the margins of administered territory in Burma, a durbar gathering in miniature held under the auspices of significant local officials was seen as a forum at which government policy statements could be made and local allegiances confirmed.

Although it is not clear exactly when British officers started to hold *manau* festivals rather than just to attend them, the annual Administration Reports on the North Eastern Frontier begin to mention this from 1917 onwards.[13] One of the first government-sponsored *manau* seems to have been held in 1918 at Shaduzup, at the extreme edge of administered territory in the Hukawng Valley, under the auspices of Mr C.W. King, the Assistant

Figure 11.3 Myihtoi or spirit medium dancing around the *manau* posts. The exact location and date of this photograph is unknown but it was probably taken in the northern Shan States in the 1920s. The carved upright posts reflect a regional variation in design (see Figure 11.8). This kind of carving was not usually found in 'The Triangle'. Jinghpaw *manau* posts in the northern Shan states tended to use fewer uprights and the geometric design seems also to have been less common. Here only four uprights were used. The Jinghpaw always used multiples of two, whereas other groups might use uneven numbers. (Photo courtesy the James Henry Green Collection, Royal Pavilion, Libraries and Museum, Brighton and Hove [A0029].)

Superintendent and Subdivisional Officer at Kamaing.[14] This event seems to have confirmed to the Government the potential this forum had for resolving local cross-border disputes, for enforcing boundary policies, and for consolidating good relations with trans-frontier Kachin chiefs and headmen.[15]

Typically on such occasions a local chief would assist with making the arrangements for the *manau*. This could add to a chief's local prestige and certain chiefs were selected above others for this role as a means of consolidating a local hierarchy in line with British administrative needs. An officer's durbar would be held on just one of the days of the festival, frequently at some distance from the main site of the *manau* itself, and the officer himself might thus not have been perceived as a particularly intrusive figure. Initially at least, the British authorities tried to maintain the animist integrity of the festival, but there were also early signs of administrative manipulation when this was deemed opportune.[16]

Yet Kachin communities had long been perceived as having shifting loyalties and there soon developed an awareness amongst administrators that these large gatherings could act as forums for opposition movements or for subversive activities. There were concerns, for example, that opium cultivators from beyond British borders were making use of such gatherings to pay tribute to Kachin chiefs inside British territory. These chiefs in turn granted to these cultivators permission to grow opium inside British borders on land over which the chiefs claimed authority.[17] This was in direct opposition to stated government policy, which prohibited opium production. There were also concerns that an incipient 'Bolshevism' might find a willing ear in the Kachin 'gumlao' villages, which were perceived as potentially revolutionary.[18] *Gumlao* is a Jinghpaw term most frequently translated as the overthrow of despotic authority. Since the 1870s there seemed to have been a steady increase in the occurrence of *gumlao* activity, particularly among the Lahpai lineages around Bhamo and in the lower part of 'The Triangle', the area of land bounded by the Mali and Nmai Rivers before they converge to form the Irrawaddy River. Although its connotations have proved variable over time, by the 1920s the designation *gumlao* was interpreted by some British officers as expressive of communist revolutionary inclinations. The closeness of these communities to the border with China also added to concerns, as did the involvement of many of them in the 1914–15 uprising. There is some evidence that large festivals and gatherings held by these communities were monitored to ensure that opposition activities did not arise directly from them.[19]

The administration was greatly assisted in their desire to control the occurrence of large festivals such as *manau* and to direct those that did take place in their own interests by the apparently deteriorating economic situation of Jinghpaw chiefs at this time.[20] This would have inhibited many from hosting these costly events without government sponsorship and thus probably rendered a more overt control by government unnecessary. That the *manau* should be increasingly focused on the government-sponsored events as its main forum was no doubt a fortuitous convergence for the administration of both circumstance and desire.

From the mid to late 1920s the government-sponsored *manau* was defined on a broader stage, being used primarily to announce key policies amongst the collective of communities now administratively and militarily defined as 'Kachin'. *Manau* festivals were sponsored by higher-ranking officials, such as the Commissioner and District Commissioner, who appended such festivities to the large durbar meetings that they held annually. This change reflected administrative alterations heralded by the creation of the Burma Frontier Service in 1922, which sought to raise the status of the four newly constituted positions for 'superior officers' (including those of District Commissioner in Myitkyina and Bhamo), in contrast to those of thirty-five 'inferior appointments', such as Assistant Superintendent and Subdivisional Officer, who previously had taken it upon themselves to host these events.[21]

Two of the most significant of these large-scale administration-sponsored *manau* festivals were those held in the presence of the Governor Sir Harcourt Butler in Maingkwan at the edge of the Hukawng Valley in January 1925 and in Myitkyina in January 1927. Both of these events were used to announce the commencement of slave release campaigns in the Hukawng Valley and in 'The Triangle' respectively and can be viewed as a continuum with the British concept of the durbar in India.[22] Just as the great imperial assemblages held at Delhi were intended to mark new phases of authority in India, officials intended that the Kachin *manau* durbars be interpreted as epoch-marking events, that is historically dated, defining moments for Kachin people (and also for Naga communities within the Jinghpaw sphere of influence). Life before and life after this event were to be inferred as different epochs of moral progress and social development, epitomised by the suppression of slavery within their midst. This concept of the *manau* had been promoted by officers such as Mr T.P. Dewar, the Subdivisional Officer at Mogoung, who seems to have had some responsibility for researching the festival for the information of the Government. Mr Dewar considered

the *manau* to be an epoch-marking event that could be held only once in a chief's lifetime, even though there was in fact no such ritual constraint, and he seems to have been oblivious to the possibility that government policy over an extended period of time might, in fact, have greatly contributed to making it appear so.[23]

Despite the pretensions towards animist authenticity, there was no doubt an increasing lack of harmony between the obligations of animist ritual and the administrative purposes of the accompanying durbar. Nonetheless, the rituals of the *manau* could be remarkably accommodating, requiring only that precautionary recitations be made to the spirits to explain any proposed novelties which would counteract any possibility of negative effects from the spirits' anger.[24] At these festivals a chief, or a *joiwa* who was also a chief, would generally have been more than happy to associate their own *manau* genealogy with a government event (as an essential prerequisite for the key offering to *Madai* to take place), knowing that both temporal and spiritual blessings and prestige would accrue to them as a consequence. However, any unforeseen errors in the conduct of the ritual were a serious matter and it was believed that they could be potentially devastating not only for the chief himself, but also for many future generations of his family line. The danger, therefore, came from those administrative adaptations that were unexpected and thus unguarded against.

The worst such 'mistake' was probably that at a *manau* durbar sponsored by Mr T.P. Dewar in April 1927. As part of the campaign against head-hunting and human sacrifice amongst the Naga peoples, Mr Dewar hoped to persuade Naga headmen from the Shingbwiyang area (Hukawng Valley area), who paid allegiance to the Jinghpaw chiefs of Shingbwiyang and Ningmoi, to abandon their ritual of human sacrifice for that of a *manau*-style buffalo sacrifice. They would see this ritual at a festival he would sponsor for their benefit. Mr Clague, the Chief Secretary to the Government of Burma, wrote to the Foreign Secretary on 6 August 1927, concerning this matter:

> The substitution of the sacrifice of *Mithun* (Bos frontalis) for the sacrifice of humans, which Mr Dewar initiated at the Durbar held by him at Shingbwiyang Ga, and in which the Nagas joined with due ceremony and apparently with delight, shows clearly that the end of human sacrifice is in sight.[25]

From Mr Dewar's description of this event, it seems that a number of adaptations were necessary to effect this administrative goal and Dewar himself tells us that on the first day of the festival:

> The Tumsa Wa (praying priest) and his assistants entered the manao hut and went into retreat to pro-

pitiate the *nats* and supplicate them regarding the change of procedure which was to be adopted as to the holding of this their most important *nat* ceremony.[26]

Not least of these procedural changes seems to have been the need to compress the Jinghpaw animist *manau* rituals and dance into one day in order to accommodate the performance of other rituals by the Naga people attending the festival. It is likely, therefore, that this was the first one-day *manau* held under the auspices of government. It was Mr Dewar's intention that the Naga chiefs should hand over at this durbar the relics of human skulls and bones in their possession as a sign of their compliance with the government's policy to abolish practices of human sacrifice and head-hunting. It seems, however, that neither the Jinghpaw chief of Shingbwiyang, in whose village this event was to take place, nor the *joiwa*, nor any of the Kachin people who attended, were aware of this prior to the festival. Mr Dewar informs us that all the Kachin chiefs had deliberately absented themselves whenever the issue of head-hunting or human sacrifice had been raised, finding the subject too discomforting. He states:

> Although the Kachins regard the sacrifice of humans with pity and abhorrence neither of these families [Shingbwiyang and Ningmoi] in the past have made any efforts whatever to stop the practice. The only marks of displeasure they appear to have shown were not to attend a human sacrifice or discuss details with the Nagas regarding such practices. That their seeming indifference was not due to lack of human feeling was abundantly exemplified during the season when the Kachin chiefs with the expedition invariably endeavoured to be absent when details regarding the practice were being recorded by the civil officer.[27]

On the third day of the gathering, 102 skulls in total and 18 human bones were handed over in the midst of the durbar arena, where the *manau* dance had also been held. Although the dance had taken place two days previously, the ritual space of the *manau*, which extended to a ritually purified area surrounding the village as a whole, was deemed auspicious for a full year after the erection of the posts, not just for the duration of the dance itself. Thus the *manau* arena and the protected space of the village would have been violated in Jinghpaw eyes by this presentation of human remains. Jinghpaw people associated such human relics with the dreaded *Sawa* spirits, which were created when people died in violent circumstances and against whose negative influence offerings would already have been made at the festival. We get some idea of the reaction of the Kachin onlookers to this sight when Mr Dewar informs us in his report that:

> On the third day the skulls were surrendered in the presence of a large gathering of Nagas and Kachins. The latter on seeing the skulls were overcome by their feelings, and passed remarks which were overheard by the Nagas, some of whom were so affected that they turned round to the Civil Officer and said, 'Chief, we too will be good from this day'.[28]

Mr Dewar clearly misunderstood the cultural implications of the surrender of the bones in this location. News of this disastrous event would have spread quickly throughout the Hukawng Valley and the Kachin hills, so great was the potential calamity for the chief of Shingbwiyang and his family line. Occurrences such as this might have lead to distinctions being made in the eyes of local people between the government-sponsored events and 'authentic' rituals and would, no doubt, have contributed to the process by which a distinct identity was to emerge for the sponsored festivals.

The British administration seems to have interpreted the *manau* in a self-fulfilling way. They considered it to be the highest ritual of chiefs, and into this they transformed it. They stated that the *manau* was the key community act of gathering and this it was to become. They considered it to be an epoch-marking event that could be held only once in a chief's lifetime, and in this failed to appreciate the impact of their own policy in making it so. By the late 1920s, private *manau* festivals seem to have more or less vanished from the scene and, as government became less generous with its sponsorship, the main forum for this event became the annual festival of the District Commissioner.

THE *MANAU* AND THE EMERGENCE OF KACHIN NATIONALISM

The festivals hosted by British officials came to have a distinct identity as a one-day gathering focused upon a community dance around a set of posts as a forum for a durbar. Indeed, the kind of festival that had emerged by the end of the 1920s appears to have been the forerunner of all government-sponsored *manau* festivals held since.[29] Kachin nationalists distinguish between all government-sponsored festivals and their own, despite the fact that neither of these forms today is a complex ritual act and outwardly they appear identical. It is the emergence of the nationalist meanings of the *manau* and *manau shadung* that will now be considered.

The *manau* as a political forum played a small but significant part in the emergence of a modern Kachin political identity during the British era. This identity was probably first expressed coherently at the government *Padang* or Victory *manau* held at Sinlum Kaba in December 1918 to celebrate the return of Kachin troops from Mesopotamia after the First World War.[30] Such events were not without significance in British attempts to structure ethnic groups as political communities at this time, the term 'Kachin' itself being both defined and emphasised on such occasions. This event, however, seems to have been initiated with the support of local Kachin chiefs and elders, not simply 'imposed' from above. Kachin elders passed resolutions on this occasion, which they presented to the District Officer, Mr Walter Scott, requesting that a Kachin school be set up and that a distinct Kachin Regiment be created within the Indian Army.[31]

The year 1920 saw an even larger Victory *manau* held at Sinlum Kaba and attended by the Commissioner of Mandalay Division, Mr Cabell, and 2,800 Kachins from the surrounding Hill Tracts.[32] This time the 'Victory' was deemed to be the suppression of an abortive conspiracy in the Bhamo-Katha region by Chinese Shans under the nominal leadership of Mintha Saw Yan Baing, a member of the Burmese Royal family.[33] The Kachin people attending this *manau* were lauded for their refusal to collaborate with such a conspiracy, their cultural and political distinctiveness being emphasised by the administration through the symbol of a politicised 'ethnic' ritual.

By the time of the 1927 Governor's *manau* in Myitkyina, which brought together 120 Kachin leaders from 'The Triangle', the chiefs and headmen were able to put forward a strong public appeal to the Governor, Sir Harcourt Butler, for non-interference with their traditional customs, notably that of 'slave' ownership. *Duwa* Nga Lang La, one of the most important of 'The Triangle' chiefs, demanded that a vote be taken on such matters, but this request was studiously ignored by the Governor.[34] Clearly these festivals were becoming significant to modern Kachin political identity.

Although two other *manau* festivals are deemed historically significant in nationalist narrative, the first to celebrate victory in the Second World War, the second to celebrate the creation of Kachin State in Independent Burma, modern nationalist *manau* folklore today focuses primarily on the event held to mark the outbreak of armed hostilities with the Burmese Government in 1961. This event, held three years after the Burmese government had ceased to support the annual Kachin State Day *manau* festival, is deemed to have heralded a fully developed expression of modern nationalist unity. This *manau* is considered distinct for a number of reasons. First, as the leadership of the main nationalist opposition movement, the Kachin Independence Army (KIA) abolished the authority of the chiefs around this time, so this *manau* is considered neither a private festival nor a government-sponsored forum. Second, participants at the *manau* included many Lisu people who had crossed into Burma as a result of political upheavals in China. Although these communities did not associate themselves with the local 'Kachin' affiliation, their support was required to ensure the maximum moral and numerical strength for a united military opposition to the government. It is popularly believed that the Lisu alone had no tradition of holding *manau* festivals. Kachin nationalist leaders have subsequently mythologised this event as the return of the lost Lisu brother, when the Lisu people also learned how to dance the *manau*. This represents Kachin cultural unity and is a symbol of the united armed struggle to follow.[35] The folklore of this event has helped to transform the *manau* into a decidedly modern symbol, a festival at which a pan-Kachin ethno-political identity is believed to be made explicit.

The nationalist concept of the *manau* as a secular expression of kinship has been important during the recent years of conflict. However, the hostilities also made it effectively impossible to hold independent events inside Burma itself during this time, not only for lack of resources but also because of the vulnerability of the participants at any such large outdoor gathering. Therefore, in the absence of both private and sponsored *manau* festivals, the nationalist concepts of the *manau* seem to have been expressed principally through the emblem of the posts as elements of graphic design. The posts themselves do not previously seem to have been considered in this way, it being the curvilinear and geometric designs that were of most significance. These patterns, abstracted from the posts, were to be found on a number of ritual and domestic architectural elements associated with the system of hereditary chiefs, such as on the *Madai* fireplace in the chief's house, but such usage largely disappeared with the abolition of the chiefs' authority. The patterns had also been used as borders on women's skirt cloths, but this usage was also prohibited by the KIA during the 1970s. The designs would lose their effectiveness as a symbol of strength and unity, it was said, by association with women's clothing, a belief in the lower status of women's skirt cloths also prevalent elsewhere in Burma. Today the structure of the posts is deemed as significant as the designs themselves and the posts have become strongly linked to a martial interpretation, the convex and concave tips being thought to resemble spears and distinctive Kachin swords.[36] The graphic design *manau* posts, with their nationalist and martial associations, have become extremely effective as contemporary ethno-political emblems.

Although it seems that secular *manau* festivals were held as political forums in China and India under the auspices of Kachin nationalist organisations prior to the recent cease-fire in Burma, by the time it was possible to hold large-scale, independent festivals inside Burma again, account had to be taken of the fact that significant changes had taken place in the socio-religious structure of Kachin communities since the 1950s and 1960s. Local oral history accounts suggest strongly that by the 1970s expressions of Christian faith had become significant in the way many ordinary Kachin people inside Burma expressed their nationalism, a political development which corresponded with a renewed missionary effort by both the Catholic and Baptist Kachin churches at that time. For many of these Christian converts, there was (and is) unease at the *manau* festival's animist origins despite its contemporary secularism, and there was (and is) a desire to distinguish more strongly between the modern event and its animist predecessor(s). A further contemporary legitimacy was obtained for the symbol of the *manau* and *manau shadung* from the 1970s onwards when both the Catholic and Baptist Kachin churches made attempts to Christianise aspects of the festival (Figure 11.4). In recent years both these large churches have used the *manau* to celebrate significant moments in their local histories. Some have attempted to reinterpret the dance patterns in the *naura* with Christian meanings.[37] For example, dance leaders may carry crucifixes, festivals may be opened with the saying of Christian prayers, new local churches might hold a *manau* as part of the consecration festivities, and on occasion a crucifix might be incorporated into the

designs on the posts. Although the process of 'Christianisation' is not without its critics, such developments within the two largest Kachin religious constituencies have undoubtedly added to the *manau*'s viability as a popular, contemporary symbol.

CONCRETE *MANAU* POSTS

The effectiveness of efforts to legitimate the *manau* and its posts as modern symbols is perhaps best exemplified by recent attempts to construct posts in concrete.[38] This development seems to have been started in Kachin communities in China in the 1980s, as they were then seen on the Chinese wall calendars imported into Kachin State. The Kachin Independence Organisation (KIO), the civil wing of the KIA, built the first concrete posts inside Burma in Kachin State in 1994, following the cease-fire. They were built in the north of KIA-controlled territory at Hkindu Yang, which is considered the site of the first overthrow of a despotic chief and has become mythologised as the birthplace of the Kachin struggle for freedom in nationalist historical writing.[39]

In 1995, however, concrete *manau* posts became an issue in the Burman cultural heartland of Mandalay. A *manau* was held to commemorate the centenary of the Jinghpaw script developed by the Baptist missionary Dr Ola Hanson, and large concrete posts were built with a stylised crucifix painted at their tip. Shortly afterwards, the government ordered that they be destroyed. *Manau* posts, they stated, had nothing to do with Christianity and were, therefore, inappropriate as a permanent memorial to the Kachin Christian mission. However, by destroying them, the government engendered a new folklore around *manau* posts and poems, stories and highly popular nationalist songs were written about them. The *manau* now had its own modern narrative moment. This event seems to have greatly increased support for the *manau* posts as an emblem amongst young Kachin people, who have adopted them as a badge of contemporary identity with enthusiasm.

Although some now feel the attempt to build concrete *manau* posts near the heart of Mandalay was naive, the desire for permanent witness to a distinct Kachin cultural presence remains. The effort has transferred to Myitkyina and concrete posts of huge dimensions can now be seen near the town centre at the site of the *manau* ground once used during the British and early Independence eras (Figure 11.5). The posts stand in a dancing circle and a concrete building has been constructed opposite (reflecting the posts' previous orientation to a chief's long house), which it is hoped may at some point be used for community cultural activities. The structures represent attempts to reclaim the identity of the *manau* in Myitkyina, and to distinguish it on a grand scale from the government-sponsored event held each year on Kachin State Day, which is otherwise the festival's most public

Figure 11.4 Manau posts erected to celebrate a church festival in Myitkyina in the Kachin State, 1998. Photograph by the author.

Figure 11.5 Large *manau* posts under construction in Myitkyina in 1997. The new *manau* ground was opened officially at the end of December 2001. The six upright posts represent the six groups within the modern Kachin ethnic grouping. Photograph by the author.

Figure 11.6 A model showing a design proposed in 1997 for the new concrete posts being erected in Myitkyina. Photograph by the author.

forum.[40] This is revealed most fully by the intention to hold the 'largest *manau* ever' at the end of December 2001 to open the new *manau* ground. This event will last eight days, recalling the length of the most prestigious animist *manau* festivals, although this event will be secular. The construction of the site and the financing of the festival have been paid for entirely from local rather than government funds. Because of this, the fact that key officials from the government will take centre stage at the opening ceremonies is the subject of local resentment, albeit mixed with resignation.

Because of the more permanent nature of the concrete *manau shadung* in Myitkyina, the *Manau* Committee responsible for their construction have also tried to standardise the meanings of the posts so that they reflect contemporary Kachin values and affirm a united, six-part Kachin identity.[41] When research began for this chapter the posts were under construction and had not

yet been painted. One of the designs under consideration at this time was that seen in the artist's model in Figure 11.6. All the main elements in this design (six colours, six uprights, six spirals and six repetitions of the geometric design) refer to the unity of the six groups. All the other elements emphasise the unity of the community. A star on the lowest beam is a sublimated reference to Christianity but principally refers to the triangulated kinship system; a gong refers to the calling together and gathering of peoples; and the hornbill-headed beam is interpreted as a metaphor for unity as it enables all the component parts to stand together equally. The colours have also been attached with meanings deemed desirable to the moral outlook of modern Kachin society: loyalty (blue), courage (red), the value of tradition (black), respect for the States' natural resources (green), etc. Although the design was later adapted, these concrete posts are clearly being used as artistic canvasses to illustrate a newly defined relationship between the present and a cultural past. This past is relevant to contemporary concerns of unity and community development, and it is hoped that all six groups will sustain the modern 'Kachin' identity in the present.

NON-JINGHPAW '*MANAU*' POSTS

These concrete posts are clearly derived from Jinghpaw models, although the elders who designed them genuinely hope they will be accepted as the standard for all the Kachin communities. This, however, leads us to one final issue concerning modern nationalist interpretations of the *manau* and *manau shadung*. This is the degree to which the different groups must subordinate themselves within the collective 'Kachin' identity to prevent them from being subsumed within the 'Burmese' or 'Myanmar' identity, and the degree to which a standardised structure may represent them all. The present cease-fire arrangements have tended to make these issues more rather than less contentious.

Two communities, the Lachik and the Lawngwaw, recently held festivals to affirm their distinctiveness within the wider Kachin identity.[42] The Lawngwaw festival (*Zham Gow*) was held in Lashio in 1997, and the Lachik event (*Jhang Kham Zoem Goo*) was held in Myitkyina in 1998.[43] The posts in both cases were accomplished creative works by designers highly skilled in the allegorical and abstract representation of the community values that their generation would like to see passed on (Figure 11.7). A committee of elders at the festival had agreed upon the interpretation of the Lawngwaw posts and there was a similar concern at the Lachik festival that all interpretations should be approved by committee. In both cases, however, the matter of interpretation should best be considered as 'work in progress' and will not be reproduced extensively here for fear of misrepresenting what is an extremely complex debate both within and

Figure 11.7 Lachik posts erected for a community festival in Myitkyina in 1998. The designer incorporated many symbols taken from Lachik oral traditions. The centre post with its interwined serpents depicts the creation story, which would have been recited at this festival in the past. Photograph by the author.

between groups as well as between generations. In both cases the posts were significantly different in structure and design from the prevailing nationalist standard, although both groups claimed that they were their communities' traditional forms (Figure 11.8). It is difficult to interpret how the term 'traditional' was being used in a wider historical context given the absence of any known historical representations or descriptions of these festivals. At the very least, the notion of 'traditional' referred to oral culture and myth depicted on the posts. Animist references were deemed expressions of a distinct cultural past, not of a religious present, as the designers of these posts were Christians of varying denominations who had converted from animism. It is these local debates about the artistic illustration of the *manau shadung* in their different forms and, indeed, whether animist symbols should be depicted at all, that contributes to making this such a worthwhile focus for serious research and consideration.

CONCLUSION

The *manau* and the *manau* posts are so dominant as symbols of identity today that Kachin culture appears to be focused only upon them. This process seems to have

Figure 11.8 Lawngwaw posts being erected at a community festival in Lashio in 1997. The post on the centre right has a design of interwined cords. It was said that these represented the various family lines of the community. Traditionally this post would have been carved (see Figure 11.3), but it proved impossible to find someone with the necessary skills to create a carved post for this festival. The design on the diagonal post on the left is another regional variation. It resembles a Chinese key-fret pattern but was here intended to represent the fireplaces within a traditional house. The number of fireplaces reflected a family's prosperity and fertility. Photograph by the author.

been initiated during the period of British rule after the First World War. At the time that the identity known as 'Kachin' was emerging as a modern political construct, the *manau* festival was objectified by the British administration; it appeared to be a community dance around a set of posts in a dancing circle. This touristic image of the Kachin peoples and their culture(s) prevails today in Burma and is perhaps best exemplified by the Burmese transliteration of the term Kachin as a people who 'love to dance'.

Nationalists have also sought to focus a pan-Kachin identity upon the *manau*, having developed an iconographic and mythological status for it and having successfully repositioned the symbol and re-articulated its meanings for the contemporary situation. However, the 'essence' of the symbol in this case is that of the meanings attached to it, including meanings of a peoples' struggle for political and cultural autonomy and the desire to make visible a complex social and cultural structure of kinship. For the community itself there is also an illustration through *manau* post designs of local debates on the modern meaning of Kachin identity, both within and across groups and between generations. These symbols are very far from being the expression simply of a people who 'love to dance'.

NOTES

1 The term 'Kachin', as it is used locally inside Burma today, refers collectively to six communities: the Jinghpaw, Lawngwaw, Rawang, Lisu, Zaiwa and Lachik peoples, and will be used here when referring to issues concerning more than one group. The term 'pan-Kachin' refers to a broader definition of Kachin ethnicity extending to communities in Arunachal Pradesh and Yunnan, and will have this connotation when used in this chapter.

2 The most extensive historical descriptions of the *manau* are to be found in W. J. S. Carrapiett, *The Kachin Tribes of Burma*, Rangoon: Government Printing, 1929, and O. Hanson, *The Kachins: Their Customs & Traditions*, Rangoon: American Baptist Mission, 1913. C. Gilhodes, *The Kachins, their Religion and Customs*, Calcutta: Catholic Orphan Press, 1922, presents an account of an oral tradition recited at a *manau*, although this narrative relates quite specifically to that of the *Gauri* community amongst whom Gilhodes worked as a missionary.

3 This work was made possible because of the intellectual generosity and support of a number of independent Kachin researchers, friends and colleagues in Burma, who shared their thoughts on these issues with me during the period 1996–9. Comments on the nature of animist rituals at *manau* festivals have been derived from these sources where not otherwise cited, although the interpretation presented here is my own and is not necessarily one with which they would concur. Research was supported financially by grants from the Green Trust, Brighton Museum, and by two SOAS Fieldwork Awards. Research in the UK has been supported by grants from the Open Society Institute (Burma Project) and the Green Trust. Particular thanks are due to Elizabeth Dell, Head of the Green Centre and Elizabeth Moore, SOAS, as well as to Patricia Herbert and Martin Smith for their continued encouragement in matters relating to

documentation research. Lastly, my thanks go to my husband, Hkanhpa Tu Sadan, who so patiently assisted with translation.

4 The Jinghpaw ritual form dominates for a variety of historical and political reasons, including the preference that British administrators gave to contact with Jinghpaw chiefs in the Kachin hills region prior to Independence. The term 'animist' will be used as a convenient shorthand for the diverse non-Christian and non-Buddhist religious practices and beliefs that once prevailed amongst 'Kachin' communities in Burma.

5 *Naura Majai* (recited by Npawt La at Mali Hkrang), 1992, unpublished typescript, Green Centre Archive, Brighton Museum.

6 P. Ja Li and Chyahkyi Brang, *Shanhpyi Laika: Lanyi*, Rangoon, 1999, p. 24.

7 Dureng Labau Komiti, *Dureng Labau*, Myitkyina, 1994, typescript.

8 For a fuller discussion of these issues, see M. Sadan, 'The Kachin photographs in the J. H. Green Collection: a contemporary context', in Elizabeth Dell (ed.), *Burma – Frontier Photographs*, London: Merrell, 2000, pp. 67–93.

9 Carrapiett, 1929, pp. 56–7.

10 This kind of imagery was also used in relation to the hornbill-headed beam which some chiefs had at the entrance to their house and which served to distinguish it from others in the village. In this case it symbolically kept all the bamboo flooring neat and controlled as a metaphor for the chief's position in relation to his lineage.

11 British Library, Oriental and India Office Collections [OIOC], India Office Records [IOR], L/PS/11/87, pp. 8–9.

12 Other community rituals did not provide the same opportunities. For example, the highest ritual prerogative of chiefs was in fact that associated with the fertility of cultivation sites, yet as this ritual was followed by a four-day period in which all villagers had to remain quietly inside their homes, it failed to excite much attention from British officials because of its unsuitability as a durbar opportunity.

13 There is a reference in the Administration Report on North Eastern Frontier [ARNEF] for the year ended 30 June 1917 that a durbar was held at Wawang 'strictly according to Kachin custom' [IOR:V/10/530, p. 15]. It is not clear whether the 'custom' adhered to was in fact that of a *manau*, but as the report states that over 300 Kachins were present, it is possibly the case. It is notable, however, that no *manau* appears to have been held to commemorate the visit of the Viceroy, Lord Chelmsford, to Myitkyina and Bhamo in 1917, suggesting that such large-scale festivities under the auspices of major officials were introduced by the Government after this date.

14 IOR: V/10/530 – ARNEF for the year ended 30 June 1918, p. 17.

15 IOR:V/10/530 – ARNEF for the year ended 30 June 1919, p. 17.

16 IOR: V/10/530 – ARNEF for the year ended 30 June 1917, p. 15; ARNEF for the year ended 30th June 1919, p. 17. In particular there were early attempts to adhere to the ritual of removing the *manau shadung* from the *naura* one year after the festival, but this was invariably taken as an opportunity for enforcing administrative goals such as revising village boundaries.

17 IOR: V/10/530 – ARNEF for the year ended 30 June 1921, p. 8.

18 OIOC: Mss Eur/F116/83 – *Slave Releasing Operations in the Triangle during the Season 1926–27*, Mr J. T. O. Barnard, Deputy Commissioner, p. 1.

19 IOR: V/10/530 – ARNEF for the year ended 30 June 1921, p. 18.

20 The oral histories of families such as the Maran clan chiefs of Namhkyek are revealing in this respect. This family resided in northern Shan State and was one of those favoured by the British throughout the 1920s for the co-operation they afforded the British civil and military authorities. They were a family of considerable wealth and standing but the Namhkyek family today recounts that the last private *manau* that the family held was in the early 1920s. Evidence of an increasingly difficult economic situation is provided by many of the government reports of the period including the Administration Reports on the North Eastern Frontier and *Report on the Hukong Valley and Upper Namkong Basin* by H. N. Thompson, Assistant Conservator of Forests, June 1896 [OIOC: Mss Eur/ F116/82].

21 IOR: L/PS/10/73 – Letter from the Chief Secretary to the Government of Burma to the Political Secretary to the Government of India, Foreign and Political Department, 5 August 1920. The obvious exception to this must be Mr Dewar's *manau* held in Maingkwan in 1927 (see below), but the intention of this was expressly to create a link with the Governor's statements on head-hunting, etc.

22 James Talboys Wheeler, *History of the Imperial Assemblage at Delhi* (fol.), London, 1878 (OIOC: RL89). H. Caldwell Lipsett, *Lord Curzon in India, 1898–1903*, London: R.A. Everett and Co., 1903.

23 OIOC: Mss Eur/ F116/82, pp. 29–31 – *Notes on the Kachin Manau*, T.P. Dewar.

24 *Naura Majai*, 1992.

25 OIOC: Mss Eur/ F116/82 – *Confidential Report on the Naga Hills (Burma) Expedition for the abolition of Human Sacrifice, Season 1926–27*, T. P. Dewar, Government Printing, 1927, p. 2.

26 *Ibid.*, p. 28.

27 *Ibid.*, p. 21.

28 *Ibid.*, p. 29.

29 The Government of Burma continued to provide financial provision for the holding of an annual Kachin State Day *manau* in Myitkyina until 1958. They were held at the special *manau* ground reserved for the purpose since the British era. During the recent conflict the government held *manau* festivals intermittently, notably on Union Day rather than Kachin State Day and in the grounds of the government's headquarters, not in the *manau* ground. Since the cease-fire, the government 'tradition' of holding *manau* festivals on Kachin State Day has been revived, although the site remains that of the administration headquarters.

30 C. M. Enriquez, *A Burmese Arcady*, London: Seeley, Service and Co., 1920, pp. 120–6.

31 *Ibid.* IOR: V/10/530 – ARNEF for the year ended 30 June 1919, p. 22.

32 IOR: V/10/530 – ARNEF for the year ended 30th June 1920, p. 59. Following this we also read that a swampy pool near the District Officer's quarters at Sinlum Kaba was cleared to provide a communal recreation ground, which strongly suggests an area was being prepared so that these events might become a regular occurrence. A similar process took place at Myitkyina where a specific site came to be used whenever a *manau* was held. See note 29.

33 *Ibid.*, p. 5.

34 OIOC: Mss Eur/F116/81c – *Sir Harcourt Butler's Diary of events from the 5th–10th January, 1927*. A photograph of this event was published in *The Tatler* on 30 March 1927, titled 'All Abroad!' It may also be viewed in the Harcourt Butler archive OIOC: Mss Eur F/116/84.

35 This argument centres upon a nationalistic interpretation of Kachin kinship which extends clan and family affiliations across the six groups identifying themselves today as 'Kachin'. In practice this construct is extremely complex, but its mythic justification is derived from the idea that all six groups are descended from six original brothers.

36 It is difficult to assess whether this interpretation is wholly contemporary but it prevails as the current understanding of the significance of the shape of the posts.

37 Lahpai Zau Nu, *Naushawng Hpaji*, Bhamo, undated.

38 Traditionally the posts would have to be dismantled one year after the event, although they could later be re-used.

39 H. Naw Awn, *Wunpawng Labau Ginshi*, publisher and place of publication unknown, 1986. This has functioned as an 'official' text book of Kachin nationalist history in recent years.

40 The willingness of the government to allow such a construction reflects complex changes that have taken place in local politics since the cease-fire of 1994. The difficulty for ordinary local people, however, is to know to what extent such developments may be attributed to a change of policy and not merely to changes in personnel.

41 Information obtained in conversations with the designer and members of the *Manau* Construction Committee.

42 Lachik is written *La:cid* in their own script, and Lawngwaw is written as *Lhaovo:*. The Lachik are sometimes called Lashi and the Lawngwaw are sometimes referred to as Maru by Jinghpaw people.

43 Information obtained in conversations with the designers and members of the respective organising committees while the festivals were taking place, and subsequently.

12 Court dress, politics and ethnicity in the Shan States

Susan Conway

Before the twentieth century the inland states of South-east Asia formed a network of principalities situated in upland valleys where the inhabitants were wetland rice farmers. The major outside influence was Theravada Buddhism that assimilated, or in some cases was grafted onto the practices of ancient indigenous spirit religion. In the surrounding hills, the people, controlled by their own rulers, practised swidden agriculture and animism. The rulers of the uplands and the valleys claimed hereditary rights through mythical kinship links to the highest guardian spirits. This inland culture was distinctive from that of coastal Southeast Asia, but was as rich and as complex. It was based on a relatively egalitarian ideology that permitted the flowering of indigenous skills and innovations, especially among women, and a complex history that involved conquest and migration.

This chapter focuses on the principalities of the eastern Shan States (Burma) with reference to the surrounding principalities of Lan Na (north Thailand), Lan Xang (western Laos) and Sipsong Pan Na (Xishuang Banna Province, southwest China). From the fifteenth century, the inhabitants of these states developed a similar culture, including a written script called *tham*, which led to their definition, the 'Culture of the Region of the Dhamma Letters'.[1] The people have been identified in ethno-linguistic and geographic terms as Lawa (Wa), Mon, Karen, Kachin and Tai. The Tai are divided into the sub-groups Tai Shan (Tai Yai), Tai Neua, Tai Lue, Tai Yuan, Tai Khoen and Tai Lao.[2] The Tai chronicles record that from the thirteenth century their lives were linked through a complex web of political treaties and marital alliances and also through trade, although local feuds and fighting between them was not uncommon.[3]

In the nineteenth century, the Tai Shan, Tai Khoen, Tai Lue, Lawa, Karen and Kachin were the main groups living in the Shan States. One hypothesis places the origins of the Tai Shan in south China, from where, it is argued they migrated south into the eastern and western Shan States.[4] The Tai Khoen (Khun) were the Tai-speaking population living in and around the Shan State of Chieng Tung (Keng Tung) and were closely related to the Tai Lue. The Tai Lue migrated from Sipsong Pan Na to the Shan States, and to Lan Na, in the nineteenth century. By

1918 it was reckoned that there were about 50,000 Tai Lue living among the Tai Khoen in Chieng Tung.[5] According to historical sources (*tamnan*), Chieng Tung was allied to neighbouring Lan Na and there was a long tradition of intermarriage between their royal families.[6] Powerful Tai Shan, Tai Khoen and Tai Lue families also intermarried with the Tai elite of other inland principalities.

The Lawa are of Tibeto-Burmese origin and were recognised by the Tai as the original inhabitants of the land. The Tai granted them land rights and invited them to lead major Tai ceremonial processions.[7] The Lawa were also asked to attend Tai family occasions, such as weddings, and were viewed by royalty as augurs of good fortune.[8] Some Lawa were Theravada Buddhists, while others practised a form of spirit religion. Less easily placated by the Tai were the powerful Karen and Kachin hill-dwelling groups, also of Tibeto-Burmese origin. Many other terms have been used to describe them and their sub-groups, and they have their own names for themselves.[9] From their elevated strongholds they levied taxes on the valley dwellers, collected in the form of silver, cattle and agricultural products.[10] The Tai chronicles state that in order to maintain peace, valley dwellers made treaties with the hill peoples and agreed to pay their levies annually. Failure to pay led to raids that might include the sacking and torching of the palace of a valley ruler.[11] Nevertheless, members of elite Karen and Kachin families intermarried with Tai royalty. These marriages were recorded in the Tai chronicles, but were disregarded during the period of 'Pan-Thai-ism' in the 1940s when there was an attempt to rewrite history without reference to ethnic diversity.

Although ethnic groups have been defined here according to ethno-linguistic and geographical data, the question of how to define ethnic identity in inland Southeast Asia has been the subject of debate for almost a century. Seidenfaden noted that the valley people of the inland states were descendants of assimilated Tai, Lawa, and hill tribe people.[12] Edmund Leach argued that hill tribe people who adopted the manners, dress and language of valley inhabitants could merge with them completely in the course of a few generations.[13] Moerman later observed that some Tai ethnic groups were so similar that the claim of being distinct from others was only a matter of their personal perceptions.[14] Keyes concluded that assertions about ethnic origin were derived from cultural interpretations of the birthplace of one's ancestors.[15] Erikson added to the debate in his observation that even linguistic affiliation did not always correlate with culture, political organisation, or territorial proximity.[16]

This debate followed late nineteenth- and early twentieth-century surveys in the inland states which had attempted to match groups defined in ethno-linguistic terms to certain forms of dress.[17] These surveys analysed 'traditional' dress at a particular time, but did not address issues of assimilation and change. The people of the inland states adapted their dress to suit mutable political and economic conditions, migration patterns and intermarriage. Eicher has examined this phenomenon in other cultures and argues that, although dress and ethnicity are linked, this phenomenon has to be considered within the context of 'time and space' relationships.[18] It is argued here that in the nineteenth and early twentieth centuries there were identifiable forms of court dress that related to perceived notions of ethnic identity and to the political, economic and cultural values of the time.

Issues of ethnicity and dress are also considered here within the context of gender and identity. In the inland states defined here, European and American writers noted that male dress adapted quickly to change, whereas female dress was defined as 'conservative' or 'traditional'.[19] Women were not subject to rigid dress codes, however. When they made clothes, they selected materials that allowed a style to be defined as 'traditional', while adding elements of their own choice. The components from which characteristic elements and personal choices were made included indigenous yarns and fabrics, a range of weaving patterns, and imported fabrics and trimmings. This introduces the important factor of trade that affected the variety and quality of yarns, fabrics and trimmings available in the inland states. By using a combination of indigenous and imported materials, women created what was considered to be 'traditional' dress.

Indigenous yarn, fabrics and dyes were traded in town and village markets. Yunnanese, Shan and Burmese itinerant traders transported materials throughout the inland states. Because they used ponies, Yunnanese traders were able to cross difficult terrain, and therefore textiles and trimmings, which were imported, were circulated in remote hills and valleys. Goods were also transported to main trading centres by riverboat and by human porters. However, even the most adventurous traders did not risk routes that were subject to attack by bandits, and at times this affected the Shan States routes that extended from Yunnan to the Gulf of Martaban.

Chinese silk yarn, Chinese silk and satin fabric, gold and silver metal thread, embroidered ribbons and trimmings, Burmese silk, floss silk, cotton and silk piece goods, skeins of wool, velvet and velveteen, aniline dyes, broad cloth, muslin, silver coins, and sequins were carried by the traders. Nevertheless, not all the elite could afford imported materials and many of them were not able to reach certain markets where they were sold. The people living in the valleys and at lower altitudes in the hills had the greatest access to imported goods. Although many finished fabrics were purchased, there was also an important market for yarn, bought by weight and woven by female weavers in the service of the regional courts.

Another factor that affected the style of textiles and dress worn at court was the presence of immigrant textile workers who brought new skills and produced woven and embroidered textiles as they were made in their original homelands. The inland states always suffered from a labour shortage and this was partly solved by taking captives during warfare, raiding neighbouring territory in peacetime and sometimes forcibly resettling whole populations from one state to another. Resettled immigrants were not generally considered alien because most were seized from the 'extended cultural area'.[20] Among the most prized captives were craft workers, including gold and silversmiths, metal workers, painters, woodcarvers, potters, lacquer makers, weavers, dyers and embroiderers. Textile workers were almost exclusively women and many were settled in palace workshops, usually under the supervision of a royal princess. They made ornate dress for ceremonial occasions, everyday court dress, and soft furnishings for the palaces. At Buddhist courts it was also their duty to make robes for the monks and textiles for use in temple ceremonies.

MALE DRESS IN THE SHAN STATES

In the Shan States everyday male dress could not be identified with a particular ethnic group or homeland.[21] Working-men's dress in the hills and valleys consisted of rectangles of hemp or cotton cloth worn as turbans, sashes and loincloths, or cut and stitched to make shirts and jackets, sleeveless tunics, loose-legged trousers and shoulder bags. Rectangular blankets were used as shawls to keep warm. This type of dress was made from indigenous materials which were considered more durable than imports. The fabric was woven in narrow strips and to make garments, two or more lengths had to be sewn together along the selvage. Stripes and simple geometric patterns in supplementary weft were the most common decoration, although jackets and shoulder bags were often embellished with imported strips of embroidery, tassels, beads, shells, coins and sequins. For 'best' dress, those who could afford it wore shirts, jackets and loincloths made from indigenous silk, Chinese silk or other imported fabrics such as mill cotton and cotton velvet, decorated with supplementary weft patterns, silk embroidery and trimmings.

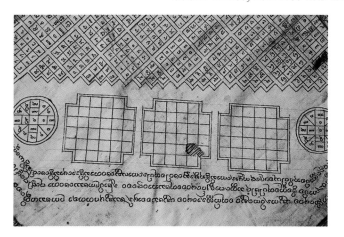

Figure 12.1 Spirit cloth, hand-spun plain cotton with illustrations of talismanic symbols and magic formulae in local script. Hand-drawn with black ink. Private collection. Photograph by the author.

Like elsewhere in Southeast Asia, Tai Shan and Karen men from the eastern Shan States were tattooed from waist to knee, a process believed to protect the wearer against all types of injury. Tai Lue men adopted the custom when they settled among them.[22] Similar forms of tattooing were also customary in Lan Na and Luang Prabang. The tattoo designs included mythical beasts, animals and birds, contained within decorative borders at the waist and knee. Opium was administered to ease the

pain of the process. To display their tattoos, men wore their loincloths high on the hips. Some Shan and Karen also tattooed their chests, shoulders and arms with talismanic symbols and mystical symbolic diagrams (*yantra*). Similar designs were hand-drawn in black ink on cotton jackets, vests and cotton cloths. They were carried into battle and were also kept in domestic dwellings to prevent the intrusion of malignant spirits (Figure 12.1)

The everyday dress of men at the inland courts, although similar in design to village dress, was more costly. The shirts were made of Chinese or Burmese silk, or imported velvet; fine muslin was used in the hot season and quilted cotton in the cool season. Patterned silk, plain silk or plain muslin was used for turbans. Loincloths were made of silk, generally checked or striped, or of light, monochrome cotton. For formal wear the fabric was worn as a sarong, pleated in the front and of ankle length. As with village dress, the fabric could be tucked between the legs to form a type of draped trouser.

The Shan princes (*sawbwa*) wore ceremonial court dress that was issued according to the sumptuary laws of the ruler to whom tribute was paid. From the sixteenth to the late nineteenth centuries, the Shan princes paid tribute to Burma or to China who acted as distant overlords, enabling the Shan princes to maintain their own spheres of interest. The Shan princes who paid tribute to Burma went annually to Mandalay where they attended a ceremony of homage (*kadaw*) to the king. They were

Figure 12.2 A Shan delegation to Chiang Mai. Detail, temple mural painting, Wat Phra Singh, Chiang Mai. Photograph by the author.

Figure 12.3 The *Duwa* Nga Lang La seated in state, *c.* 1920. Photo courtesy the James Henry Green Collection, Royal Pavilion, Libraries and Museum, Brighton and Hove [0166].

entitled to civil court dress, as issued to Burmese governors. This included a curved shaped conical headdress, framed with a circle of gold leaf, a long sleeved silk or velvet coat, trimmed with gold and silver metal thread, and embellished with sequins and beetle carapaces, worn over an ankle-length silk loincloth. The princes were also assigned, according to sumptuary law, jewellery, ceremonial vessels and betel boxes; these are illustrated in court books (*parabaik*).

The most valued loincloths, worn by the Shan princes and the elite, were made of silk *luntaya*, a complex tapestry weave fabric with interlocking 'wavy line' patterns and complex geometric and floral designs (*acheik*). The weaving technique involved the use of many small shuttles, up to two hundred for the most complex patterns. Although the cloth could be worn as an ankle-length sarong, Shan princes and senior officials are portrayed in temple mural paintings and in *parabaik* wearing *acheik-luntaya* cloth, long enough to wrap around the waist, tuck between the legs, and pass across the chest and over one shoulder. Tattooing of the thighs was common among the princes of the inland states and the cloth was folded to knee length so that the tattoos were just visible below the hemline (Figure 12.2). Some princes retained their own tattoo artists, although there were no special symbols to denote rank.[23]

The rulers of autonomous and semi-autonomous states, whose loyalties fluctuated according to local power politics, wore forms of ceremonial dress that reflected their personal wealth and prestige.[24] Their dress was a combination of imported fabrics and cloth woven by women employed at court. Court weavers used indigenous silk yarn or imported Chinese silk yarn, adding a supplementary weft of silver and gold metal thread. The finished cloth might then be embellished with beetle carapaces, silver sequins, and silk embroidery. These princes enforced their own sumptuary laws, and allocated regalia and ceremonial silver to their courtiers, advisers and tributary chiefs.

The artist L. Delaporte, who accompanied the French explorer François Garnier on his journey through the upper Mekong River region, portrayed senior princes at court ceremonies wearing Chinese dragon robes, Chinese silk shirts and embroidered silk turbans, surrounded by silverware made by their captive craft workers. Half a century later, Colonel Green photographed a powerful Kachin chief (*duwa*) wearing a Chinese silk dragon robe, a Chinese hat couched with circles of coloured glass and mother of pearl, and a fine cotton loincloth. The chief's silver pipe was made either by silversmiths under his control or acquired through trade or gift exchange (Figure 12.3).[25] Chinese silk was also used for religious ceremonies and rituals. Taoist priests (*siep mien mien*), practising among hill tribe groups wore Chinese silk, particularly dragon robes, which they modified and combined with indigenous garments and accessories. Buddhist priests used Chinese silk to wrap up sacred manuscripts kept in monastery libraries. At the Tai courts, indigenous silk was considered to be inferior to Chinese silk.[26]

It is evident that the style of male court dress worn by Shan rulers can be linked to political affiliations, personal wealth, and access to imported goods. Burmese court robes and regalia were issued to senior princes who paid allegiance to Burma, while those with political links to China, wore Chinese robes. The rulers of autonomous and semi-autonomous states commissioned clothing and personal regalia, and regalia for their courtiers, from craft workers who were their subjects or their slaves. Female textile workers produced woven fabrics and also made garments from imported materials. Less powerful rulers of the valleys and hills who could not maintain their own craft workers, wore prestige dress imported from other Shan states, from the surrounding inland states, or from Burma and China. Some textiles were received as part of a gift exchange.

FEMALE DRESS IN THE SHAN STATES

While men adapted their dress to meet political circumstances, women maintained certain 'essential elements' that were purposefully selected to allow a style to be defined as 'traditional'.[27] 'Traditional' dress in this context means dress identified with a particular ethnic group or with a homeland. Identification is based on the cut and style of individual garments, the type of yarns and dyes, the weaving, dyeing and embroidery techniques, and the patterns that were created. Where the fabric was not locally made, the choice of imported materials and how they were used may assist in identification.

Within the framework of 'tradition', women adapted their dress to suit environmental conditions. Lawa, Kachin and Karen women wore tubular skirts to the knee or to mid-calf, and leggings that allowed easy movement for climbing steep hills while protecting their legs from thorny plants, insects and leeches. At lower altitudes and in settled valley communities, they did not change the weaving patterns or the dye colours used for their skirts, but altered the length to reach the ankle. Padded cotton jackets that were essential dress in the cold season at high altitude were substituted at lower altitude with lighter jackets, blouses and shoulder sashes.

Figure 12.4 A Tai Khoen or Tai Lue 'ordinary' court skirt, with multicolour stripes and a green silk hem. Private collection. Photograph by the author.

Valley and hill tribe immigrants exchanged textile techniques and patterns over many centuries. For example, the Lawa incorporated narrow bands of ikat and coloured stripes in their tubular skirts, and the Karen also produced similar designs. In many instances it is difficult to distinguish between them, although the Karen tend to use red as the main colour, while the Lawa use indigo. In his study of the Lawa, Young suggested that Lawa women borrowed patterns from the Karen, although he noted that assimilated Lawa wore identical dress to the Tai.[28] In some areas the Tai and Lawa lived close to each other, and as a result both groups wore skirts with ikat designs. There are strong similarities in the supplementary weft patterns woven by the Karen and the Kachin to decorate their skirts and bags. Foreign writers also noted the similarity between Tai Khoen and Tai Lue 'ordinary' court dress, describing the multi-coloured striped skirts and green hems worn by both groups (Figure 12.4). Groups also took elements of dress as 'fashion'. For example, in the 1880s some wealthy women at the inland courts developed a taste for European-style blouses, described as 'ladies jerseys', while in the 1920s some Kachin women took a fancy to voluminous turbans that replaced their more modest head coverings at festivals.[29]

Figure 12.6 Detail of a Tai Khoen court skirt. Silk and silver metal thread in horizontal stripes in the top panel, a band of Chinese embroidery bordered by silver sequins in the centre and a green silk hem. Private collection. Photograph by the author.

The similarities that can be identified in hill and valley dress do not alter the fact that when necessary women wore certain elements that identified them with a particular group or homeland. This was noted by many foreign writers, including Colquhoun who wrote in 1885 that female immigrants to Chiang Mai (the capital of Lan Na) are 'more conservative than their male folk and still adhere to costumes worn by their race previous to leaving the Burmese Shan States for these parts'.[30] The missionary W.C. Dodd recalled that when the Shan princess Nang Wen Tip married the Prince of Chieng Rung in Sipsong Pan Na, she moved to 'the Lu [Tai Lue] country' but continued to wear Tai Khoen dress.[31]

For women who married into a powerful family from another state, the wearing of 'traditional' dress had strong political overtones. The rulers were polygamous and on public occasions they ensured that the consorts they had gained through marital alliances were seated together and dressed in the costumes of their homelands as a way of

Figure 12.5 A Shan skirt of silk *luntaya* with a plain black cotton waist band. Private collection. Photograph by the author.

signalling the extent of their influence. This was an important gesture within the polity of the inland states, but in the nineteenth century it was aimed at a wider audience, as the British and the French were expanding their interests in the region. It was then particularly important to use dress as a show of strength by displaying the alliances that existed between the Shan States, Sipsong Pan Na, Luang Prabang and Lan Na. Whether the colonial authorities understood the significance of these displays is difficult to assess.

When a princess married and moved to a foreign court, she wore the dress of her homeland throughout the time of her marriage. If she were accompanied to her new residence by a number of attendants, they might include weavers who could make her 'traditional' dress, obtaining the necessary yarns, fabrics and notions from itinerant traders who served all the main cities of the inland states. When familiar materials were not available, new sets of dress were sent from the home court.[32]

Tai Shan princesses wore tailored blouses with flared bodices, long straight sleeves and front or side fastenings, trimmed with embroidery, lace and ribbon. They wore Chinese silk, Chinese satin or cotton lawn in the hot season, and padded and quilted cotton, or silk and velvet lined with cotton, in the cool season. Their long hair was oiled and twisted into shiny coils, and decorated with fancy combs and flowers. They wore ankle-length skirts, made from flat rectangles of fabric that either wrapped around the waist, or were sewn lengthways into tubular forms. Both styles were tucked at the waist to form a pleat in the front. The wrapped skirt revealed the ankles when the woman walked and created a short train at the back. The skirts were made of Burmese *luntaya* silk fabric or plain Chinese silk and satin that was embroidered and beaded, or couched with strips of Chinese brocade, Chinese embroidery, silk velvet and imported printed fabric (Figure 12.5).

Tai Khoen women wore blouses with flared bodices, long, straight sleeves and crossover fronts with side fastenings, trimmed with lace, ribbons and embroidery. In the cool season they wore quilted cotton or lined silk and velvet jackets. They also wore turbans. The most spectacular part of their costume was the tubular skirt, described by the missionary William Dodd (Figure 12.6).

The skirt with the many coloured stripes and the dark green border is the ordinary court dress. To this is added a second border of large flowers solidly embroidered in gold thread, each flower four or five inches in diameter and costing a rupee a flower. In the body of the skirt also is there wove much gold thread, and the border of green velvet is bordered on either edge with sequins in silver tinsel put on in points. The same sequins trim the two or three inches of underskirt showing, which usually trails on the ground.

With gold embroidered slippers, gold bracelets and many gold ornaments in the hair set with spangles, you want to get a kun [Khoen] princess out in the sunshine to see her sparkle.[33]

Tai Lue princesses wore Chinese silk, satin or cotton blouses with flared bodices, long straight sleeves and crossover fronts with side fastenings, trimmed with ribbons and embroidery. In the cool season they wore quilted cotton or lined silk and velvet jackets. They also wore turbans. Their tubular skirts had a plain waistband and a central panel with horizontal stripes woven in supplementary weft patterns with gold and silver metal thread in floral and geometric designs. Hallett described the typical Tai Lue skirt as having horizontal red stripes interwoven with lines of gold metal thread with bands of black, blue and red in the border.[34]

From the twelfth century, the Tai chronicles document intermarriage between powerful Tai and hill tribe families and in the nineteenth and early twentieth centuries, foreign observers also record this custom. In the 1860s, during an expedition with François Garnier in Sipsong Pan Na and Laos, L. Delaporte sketched the hill tribe consorts of Tai princes (Figure 12.7). In the 1930s, Colonel Green recorded the marriage of a powerful Kachin chief to the daughter of the ruling Shan family of Hsenwi.[35] Like Tai women, Karen and Kachin women tended to be conservative, and when they resettled in the valleys continued to wear 'traditional' dress. Evidence from textile collections and photographs indicates that elite women maintained certain elements of dress that enabled them to identify with their particular group. Karen and Kachin women wore tunic style blouses (*hse*) constructed from narrow strips of cloth joined along the selvage with a slit in the centre as a neck opening. They

Figure 12.7 The King of *Muang You* (right) with two consorts, one in Tai dress and one in hill tribe dress. Illustration by L. Delaporte in François Garnier, *Voyage d'Exploration en Indo-Chine,* Paris: Hachette et Cie, 1885.

were decorated with complex supplementary weft patterns in multicoloured silk or cotton, embellished with silver discs, seeds (Job's Tears), cowrie shells, mother of pearl buttons, and silk and cotton tassels. Their skirts were either flat rectangles of cotton fabric that wrapped around the waist, or they were sewn lengthways into a tube. The skirts were highly decorated with complex supplementary weft 'zigzag' patterns and ikat. When living among the Tai, they often replaced the *hse* with a Chinese silk or satin blouse as worn by Tai women. They also substituted silk yarn for cotton yarn to weave their skirts, in keeping with local values that rated silk as a superior fabric.

In the twentieth century many rulers abandoned the practice of polygamy and as a result there were no longer consorts in different forms of 'traditional' dress residing at court. Interestingly, from this time there are photographs showing princesses wearing the 'traditional' dress of other groups, probably connected to them or their husbands by the political alliances of the time. This can be seen in photographs portraying the *Sawbwa* and the *Mahadevi* of Yawnghwe in the Shan States. The *Mahadevi* is photographed in Shan dress and in hill tribe dress (Figures 12.8 and 12.9).

Although the display of 'traditional' dress was important in terms of the politics of the inland states, where there was tributary allegiance to Burma, the Shan princesses, like their husbands, conformed to sumptuary laws when they went to pay tribute in Mandalay. They were issued with a headdress made of velvet, decorated with gold tinsel and surmounted by a gilt finial. It was worn with a long-sleeved coat trimmed with gold brocade, a scalloped gold collar and a flat, scalloped breastplate, embroidered with gold metal thread, sequins and beetle carapaces. An ankle-length, wrap-over skirt of Burmese *luntaya* fabric, or of locally woven silk, completed the outfit.

CONCLUSION

The dress and textiles of the Shan States developed from the cohesion of local inland cultures and societies and the

Figure 12.8 The *Sawbwa* and *Mahadevi* of Yawnghwe, Shan States. The *Mahadevi* wears Shan dress. Photo courtesy the James Henry Green Collection, Royal Pavilion, Libraries and Museum, Brighton and Hove [1471].

Figure 12.9 The *Sawbwa* and *Mahadevi* of Yawnghwe, Shan States. The *Mahadevi* in hill dress. Photo courtesy the James Henry Green Collection, Royal Pavilion, Libraries and Museum, Brighton and Hove [1472].

integration of indigenous designs, enriched by yarns, fabrics and trimmings obtained from overland traders. The ruling elite adapted their dress to suit prevailing political authority. When tributary to Burma they wore ceremonial dress and regalia that was allocated to them according to sumptuary laws; if tributary to China, they received Chinese textiles and robes. In contrast, autonomous Shan and hill tribe rulers wore dress that was considered to be prestigious by the standards of local society. Their ceremonial dress included imported garments, mainly of Chinese origin, or locally made garments woven and embroidered with imported Chinese silk yarn or indigenous yarn and some imported trimmings. Court regalia was generally made by indigenous craft workers. The allocation of dress and regalia to subordinates depended on the power and hierarchical nature of individual courts. Body decoration among men, particularly tattooing, was not hierarchical and there were no particular symbols to denote rank.

In contrast to male dress, female dress was conservative and women maintained certain elements in their clothing that enabled them to be identified with a particular group or homeland. The ankle-length skirt is the garment that can consistently be seen to represent group identity and homeland. Court dress and village dress were similar in terms of weaving patterns and structure although at court the yarns and fabrics were more expensive, usually imported, and the weaving and embroidery was more refined. Forms of 'traditional' dress, worn on official occasions, were intended as a way of visually communicating marital unions between ruling families and demonstrating strategic political alliances to a wider audience. However, there were periods, as in the 1940s, when certain forms of 'traditional' dress did not fit political notions of cultural uniformity and were suppressed.[36]

NOTES

1 Hans Penth, *A Brief History of Lan Na*, Chiang Mai: Silkworm Books, 1994, p.13.

2 Frank M. Le Bar, Gerald C. Hickey and John Musgrave, *Groups of Mainland Southeast Asia*, New Haven: Human Relations Area Files Press, 1964, pp. 95 and 193–215. William Clifton Dodd, *The Tai Race: Elder Brother of the Chinese*, Cedar Rapids: Torch Press, 1923, repr. Bangkok: White Lotus Press, 1996, pp. 170–274.

3 Ruyaya Abhakorn, 'Chiang Tung and the Thai State Before 1948', *Proceedings of the 16th Conference of the International Association of Historians of Asia*, Kota Kinabalu, Sabah, Malaysia, 2000 (at press).

4 D.G.E. Hall, *A History of South-East Asia*, London: Macmillan, 1955, repr. 1968, pp.10–11.

5 Maurice Collis, *Lords of the Sunset: A Tour in the Shan States*, London: Faber and Faber, 1938.

6 There are at least five important families in north Thailand who can trace their ancestry to Chieng Tung.

7 Kraisri Nimmanhaeminda, 'An Inscribed Silver Plate Grant to the Lawa of Boh Luang,' in *Felicitation Volumes of Southeast Asian Studies Presented to Prince Dhaninivat on his Eightieth Birthday*, Bangkok: the Siam Society, vol. 2, 1965, pp. 233–40.

8 E.W. Hutchinson, 'The Lawa in Northern Siam,' *Journal of the Siam Society*, vol. 27, no. 2, 1935, pp. 153–82.

9 Kachin is a Burmese term loosely translated as 'barbarians of the north-east' (Edmund R. Leach, *Political Systems of Highland Burma*, London: G. Bell, 1954, p. 41). Military officers and missionaries used the term Jinghpaw (Mandy Sadan, 'The Kachin Photographs in the J.H. Green Collection: A Contemporary Context', in Elizabeth Dell (ed.), *Burma Frontier Photographs*, London: Merrell, 2000, p. 187). The Karen call themselves 'pak ayor' (the people).

10 O. Hanson, *The Kachins: Their Customs and Traditions*, Rangoon: American Baptist Mission Press, 1913, p.12.

11 Oral communication from Eleanor Gaudoin, descendant of the ruler of Hsenwi, Shan States, Brighton, 1995.

12 Erik Seidenfaden, 'The Lawa: additional note', *Journal of the Siam Society*, vol.17, 1923, pp. 101–2. For further information, see Erik Seidenfaden, *The Thai Peoples*, Bangkok: the Siam Society, 1963.

13 Leach (1954) argued that these ethno-linguistic classifications were full of inconsistencies.

14 Michael Moerman, 'Who are the Lue: Ethnic Identification in a Complex Civilisation', *American Anthropologist*, vol. 67, 1965, pp. 1215–29.

15 Charles Keyes, 'Kin Groups in a Thai-Lao Community', in G. William Skinner and A. Thomas Kirsch (eds), *Change and Persistence in Thai Society: Essays in Honor of Lauriston Sharp*, Ithaca, NY: Cornell University Press, 1975, pp. 278–97.

16 Thomas Hylland Erikson, *Ethnicity and Nationalism: Anthropological Perspectives*, London: Pluto Press, 1993.

17 H.R. Spearman, *British Burma Gazeteer*, Rangoon: Government Press, 1880. J.G. Scott and J.P. Hardiman, *Gazeteer of Upper Burma and the Shan States*, vol. 1 and vol. 2, Rangoon: Superintendent of Government Printing, 1900, 1901. J.G. Scott, *Burma: A Handbook*, London: Alexander Moring, 1911. O. Hanson, *The Kachins: Their Customs and Traditions*, Rangoon: American Baptist Mission Press, 1913. C. Gilhodes, *The Kachins, their Religion and Customs*, Calcutta: Catholic Orphan Press, 1922, pp. 111–14. Harry Marshall, 'The Karen People of Burma: A Study in Anthropology and Ethnology', *Ohio State University Bulletin*, vol. 26, no. 13, Columbus: Ohio State University, 1922.

18 Joanne Eicher (ed.), *Dress and Ethnicity*, Oxford: Berg, 1995, pp.1–4.

19 Archibald Ross Colquhoun, *Amongst the Shans*, London: Field and Tuer, 1885. Also, Dodd, 1996.

20 Michael Vatikiotis, 'Ethnic Pluralism in the Northern Thai City of Chiang Mai,' PhD dissertation, St Catherine's College, University of Oxford, 1984.

21 Leslie Milne and Wilbur Cochrane, *Shans at Home*, London: John Murray, 1910.

22 The British described men tattooed in this way as 'the black bellied Lao' because in many cases their stomachs and thighs were tattooed.

23 Carl Bock, *Temples and Elephants, Travels in Siam 1881–1882*, Oxford: Oxford University Press, 1884; repr. Oxford University Press, 1986, p. 171.

24 E. Lefèvre, *Un Voyage au Laos*, Paris: Plon, Nourrit et Cie, 1898; repr. in translation (*Travels in Laos*, W. Tips, trans.), Bangkok: White Lotus, 1995.

25 The chief owned many slaves and it is possible that there were craft workers among them. On the artist, L. Delaporte, see François Garnier, *Voyage d'Exploration en Indo-Chine*, Paris: Hachette et Cie, 1885.

26 Oral communication, Princess Vilai na Chieng Tung, interviewed in Chiang Mai, 1996.

27 E. Shils, *Tradition*, Chicago: University of Chicago Press, 1981, p. 14.

28 George Young, *The Hill Tribes of Northern Thailand*, Bangkok: the Siam Society, 1962.

29 Bock, 1986, p. 327. Sadan, 2000, p. 72.

30 Colquhoun, 1885, p.127.

31 Dodd, 1996, p. 201.

32 Collections of 'traditional' female court dress from one state may include samples of 'traditional' dress from other states, a legacy of intermarriage.

33 Dodd, 1996, p. 201.

34 Holt Hallett, *A Thousand Miles on an Elephant in the Shan States*, Edinburgh and London: Blackwood and Sons, 1890; repr. Bangkok: White Lotus, 1988.

35 Sadan, 2000, p. 70.

36 A further reference is Paul and Elaine Lewis, *Peoples of the Golden Triangle*, London: Thames and Hudson, 1984. The journal of Sir Ernst Satow also includes relevant information. See Sir Ernst Satow, 'Journal of Sir Ernst Satow', 1885–1886, Mss 206, Public Records Office, Kew, London, 1885.

13 Diversity, identity and modernity in exile: 'traditional' Karenni clothing

Sandra Dudley

This chapter, based on long-term anthropological field research, concerns forms of so-called 'traditional' Karenni clothing and the meanings and values associated with them in exile.[1] Dress, I argue, plays an important role in the ongoing forging and changing of Karenni cultural and political identities.

Clothing – especially women's – is an aspect of 'tradition' that in the refugee camps is important in the processes concerned with what it means to be a modern Karenni person and what it means to become and be a Karenni refugee. These processes and the clothing itself are highly politicised, embedded in webs of myth, history and nationalist aspiration. Here, I consider both the clothing of newly arrived refugees and its meanings for different sectors of the refugee population, and other interpretations of 'traditional' clothing in the camps.

I focus on women's dress. The basic forms of male dress in the camps show a greater variety, with men wearing shorts, skirt-cloths, or trousers. Women dress far more 'traditionally' (this may mean different things to different sectors of the population) than do men. Indeed, amongst the Karenni as elsewhere in the world, women seem 'charged more than men with upholding a group's culture and identity'.[2] Ideas about 'Karenni-ness' and sub-Karenni ethnicities are expressed through appropriate women's clothes worn especially at religious, national and traditional occasions. But the significance of women's dress lies not only in its ability to signal ethnic similarity and distinction; it lies too in the preservation of prevailing morality. Female clothing is caught up in processes by which those with most power in determining political and communal agendas seek both to uphold morality and to strengthen national identity.

KARENNI REFUGEES

The subjects of this chapter are refugees from Kayah (Karenni) State now living in refugee camps near the Burmese border in northwest Thailand, under the auspices of the Karenni National Progressive Party (KNPP). Karenni refugees are highly diverse in ethnicity, language, level of education, religion, awareness of the wider world, political aspirations, and the experience of displacement itself. Exile has brought together people who all originate

in Kayah State but who are otherwise disparate. Some have elements of shared history, ethnicity and language, but all had less direct contact with and influence upon each other prior to their relocation to refugee camps. Nonetheless, they all call themselves 'Karenni'. What 'Karenni' actually means, however, depends upon whom one talks to; this term is itself diverse and changing, variously defined in terms of ethnicity, territoriality and history. There are at least eleven ethnic groups and associated languages in the camps,[3] all originating in Karenni State and all referring to themselves as 'Karenni', but simultaneously describing themselves as ethnically distinct. Identities are multiple. Most refugees who have been in the camps for some time, emphasise that while they are, for example, Kayan, they are of course 'Karenni'; they then add that 'we are all Karenni, we are the same family'.

In the camps, people's lives, the things that give meaning to their lives, their sense of belonging to a particular group, and the labels they give themselves, are all in a state of flux. From within this fluid, heterogeneous population is emerging a pan-Karenni national identity for which there was no real precedent before independence from the British in 1948.[4] This continual re-defining of what it means to be Karenni involves self-conscious appropriations and rejections of elements of tradition, on the one hand so as to bring together disparate Karenni groups and, on the other, so as to reinforce the differences between the Karenni and other, non-Karenni communities. Some sectors of the Karenni population are more dominant than others in these processes, attempting to create and enforce what they see as a modern, desirable Karenni identity. These dominant groups come from the longer-staying refugee community and comprise relatively well-educated, Christian individuals in the highest levels of the social and political hierarchy.

The first significant numbers of Karenni came to Thailand in 1989, but some political leaders have been in Thailand for thirty years or more. Indeed, a number of today's Karenni adolescents were born in Thailand and have never been to Karenni State. Yet, many others have become refugees very recently, particularly in and after June 1996, when the Burmese army enforced widespread

Figure 13.1 Recently arrived women sitting on house steps in a Karenni refugee camp in 1996, wearing traditional Kayah dress. Photograph by Richard.

Figure 13.2 Recently arrived Kayah women and children at a standpipe in a Karenni refugee camp 1996. One woman's ornament made of old silver rupees is clearly visible. Photograph by Richard.

Figure 13.3 Naw Sarah sitting in her house in a Karenni refugee camp, 1997. She wears a polycotton skirt-cloth printed with mock batik designs, of the kind ubiquitous throughout Southeast Asia. Photograph by the author.

relocations of villages inside Karenni State. These recent arrivals doubled the total Karenni refugee population from around 5,500 to nearly 11,000 by March 1997 (by the year 2000, numbers stood at almost 20,000). Ethnically Kayah, they came from very remote hill villages between the Pon and Salween Rivers. They differed from the pre-existing refugee population in religious and curative practices, dialect, education, female dress, and awareness of the wider world. Most claimed never to have seen motor vehicles or foreigners before, nor even women of their own ethnic group who did not dress as they did. Most of their villages had not yet received Christian missionaries, and most follow 'traditional' Kayah religion and curative practices rather than Christianity. Furthermore, unlike their ethnic cousins amongst the longer-staying refugee community, almost all of these people had little if any awareness of the KNPP's nationalist agenda. Once in the camps, they suddenly found themselves in the midst of the politicised moulding of a pan-Karenni national iden-

tity, a process over which their lack of education and political awareness gave them little influence.

It was evident that for these new arrivals the three things particularly emblematic of who they were and had been, were their main occupation of farming, the clothing traditionally worn by women, and the annual *ka-thow-bòw* festival and its associated beliefs and practices. Here, I turn to women's clothing, a distinctive element of culture that for the recent arrivals represents and reproduces the essence of who they are.

THE 'TRADITIONAL' DRESS OF THE NEW ARRIVALS

All the newly arrived women wore home-made clothing that exposed their knees, lower thighs, back, and often one breast (Figures 13.1 and 13.2). The marked dis-

144

tinction between this and the ubiquitous T-shirts (always with brassieres underneath) and *longyi* worn by women in the pre-existing Karenni refugee community (Figure 13.3) both indicated and generated some important differences between new and old refugees concerning ideas of history, morality, and what it means to be 'Kayah' and 'Karenni'. Once the women were in the camps, this 'traditional' dress also became subject to changes that were a direct cause of distress to the new arrivals.

I use 'traditional' in describing the clothing worn by the newly arrived female refugees for two reasons. Firstly, this clothing is regarded as 'traditional' by the pre-existing refugees and by the new arrivals themselves, although what each group means by 'traditional' differs. And secondly, archive photographs and early descriptions by missionaries, colonial officers and others, indicate that this kind of costume has indeed been the customary dress of Kayah women for a long time, and certainly for much longer than the so-called 'national costume' favoured in the camps (see the section on 'national dress' below).

'Tradition' and value: the meanings of female dress for new refugees

Briefly, the new refugees' female dress consists of: a skirt-and head-cloth both always home-made of home-grown cotton; a breast-cloth usually made of commercial fabric; a fabric belt-cum-purse; a string of old silver British India one rupee coins worn as a belt, sash or necklace; necklaces of glass beads; large silver ear ornaments; and a great number of black, lacquered, 2-ply cotton rings worn around and just below the knee. It is important that the full dress, with the occasional exception of the head-cloth, is worn at all times. Other than the head-cloth, no items, including jewellery, are removed, even at night. The silver functions not only as ornament, but also as family wealth and as an heirloom for safe-keeping and passing on to the next generation. In general, the clothes and jewellery worn by a Kayah woman are an extension of herself, with which she signifies her identity on a number of levels: as a Kayah woman, as a woman of a certain age and marital status, and perhaps as a woman from a particular village. This dress is more than a repository and expression of the identity of its wearer alone. Both women and men are proud of the women's weaving and clothes, and invariably describe them as 'more beautiful' and 'more comfortable' than the ubiquitous T-shirts and skirt-cloths worn by other women in the camps. Recently arrived women do not appear to feel stigmatised now that they are living amongst their Kayah cousins who wear a less traditional style of dress, although a few have encountered problems. Four years after arrival, the overwhelming majority continues to wear only traditional clothing.

Together with farming and the annual *ka-thow-bòw* festival, women's dress was one of the most significant topics of conversation among the new refugees when they first arrived in 1996. It was also the focus point for anxiety about leaving the village and becoming a refugee. There was much distress amongst women *and* men about the women's present inability – due to lack of cotton or money to buy it – to continue weaving. That is, distress did not pertain solely to the desire to continue wearing these clothes; it directly related also to the desire to continue *making* them. Like farming, this is an occupation intrinsic to being Kayah and to the meaning of women's lives. The *process* of weaving, like the process of farming, is as important to the integrity of Kayah culture as its end-products. Weaving is simultaneously connected to what has been left behind and the painful nature of the leaving-behind process itself. Also, like traditional festivals, it is one of the things refugees prioritise in their desire to make their current situation more familiar. It is both a symbol of the past and an important factor in trying to make the present more bearable and familiar.

Female dress symbolises the past for new refugees in a positive and short-term sense. It stands as a reminder of 'home' and of everyday life in the recent, village-based past. Furthermore, this connection of female dress with the recent past is intrinsic to the process of becoming a refugee. As soon as they arrive in a camp, see large numbers of other people wearing T-shirts and *longyi*, and realise the impossibility of growing or purchasing cotton in this new environment, Kayah refugees immediately begin to express anxiety about the likelihood of women not being able to continue to wear their existing style of clothing. This is not necessarily the same, however, as immediately seeing female dress as 'traditional', in the sense either of how things have always been done or in the sense of how they always used to be done.

Nevertheless, within a short time of the new refugees coming to the camps, both the pre-existing and the new refugee communities had indeed come to regard this female dress as 'traditional'. However, the values and meanings each group ascribes to female dress in particular and to 'tradition' in general, vary. For the recent arrivals, their clothing is beautiful and for both women and men is the most immediate signifier of their identity as Kayah; immediately on arrival in a refugee camp in Thailand, it was the only tangible remaining sign of what and who they were and had been. It is an obvious visual marker of difference between these Kayah and others, from which derive self- and other-defined ideas of who they are. This difference only becomes important after the Kayah have become refugees, as in their villages difference in female dress is not important. There, most if not all women wear similar clothes (it was simply the way women dressed) and most villagers, male or female, rarely if ever, encounter non-local Karenni women who dress otherwise. On arrival in the camps, however, this immediately changes, as the new refugees are suddenly exposed to large numbers of *longyi*-clad women on a daily basis. Such exposure and the associated awareness of difference combine with the attitudes and comments of pre-existing refugees (see below) to stimulate a rationalisation by new refugees of why their women dress as they do. They begin to explain it in terms of 'as things have always been done', 'as our mothers and grandmothers did before us', or 'because, long ago, the old man told us to'.[5] I suggest that the shift in self-perception and its presentation, shown by these Kayah after they have become refugees, can in some sense be defined as them coming to regard themselves as 'traditional' when compared to other Kayah and non-Kayah Karenni. This shift is subtle, operating on the level of how existing ideas of identity are rationalised, rather than on the level of changing identity itself. Nonetheless, what is essentially a raising of consciousness facilitated by a change of context has impact not only on the Kayah's experience of refugeeness, but also on ways in which they increasingly become aware of their place in a wider, Karenni 'nation'.

Attitudes of the pre-existing refugee community

Longer-staying Karenni refugees all discussed the new arrivals in similar, double-edged terms. On the one hand, they were Karenni people, 'the same as us', whose treatment by the Burmese army and subsequently awful journeys through the jungle to the border were seen as a tragedy to be shared and grieved over by *all* Karenni people; they were brethren, united by misfortune, a common geographical origin, a common enemy, and for some a common language or ethnic origin. On the other hand, longer-staying refugees also talked continually of the differences between the new arrivals and themselves. The focal point was always female dress, which was, like many aspects of the culture of the new arrivals, described by other Karenni as 'traditional'.[6] They talked of the new arrivals as *defined* by wearing clothes and adhering to religious and curative practices worn and practised long ago by all Kayah people, but now by only a few who had stayed with their old-fashioned ways because of their geographical remoteness and – as the longer stayers saw it – unfortunate lack of exposure, thus far, to education, Christianity and modernity.

This indicates a possible paradox in pre-existing Karenni refugee attitudes to the new arrivals. It seems as if the second Karenni view of the new arrivals as 'different' and highly 'traditional' in some way conflicts with the concurrent view that the new arrivals are 'the same as us'. Yet, notions of difference do not necessarily contradict the idea of the recent arrivals belonging to the Karenni family as a whole. It is rather that these new refugees are seen by other Karenni to be the most traditional members of the Karenni family, in some ways representative of its past, of threads common to the fabric from which all Karenni or, at the very least all Kayah, are

cut. It is this perception of the newly arrived Kayah as the epitome of 'tradition' that is the essence of the contradictions in the attitudes of longer-staying Karenni.

The perception of tradition and the consequently contradictory attitudes of the longer-staying refugees are derived from the obvious visual stimulus of female dress. Some longer-staying refugees, particularly young adults who have been in Thailand most or all of their lives, or who have come to Thailand from places of origin outside Karenni State, prior to 1996 had never seen traditionally-dressed Kayah women *en masse*. Others, including other young adults, come from villages where most women, including their own mothers, used to wear such clothes (and perhaps still do, if they remain inside Karenni State). Most longer-stayers I knew fell somewhere between these two extremes, having seen traditionally-dressed Kayah women before, but not in such large numbers as began to arrive in 1996. The excitement engendered in some of my Karenni friends by the new arrivals was not dissimilar to the excitement I felt myself; where we differed, however, was in the meanings we attributed to the traditional dress.

On my way to the new arrivals' camp for the first time, I stayed overnight in another camp with the family of Klaw Reh, my companion and translator. Klaw Reh's older brother, a relatively senior member of the Karenni political community, himself ethnically Kayah, was concerned that I would be shocked when I first saw the new arrivals. 'They are very, errm, *natural*', he said, laughing nervously. He wanted to forewarn me of the semi-nudity of the new refugees, with women's knees, lower thighs and, worst of all, breasts on show. He was worried not about my sensibilities alone, but also that I may judge the new arrivals harshly. By extension, I might also then judge all Kayah and ultimately all Karenni people in a similar manner.

From the beginning then, the new arrivals' clothing has been a complex issue for members of the largely Christian, pre-existing refugee population. They regard it as a 'traditional' form symbolic of the ethnic and historical roots of contemporary Karenni culture, yet it also represents to them backwardness, lack of education, poor hygiene and, above all, an unchristian immodesty on the part of the women. In this sense, it is for them a metaphor for the negative aspects of a past without the apparent moral and practical benefits of Christianity and modernity. Furthermore, the pre-existing refugee population immediately began also to act intentionally and unintentionally to influence the experience and self-perceptions of the new arrivals. At the most basic level, this involved comments being made to new arrivals and in their hearing about the revealing nature of the women's clothing. For example, on first arrival many of the women wore their breast-cloths in such a way that one breast was exposed, but within a short time as a result of comments made they had begun to wear the breast-cloth more self-

146

consciously, ensuring that both breasts were covered. Particularly influential amongst those who made such comments were the refugee staff of the camp clinic and the Camp Committee. More specifically, certain groups within the longer-staying refugee community made a deliberate decision to 'help' the new arrivals. Residents of one camp, for example, organised their own collection of used clothing within the camp, for donation to the new refugees. Such donated clothing included items for children and men, but also T-shirts and *longyi* for women. Even if these longer-staying refugees did not deliberately intend their donations to alter the way these new female refugees dressed, the effect of the composition of their donations (as of course with other donations made by international organisations) was to reinforce the fact that newly arrived women had to change their mode of dress if the particular clothes in which they had arrived were eventually to fall apart (as many women's did).

Even more significantly, soon after the first large waves of arrivals in 1996 the Karenni Border Catholic Association held an extraordinary meeting of its officers in order to plan systematic missionary activity amongst the new refugees. These evangelists and the initiative for their work all came from within the existing Karenni refugee community itself. They included a number of ethnic Kayah, but were dominated by Kayans. Certainly, the main objective was not to persuade women to wear different style of clothing; rather, it was to convert people to Christianity and at the same time, to the value of education. However, in practice, for the dominant, longer-staying Karenni refugee community, ideas of Christianity, education, female propriety, and what it means to be a modern Karenni person, are all intertwined. Most Christian Karenni would consider that a side-effect of Christianity is its 'civilising' influence, including encouraging women to cover themselves decently. There is little separation of a biblically derived Christian morality on the one hand, and an historically derived, Victorian morality repressive of women and originating with the nineteenth-century American and European missionaries, on the other.

More general issues raised by this mesh of ideas of Christianity, propriety, modernity and education cannot be discussed here; suffice to say that these ideas were no more separable for those planning missionary work with the new arrivals than for any other Christian member of the pre-existing population. Most members of this population, and certainly its leadership and educated youth sectors, whether Catholic missionaries or not, found it hard to separate such ideas in their attitudes towards and interaction with the new refugees. Even in 1998, two years on, members of the longer-staying community continued to hold onto their ideas about the 'traditional' Kayah. Paw, for example, a young woman who had herself conducted human rights interviews with the new

refugees back in 1996, giggled in horror with her friends about how, when these refugees first came to the camp, 'They didn't even know how to *wash*! They had to be taught how to keep themselves *clean*!'

Such attitudes are complex, not least because of their co-existence with feelings of fraternal sympathy. What matters here, is that they are always associated with traditional Kayah female dress. As a visual fact it stimulates these attitudes, and is returned to repeatedly in the ways in which the pre-existing refugee community thinks of its traditional Kayah cousins. Ideas about the new arrivals' cleanliness – or lack of – are intimately bound up with traditional dress (not least because it is well known that this dress is never removed, even at night and even when washing). Similarly bound up with dress are notions (often pitying) about the new refugees' unawareness of Christian soteriology and what are believed to be Christian ideas about propriety and decency. By extension, there is pity too for their ignorance of the modern world, how to live in it, and how to deal with its politics. In sum then, female dress is central to a set of existential processes whereby pre-existing refugees make moral judgements about their newly arrived cousins.[7] Such attitudes, together with those of outsiders, gave to the new refugees an impression of the camp as an area apart, a place of mixed messages. In the face of such confusion, rather than turning their back on this clothing, the new arrivals instead clung tighter to it, its significance in their everyday conversation and concerns growing, rather than diminishing with time.

'TRANSITIONAL' CLOTHING IN THE CAMPS

Amongst the longer-staying refugee population, the particular kinds of *longyi* worn by men and women with their T-shirts are usually varied and personal. Women's are generally either woven commercially in Malaysia or Thailand and printed at source with designs mimicking traditional Malay and Indonesian *batik* patterns, or are more traditional-style cloths made by women on back-strap or non-automated frame looms in the camps. The first type is ubiquitous in markets throughout Southeast Asia. The second type, however, is important in what I call 'transitional' dress.

On Sundays, during festivals, and on other special occasions, many people choose to dress in what they refer to as 'traditional' or 'national' dress. Many women also wear this style of clothing or at least a 'traditional' hand-woven *longyi* rather than a Malaysian or Indonesian printed one on an everyday basis, particularly in the cold season (hand-woven *longyi* being thicker and warmer).

Nonetheless, these transitional types of clothing are not worn daily by large numbers of people on the kind of scale on which recent arrivals wear their traditional Kayah costume. Furthermore, with the exception of so-called 'Paku' cloths (i.e. cloths identified as belonging to the Paku Karen Karenni sub-group, further discussed

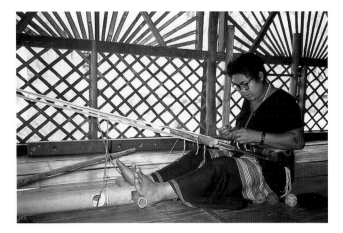

Figure 13.4 Naw Rebecca weaving at a backstrap loom in her house in a Karenni refugee camp in 1997. She wears a 'transitional' Paku Karen skirt-cloth that she wove herself, and a Paku married woman's shirt. Here, she is weaving a dress for an unmarried girl, an item later collected for the Pitt Rivers Museum, University of Oxford. Photograph by the author.

'universal' sorts of dress and, on the other, highly 'traditional' clothing worn by recently arrived refugee women. It is because of its location midway along the continuum that I refer to this style of dress as 'transitional'.[9]

There are a number of different sorts of the transitional skirt-cloths hand-woven in the camps, differentially characterised as 'traditional' to and by various Karenni groups. Other than the so-called 'Karenni national' cloths (see below), the most common types are 'Paku (Karen)' (Figure 13.4) and 'Padaung' cloths. Women make these on continuous warp back-strap looms, using yarn purchased ready-spun and ready-dyed in Mae Hong Son market or in a camp shop. They may be made by the eventual wearer herself, or subsequently sold. They are often worn as everyday wear with T-shirts, but they are also worn on occasions that are more formal. Both types are predominantly black, with thin coloured stripes near the top and bottom of the skirt, and stripes and subtle patterning in the central portion.

The characterisation of these two types of cloth as 'Padaung' and 'Paku' is not mine, but that of my informants. They describe each type of cloth as being the traditional, typical type for each of these two ethnic groups. Yet, this neat labelling does not necessarily fit with a complex ethnographic reality. 'Padaung' here refers to all Kayan, each of the self-defined sub-groups of which

below), the skirt-cloths in these types of so-called 'traditional' outfits are notably absent from early archive photographs and museum collections. Indeed, I suggest that these clothes represent a mid-point on a continuum between, on the one hand, increasingly 'Burmese'[8] and

Figure 13.5 High school students in a Karenni refugee camp in 1996. They are performing the *dïy küw* dance as part of the annual *dïy küw* festival. The dance represents the activities of the agricultural year. They wear 'national' Karenni dress. Photograph by the author.

actually has its own traditional cloths that do not correlate to the type described as 'Padaung' in the camps. Indeed, some Kayan informants[10] said the cloths described as 'Padaung', and thus implied to be in some way representative of and traditional to all Kayan groups, were in fact typical only to Kayan Kang-Ngan, and inside Karenni State were to be found mainly in two particular villages near the state capital of Loikaw.

NATIONAL DRESS AS TRANSITION AND TRANSFORMATION: KARENNI 'NATIONAL' CLOTHS

I have indicated that traditional Kayah clothing is a female repository and expression of Kayah (and a form of Karenni) identity. At the same time, the diverse Karenni community as it exists in its refugee context, is continually developing a highly politicised sense of 'Karenni-ness', a national identity dependent on real and imagined shared pasts. Yet, traditional Kayah women's dress, an obvious marker of the legacies of the past and of difference between Karenni and non-Karenni, is not directly appropriated as a symbol in this process. This is because it is emblematic of aspects of the past not wanted in dominant groups' formulations of 'Karenni-ness'.

Instead, a transformation of traditional Kayah dress has become a metaphor for an emerging pan-Karenni national identity. Female school students and others, on occasions of annual festivals and ceremonies, wear what they describe as 'traditional' Karenni/Kayah dress, but which bears little resemblance to the clothes worn by the recently arrived refugee women. It comprises a striped, red *longyi* reaching to mid-calf length, a similar cloak, a white or pale pink blouse, and a white sash (Figures 13.5 and 13.6). In colour and patterning the skirt-cloth and cloak are clearly related to the skirt- and head-cloth worn by newly arrived refugees. There are two important differences to this wider form of dress, however. Firstly, it does not expose the amounts of female flesh seen with the 'traditional' version. And secondly, it is considered 'national Karenni', not 'Kayah', dress, not only by Kayah members of the longer-staying refugee population, but by all that population's other members too. Seng and Wass, writing about Palestinian wedding dress in the USA, similarly explore 'how the concept of tradition has changed, like the garments, over time, and how that change is linked to a search for national identity'.[11] They point out that contrary to outsiders' understandings of 'tradition' as implying an unchanged form, 'the [insiders'] definition of what is traditional involves a selective process, for as long as an object contains certain determined elements it may still be considered as 'traditional'. Both process and definition are dynamic'.[12] For longer-staying Karenni refugees, the 'certain determined elements' include colour and patterning on the skirt-cloth and cloak.

This form of dress was developed by members of the growing national movement after 1948,[13] and is a transformation of 'tradition' which includes elements of traditional Kayah dress.[14] Like promulgations of 'tradition' discussed by Knauft in the cases of Melanesia and the Amazon, it 'actively appropriates aspects of perceived modernity in reconstruction of indigenous identity'.[15] In this case, the appropriated 'aspects of perceived modernity' concern propriety, with women becoming more covered up. Furthermore, concurrently with ideas about dress, notions of proper feminine behaviour are also transformed. For example, young, unmarried, traditional Kayah girls joke about their breast-cloth (which usually only covers one breast), saying their boyfriends can have the exposed breast now, but they have to wait until marriage to get their hands on the other one. Such sexual banter is in sharp contrast to the self-consciously demure way in which most other refugee Karenni girls behave.

Figure 13.6 A non-traditional Kayah couple at their wedding in a Karenni refugee camp in 1997. She wears 'national' Karenni dress, and he wears a striped red skirt-cloth. Photograph by the author.

Increasing nationalism, here accompanied by increasing Christianity, seems also to imply increasing conservatism, especially with respect to women and their sexuality. In this case, it is female dress that undergoes the most obvious conservative transformation.

Friedman suggests that an engagement with modernity frequently implies devaluation of local culture.[16] In the case of traditional Kayah female dress, an essentially female signification and reinforcement of cultural identity has in its untransmuted, traditional form, been devalued and ultimately rejected by the mainly male groups that dominate contemporary ideas of 'Karenni-ness'. For these dominant groups, transformation of traditional female dress represents continuation of a body of tradition that identifies Karenni people as having a distinct and glorious history, and emergence as a modern, Christian, educated and united people. The continuation and transformation of tradition is part of a set of processes aimed at ensuring Karenni identity remains Karenni, and at keeping Karenni people clearly distinct from others.

But transformation of female dress is only one of a number of ways in which Karenni groups to different extents use past- and future-oriented ideas of self, community and belonging, both to give meaning to their present displaced state, and to attempt to re-define identity and control a set of realistic and semi-mythical futures. For the new arrivals in their first months in the camp, in the initial and distressing stages of becoming a Karenni refugee, the only way they could give meaning to this experience was to tighten their grip on the visual markers of self that they had brought with them, particularly women's clothing, grasping firmly the most emblematic aspects of traditional Kayah culture and village life. As time has passed, the new arrivals have been drawn into the constant re-assessment and re-negotiation of identity experienced by all members of the Karenni refugee community.

Traditional dress, like festivals, exemplifies not only the complexities involved in emic interpretations of 'tradition', but also the extent of the elite's role in continuity and change in the context of Karenni nationalism. Clothing especially demonstrates too that actors other than the elite also have an important part to play in the ascription of identities, i.e. they 'are involved in *making* classifications as well as in simply following them . . . [they are] making decisions, choosing to some extent their own self-image, playing with identities and recognising the role of clothes in image construction and interpretation'.[17] In a process by which Karenni identity is self-consciously, and reasonably successfully, strengthening and remoulding itself, elements of 'tradition' are selectively appropriated, transformed or rejected. This is part of a general process in which clothing, annual festivals, and other aspects of real and imagined shared pasts articulate political aspirations and revolutionary ideologies. Ideas of the past and the future combine to define a Karenni nationalism and national identity which rise above and are inclusive of all the related but distinct ethnic identities. Clothing plays an important part in this process.

NOTES

1 An important form of traditional Karenni clothing not discussed in this article is the dress and ornament worn by Kayan Kung-Kaw ('Padaung' or 'Long-neck') women.

2 F. Wilson and B.F. Frederiksen, 'Introduction: Studies in Ethnicity, Gender and the Subversion of Nationalism', in F. Wilson and B.F. Frederiksen (eds), *Ethnicity, Gender and the Subversion of Nationalism,* London: Frank Cass & Co., Ltd., 1995, p. 4.

3 These include the Kayah, Paku Karen, Bre Karen, Yintale, Kayaw, Manu Manaw, and at least four different Kayan sub-groups. All are linguistically related (some more closely than others), and all are, in differing degrees of classification, sub-groups of the overall Karen family. Scholars differ on precise classifications, but see, for example: R. B. Jones, *Karen Linguistic Studies,* Berkeley: University of California Press, 1961; F.M. Lebar, G.C. Hickey and J.K. Musgrave (eds), *Ethnic Groups of Mainland Southeast Asia,* New Haven, CT: Human Relations Area Files, 1964; and J. Matisoff, 'Linguistic Diversity and Language Contact', in J. McKinnon and W. Bhruksasri (eds), *Highlanders of Thailand,* Singapore: Oxford University Press, 1986.

4 Cf. F.K. Lehman, 'Burma: Kayah Society as a Function of the Shan-Burma-Karen Context', in J.H. Steward (ed.), *Contemporary Change in Traditional Societies II: Asian Rural Societies,* Urbana, Chicago and London: University of Illinois Press, 1967, pp. 1–104.

5 The 'old man' often invoked in Kayah explanations of various myth and traditional practices, is generically a wise ancestor figure who set down the Kayah ways of doing things.

6 They frequently used the English word.

7 Judgements made by outsiders are also important, and can play a significant role in the new arrivals' experience of what it is to be refugees. See S. Dudley, '"Traditional" Culture and Refugee Welfare in North-west Thailand', *Forced Migration Review,* vol. 6, 1999, pp. 5–8.

8 This is a contentious term for the Karenni. See also note 13.

9 There is another way in which this form of dress acts as a transitional or connecting phase, this time in connection with memories of 'home'. See S. Dudley, *Displacement and Identity: Karenni Refugees in Thailand,* Unpublished DPhil. thesis, University of Oxford, 2001.

10 E.g. Augustino, personal communication, 1996.

11 Y.J. Seng and B. Wass, 'Traditional Palestinian Wedding Dress as a Symbol of Nationalism', in J.B. Eicher (ed.), *Dress and Ethnicity,* Oxford: Berg, 1993, p. 229.

12 *Ibid.*, pp. 229–30.

13 It appears in many ways to be a Burmanisation of older forms of Kayah dress, although when I put this to the Secretary of the Karenni National Women's Organisation, she rejected the suggestion angrily, saying that in no way was it a Burmanisation, and didn't fashions in my country change too? This deliberate development of a 'national' costume is also documented elsewhere; e.g. Eriksen on the self-conscious selection of national 'folk costumes' and other invented traditions in Norway (T.H. Eriksen, *Ethnicity and Nationalism: Anthropological Perspectives,* London: Pluto Press, 1993).

14 It does not, however, utilise elements of Kayan, Kayaw or Paku Karen traditional forms of female dress.

15 B.M. Knauft, 'Gender Identity, Political Economy and Modernity in Melanesia and Amazonia', *Journal of the Royal Anthropological Institute*, vol. 3, part 2, 1997, pp. 233–59. Transitional and national forms of dress could also be said to be 'symbolic inversion, on high days and holidays, which tells people what it is that they are in their ordinary daily lives . . . [in which] they are, in their own eyes, "modern"' (M. Chapman, '"Freezing the Frame": Dress and Ethnicity in Brittany and Gaelic Scotland', in J.B. Eicher (ed.), *Dress and Ethnicity*, Oxford: Berg, 1995, p. 27).

16 J. Friedman, 'Narcissism, Roots, and Postmodernity: the Constitution of Selfhood in Global Crisis', in S. Lash and J. Friedman (eds), *Modernity and Identity*, Oxford: Basil Blackwell, 1992, p. 338.

17 E. Tarlo, *Clothing Matters: Dress and Identity in India*, London: Hurst, 1996, pp. 7–8, emphasis original.

14 Burmese arts and crafts: the Scherman Collection in the Ethnographic Museum, Munich

Uta Weigelt

While considered an authority on Indian ethnography, philology, and culture during his lifetime, Lucian Scherman and his work have been almost forgotten by the scholarly community. As a result, the large collection of Burmese arts and crafts which Scherman brought back from Burma in 1911 remains largely unknown to the public today.

LUCIAN MILIUS SCHERMAN

Lucian Milius Scherman was born in Posen on 10 October 1864. He studied Romance languages and literature, as well as Indian philology, in Breslau and Munich. He obtained his doctorate in 1885, with a comparison of the philosophies espoused by the hymns of the Rig- and Atharva-Veda-Sanhitâ in relation to those of the older Upanishads,[1] and qualified as a university lecturer in 1901. In 1916 Scherman was appointed to the first chair of ethnography at the Ludwig Maximilian University in Munich.

Scherman also edited *Oriental Bibliography*, the premier reference work for scholars of Oriental studies, until 1928, when publication ceased due to financial problems.[2] Being the editor of the bibliography and working together with colleagues of similar interests, including Berthold Laufer (1874–1934) and Aurel Stein (1862–1943) among others, made Scherman well known in Germany and abroad.

Scherman, however, met his true calling in 1907 when he was appointed director of the Royal Ethnographical Collection of the House of Wittelsbach in Munich, one of the oldest collections of its kind in Germany. Since 1868 the collection had been stored in the Galeriegebäude, which was originally built to house a collection of paintings. However, this venue was too small for the ethnographic collection, with the result that none of the objects could be shown in an appropriate way. Only in 1926, however, did Scherman finally realise his plan to move the collection to a more spacious building. The new site was located on Maximilianstrasse, and the collection is still housed there today.[3] The re-arrangement of the collection, which was enlarged many times over during Scherman's directorship, made the museum – to use the words of Franklin Edgerton (1885–1963), lecturer in

Sanskrit at Yale University and a former student of Scherman – 'a new sort of model for what such a place should be'.[4] Scherman devoted all his energy and attention to the museum until in 1933 the Nazis forced him to resign from all his offices because he was Jewish. He stayed in Munich until 1939, when he and his wife Christine (1865–1940) emigrated to the United States to live with their son and his family in Hanson, Massachusetts. Scherman continued studying, and only a few weeks prior to his death in 1946, he received the message that he had been reinstated as professor emeritus at the Ludwig Maximilian University.

COLLECTING

In his position as the director of the Ethnographic Museum, Scherman, together with his wife Christine, made a study trip through Burma from January to August 1911.[5] They started their trip in Rangoon and travelled to Mandalay via Pegu, where they stayed for a couple of days. Using Mandalay as a base, they made several short journeys into different regions of the country. The first journey lasted about a month and took them by boat up the Chindwin River as far as Khamti in the north. On the way they stopped several times to visit villages and other interesting sites on the river. After a six-week stint in Mandalay, they embarked on another tour, which led into the southern Shan States via Thazi, Pyinyaung, Nampandet, Kalaw, Heho, Ta-yo, and Inle Lake. They also travelled on to Loikaw and Taunggyi before returning to Mandalay via Nampandet and Hlaindet. Back in Mandalay, they immediately prepared for their next trip into the northern Shan States to visit Hsipaw, Lashio, and Namshan. The final tour took them north up the Irrawaddy River to Bhamo and then to Namhkam on the Chinese border.[6]

By visiting craftsmen, manufacturers, monasteries, missionaries, schools, and villages, the Schermans acquired a large collection of Burmese arts and crafts from many different ethnic groups, including the Burmans, Nagas, Palaungs, Shans, Karens, and other hill tribes. In bringing together this collection the Schermans were assisted by European and American missionaries, British govern-

Figure 14.1 Lucian and Christine Scherman with Deputy Commissioner Grant Brown and purchased objects, February 1911. Photograph by L. Scherman, Ethnographic Museum, Munich, Ch 95.

ment officials, and local residents. The government translator and archaeologist Taw Sein Ko was of particular assistance during their stay in Burma. He organised meetings with locals, ordered models of houses and copies of books for the Schermans, and in long discussions explained Burmese culture to them. In a letter to his mentor and teacher Ernst Kuhn (1853–1920), Scherman described the necessity of being supported by officials of the British government.[7]

Grant Brown, who held the office of the Deputy Commissioner of the Upper Chindwin District, invited the Schermans to join him on a census tour of the area (Figure 14.1). On this occasion the Schermans collected 370 objects from different ethnic groups, made phonographic records, and took many photographs. On their trip to Bhamo and Namhkam, the Schermans were invited to stay at the house of the head of the American Baptist Mission, Reverend Roberts, in Bhamo. The pupils in the mission were mainly Kachin, and the Schermans were able to acquire valuable information about this ethnic group and were able to take numerous photographs (Figure 14.2). Reverend Roberts also organised the recording of Kachin proverbs and Atsi and Jinghpaw numerals.

Thus, having invited Lucian and Christine Scherman to stay, their various hosts put together collections for them, organised meetings, and dealt with local residents in order to gain further information and material. Without the help of these men, and many others, the journey through Burma would not have been so successful.

THE SCHERMAN COLLECTION OF BURMESE MATERIAL

The Scherman Collection, kept in the Munich Ethnographic Museum, comprises about 2,000 items, including Buddhist sculptures, *nat* figures, decorative architectural

Figure 14.2 Reverend Roberts and the teacher Miss Ragon, with five Kachin wearing their traditional dress, Bhamo, 13 July 1911. Photograph by L. Scherman, Library of the Ludwig Maximilian University Munich, Estate E. Kuhn, correspondence Scherman, No. 87.

elements, textiles, silverware, jewellery, pottery, musical instruments, puppets, basketry, weapons and shields, and models of fishing equipment, boats, and houses of different ethnic groups. The travel diaries of the Schermans, which are also kept in the Ethnographic Museum, allow a detailed reconstruction of their itinerary and the origin of many of the purchased objects.[8] A large number of photographs, taken by Christine Scherman, with a list of the subject matter of each and the date and place they were taken provides valuable information. Phonographic recordings complete the collection.[9]

Despite the extensive records kept in the museum and the Schermans' travel diaries, it is not always evident how the Schermans purchased the items. Some of them were bought at the markets and, as mentioned before, some objects were given to them as gifts. For example, Taw Sein Ko bought for the museum a series of fifteen plates illustrating the *yun* process listed as 'Lacquerware for Rs 17– 8' (Inv. Nos. P 67a-h, j-p).

To date, only a small part of the collection has been studied. Some of these studies were undertaken by Scherman himself. Using an earlier article, 'Frauenleben im buddhistischen Birma', as a basis, Scherman wrote the lavishly illustrated monograph, *Im Stromgebiet des Irrawaddy. Birma und seine Frauenwelt*, with his wife.[10]

This book provides an insight into the life and customs of the different ethnic groups in Burma. His article, 'Brettchenwebereien aus Birma und den Himalayaländern' gives a unique eye-witness account of the production and the use of tablet weaving.[11] Together with his wife, Scherman also researched the weaving patterns of the Kachin.[12] In the essay, 'Buddha im Fürstenschmuck', Scherman illustrated Buddhist sculptures owned by the museum and drew comparisons with other objects that he had seen during his stay in Burma.[13] Several other essays focus on the *nat* cult.[14]

The Scherman collection of musical instruments was studied by Curt Sachs in 1917.[15] Later, Kurt Reinhard used part of the phonographic records made by Scherman to examine the traditional music of Burma.[16] A catalogue of the Scherman collection of *yun* lacquerware with detailed descriptions of thirty-one objects was published by this author in volume six of the series *Münchner Beiträge zur Völkerkunde*. In the same volume, an essay on *nat* figures, a bibliography of Scherman's complete work, a biography focusing on Scherman's Indian studies and his academic career, and an itinerary of his travels in Burma were published. A doctoral dissertation about the life and work of Lucian Scherman is in progress by the author.

THE SCHERMAN COLLECTION OF *YUN* LACQUERWARE

The Schermans also collected lacquer items and recorded production processes. Two photographs of lacquer workers taken by the Schermans at Pagan in 1911 show the different steps in the manufacture of *yun* lacquerware, from splitting the bamboo, weaving the substrate (in this case for a box), applying the first layer of lacquer mixed with ashes or other substances, smoothing the surface, to applying the lacquer, polishing, and engraving the object.[17] These images provide detailed information about the process of manufacturing *yun* ware which complements that given by Scherman in his travel diaries.[18]

Scherman also bought tools and materials used in making lacquer vessels, such as a bow-operated lathe, devices for engraving parallel lines and other engraving tools, compasses for engraving concentric lines, blades for smoothing the surface, whetstones, a piece of petrified wood for smoothing the surface, a mandrel for weaving lacquer cups, and six colouring agents.[19] Apart from the mandrel and the stones, all these items have unfortunately been lost, but the museum's records can still be consulted for the specifications of these items, such as their size.

The Scherman Collection contains more than one hundred pieces of lacquerware. All of the techniques used in Burma are represented: gold leaf lacquerware, relief moulded lacquerware with glass inlay, as well as dry lacquer items. The last includes several pieces given to Scherman by the grand-nephew of King Mindon, Hteik Tin Galay. A palanquin with a seven-tiered roof, which was originally presented to a monastery by the Burmese king, was offered to Scherman by the head of a monastery near Mandalay.[20] In addition, the hermit U Khanti presented a gilded hat of his order to Scherman (Inv. No. Md 3).[21]

Yun lacquerware is represented in the collection by about forty pieces. The forms of the objects vary, and include betel-boxes, plates, cups, bowls, cosmetic boxes, covers for water vessels, and a hat box. The shapes of some of the pieces are highly unusual. For instance, there is a box-like object with tapered sides and lid showing a *kunan kanbyat* design, also known as the Yunnan semi-circular design (Inv. No. P 16).[22] It may have been used as a tea cup.[23]

The hat box with a domed lid decorated with a variant of the *kunan kanbyat* design (Inv. No. Md 75) is similar to a betel-box with a similar shape published in the exhibition catalogue, *Visions from the Golden Land: Burma and the Art of Lacquer*.[24] The five layers of the domed lid may indicate that this box was owned by a member of the royal family, but there is no reference to the original ownership in Scherman's diaries. Two lids for water vessels (Inv. Nos. P 17 and P 18) and an offering vessel consisting of five separate parts with a simple *Myin-mo* (Mount Meru) design filled with the twelve signs of the zodiac and floral bands (Inv. No. Md 329) are further examples of pieces with unusual profiles in the collection.[25]

LACQUER WORKSHOPS

Several *yun* lacquer pieces in the Scherman Collection bear inscriptions. These inscriptions were primarily added by the makers, indicating the name of the workshop, the date of the item, and claiming high quality for it. The story scenes depicted on some pieces are usually also explained by several captions. None of the names of lacquer masters represented in the Scherman Collection have been previously mentioned in the writings of Western scholars.[26] The identification of these lacquer masters, their workshops, and the dates of manufacture will help piece together the history of Burmese lacquer production.

One piece bears the name of the owner on the bottom. It is a bowl (Inv. No. P 15), similar to the one published in *Burmese Lacquerware* by Sylvia Fraser-Lu,[27] showing the name Tha Wan, one of the four ministers of a king.

A very fine example of a thin-walled, light and flexible piece decorated in the typical Pagan style is a betel-box with two inner trays (Inv. No. P 5).[28] The substrate of the box consists of a mixture of fine bamboo splints and horsehair, the latter forming the weft of the basketry. Around the top edge of the cover and the bottom edge of the box are four inscriptions in yellow which read:

မြန်မာနိုင်ငံ ပုဂံမြို့တိုက်စု
ရွာပဲတိုက်ထွက်အခင်ပါ
. သက္ကရာဇ် ၁၂၇၂ ခါဆိုလ
. လုတ်ကိုင်သာည့် ယွန်ထည်
ဝယ်ယူသူ မိတ်ဆွေတို့
အဆင်: ပါ.မြို့ ရှိသော
လက်ဆောင်: အမြို့ ဖို
အသိတ် အကောင်ဆို;

'Burma, Pagan, Taik-su ward, a betel box from the workshop of Master Hpe, in the year 1272 BE [AD1910], Wazo [July], handmade lacquer work. To friends and customers: this work in five colours is up to the same standard as traditional ware. It is precious. It is the best.' This piece was evidently manufactured in July 1910 in the workshop of a certain Hsaya Hpe of the Taik-su ward of Pagan. The illustrations depicted on the drum show scenes from the Mahosadha Jataka as indicated by the captions accompanying the narrative. The side of the base piece shows a palace scene, and the two trays are equally finely embellished.

Another betel-box in the collection which is from the same workshop shows floral netting or lace work (Inv. No. P 7), which derives from textile patterns.[29] Like the box described above, the frame is also made of horsehair and split bamboo. The literature on *yun* lacquerware often mentions that the design is done freehand and not measured out before applying the decoration, and therefore the errors the artist made in dividing the space on this item are not surprising. On the side of the drum and the trays, he added a filler motif to hide the fact that the pattern does not fit perfectly around the vessel. Nevertheless, the inscriptions on the box praise it as being of the highest quality manufactured by the above mentioned Hsaya Hpe in the month Wagaung of the year 1272 (August 1910). Another inscription on this betel-box provides very valuable information about the origin of the pattern. The four lines of inscription on the foot are as follows:

ဇာယွမ်းထည့်အဆန်း
အမျိုးဖွဲ့လက်ဟောင်း
အကို့တံအရကောင်းဆွဲ
ဇာ့ရောင်ဝင်အနှစ်ပါ

'This box is of royal quality, made with the latest novel pattern, the *za-yun* pattern; it is of authentic traditional workmanship; and is a valuable piece of the best quality.'

Since the date of manufacture is given as 1910, the *za-yun* or netting pattern was clearly fashionable then, and may perhaps have been entirely new. This piece is the only one known so far to name its pattern and claim novelty for it.

A legendary adventure of the founder and later king of Pagan, Pyazawhti (AD 168–243) embellishes another betel-box (Inv. No. P 6).[30] The inscription names the workshop of Hsaya Sein as also situated in the Taik-su ward at Pagan. Other captions praise the quality of the item and claim that it was produced in the traditional way.

Another piece, this time from the workshop of Hsaya Hla, which was also located in the Taik-su ward of Pagan, is a shallow box (Inv. No. P 10).[31] As recorded in the inscription on the top of the lid, a scene from the Paduma Jataka is depicted. On the side of the box running figures alternate with cows and palm trees. A cup with minute yellow dotting all over the cinnabar red ground (Inv. No. Md 86), which also bears the name Hla engraved on the bottom, might originate from the same workshop.[32] This piece was given to Scherman by Taw Sein Ko in Mandalay. On a third item, a very fine betel-box with one

inner tray decorated with *kunnan kanbyat*, or the 'Yunnan semicircle' pattern (Inv. No. Md 81), the name Hla also appears on the base in very delicate calligraphy.[33] The last object bearing the name of the workshop Hla is a box with one tray decorated with yellow dotting over the cinnabar red ground (Inv. No. Md 80).[34]

Another workshop that can be identified by the inscriptions on two similar *yun* lacquer water vessels (Inv. Nos. P 8 and P 9), executed in the Pagan colours of red, orange, green and yellow, are from the workshop of Hsaya San in the centre of Pagan.[35] One of the inscriptions, in a cartouche embedded in a floral band, praises the item as being of first quality. The depicted scenes have not yet been identified although the name of a certain minister, Velusara, is mentioned.

Finally, a piece in the Scherman Collection identifies the lacquer master U Tha Shein as an imperial prize winner. He is introduced in one of the inscriptions on a circular tray on which vivid scenes from the Kusa Jataka are shown (Inv. No. P 14).[36] The scenes depicted here illustrate an elephant fair, which Prince Kusa attended disguised as a mahout and at which he threw dirt at his own wife. Five captions record this episode. U Tha Shein's work was shown at the 1902–3 Exhibition of Indian Arts Manufactures at Delhi, held as part of the celebrations of the coronation of the Emperor, King Edward VII. He won special commendation for a lacquered table, and a bronze medal (third prize) for a collection of lacquered work.[37] In 1910, he therefore signed the tray as follows:

မြန်မာနိုင်ငံအထက်ပိုင်း ပုဂံမြို့မ
တံဆိပ်ဆက်ရ ဦးသာရှိန်ထိုက်ဖြစ်
အဆောင်ဒါးမျိုးရှိသော မျှန်ထည့်
အမျိုးဖွန် အဆို့တန် လက်ဟောင်း

'Upper Burma, the major town Pagan, [from the] Workshop [of] U Tha Shein, imperial prize winner. This five coloured lacquer piece is of authentic, valuable, and traditional craftsmanship.'

YUN LACQUERWARE OF THE SHAN STATES

In the town of Myn-ma-ti in the Shan States, Scherman bought a stemcup-like vessel with one tray embellished with a simple band of flowers (Inv. No. Ss 25; Figure 14.3). According to the entry in the museum register, it originates from Laihka in the Shan States. Vessels of this kind were used for holding flowers and other offerings when going to the temple.[38]

A beautifully embellished betel-box (Inv. No. Br 71; Figure 14.4) was, along with several other lacquer objects, presented to Scherman by a Superintendent called C. S. Browne. It is very similar to a piece published in the cat-

Figure 14.3 Vessel with one tray decorated with floral design. Early twentieth century. Photograph by Norbert Hein, Ethnographic Museum, Munich, Ss 25.

alogue of the British Museum exhibition.[39] The *yun* decoration of this betel-box with two trays shows great draughtsmanship. The top of the lid and the drum depict dancing figures against a background of foliage in gold and black. They wear their waist cloths caught up high between the legs in typical Shan style to form baggy breeches. The side of the base is covered only with foliage and clouds, while on the bottom of the base there is a very elaborate scene which is not easily identifiable (Figure 14.5). In this scene a prince is sitting on a horse, holding the reins in his hands. The neck as well as the ears and the top of the head of the horse are shown. A servant is cleaning the prince's left foot with a towel, yet not daring to look his master in the face.

A comparatively large cylindrical box with one tray was probably meant to be used to store hairpieces, combs, cosmetics, and toiletries (Inv. No. Md 73) (Figure 14.6). Several narrow hoops of bamboo are attached to the drum of the lid and to the base, and on the base a moulded band of *thayo* shows a fine design which imitates turned slivers or pegs of wood.[40] On the lid a scene in a palace is depicted, and on the drum, a very vivid hunting scene. A king is standing on a cart drawn by two horses accompanied by servants holding three fans, while servants with guns lead the way (Figure 14.7). The queen is

Figure 14.4 Betel-box with two trays showing dancing figures in *yun* decoration. Early twentieth century. Photograph by Norbert Hein, Ethnographic Museum, Munich, Br 71.

sitting on an elephant behind the king, followed by guards with bows. Deer, monkeys, and birds are also depicted. The execution of the detailed scenery shows great draughtsmanship.

The collection of Shan lacquerware also includes three small cups of the northern Shan States, with a simple green ornamental decoration on a black background (Inv. Nos. Ns 379, Ns 381 and Ns 382), and two trays. One of the latter items is a large, deep platter embellished with floral designs in silver (Inv. No. Ss 507); the other one is a rather shallow platter with a floral design in gold (Inv. No. Br 70) (Figure 14.8).

CONCLUSION

The Scherman Collection of Burmese arts and crafts provides a very specific and valuable record of Burma and its inhabitants during the early twentieth century. The detailed documentation of the production of *yun* lacquerware in Scherman's diaries, combined with the photographs and the purchased objects, contributes valuable information to the study of Burmese lacquerware. The pictures, phonographic recordings, and the

Figure 14.5 Bottom of the betel-box showing two figures. Early twentieth century. Photograph by Norbert Hein, Ethnographic Museum, Munich, Br 71.

Figure 14.6 Large box with one tray decorated with several narrow hoops of inset bamboo showing a hunting scene. Early twentieth century. Photograph by Norbert Hein, Ethnographic Museum, Munich, Md 73.

Figure 14.7 Detail of Md 73 showing a hunting scene. Early twentieth century. Photograph by Norbert Hein, Ethnographic Museum, Munich, Md 73.

Figure 14.8 Platter with floral design. Early twentieth century. Photograph by Norbert Hein, Ethnographic Museum, Munich, Br 70.

diaries that the Schermans brought back from their journey, along with this large collection of objects, still awaits a comprehensive analysis.

NOTES

1 Lucian Scherman, *Philosophische Hymnen aus der Rig- und Atharva-Veda-Sanhitâ verglichen mit den Philosophemen der älteren Upanishads* [Philosophic Hymns from the Rig- and Atharva-Veda-Sanhitâ Compared with the Philosophic Concepts of the Upanishads] (Diss. München 1885), Strasbourg: Karl J. Trübner; London: Trübner & Co, 1887.

2 Lucian Scherman (ed.) [from vol. 7], *Orientalische Bibliographie* [Oriental Bibliography], Berlin: Reuther und Reichard, 1894–1911, 1922, 1928.

3 For further information on the history of the Ethnographic Museum in Munich under the directorship of Scherman, see Wolfgang Smolka, *Völkerkunde in München. Voraussetzungen, Möglichkeiten und Entwicklungslinien ihrer Institutionalisierung (ca. 1850–1933)* [Ethnography in Munich. Origins, Options and Ways ahead in its Institutionalisation (*c.* 1850–1933)], Berlin: Duncker & Humblot, *c.* 1994, pp. 188–206.

4 Archives of the Ludwig Maximilian University, Munich UAM E-II-2942 [Personal file, Lucian Scherman] (Unpublished).

5 The trip to Burma was preceeded by a two-month journey through Ceylon and India. After their stay in Burma, the

Schermans spent another two months in Northern India.

6 Lucian Scherman, *Reisedatenbuch 1. 9 Oktober 1910 (München) bis 26. Mai 1911 (Yawnghwe – Taung-gyi)* [Travel data 1. 9 October 1910 (Munich) until 26 May 1911 (Yawnghwe – Taung-gyi)]. Dorothee Schäfer (trans.), (unpublished) Munich: Staatliches Museum für Völkerkunde, 1910–11. The results of his journeys in India are also summarised in several articles. For a bibliography of the works of Scherman, see Uta Weigelt, Hartmut Walravens, and Wolfgang Stein, 'Lucian Milius Scherman (1864–1946) – Bibliographie' [Lucian Milius Scherman (1864–1946) – Bibliography], *Münchner Beiträge zur Völkerkunde*, vol. 6, 2000, pp. 51–5. The collected articles of Lucian M. Scherman have also been published. See Friedrich Wilhelm, *Kleine Schriften*, Stuttgart: Franz Steiner Verlag, 2000.

7 Library of the Ludwig Maximilian University, Munich. *Nachlass E. Kuhn* [Estate of E. Kuhn]. Letter from Scherman to Kuhn, 01.03.1911 (Unpublished).

8 Scherman, 1910–11. Also, *Indien-Reise Prof. Scherman 1910/11 II* [The Indian Journey of Prof. Scherman, vol. 2, 1910–11], Archives of the Ethnographic Museum, Munich, Umschlag zu 41; letter from Taw Sein Ko to Scherman, 21.08.1911 (Unpublished). Lucian Scherman, *Reisedatenbuch 2: 27 Mai 1911 (Taunggyi) – 30 Juli 1911 (Namkam)* [Travel Data 2. 27 May 1911 (Taunggyi) – 30 July 1911 (Namkam)]. Dorothee Schäfer (trans.), Munich: Staatliches Museum für Völkerkunde, 1911a (Unpublished). Lucian Scherman, *Reisetagebuch 2: Birma. Chindwintour. 2 Februar – 20 Februar 1911* [Travel Diary 2: Burma. Chindwin tour. 2 February – 20 February]. Dorothee Schäfer (trans.), Munich: Staatliches Museum für Völkerkunde, 1911b (Unpublished). Lucian Scherman, *Reisetagebuch 5: Birma. Südliche Shanstaaten. 16 April – 1 Mai 1911* [Travel Diary 5: Burma. Southern Shan States 16 April – 1 May]. Dorothee Schäfer (trans.), Munich: Staatliches Museum für Völkerkunde, 1911c (Unpublished). Lucian Scherman, *Birma Tagebuch Nr. 11. 13.08–31.08.1911 [25.08.1911] Mandalay – Pagan – [Rangoon]* [Burma Diary 11.13.1908–31.08.1911 (25.08.1911) Mandalay – Pagan – (Rangoon)]. Dorothee Schäfer (trans.), Munich: Staatliches Museum für Völkerkunde, 1911d (Unpublished).

9 The phonographic records are now kept in the Phonogramm-Archiv of the Ethnographic Museum in Berlin.

10 Lucian and Christine Scherman, 'Frauenleben im buddhistischen Birma' [The Life of Women in Buddhist Burma], *Zeitschrift für Buddhismus*, vol. 4, 1922a, pp. 73–104. Lucian and Christine Scherman, *Im Stromgebiet des Irrawaddy. Birma und seine Frauenwelt* [In the Irrawaddy River Region: Burma and the Life of its Women], Munich-Neubiberg: O. Schloss, 1922b.

11 Lucian Scherman, 'Brettchenwebereien aus Birma und den Himalayaländern (Völkerkundliche Notizen aus Oberbirma 3)' [Tablet Weaving from Burma and Himalayan Lands (Ethnographic Notes from Upper Burma 3)], *Münchner Jahrbuch für bildende Kunst*, vol. 8, 1913b, pp. 223–42.

12 Lucian and Christine Scherman, 'Webmuster der birmanischen Kachin, ihre Namen und ihre Stilgrundlagen (Völkerkundliche Notizen aus Oberbirma 5)' [Weaving Patterns of the Burmese Kachin, with their Names and Origin of their Styles (Ethnographic Notes from Upper Burma 5)], *Aufsätze zur Kultur – und Sprachgeschichte vornehmlich des Orients, Ernst Kuhn zum 70. Geburtstage am 7. Februar 1916, gewidmet von Freunden und Schülern*, 2 vols, Munich and Breslau: H. & H. Marcus, 1916, pp. 505–23.

13 Lucian Scherman, *Buddha im Fürstenschmuck. Erläuterung hinterindischer Bildwerke des Münchener Museums für Völkerkunde* (Abhandlungen der Bayerischen Akademie der Wissenschaften, Philosophisch-historische Abteilung, NF 7) [Buddha in Royal Attire: Remarks on South-East Asian Sculpture in the Ethnographic Museum Munich (Paper of the Bavarian Academy of Science, Philosophical-historical Department, NF 7], Munich: Verlag der Bayerischen Akademie der Wissenschaften, 1932.

14 Lucian Scherman, 'Ein volkstümliches Geisterfest in Birma' [A Folkloristic Spirit Festival in Burma], *Einkehr 1*, vol. 33, 1920a, pp. 257–60. Lucian Scherman, 'Musizierende Genien in der religiösen Kunst des birmanischen Buddhismus (Völkerkundliche Notizen aus Oberbirma 6)' [Music-making Celestials in Burmese Buddhist Art (Ethnographic Notes from Upper Burma 6)], *Ostasiatische Zeitschrift*, vol. 8 [commemorative publication, Friedrich Hirth, Berlin], 1920b, pp. 345–53. Lucian Scherman, 'Geisterfeste im buddhistischen Birma (Völkerkundliche Notizen aus Oberbirma 8)' [Spirit Festivals in Buddhist Burma (Ethnographic Notes from Upper Burma 8)], *Ararat*, vol. 12, 1921, pp. 323–33.

15 Curt Sachs, *Die Musikinstrume Birmas und Assams im Königlich Ethnographischen Museum zu München* [The Musical Instruments from Burma and Assam in the Royal Ethnographic Museum in Munich], Munich: Verlag der Bayerischen Akademie der Wissenschaften, 1917.

16 Kurt Reinhard, *Die Musik exotischer Völker* [The Music of Exotic Peoples], Berlin: Wigankow, 1950.

17 Uta Weigelt, 'Kunsthandwerk aus Birma. Yun-Lacke aus der Sammlung Scherman' [Burmese Crafts: *Yun* Lacquerware in the Scherman Collection], *Münchner Beiträge zur Völkerkunde*, vol. 6, 2000, pp. 71–122, figs 1 and 2.

18 Scherman, 1911d.

19 For a list of the objects, see Weigelt, 2000.

20 A detailed description of this palanquin is given in Scherman, 1913a, pp. 313–15. Lucian Scherman (ed.), 'Berichte des Kgl. Ethnographischen Museums 5' [Reports of the Royal Ethnographic Museum 5], *Münchner Jahrbuch für bildende Kunst*, 1913a, pp. 312–35.

21 Scherman and Scherman, 1922b, p. 35, fig. 15.

22 Sylvia Fraser-Lu, *Burmese Lacquerware*, Bangkok: Tamarind Press, 1985, p. 40.

23 Weigelt, 2000, cat. 12.

24 Ralph Isaacs and T. Richard Blurton, *Visions from the Golden Land: Burma and the Art of Lacquer*, London: British Museum Press, 2000, p. 111, cat. 53.

25 Weigelt, 2000, cat. 24, 25 and 13.

26 For a list of names and workshops, see Isaacs and Blurton, 2000, pp. 41–64 and 229–33.

27 Fraser-Lu, 1985, p. 76, ill. 64.

28 Weigelt, 2000, cat. 5.

29 *Ibid.*, cat. 4.

30 *Ibid.*, cat. 6, fig. 11. These images present a contour drawing of the top of the lid showing Pyazawhti fighting a big bird.

31 *Ibid.*, cat. 10.

32 *Ibid.*, cat. 28.

33 *Ibid.*, cat. 9.

34 *Ibid.*, cat. 8.

35 *Ibid.*, cat. 22 and 23.

36 *Ibid.*, cat. 16.

37 I am indebted to Ralph Isaacs for this information. See also Isaacs and Blurton, 2000, Appendix, no. 69.

38 Many thanks to Sylvia Fraser-Lu for this information.

39 Isaacs and Blurton, 2000, p. 180, cat. 131.

40 *Thayo* is a putty made of lacquer sap mixed with clay, sawdust, or ash, which can be sculpted or pressed into stone or metal moulds.

15 Photographs by Max and Bertha Ferrars

Joanna Wright

From the date it was founded, the Royal Geographical Society has sought to collect books and maps and, as its Royal Charter states 'advance geographical science and improve geographical knowledge'. Once photography was established as an empirical recording device, the Society actively began to encourage its use by members and to collect the photograph in all its forms. From the 1880s onwards, a note was included in the *Geographical Journal* asking Fellows to forward copies of the photographs they took on their travels to the Society's Map Curator. This was the beginning of the photographic collection. Today, some 170 years after its foundation, the Society estimates that its photographic holdings number more than half a million objects, including original prints, negatives and lantern-slides. Among these are a large number of original glass-plate negatives, many of which have no original photographic print or other information by which to identify them. Several years ago, through routine conservation work in the Picture Library, a collection of particularly detailed and sharp negatives caught my eye. It was only when Richard Blurton, curator of the exhibition 'Visions from the Golden Land: Burma and the Art of Lacquer', visited the Picture Library to research images for the exhibition that these negatives were identified.[1] The images that came to light were of Burma and had been taken by Max and Bertha Ferrars during the 1890s. In total, 467 half-plate glass negatives were rediscovered. These negatives had been given to the Society in 1937 by Mrs M. MacTaggart through V.C. Scott O'Connor.[2]

Max Ferrars was born in Ireland in 1846, the son of a clergyman and a German mother. He studied at Trinity College, Dublin and at the Royal Saxonian Forest Academy of Tharnath. He passed the entrance examination of the Imperial East India Forestry Service and served the British colonial authorities for twenty-five years in various parts of India. He held the posts of Forestry Assistant, Forestry Superintendent, Inspector of Schools, and Superintendent of the Colonial Educational Services. He appointed himself First Deputy of the Anglo-Oriental Society for the Suppression of the Opium Trade. This engagement caused him to come into conflict with British authorities, however, and in 1896 he had to retire from the colonial services. Together with his wife Bertha (née Hensler, born 17 November

1845), he moved to Freiburg, Germany. In Freiburg, he lectured at the English Seminary of the University from 1899 to 1921. In addition, he voluntarily worked as the head of the University Photographic Laboratory until

Figure 15.1 'Thami-u arrayed for her Fete' (Ferrars, p. 14, pl. 30). The image shown here differs from that in *Burma* in the position of the hands and head. '[A] holiday answering to that of the boy's novitiate is held in honour of the girl, especially when she is the first born child – *thamî-u*. In her case the ear-boring ceremony, if not the piercing itself, is deferred to the age of ten or twelve. The child, equipped in royal attire, or an imitation of it, and wearing a queen's crown (*sîbôn*), is the centre of a great gathering of relatives and friends, who are entertained with music and plays.' RGS reference: B5739.

1920.[3] The Ferrars also donated a collection of twenty-eight Burmese marionettes to the town museum in Freiburg.[4] Max Ferrars died in 1933 and Bertha in 1937.[5]

In 1900, the Ferrars published a highly illustrated account of Burma and its people called *Burma*.[6] Some of the recently rediscovered glass-plate negatives are similar to the material in that publication. A small handful in fact match images in the publication identically, but the vast majority are previously unpublished images.[7] Why the Ferrars documented Burma so rigorously is unknown, and further research will be required to contextualise this

Figure 15.2 'Shinlaung Pageant (Pegu)' (Ferrars, pp. 14–15, pls 33 and 34). This image is not in *Burma*, though similar images are shown. '[T]he lad who has prepared to renounce the world for a season, or it may be for life, is called a *shinláung* . . . In order to accentuate the renunciation of the world which the lad is making, he is arrayed and attended like a prince and makes a royal progress on horseback or in a chariot to the monastery.' RGS reference: B5778.

collection. It is hoped that this publication might provide the impetus for this.

Burma has a long tradition of being "represented" photographically. John Falconer's account of photography and ethnography in Burma demonstrates that from the 1850s onwards a vision of Burma has been constructed through Europeans' use of the camera.[8] Numerous professional photographers, including Felice Beato, used photography to portray and define Burma; similarly, many amateur photographers also recorded their distinctive vision of the country and its people.[9]

What is impressive about the images by Max and Bertha Ferrars is the meticulous rigour with which they set out to record the Burma they knew. The list of illustrations in *Burma* states that: 'Illustrations with ★ prefixed are by Bertha Ferrars (the late Mrs. Ll. W. Lewis), by whom all the plates were developed (1892–96). The remainder are by Max Ferrars, with the exception of No. 104.'[10] This therefore indicates that Bertha took 20 images whilst Max took 434. I assume, however, that they worked as a partnership, to set shots up, liaise with subjects, change the glass negatives, and calculate exposure times. The Ferrars' photographs often show people in their 'natural settings', rather than subjected to studio set-ups and pictorial backdrops, as was the case with many images of Burmese people from this period. In contrast, their photos are almost documentary in style; the images are taken in the village, at a local house or in a shrine. Yet, these images are also constructed; individuals have been asked to pose, although this may have been due to the long exposure times required.

It is important to the Society to bring these photographs to the attention of scholars of Burma worldwide. It would also be useful to understand how these images reflect contemporary Burmese society, how they inform us about Burma, and how they form part of Europe's mythologising of Burma. As Tractenberg has pointed out: 'Representing the past, photographs serve the present's need to understand itself and measure its future. Their history lies finally in the political versions they may help us realize.'[11]

A few of the Ferrars' unpublished photographs are shown here, usually with the title of the similar published picture. A quote from the Ferrars' text is also included to exemplify some relevant Burmese customs (see Figures 15.1–15.14). The following images are only a selection of the material now available to scholars of Burma at the Royal Geographical Society Picture Library. It is hoped that through this publication, interest will be generated in the photographs taken by Max and Bertha Ferrars.

Figure 15.3 'Shinlaung renewing his prayer' (Ferrars, p. 17, pl. 37). Like Figure 15.2, this image is very similar to that in *Burma*; the differences lie in the position of the hands and head. 'Having acquiesced in the rule of life, the candidate is admonished to divest himself of worldly state and personal adornment, and after that to renew his prayer for admission.' RGS reference: B5780.

Figure 15.4 'Dautcha Yathé' (Ferrars, p. 39, pl. 83). This particular image is not found in *Burma*, though similar pictures exist. 'The *Yathé*, who are few in number, live in forest caves or derelict shrines, and shift for themselves, singly or in small colonies. . . . Certain of them use a headgear called *dautcha*, which forms a receptacle for an image of the Buddha.' RGS reference: B5630.

Figure 15.5 'Family of Burman notable leaving a shrine' (Ferrars, pl. 95). Only images similar to this one are found in the Ferrars' book. The impressive family grouping illustrates the range of items carried to the monastery as food offerings (*hsun*). The first three ladies carry respectively, an offering vessel with a cone-shaped lid, a repoussé silver bowl containing pineapples, and a betel-box (*kunit*), while the man behind carries a spired offering vessel (*hsun ok*). With the exception of the silver bowl, these elegant vessels are lacquered and decorated baskets. RGS reference: B5668.

Figure 15.6 'Tattooing (togwin)' (Ferrars, p. 13, pl. 152). This image is very similar to the one in *Burma* with differences only in the hand and head gestures. '. . . it is the custom for the Burman lads to have themselves tattooed from the waist to the knee . . . Not to submit to the ordeal is to incur the reproach of cowardice. The tattooing is an intricate pattern of animals and tracery. Owing to the extent of surface involved, the process is most painful. It occupies days or weeks, according to the fortitude of the subject, who is drugged with opium for the occasion.' RGS reference: B5650.

Figure 15.7 'Burman cartwrights' (Ferrars, pp. 138–9, pl. 305). This specific image is not in *Burma*. 'The cart-building exemplifies the Burmese love of curves. . . . The Burman has proved the best wheelwright of the East, both for heavy wheels and the light spider wheels he uses in pleasure and racing-carts.' RGS reference: B5669.

Figure 15.8 'Shan camp in the frontier hills' (Ferrars, p. 146, pl. 340). This picture only differs very slightly from the one published in *Burma*. 'But it is as caravan traders that the Shans chiefly figure in Burma. They carry produce and wares between the emporiums of Burma, and the land-locked areas of their own and contiguous territories. On their homeward journey they take salt, salt fish, and *ngapî* . . . The caravans bring down tobacco, lac, ground-nuts, *thanakkâ*, garlic, and seeds. . . . The goods are carried either by men or by pack-bullocks.' RGS reference: B5766.

Figure 15.9 'Burman juggler' (Ferrars, p. 181, pl. 409). Again, it is only variations in head and hand gestures that differentiate this photograph from the Ferrars' published one. The showman holds up a puppet, perhaps in a display of ventriloquism. To his right is a large lacquered basketry box, of cylindrical shape, apparently decorated with raised *thayo* work and inset glass. 'The showmen in Burma are the conjuror and the snake-charmer.' RGS reference: B5652.

Figure 15.10 'Koyin receiving higher instruction' (Ferrars, p. 18, pl. 40). This image is identical to that in *Burma*. 'Those probationers who remain in the monastery for several years – reckoned by Lents (*wa*) – and who aspire to full membership of the Assembly, read with the recluse Pâli texts of the Tripitaka, and the commentaries on these, and commit portions, sometimes whole books of the canon, to memory.' RGS reference: B5662.

Figure 15.11 'Cutting bamboo' (Ferrars, p. 56, pl. 122). This image differs considerably from the published one. Here the bamboo trees are thin and wild looking, and the focus is upon the cutter. The poses of the cutters are very similar in both photographs, however. In this picture the tattoos on the cutter's legs are faintly visible. The Ferrars comment on how difficult it is to capture tattoos photographically (Ferrars, p. 13). 'The giant bamboo (*wabô*), a denizen of the evergreen hills, is cultivated in the plains for house-posts and masts and side-buoys of boats. Its culms attain a height of eighty feet and a girth at the butt of two feet. Every bamboo jungle supplies the rest of the material for the house. No tools are needed for bamboo work, but the universal *dâ* – a sabre, trimmer, chopper, according to its proportions . . . With the *dâ* [Burmese multi-purpose hafted blade] the bamboos are hewn, split open and slit into withes (*hnî*) for lashing.' RGS reference: B5750.

Figure 15.12 'The suitor's visit' (Ferrars, p. 68, pl. 149). Like many of the other photographs, only the head and hand positions indicate the difference between the published and unpublished versions. 'The young men are expected to make short calls only, so as not to keep the old people up late. . . . The suitor brings presents of flowers and fruit and ornaments. Oranges, expensively stored one by one, long past the season, are for this sole purpose.' RGS reference: B5759.

169

Figure 15.13 'Peingaw sailing up-stream' (Ferrars, pp. 136–7, pl. 299). The photograph here is not the same as the published one. 'They only sail before the wind and carry an immense expanse of sail, to stem the current of the Irawadi, which runs four to five knots in the rains. . . . They convey the produce of Pegu to Burma Proper, – *ngapî*, dried fish, salt and rice, besides imported goods. They bring down the manufactures of the North – cutch, lacquer, images, and *paréikaya* wares.' RGS reference: B5675.

Figure 15.14 'Swing net (yagwin)' (Ferrars, p. 89, pl. 191). Images similar to this one can be found in *Burma*. 'Next to the rice industry the greatest industry of Burma is the catching and curing of fish. Unlike the rice, the fish is entirely for local consumption.' RGS reference: B5744.

NOTES

1 Ralph Isaacs and T. Richard Blurton, *Visions from the Golden Land: Burma and the Art of Lacquer*, London: British Museum Press, 2000.

2 It is unknown who Mrs M. MacTaggart was, though probably she was the wife of Peter MacTaggart, son of Max and Bertha Ferrars. Why the Ferrars' son should bear a different surname is puzzling. Vincent Clarence Scott O'Connor was a Fellow of the Royal Geographical Society who wrote several books, including two on Burma titled *The Silken East: a Record of Life and Travel in Burma* (London: Hutchinson and Co., 1904) and *Mandalay and Other Cities of the Past in Burma* (London: Hutchinson and Co., 1907). During his long and varied career, O'Connor at one time held the position of Accountant-General, Government of India. It is assumed that he knew the Ferrars and that this is how the donation of these negatives came about.

3 In May 1994 Christie's auctioned material of the descendants of Max and Bertha Ferrars. The catalogue states that an album includes pictures of Burma, Freiburg, family members, and other portraits. In addition to the pictures by the Ferrars, there were examples by P. Klier of Rangoon and Peter MacTaggart, as well as a four-part panorama of Freiburg by G. Robeke.

4 A few photographs in the Ferrar's publication are of objects in the Freiburg Museum (see illustrations 7, 62, 63, and 384).

5 Thanks are due to Hans-Bernd Zöllner who supplied this information. Thanks are also due to Patricia Herbert and Ralph Isaacs who passed the information on to me.

6 Max and Bertha Ferrars, *Burma*, London: Sampson Low, 1900.

7 In the Ferrars' book there are 455 images, and in the Royal Geographical Society collection there are 467 negatives. It appears that, as with all good photographers, the Ferrars took more than one image of a subject and also took more images than were used in the publication. The negatives now held by the Royal Geographical Society are probably those images not chosen for the book, though taken at the same time and of the same subject. The location of the negatives used in the publication is not now known.

8 John Falconer, 'Photography and ethnography in colonial period Burma', in E. Dell (ed.), *Burma: Frontier Photographs 1918–1935*, London: Merrell, 2000, p. 29.

9 For further information on Beato, see Noel Singer's article, 'Felice Beato's Burmese Days', *Arts of Asia*, vol. 28, no. 5, September–October 1998, pp. 96–107.

10 Ferrars, 1900, p. vii. It is unclear why Bertha Ferrars is refered to as the 'late Mrs. Ll. W. Lewis'.

11 A. Tractenberg, *Reading American Photographs*, New York: Hill and Wang, 1989, p. xvii.

Index

This index covers the fifteen chapters of this volume and the illustration captions. Preface, Foreword and footnotes are excluded. Please note that entries appear in Sanskrit, Pali and Burmese and – according to the style of the authors – with or without diacritical marks; please check for variant spellings.